The Muslim Difference

The Muslim Difference

Defining the Line between Believers and Unbelievers from Early Islam to the Present

Youshaa Patel

Yale UNIVERSITY PRESS

New Haven & London

Published with assistance from the foundation established
in memory of Calvin Chapin of the Class of 1788, Yale College.

Set in Adobe Garamond type by Integrated Publishing Solutions.
Printed in the United States of America.

Library of Congress Control Number: 2022930222
ISBN 978-0-300-24896-8 (hardcover : alk. paper)

A catalogue record for this book is available from the British Library.

This paper meets the requirements of ANSI/NISO Z39.48-1992
(Permanence of Paper).

10 9 8 7 6 5 4 3 2 1

To my mother

Contents

Preface

EDINBURGH, SCOTLAND (1982)

"I'm in a group all by myself," I told my mother one day after returning home from primary one, the equivalent of kindergarten. I was five years old, quiet, and well behaved. Yet Ms. McGowan had chosen to physically set me apart from my classmates, seating me alone at a desk in a corner while everyone else learned together in groups. A former teacher, my mother was shocked. School was a place not only to learn but to socialize—a place where children learn how to conform, respect authority, and belong. The following day, she visited my class and witnessed firsthand how I was being segregated from the other children. Always ready to speak her truth, despite her diminutive size (she was barely five feet tall), she confronted Ms. McGowan. She argued that isolating a child is psychologically damaging: "He needs to socialize with his peers or he will think that something is wrong with him, that he is *different.*" But Ms. McGowan countered that I was simply too different to be included in group activities. She reasoned that it was in "the best interest" of both me and my peers that I learn alone. But in her reasoning, my mother saw discrimination. I was, after all, the only student of color in my class. Hurt and frustrated, my mother took her case to the school administration, hoping for support. But those officials, too, refused to acknowledge what had become obvious to my mother—that Ms. McGowan's teaching methods were discriminatory. The incident was a tipping point for my mother, who had been told to "go back to your own country," among other racist insults, blatant and subtle, since moving from Bombay to Edinburgh with my father in 1973. We may have looked different, but we did not deserve to be treated differently. My mother resolved to move our family to the United States, a nation of immigrants, hoping to find greater equality. We emigrated that same year.

CHICAGO, ILLINOIS (2002)

I pick up the story two decades later in Chicago, where I am now a recent college graduate pursuing a career in management consulting. One Friday, I was sitting in a mosque on the North Side of Chicago listening to a sermon (*khuṭba*). The preacher, a well-known Sufi shaykh in the local Muslim community, proclaimed that "Muslims must be different"—not just on the inside, by cultivating virtuous character, but on the outside as well, by dressing distinctively. Delivered as the U.S. government was launching its post-9/11 war on terror and intensifying its surveillance of American Muslims, the sermon urged the congregation to resist the mounting pressure to assimilate. I listened attentively, waiting to hear how the Sufi shaykh would draw from Islamic tradition. But instead of citing the Quran, he invoked the charismatic authority of the Prophet Muhammad, citing hadiths that urged Muslims to be different from Jews and Christians, including the well-known saying "Whoever imitates a people becomes one of them"—implying that if Muslims copied the ways of other people, they would eventually become like them and lose their religion. Being different, he argued, was in fact an Islamic doctrine. But as I left the mosque that day, I was still not convinced. If Muslims must indeed be different, *how different* must they be?

That question lingered in my mind as I made the decision later that year to change my profession and enter the academy. I enrolled in Duke University's graduate program in religious studies, with a focus on Islam.

DAMASCUS, SYRIA (FEBRUARY 2010)

The sermon in Chicago on Muslim difference inspired a term paper that gradually evolved into a dissertation directed by my advisor, Professor Ebrahim Moosa. Although I was initially reluctant to devote several years of my life to this subject, during a visit to Princeton University, Professor Michael Cook convinced me that this topic was indeed worthy of my time: "It would be like throwing a small brick into a large window." With this small act of destruction in mind, I opted to undertake my dissertation research at the Asad National Library in the ancient city of Damascus, home to a monumental yet unpublished manuscript of the Ottoman Arab Sufi jurist Najm al-Dīn al-Ghazzī. The civil war that would soon engulf the country had yet to break out, although some signs indicated that all was not well.

As part of my research, I was attempting to acquire all available copies of the manuscript. I had already obtained digital copies from the Chester Beatty Library in Dublin and Süleymaniye Library in Istanbul, but had yet to obtain the two copies held by the Asad National Library, which, according to its manuscript catalogue, included the author's original handwritten copy. It was conventional practice among researchers and libraries across the world to trade manuscripts of comparable value, a custom that reminded me of my childhood days trading baseball cards. I was hoping to trade my gorgeous copy from the Süleymaniye Library—a complete copy—for the ones held in the Asad National Library. Having visited the institution regularly over the course of nearly a year, I had built relationships with several administrators. I had good reason to be optimistic when I offered to trade my digital copy for theirs. I waited several days but didn't hear back. Finally, an administrator notified me that the library had rejected my request for a trade, claiming that my digital copy was, in fact, incomplete. I was shocked. I had reviewed my copy of the manuscript thoroughly and had no reason to believe that it was incomplete. In my mind, this was a fair trade.

I was now in the final month of my stay. Prepared to leave Damascus with my mission only partially accomplished, I received a message from one of my Arabic and Islamic studies teachers, Dr. Issam Eido, a graduate of the University of Damascus who had trained under the hadith master Shaykh Nūr al-Dīn ʿItr. He informed me that while visiting Dr. Tawfīq Ramaḍān al-Būṭī, son of the late Shaykh Saʿīd Ramaḍān al-Būṭī, he heard someone mention a "top secret" project: a plan to publish a critical edition of Najm al-Dīn al-Ghazzī's treatise! Dr. Issam mentioned my interest in the treatise to the source of this news, who agreed to arrange a meeting for me with the managing editor, Nūr al-Dīn al-Ṭālib.

Several days later, I found myself sitting in the office of Nūr al-Dīn al-Ṭālib, who was planning to publish Ghazzī's treatise the following year—a project that been kept secret for five long years. As we began talking, Nūr al-Dīn surprised me with his candor. He first apologized on behalf of all Arabs for their *sūʾ al-adab,* or bad manners. He explained that administrators at the

Asad National Library had misled me—on purpose—to deny me access to the manuscript, most likely because of my American nationality. He reassured me that the copy I possessed was in fact complete. He also explained that the library was mistaken about the copies of the manuscript that it possessed. The library did not own every volume of the original handwritten manuscript; it possessed only two of the three surviving volumes. The third volume was held in the Chester Beatty Library in Dublin—a copy of which I already had. At the end of our conversation, he handed me a wonderful gift: a CD with all the digital copies of every manuscript of the treatise in existence, including the ones the Asad library had refused to share with me. He also promised to send me the entire twelve-volume publication gratis—a traditional display of Arab hospitality and generosity.

SPRINGFIELD, NEW JERSEY (2021)

I tell this compressed intellectual autobiography at the outset because the story of Muslim difference that I narrate in the following pages cannot be disentangled from my own story. Nevertheless, this book is not about me. It is about the Muslim thinkers across Islamic history who struggled to define what it means to belong to a salvific community in a shared world where the line between self and other is often undefined.

Acknowledgments

bi-smillāh al-raḥmān al-raḥīm

"A good word is a like a good tree—its roots are firm and its branches reach the sky" (Q 14:24). I planted the seed for this project more than a decade ago. I continued to water the seed and expose its shoots to light from above until it grew and matured into the book before you. The reader can judge whether the tree I have planted is indeed good—how firm its roots are and how high its branches reach.

I wish to thank my mentors in the graduate program of religious studies at Duke and UNC–Chapel Hill, beginning with my supervisor, Ebrahim Moosa, who showed me how a critical engagement with the Islamic tradition can be born of deep reverence. I am also incredibly grateful for the mentorship of Bruce Lawrence, Leela Prasad, and Carl Ernst, who stand out for their brilliance, humor, and humanity.

Within my broader circle of mentors and colleagues, I thank miriam cooke, Omid Safi, David Morgan, Engseng Ho, Sherman Jackson, Muhammad Qasim Zaman, Christian Lange, Eric Tagliacozzo, David Powers, and Michael Cook for sharing valuable guidance, and I thank Rob Rozehnal and the entire Lehigh University religion studies department for their warm hospitality during my fellowship at the Center for Global Islamic Studies in 2011–12. I also thank Martin Nguyen and Ahmed El Shamsy for meticulously reading and critiquing the entire manuscript during its later stages.

At Lafayette College, I thank Neha Vora, Rachel Goshgarian, Hafsa Kanjawal, Jessica Carr, Herman Tull, and Laura McKee for their friendship, support, and inspiration. I also thank Abdul-Manan Bhat and Riddhima Gooptu for their spirited engagement with this project while serving as my research assistants.

At home and abroad, I have been fortunate to study the Islamic tradition with several of its modern-day custodians, including Shaykh Husain Sattar, Mohammad Amin Kholwadia, and Dr. Umar Faruq Abdallah (Chicago); Mawlana Hifz al-Rahman Nadwi (Lucknow); Shaykh Mushtaq Nadwi and Dr. Abdallah Abdallah (Doha); Shaykh Amienoeallah Abderoef and Shaykh Ali Hani (Amman); Dr. Issam Ido and Shaykh Ali al-Zaytun al-Azhari (Damascus); and Habib Umar bin Hafiz, Habib Ali Jifri, and Shaykh Ibrahim Osi-Efa (Tarim).

The following institutions deserve recognition for granting me funding to carry out this study: Lafayette College, Duke University Graduate School, Fulbright-Hays Foundation, Mellon Foundation, University of Qatar, American Institute of Indian Studies, American Institute of Yemeni Studies, and FLAS fellowship programs. The following libraries provided invaluable research support: Skillman Library at Lafayette College, the library systems at Duke University, Columbia University, and Princeton University, as well as the Asad National Library (Damascus), Süleymaniye Library (Istanbul), and Chester Beatty Library (Dublin).

The following institutions and organizations merit acknowledgment for giving me the opportunity to present my research and to receive scholarly feedback that enhanced this book: American Academy of Religion, Middle East Studies Association, School of Mamluk Studies, American Oriental Society, British Association for Islamic Studies, British Society for Middle Eastern Studies, International Association for the History of Religions, Franklin Humanities Institute at Duke University, Comparative Muslim Societies Program at Cornell University, Princeton University Islamic Studies Colloquium, SENSIS Project at Utrecht University, and the departments of religion/religious studies at Lehigh University, Stanford University, Vanderbilt University, University of Tennessee–Knoxville, and University of Hawaii–Manoa. I am also grateful to Brill and Taylor & Francis for permitting me to reprint, with modifications and elaborations, previously published material.

At Yale University Press, I thank my editor, Heather Gold, for seeing the potential of this project, offering critical feedback on later drafts, and patiently seeing it through to completion. I am grateful to Eva Skewes and Joyce Ippolito for their assistance during the production process, and to Robin Du-

Blanc for her marvelous copyediting. I am also grateful to the anonymous readers commissioned by Yale University Press and Oxford University Press for their constructive feedback on the manuscript.

I owe a great debt to friends and colleagues who encouraged me at different stages of this project, especially Brett Wilson, Brad Underwood, Ali Aslam, and Eilene Bizgrove. I am particularly grateful to the household of Umm Zaheer for giving me a second family in Damascus.

Finally, I apologize to my father, Yusuf Patel, and brother, Zubair, for my oddball ways throughout this long journey and thank them for patiently bearing with me. They have taught me what family means. They certainly deserve more from me, as does my wife, Maria, a force of nature who fills my life with joy, exuberance, and love. Whether it meant carefully reading and commenting on the manuscript from beginning to end or helping to design the exceedingly complex *isnād* maps, she saw my triumph as her own. I can't wait for all the adventures that lie ahead of us.

This book is dedicated to my mother, Zainab Patel. Although she did not live to see it finally enter the world, this book would have never happened had she not sacrificed her own happiness so I could pursue mine. In matters big and small, private and public, she set incredibly high standards of excellence. Her person was, and always will be, defined by sagacity, courage, sincerity, integrity, beauty, and compassion. I have tried to emulate her model, aware that I fall woefully short. May God reunite us in the world to come—for the Prophet reassured us that people belong with the ones they love.

Note on Style

I use a modified version of the Arabic transliteration system established by the *International Journal of Middle Eastern Studies.* I omit diacritics for words that are commonly used in English, such as Quran, hadith, Sufi, shariʿa, Sunni, Abbasid, Mamluk, and fatwa. The definite article (*al-*) in individual Arabic proper names is omitted except when preceded by a forename or when mentioned in the references. I occasionally add the suffix "-s" to pluralize Arabic terms. Hadiths collected in The Sound Six are referenced by chapter (*kitāb*) and section (*bāb*), not page number, as with other compilations. Dates refer to the Common Era unless otherwise noted. And translations are mine unless otherwise noted.

Introduction

"WHOEVER IMITATES A PEOPLE BECOMES ONE OF THEM"

THE VIRTUE OF SOCIAL DISTANCING

In *Islam at the Crossroads,* completed in the fall of 1933, the prominent Austrian Jewish convert to Islam Muhammad Asad warns his readers: "The imitation—individually and socially—of the Western mode of life by Muslims is undoubtedly the greatest danger for the existence—or rather, the revival—of Islamic civilization."[1] The ongoing clash between Islam and Europe, in Asad's view, was not limited to the battlefield, but was a drama that unfolded on the stage of everyday life. To Asad, still haunted by the collapse of the Ottoman caliphate as European nations extended their colonial domination over Muslim lands from South and Southeast Asia to the Middle East and North Africa, the imitation of Western—coded as secular and non-Muslim—civilization was not simply a sign of "inferiority"; it posed an existential threat to Islamic civilization itself.

In this clash of civilizations, Asad cautions his fellow believers against belittling surface-level matters that seem unrelated to Islam, such as physical appearance: "As soon as we begin to adopt the outward forms [of Western civilization] . . . its inherent currents and dynamic influences set to work in ourselves and mould slowly, imperceptibly, our whole mental attitude."[2] The external practices that define a culture eventually seep beneath the surface of the human skin and shape a people's internal attitudes and feelings. There was thus no distinction between outside and inside or between "important" and "unimportant" aspects of social life. Taking the example of dress, Asad explains, "Fashion corresponds to the aesthetic conceptions of that people, and so to its inclinations," which, in the case of Europeans, "thoroughly correspond to the intellectual and moral character of the modern West."[3] So when a Muslim imitates European fashions, he "unconsciously adapts his tastes to those of the West and twists his own intellectual and moral Self in such a way that it ultimately 'fits' the new dress."[4] Asad claims—wrongly—that Europe "never imitated the outward appearance and the spirit of Arabian culture."[5] With biting sarcasm, Asad argues that the only way that Muslims should imitate Europe is in "how they did not imitate Arabs": by crafting an independent and distinct collective identity. The aesthetic values of a civilization were thus anything but superficial. The outward imitation of Western civilization leads to an inauthentic Muslim self.

Asad warns the reader that the slippery slope of imitation descends all the way to assimilation—the total loss of Muslim religious and cultural norms. This bleak outcome, he suggests, was in fact anticipated by the Prophet Muhammad, who said, "Whoever imitates a people becomes one of them."[6] Asad explains, "This well-known prophetic tradition (*hadith*) is not only a moral admonition but also an objective statement of fact—in this case, the fact of the inevitability of Muslims being assimilated by any non-Muslim civilization which they imitate in its external forms."[7] Continuing his commentary, he employs a dramatic metaphor of a tree being blown away by a strong wind to illustrate how Islamic civilization was on the verge of being uprooted from its illustrious past by the overwhelming force of Western influence.

To change this narrative, Asad recommends that Muslims reclaim their self-respect: "A Muslim must live with his head held high. He must realize that he is distinct and different from the rest of the world, and he must learn to be proud of his being different. He should endeavor to preserve this difference as a precious quality, and pronounce it boldly to the world instead of apologizing for it and trying to merge into other cultural circles."[8] The solution to the problem of imitation was its opposite: difference.

One might dismiss Muhammad Asad as a provincial Muslim "fundamentalist" who sees the world in stark black-and-white hues. But this portrayal is a gross mischaracterization of Asad, a habitual boundary-crosser. Born into an Orthodox Jewish family, Leopold Weiss converted to Islam when he was twenty-six years old, becoming Muhammad Asad. He experienced firsthand the radical transformation of leaving the fold of one people and entering the fold of another, becoming "one of them." Throwing himself, body and soul, into his new religious identity, Asad spent six years in Arabia, living among the Bedouin and consorting with royalty, an adventure documented in his widely acclaimed autobiography, *The Road to Mecca.* But his stay in Arabia was just one stop on a lifelong journey that took him across four continents, from his birthplace of Lviv, Ukraine, to Vienna, Berlin, Jerusalem, Mecca, Pakistan, New York, Morocco, and finally to Granada, Spain. A linguaphile, Asad gained competence in at least eight languages: Polish, Aramaic, Hebrew, German, English, French, Arabic, and Persian. Due to his role in founding the nation of Pakistan, Asad was chosen to represent his adopted country at the United Nations in 1951, an honor that figured into Austria's decision after his death to name the square adjacent to the United Nations building in Vienna Muhammad Asad Platz. And although he stressed the value of maintaining distinctive styles of Muslim dress, Asad usually dressed in European attire (see figure 1). He was thus perceived by some as the ultimate liminal figure: "He was one of us and one of them."[9]

And yet despite his cosmopolitan lifestyle, Asad held onto the conviction that Muslims must be different. In 1981, nearly a half century later after the publication of *Islam at the Crossroads,* Asad issued a new edition in which he restated his original purpose for writing the book: "What I had in mind when I wrote this book was a re-awakening of the Muslims' consciousness of their being socially and culturally *different* from the all-powerful Western society, and thus a deepening of their pride in, and their desire to preserve, such of their own traditional forms and institutions as would help them to keep that essential 'difference' alive."[10] Apparently, Muslims had not grasped this message the first time.

The space of contradiction between Asad's spiraling manifesto against imitation, which drew clear lines between East and West, and the person of Asad, whose life was defined by crossing them, furnishes an appropriate point of departure for this book. Asad was just one among many Muslim thinkers during the nineteenth and twentieth centuries who called upon fellow believers to maintain their distinct religious identity. This chorus of appeals to be different, though distinctly modern, also had deep roots in the Islamic tradition that go all the way back to the origins of Islam. Indeed, it was not the majestic words of God, the Quran, but the charismatic words of the Prophet, a hadith, that rallied Muslims around this cause: "Whoever imitates a people becomes one of them"—transmitted on the authority of the prominent Companion ʿAbd Allāh b. ʿUmar and collected by the famous traditionist Abū

Figure 1. Muhammad Asad addressing his audience on Radio Pakistan in 1947. (Courtesy of Mischief Films.)

Dāwūd of Sistan. But scholars of Islam have yet to tell the story of how this anodyne statement snowballed into a prescriptive doctrine to be different from all others, and why this imperative gained urgency in modern times.

In this book, I present a genealogy of Muslim difference—a narrative of how Muslims have defined the line between themselves and others—from the origins of Islam to the present.[11] I explain and contextualize the anxieties of Muslim thinkers like Asad who wrestled with the ambiguities of otherness implicit in their quest to define how Muslims are different. For it is through differences—symbolic acts that set oneself apart from others—that all people, individual and collective, form a sense of identity.[12] "The assertion of identity," observes the philosopher Kwame Anthony Appiah, "always proceeds through contrast or opposition."[13] A humorous exchange in one of Mark Twain's lesser-known novels, *Tom Sawyer Abroad,* nicely illustrates this idea. When asked "what a Moslem was," Tom Sawyer answered: "It was a person that wasn't a Presbyterian." Sawyer's companion, Huck Finn, then wrongly concluded, "So there is plenty of them in Missouri, though I didn't know it before."[14] Not knowing who Muslims were, Sawyer could only define them by who they were not (even though the reader still learns nothing about who Muslims are). But the habit of defining something—or someone—by what it is not is universal. When the Prophet exhorted Muslims, "Be Different!" from Jews, Christians, and Zoroastrians, he, too, was defining what it meant to be Muslim. And so, the story of Muslim difference told in this book is also a story of how Muslimness was made.[15]

The fundamental question posed in the book goes to the heart of Muslim identity: how does a religious community adapt to its broader cultural landscape, while preserving and valuing what makes it different? Drawing on a wide range of Islamic literary and documentary sources, my research demonstrates that the Prophet Muhammad never intended for Islam to become something entirely foreign and strange to others, but rather selected distinctive markers that were small in scale (such as growing a beard) to at once set apart *and* connect Muslims to the cosmopolitan world around them. Choosing to be different in a way that is not entirely oppositional is a choice. For not all differences are alike. Differences are expressed in an array of forms and exist in varying degrees. *Big differences* are starkly oppositional, while *small differences* are subtle and may not even be noticed. Difference thus resides along a spectrum. The crucial question for Prophet Muhammad and subsequent generations of Muslims, then, was not whether or not to be different, but rather *how* to be different.

Today, *difference* has become an ideologically charged term that reflects the value of diversity in secular democratic societies. Difference is to be tolerated, and ideally embraced. To embrace difference means to value the diversity of human identity through the equal treatment of marginalized groups across race, class, age, gender, sexuality, ability, ethnicity, nationality, and religion. Religious difference, in particular, alludes to the distinctive way that secular states regulate religion which, in the words of the late Saba Mahmood, "promises to demolish premodern forms of hierarchy in order to create a polity where all citizens are supposed to be formally equal in the eyes of the law."[16] The primary ethical concern underlying this contemporary view of difference is the promise of equality. But what happens to difference if it is imagined outside the political context of the secular state and the promise of equality is no longer the primary ethical concern? The majority of the Muslim thinkers encountered in this book did not live within nation-states but within empires in which hierarchy, not equality, between different subjects was the norm. In this book, I demonstrate how their imaginations of difference reflect distinct conceptions of the good that were entangled with their historically contingent political context. But we must first set aside our expectations of equality to avoid anachronistically projecting them back onto Muslim discourses of difference, viewing them instead within their original historical context.

I propose a novel interpretation of Muslim differences that avoids reducing them to singular expressions of psychological anxiety or an aggressive will to power. These differences were creative and connective acts. Instead of adopting differences that were unrecognizable or so strange that foreign communities were unable to decode their meaning, Muslims adopted shared cultural idioms that were intelligible to their rivals and conformed to their expectations of what difference should look like. Muslims avoided expressing difference in starkly oppositional or grandiose ways. Most Muslim differences, in other words, were small, not big. The particular shape of these differences harmonized the relationship between Muslims and their cultural environment. This deliberate strategy aligns with a broader narrative, advanced in the Quran, that positions Islam as a middle path between Judaism and Christianity—and Muslims as a moderate community (*umma wasaṭa*) that shuns extremes.

This book is not intended to be a general history of Muslim interreligious relations but a focused study of Islam's *difference-makers*—Muslim religious scholars, the *ʿulamāʾ*. Having been anointed as "the inheritors of the prophets," the *ʿulamāʾ* are the custodians of the Islamic discursive tradition and are differentiated along disciplinary lines, as hadith collectors, jurists, Quran exegetes, historians, theologians, and Sufis. How did these thinkers across time and place understand and respond to the Prophet's exhortations to be distinct from other religious communities, especially Jews and Christians? Did they understand the Prophet Muhammad's "moral admonition" against imitation to be equivalent to a religious obligation for Muslims to be different? And if so, what spheres of life does this obligation encompass? Put differently, what should Muslim difference *look like* in everyday life? Can foreign practices perceived as virtuous or beneficial ever be adopted by Muslims and become, as it were, "Islamic"? The responses of *ʿulamāʾ* to these and other questions, as expressed in the religious discourses examined in this book, offer a window into how Islam both configured, and was configured by, encounters with other religious communities. These discourses are normative because they make claims upon ordinary Muslims, prescribing their everyday behavior and defining their ideals of how to interact with others.

At its heart, *The Muslim Difference* is concerned with the moments and spaces of encounter between different people, especially religious communities, a subject that is more timely today, in our globalized and interconnected world, than ever. This book thus contributes to the voluminous literature on interreligious relations, which encompasses a range of subfields and, more specifically, the still poorly understood subject of interreligious boundaries. Although the few existing studies of religious boundary-making within Muslim societies have greatly enhanced our understanding of the subject, they are nonetheless sharply delimited in both historical and geographic scope. And the pioneering scholars who have examined the Islamic doctrine against imitation have limited their studies to journal articles or book chapters. *The Muslim Difference* is the first book-length study of this subject.[17]

Among the features that set apart this book from existing studies is its ambitious historical scope. The synthetic but focused historical narrative takes the reader on a winding journey across time and space—from Arabia during Islam's formative period to Damascus during the Mamluk and Ottoman periods and finally to Egypt during British colonial rule—moments encompassing situations when Muslims were a vulnerable minority and when they were a powerful majority. Because these moments were marked by dramatic political and social transformations, they were perceived as dangerous times of crisis by the *ʿulamāʾ* who are the main actors in this story. Despite widespread misconceptions that they inhabited an intellectual and social bubble, their religious imaginations, while grounded in a sacred Islamic past, were entangled with the popular attitudes and practices of elite and nonelite subjects, Muslim and non-Muslim, living in the present.

I explain how the first Muslims began to set themselves apart from other religious communities—especially Jews and Christians, dubbed by the Quran as the "People of the Book" (*ahl al-kitāb*), an honorific that acknowledges their shared claim to divine revelation. While the religious boundaries dividing Muslims from Jews and Christians may seem obvious today, that was not always the case; there was a time, according to Companion and cousin Ibn ʿAbbās, when Muhammad intentionally emulated Jewish and Christian religious practices, when the lines distinguishing these communities were largely undefined. This state of affairs did not last, reaching a point where one of Muhammad's Jewish interlocutors hyperbolically exclaimed, "This man [Muhammad] just does the opposite of what we do!"[18] I show how succeeding generations of religious authorities drew on the precedent of early Muslim exemplars to preserve communal boundaries amid historical transformations by criticizing those who celebrated foreign holidays such as Maundy Thursday in Mamluk Damascus, socialized with the wrong people at coffeehouses in Ottoman Damascus, and followed foreign fashion trends such as donning European-style brimmed hats in colonial Egypt. In the epilogue, I reframe this historical narrative as a point of entry into the critical task of reimagining Muslim difference in late modernity. This diachronic approach reveals both continuity and rupture, demonstrating that Muslim difference was defined by the present as much as the past.

This genealogical history reveals that the shape of Muslim difference we see today was not an inevitable outcome.[19] So many of the markers that came to set apart Muslims emerged not from a series of divine commandments from above, disconnected from history, but rather from below, through a sequence of chance encounters across time and place between Muslims and others—pagans, Jews, Christians, Zoroastrians, Persians, Byzantines. The making of Muslim difference has always been a dialogical process grounded in a history of contingency, of accidental encounters that could have been otherwise. We thus find that these differences took forms that often defy our expectations of what religion—and Islam—should be. They not only encompass the familiar realm of ritual, where we expect to find Islam, but also the realm of ordinary life, where we may not expect to find it. In demonstrating how the differences that come to define a people can appear anywhere at any time, even in the most unexpected situations, this study makes an important contribution to understanding the relationship of Islam (religion) to culture and public life.

Complementing this deep history, *The Muslim Difference* offers a broad, panoramic view of Muslim interreligious relations. Instead of viewing these relations in a conceptual vacuum, through the lens of religious identity alone (as most studies do), this book stresses the intersection between religious identity and other categories of identity—ethnicity, gender, status, age, and the human. Artificially sequestering Muslim religious identity from other building blocks of identity risks misunderstanding Muslim constructions of difference, which some inaccurately attribute to religious "intolerance." Whether at the mosque, the marketplace, or the halls of government, Muslims across time and place were not only encountering members of different religions but also different kinds of Muslims. Muslims were not all cut from one cloth. Yet numerous hadiths seek to define clear lines between different ranks of Muslims across Islamic society—men and women, free persons and slaves, Arabs and non-Arabs, old and young people, humans and nonhumans (animals and demons). How do we explain this? Drawing on philosopher Charles Taylor's concept of the "social imaginary," I argue that the preservation of religious differences was not merely a product of Islam; it reflected the deeply embedded ethos of empire—the hierarchical ordering of society under a single imperial sovereign that I call an *imperial imaginary.*[20] And drawing on the research of Louise Marlow, I demonstrate how Muslims ironically inherited a hierarchical worldview from their Byzantine and Sasanian rivals, who ordered society along lines of religious and other differences.[21] What this study reveals, then, is not only how Muslims were differentiated from non-Muslims but also how Muslims themselves were differentiated. We may thus conceive "Muslim difference" not as a simple binary opposition to non-Muslims but as multiplicity—a continuum that cuts across heterogeneous groups of both Muslims and non-Muslims.[22]

Enhancing this panoramic view, this book brings to the center a topic that has remained on the margins in existing histories of Islam (especially premodern Islam): the pivotal role of the body in mediating Muslim identity. As discussed above, physical appearance was a focal point in Muhammad Asad's appeal for Muslims to be different. Muslims, including Asad, drew inspiration from the Prophet himself, who exhorted Muslims to set themselves apart from Jews, Christians, and idolaters through distinctive styles of dress, hairstyle, and small gestures in both ritual and cultural practice. Against prevailing studies that emphasize the role of grand theological doctrine in distinguishing Islam from other religions, I contend that seemingly minor quotidian practices involving the body, such as dress, ritual prayer, and funerary rites—what Sigmund Freud dubbed "Small Differences"—played a more significant role in defining Muslim difference in public life.

For many readers, the unexpected ways identity, difference, and the body converge in the Islamic past bring to mind contemporary debates over Muslim assimilation in Western countries, which have boiled over into public disputes over material symbols, from bans on headscarves and minarets in Europe to legal battles over the call to prayer and long beards in the United States.[23] But, as I hope this book makes abundantly clear, these modern-day spectacles are just the latest iterations in a long history of interreligious conflicts over how to configure public space.

The conceptual value I place on concrete and visible practices of Muslim difference is reflected in my attempt to balance literary with material sources, which span the Quran, hadith and their commentaries, theological tracts, Sufi manuals, treatises on legal theory and positive law, historical chronicles, biographical dictionaries, poetry, and newspapers as well as numismatics, archaeology, architecture, manuscript studies, and miniature paintings.

Despite widespread skepticism over the historicity of the hadiths, they were of indispensable value to early Muslim imaginations of difference. Moving from the hadiths' historical origins to their destinations, I examine their afterlife in an overlooked genre of post-classical Islamic texts I have dubbed "the treatises against imitation." My historical narrative converges on two colossi of Islamic scholarship from the cosmopolitan city of Damascus, Ibn Taymiyya (d. 1328) and Najm al-Dīn al-Ghazzī (d. 1651), who authored the two most historically significant treatises on imitation amid political crisis.

The most polarizing premodern Muslim scholar in Islam today, Ibn Taymiyya composed the first and most influential treatise against imitation as the Mongol menace loomed on the horizon of the Mamluk Sultanate. This precarious state of affairs is reflected in his treatise's incendiary title, *The Obligation of Following the Straight Path Is to Be Different from Those Damned to Hell* (*Iqtiḍāʾ al-ṣirāṭ al-mustaqīm mukhālafat aṣḥāb al-jaḥīm*). But most scholars have overlooked Ibn Taymiyya's fierce critique of imitation, the cornerstone of his argument, focusing instead on his diatribes against Muslim ritual innovations (*bidʿa*) and participation in unsanctioned holidays (*ʿīds*), such as the Prophet Muhammad's birthday (*mawlid*). In my close reading of the treatise, I bring to light Ibn Taymiyya's groundbreaking argument that being different from unbelievers is a religious obligation and a fundamental doctrine of Islam.[24]

An Ottoman Arab Sufi jurist and litterateur, Ghazzī spent nearly forty years composing his monumental treatise, *The Virtue of Awakening to What Has Been Transmitted regarding Imitation (Ḥusn al-tanabbuh li-mā warada fī al-tashabbuh)*, which spans twelve volumes in the published edition and is, according to his preeminent biographer, "unprecedented."[25] Ghazzī strikes a very different tone from Ibn Taymiyya. A reflection of Ghazzī's social imaginary, *The Virtue of Awakening* envisions humans and nonhumans as part of a single cosmic ecosystem connected to one another by mimesis. Yet remarkably, *The Virtue of Awakening* has been almost ignored by Euro-American academic and Muslim scholarship alike.[26] In *The Muslim Difference,* I present the first in-depth examination of Ghazzī's magisterial treatise in a European language, drawing attention to its remarkable intellectual synthesis of spirit (Sufism) and law (shariʿa) and emplacing it within a broader historical landscape of the Ottoman Empire at the turn of the seventeenth century in which several transformations—a currency inflation catastrophe, population swells, peasant lawlessness, climate change, and new forms of entertainment—disrupted established social distinctions and hierarchies that Ghazzī sought to reclaim.

The narrative concludes with a close study of a fatwa designated by one historian as the most controversial of all time.[27] Delivered in 1903 by the Egyptian reformer Muḥammad ʿAbduh (d. 1905), the fatwa permitted the minority Muslim population of Transvaal, South Africa, to wear European-style brimmed hats. The fatwa set off a firestorm of debate within and beyond Egypt that endured for decades, coinciding with the rapid political, economic, and cultural transformations of colonial modernity that brought Muslims closer to—and more dependent upon—Europe.

By reading these sources through an interdisciplinary lens that draws upon religious studies, anthropology, sociology, and cultural studies I attempt to move our inquiry beyond a mere factual retelling of the past to a deeper grasp of what Muslim difference *means.*[28] And by thinking with intellectuals from both the Islamic discursive tradition and the Euro-American academy, I employ an expansive and heterogeneous conception of "theory" that is not limited to the elite academic circles of continental Europe but encompasses the main subjects of this study, Muslim thinkers. The theory these thinkers generate from below enhances our understanding of several concepts, often conceived as dyads, by blurring the lines between them, including representation and reality, similarity and difference, individual and community, religion and politics, self and other.

Some may dismiss the Muslim sentiments on foreignness expressed in this book "as xenophobic and insecure" but, as Beth Berkowitz observes in her study of Jewish difference, defining communal boundaries "is also an important strategy of cultural preservation."[29] Islamic discourses suggest that cultural preservation was, and is, a key objective of Muslim difference. It is thus important to view Muslim difference within a wider cultural field, originating within the cosmopolitan milieu of the late antique Near East and Mesopotamia. Late antique Greek, Jewish, and Christian thinkers paradoxically shared with Muslims anxieties over the other. The rabbinic doctrine of *hukkat ha goyem* forbade Jews from imitating gentile practices in order to ensure that Jews remained a people set apart.[30] The Apostle Paul commanded his followers, "Be imitators of me as I am of Christ," prefiguring the Christian ideal of imitatio Christi.[31] As Elizabeth Castelli has noted, "The call to sameness (with Paul) . . . is paradoxically bound up with the call to exclusivity (difference) from the rest of the world"—to an exclusive community of Christian believers.[32]

The Sasanian and Byzantine Empires, preeminent rivals to the caliphate, also struggled to safeguard communal boundaries.[33]

But the most important way this book situates Muslim difference within a wider frame of reference is to view difference, as both a concept and practice, in relation to imitation—a dialectic expressed through the language of Muslim religious discourses themselves. Based on a careful critical and historically sensitive reading of these discourses, I argue that it is precisely because ordinary Muslims across time and place habitually interacted with and emulated Jews, Christians, and other foreigners that religious authorities from Ibn Taymiyya to Muhammad Asad struggled to set them apart. To the chagrin of these intellectuals, the collective body of Muslims never ceased imitating others. Put differently, it is because Muslims share so much in common with others that being different took on so much value. Sociologists, after all, claim that similarity and difference are two sides of the same proverbial coin—the construction of community and, more broadly, identity.[34] This book thus reveals the paradox of Muslim identity: that Muslim difference was built on a vast landscape of similarity.

The moral ambiguity implicit in the dialectical tension between difference and imitation is laid bare in the Prophet's statement "Whoever imitates a people becomes one of them." The hadith frames the conceptual and narrative trajectory of the entire book, which is a story of boundary-making as much as it is of gray zones and blurry lines between Muslims and others.

IMITATION BETWEEN GOOD AND EVIL

"Whoever imitates a people becomes one of them" is one of the Prophet Muhammad's most "well-known sayings" (*al-aḥādīth al-mushtahara*).[35] This pithy saying, what I dub "the imitation hadith," appears at first blush to be an unambiguous and objective statement about group belonging—that when a person emulates the behavior of a specific group, she or he comes to resemble the members of that group, eventually becoming "one of them." More generally, it suggests that personal identity is determined less by individual attributes than by membership in a community, which aligns with the view of Émile Durkheim, one of the founders of modern sociology, that religion is "eminently a collective thing."[36] And yet, the hadith's lack of specificity raises more questions than it answers. We lack basic information about the identity of the "people" and scope of imitation intended by the hadith. With so many blanks left unfilled, interpreters were free to apply the hadith to nearly any situation, making it one of the Prophet's most famous sayings.

However, the epistemic value of the hadith is best understood in light of the importance of imitation to human behavior, which European intellectuals since the Enlightenment have downplayed: "In the science of man and culture today," observed French philosopher and critic René Girard, "there is a unilateral swerve away from anything that could be called mimicry, imitation, or mimesis."[37] He reasoned, "The role of imitation would unduly emphasize . . . all that transforms us into herds," that is, it would erase our sense of individuality—a sacrosanct pillar of Enlightenment thought.[38] The cultural shift away from imitation to innovation, from conformity to individuality, is captured in a pointed statement of the German philosopher Immanuel Kant: "Genius must be considered the very opposite of the spirit of imitation."[39] Kant's portrayal of imitation as the antithesis of originality, creativity, and the free exercise of reason aligned with his views on adherence to tradition as a form of slavish imitation and cast a shadow over pre-Enlightenment views that expressed reverence for tradition and the imitation of past exemplars. More recently, however, a growing number of Euro-American thinkers have attempted to restore imitation to its exalted status at the center of human activity, eliciting what may be called a "mimetic turn."[40] The present study draws inspiration from this broader intellectual movement.

Imitation, after all, is at the root of human nature and culture. The classical French sociologist Marcel Mauss described imitation as a powerful integrative force that brings together the psychological, biological, and social elements of human life—what he called "physio-psycho-sociological assemblages."[41] Imitation thus encompasses the entire human being, "l'homme total."[42] There is, in other words, no dimension of human life that imitation does not affect; imitation is everywhere. Aristotle thus called the human being "the most imitative creature in the world."[43] Postwar German philosopher Theodor Adorno went further, proclaiming that imitation is a precondition of our humanity: "A human being only becomes human at all by imitating other human beings."[44] Validating these philosophical observations, cognitive scientists have demonstrated that imitation is hardwired into human physiology.[45] Through the emergence of mirror neurons in the brain at a very young age, children gain the capacity to imitate other human beings, illustrating why imitation plays a crucial role in both child development and pedagogy.

Imitation's role in human nature anticipates its role as a conduit of culture—

as a mechanism for circulating practices across space and time. Girard observes, "If human beings suddenly ceased imitating all forms of culture would vanish."[46] Art, photography, and cinema—expressions of human creativity that shape modern culture—are forms of mimesis. The fashion industry utilizes the desire to imitate to drive consumer behavior and disseminate new trends in style. In the 1990s, the advertising executives at Nike realized the powerful effect of imitation on consumer purchasing habits when they told TV viewers, "Be like Mike"—become like the legendary NBA basketball player Michael Jordan. Advocates of banning violence in popular culture—television, movies, video games, and other forms of mass media—often reference the danger of people's natural tendency to mimic these representations in real life.[47] It is thus difficult to imagine human life—individual or collective—without imitation.

Brimming with the unruly potential to cross all social boundaries, imitation could at once disrupt the normative order and unleash humanity's creative potential. This capacity for disruption elicited divergent views of the concept among the classical Greek philosophers Plato and Aristotle. Plato saw the worst in imitation, fearing the "terror of mimesis."[48] In *The Republic,* Plato wanted to exclude artists, imitators par excellence, from the Greek polis to prevent its citizens from being corrupted, because "the imitator cannot avoid a certain contamination by the object of imitation."[49] Poets, in Plato's view, could only imitate the appearance of an original, never duplicate the original itself.[50] Imitations were thus derivative, inauthentic, inferior. By contrast, his student Aristotle conceived of imitation as poiesis—a creative process that could supersede the original.[51] The contrasting attitudes of Plato and Aristotle toward imitation presaged the diverse ways Muslims approached the subject.

The multivalence of the imitation hadith hinges upon an Arabic term that is central to this book, *tashabbuh,* which I have rendered as "imitation" ("Whoever imitates [*tashabbaha*] a people becomes one of them"). However, *tashabbuh* is a potent term whose lexical field not just overlaps but exceeds the conceptual limits of imitation and encompasses a broad range of interrelated concepts, including "resemblance," "assimilation," "conformity," "mimesis," and "mimicry."[52] These terms all express relationships of congruence between things. But while *tashabbuh* is a relational or connective concept, its morphology (form V) indicates that it also is a self-reflexive behavior that encompasses the person of the imitator.

While many Muslim thinkers viewed *tashabbuh* merely as a phenomenon, in the original Greek sense of "something that appears," Najm al-Dīn al-Ghazzī defines it as a dynamic process that encompasses the whole person—a holistic self-transformation that takes place by means of another: "*Tashabbuh* refers to humans seeking [sometimes by artifice or deceit] to be a likeness of the imitated [*shibh al-mutashabbah bihi*]—its appearance, qualities, characteristics, and attributes. It means undertaking (both) its intention and implementation."[53] In Ghazzī's capacious understanding of the term, *tashabbuh* is a type of subject formation that carries the potential to blur, and even erase, the line between self and other. This portrayal of imitation converges with that of the German Jewish intellectual Walter Benjamin, who defines the parallel concept of mimesis as the faculty "to become and behave like something else" or, as reformulated by anthropologist Michael Taussig, to "explore difference, yield into and become Other."[54] We may thus include *tashabbuh* in what historian Fred Donner has termed "boundary themes," which "define the community or group in relation to others."[55] *Tashabbuh* is a key term in the grammar of Muslim identity and alterity.

By blurring the lines between imitator and imitated, self and other, imitation becomes a process fraught with ambiguity. The family of Arabic words derived from the triliteral root of *tashabbuh,* SH-B-H, also evokes a sense of ambiguity—doubt (*shibha*), uncertainty (*shubha*), confusion (*tashbīh*), comparison (*tashbīh*), and even fool's gold (*shabaha*).[56] Erasing the line between real and fake, appearance and reality, fool's gold represents the worst-case scenario, where ambiguity deteriorates into deception and mistaken identity.

The question of identity, of course, is at the heart of the imitation hadith. But the thick fog of ambiguity surrounding the term *tashabbuh* encircles the hadith as well, laying bare Muslim anxieties of identity and difference. Not only do Muslim readings of the imitation hadith inhabit a gray zone between objective statement and morally charged exhortation, the morally charged readings themselves occupy a gray zone between virtue and vice—between polemically charged admonition and encouraging homily.

Most Muslim thinkers leaned toward a morally charged reading of the hadith. But to know which reading to employ, interpreters had to first determine the moral status of the "people," or *qawm,* being imitated: are they good or bad? A polyvalent Arabic term, *qawm* signifies a set of social relationships—a people, nation, or community and, more fundamentally, a collectivity or group.[57] Although its semantic field is enriched by a cluster of other Arabic terms of sociological import—*umma, milla, dīn, qabīla, jamāʿa,* and *shaʿb*—its shades of meaning are nonetheless distinct.[58] In the Quran, *qawm* often has overlapping ethno-national, moral, and religious undertones, as in the "*qawm* of Noah," "corrupt *qawm,*" and "*qawm* of unbelievers."[59] It can even take on a gendered valence, referring to men alone, to the exclusion of women.[60] My rendering of *qawm* as "people," however, evokes the term's general sense: a community united by some marker(s) of identity, such as language, history, culture, gender, or religion.

How and why did religious scholars lean toward a polemical reading that assumed a corrupt *qawm?* Framed as an admonition, the hadith becomes an exhortation for Muslims to be different from people whose moral credentials are dubious—non-Muslims and lower-ranking Muslims. This reading authorizes *ʿulamāʾ* to draw sharp lines defining who belongs to the Muslim community and to answer the theological question "Who is a true Muslim?" in social terms. It warns believers that conforming to foreign ways will spiral into stigma, sin, and ultimately exclusion from the fold of the Muslim community. In defining firm boundaries between "us" and "them," this polemical reading brings Muslims together by setting them apart from others, eliminating the possibility that someone can be one of us and one of them at the same time. The influence of this polemical reading endowed the term *tashabbuh* with a negative connotation of reprehensible imitation and transformed the hadith "Whoever imitates a people becomes one of them" into the keynote expression of this idea among mainstream *ʿulamāʾ*.

Yet, from at least the tenth century, an alternative reading of the hadith—one that has been overlooked in contemporary scholarship—persisted among Sufis. In stark contrast to mainstream interpreters who read the tradition as a stern admonition to be different from sinful unbelievers, some Sufi masters molded the imitation hadith into an encouraging homily to emulate pious Muslims. Imitation, in this contrarian view, not only mediates belonging in a community of pious Sufis but also becomes a powerful technology of individual spiritual transformation. A means to social inclusion, *tashabbuh,* as both concept and practice, transforms from a vice to a virtue, taking on a positive connotation.

Shaped by distinct social and literary contexts, these two readings correspond to "the two bodies" of the Prophet Muhammad—the divergent but overlapping forms of authority embodied by the Prophet as both lawgiver and moral exemplar.[61] As lawgiver, the Prophet established a collective political order, while as moral exemplar, he established a pattern for individual spiritual excellence. As we shall see, the imitation hadith—and the Islamic discourse it inspired—expresses both voices of the Prophet.

Over time, the Prophet Muhammad's exemplary conduct, known as the *sunna,* became the most authoritative normative source of Islam after the Quran.[62] The related notion of following the *sunna* (*ittibāʿ al-sunna*) expressed the obligation for all Muslims to emulate the Prophet. But *taqlīd,* adhering to a specific Islamic school of law (*madhhab*), codifies how Muslims should embody the *sunna* in their everyday lives.[63] Both concepts, following the *sunna* and *taqlīd,* are types of imitation—like *tashabbuh.* But there is one key difference. While *sunna* and *taqlīd* encourage Muslims to imitate pious exemplars of the past, *tashabbuh* discourages them from imitating corrupt peoples of the present.[64] A different type of imitation, *taqiyya,* a fundamental doctrine in Shiʿism, encourages, and sometimes requires, dissimulation—the precautionary practice of disguising one's religious identity in moments of persecution or duress.[65] *Tashabbuh,* while commonly found in Sunni hadith collections, rarely appears in Twelver Shiʿi hadith collections, suggesting that the term represents a distinctive Sunni Muslim vocabulary of religious difference.[66]

In different ways, each of the above-mentioned mimetic concepts anchors Muslims, Sunni and Shiʿi, in an authoritative past, defining the contours of community and orthodoxy in Islam. Community and orthodoxy, after all, are inseparable. A rebel who runs afoul of orthodoxy may be expelled from the community of believers.[67] Orthodoxy is not disembodied opinion but authoritative truth embodied within a community and thus, as Talal Asad observes, "a relationship of power."[68] But, as the medieval historian and social thinker Ibn Khaldūn (d. 1406) argues, so too is imitation a relationship of power.[69]

Having noticed that the weak tend to imitate the strong, Ibn Khaldūn portrays imitation as a hierarchical relationship in which the imitator is inferior to the model: the conquered imitate their conquerors; children imitate their parents; commoners imitate their rulers; students imitate their teachers; and, in his era, the Spaniards imitated the Galicians.[70] In his famous introduction to history, *The Muqaddima,* Ibn Khaldūn explains why imitation follows this arc: "The reason for this is that the soul always sees perfection in the person who is superior to it and to whom it is subservient. It considers him perfect, either because the respect it has for him impresses it, or because it erroneously assumes that its own subservience to him is not due to the nature of defeat but to the perfection of the victor. If that erroneous assumption fixes itself in the soul, it becomes a firm belief. The soul, then, adopts all the manners of the victor and assimilates itself to him. This, then, is imitation."[71] Ibn Khaldūn would have agreed wholeheartedly with the eccentric British author Charles Caleb Colton (d. 1832) that "imitation is the sincerest [form] of flattery."[72] Imitation, in Ibn Khaldūn's view, is driven by the imitator's perception, or rather misperception, of the model's superiority. True or not, if the imitator idealizes the model and internalizes this misperception, he will adopt the model's distinctive attributes until he becomes like him. Put differently, the imitator emulates the model due to the prestige he confers upon him—an explanation that anticipates Marcel Mauss's notion of "prestigious imitation," which is driven by the imitator's desire to attain the model's prestige.[73]

Power is also at the root of Muhammad Asad's anxiety of influence: "It lies in human nature that nations and civilizations which are politically and economically more virile exert a strong fascination on the weaker or less active communities, and influence them in the intellectual and social spheres without being influenced themselves. Such is the situation today with regard to the relations between the Western and the Muslim worlds."[74] But, as we shall see, religious authorities warned Muslims against imitating Jews and Christians in the Realm of Islam (*dār al-Islām*), the territory in which Muslims enjoyed political and military supremacy over their non-Muslim subjects. They were, in other words, envisioning dramatic role reversals of the conquerors imitating the conquered, the "strong" imitating the "weak." But to make sense of these anxieties, we need to conceive power beyond the conventional idiom of political and military might and view it through the lens of social and cultural prestige.

We are now in a position to theorize how imitation and orthodoxy are bound together by their relationships to power. When sanctioning which models and practices to imitate (and not imitate), Muslims exercise "the power to regulate, uphold, require, or adjust *correct* practices, and to condemn, exclude, undermine, or replace *incorrect* ones," which Talal Asad describes as "the domain of orthodoxy."[75] This domain is defined not only by Muslim religious elites who officially proclaim what counts as good and bad imitation, but also by ordinary Muslims who choose to follow these norms or to create new ones of their own. The relationships of power that define both imitation and orthodoxy are thus multidirectional. In this way, orthodoxy both circumscribes, and is itself circumscribed by, imitation.

Imitation brings into focus another important theme in this book: how the relationships of power that define Islamic orthodoxy extend beyond the Muslim community. Islam is not (nor ever has been) defined by the behaviors of the Muslim community alone. Imitation mediates relations of power *within* a single community as well as relations of power *between* different communities (Muslims and non-Muslims). It illuminates the role that non-Muslims played in shaping Islamic orthodoxy; whenever Muslims adopt practices associated with non-Muslim populations, which are then deemed within or outside the bounds of orthodoxy, non-Muslims participate in the process of shaping Islamic orthodoxy. Orthodoxy is thus a dialogical process, dependent upon both insiders and outsiders, believers and unbelievers.

Taken together, the distinctive features of the imitation hadith—semantic indeterminacy, potential to carry a positive or negative moral valence, and relevance to orthodoxy, power, and Muslim interreligious relations—explain how the tradition became so highly reactive, provoking conversation and debate among Muslims for centuries to come. The imitation hadith's liminal state between objective statement and moral exhortation, between stern admonition and encouraging homily, anticipates the contrasting but overlapping historical trajectories of Muslim difference.

The Islamic ethos against imitation continued to adapt and expand over time, diffusing from the canonical collections of hadiths into compendia on law and theology, where it became doctrine, and ultimately crystallizing into its own distinct genre of treatises. Although, to my knowledge, no one prior to the late medieval scholar Ibn Taymiyya systematically argued that being different was a religious obligation, I take the view that we may call the reprehensible imitation of others (*tashabbuh*) an Islamic "doctrine," a principle or teaching, from at least the eleventh century, when Muslim jurists appear to have arrived at an undeclared consensus on its reprehensibility. One reason why historians of Islam have been slow to realize the significance of this doctrine to Muslim intellectual and social life is due to a fixation on its textual origins in the hadith, not its dynamic transformation over the *longue durée.* It is also for this reason that the post-formative literary development that I call "the treatises against imitation" has only recently been identified.[76] In this book, I examine how *ʿulamāʾ* defined difference in these treatises against imitation, revealing a dynamic Islamic discourse that reflects, and is reflected in, the transformations of Muslim interreligious relations across time and place, especially in moments of crisis.[77]

Although the domains of mysticism and law, Sufism and shariʿa, are very much intertwined in Islam, my study brings into relief dislocations between these discourses, which are laid bare in the treatises on imitation of Ibn Taymiyya and Najm al-Dīn al-Ghazzī. Both Ibn Taymiyya and Ghazzī may be characterized as Sufi jurists. Ibn Taymiyya was a jurist of the Ḥanbalī school, while Ghazzī was a jurist of the Shāfiʿī school. Ghazzī was a Qādirī Sufi, and Ibn Taymiyya was likely one too. Yet their portrayals of *tashabbuh* are very different. Although no single factor can explain this divergence, I argue that their contrasting discursive styles play an important role. In *The Obligation of Following the Straight Path,* Ibn Taymiyya employs what I describe as a shariʿa-oriented discourse that stresses the value of collective order, while in *The Virtue of Awakening,* Ghazzī draws heavily on Sufi discourses that stress the value of individual spiritual becoming. This distinction, which is tied to their specific motivations for composing their treatises, helps to explain why Ibn Taymiyya portrays *tashabbuh* in exclusively negative terms, whereas Ghazzī sees *tashabbuh* as a potentially positive force for the transformation of the individual human soul—an outlook that sets his treatise apart from nearly all other treatises on imitation.

SMALL DIFFERENCES

Sigmund Freud harnessed the dialectical tension between the twin forces of similarity and difference that shape identity to advance his powerful theory known as the "narcissism of small differences." "It is precisely the little dissimilarities in persons who are otherwise alike," observed Freud, "that arouse feelings of strangeness and enmity between them."[78] Put differently, human beings, individual and collective, have an uncanny tendency to differentiate themselves from those whom they resemble most—through small differences.

Freud first advanced this theory as a misogynistic explanation of why men have a "dread of woman," that is, of "becoming infected with her femininity."[79] But Freud realized the power of his theory to explain the hostility "in all human relations," including ethno-national conflicts between the Spaniards and Portuguese, Southern Germans and Northern Germans, and Britons and Scots, as well as interreligious conflicts between Jews and Christians.[80]

In *Civilization and Its Discontents,* Freud expands the social import of his theory, observing that "the inclination to aggression" facilitates "cohesion between the members of the community."[81] Small differences, in other words, enhance group solidarity by uniting a group against a common enemy. In this vein, Freud explains, sarcastically, that "the Jewish people, scattered everywhere, have rendered most useful services to the civilizations of the countries that have been their hosts; but unfortunately all the massacres of the Jews did not suffice to make that period more safe and secure for their Christian fellows."[82] The "most useful" service of the Jews was thus to be the object of hostility—a scapegoat—that united Christians together. Freud then draws readers' attention to a paradox: that the "inevitable consequence" of the Apostle Paul's command of universal love was "extreme intolerance" throughout Christendom.[83] In sum, Freud argues that human beings need a scapegoat to achieve group solidarity. These hostilities are most intense, paradoxically, when the rival is most similar, and may thus materialize in everyday life as "small differences."

I believe that Freud's theory helps to explain why Muslim differences were frequently small in scale—especially in relation to those who were most similar to them, Jews and Christians. Whether these small differences encompassed fashion such as beard length and headgear or physical gestures such as standing at funerals and kneeling during prayer, Freud's theory deepens our insight into why Muslim difference took the shape it did.[84]

But Freud's theory also has several blind spots. Difference-making, after all, is a dynamic and complex process. As I argue in this book, small differences in fact made a very *big difference* to Muslims. Refining Freud's theory, I contend that small differences are small only in scale, not value. It is also reductionist (and inaccurate) for Freud to attribute this value exclusively to "narcissism," a psychological abnormality and moral vice, to the exclusion of social, political, and spiritual factors that also play integral roles. Finally, while Freud's attention to the scale of these differences is important, we must also consider another distinctive feature—how these small differences are mediated externally through the physical body.

OUTSIDE IN

Readers expecting to encounter arcane theological discourses comparing Islamic models of monotheism, prophecy, and soteriology to those of Judaism, Christianity, and other religious traditions may be disappointed in this book. Instead, they will read about the physical and material markers that set apart Muslims—dress and hairstyle, corporeal techniques of ritual prayer, proper conduct at funerals and festivals, and other apparently surface-level matters that focus on physical appearance. Why was it so important for Muslims to *look* different?

Looking different became an integral feature of normative Islam because being Muslim cannot be reduced exclusively to a private, interior, abstract, disembodied experience; it encompasses a public, exterior, material, and embodied dimension as well. The habit of adopting physical markers to set apart religious communities, Michael Morony has shown, intensified in late antiquity, culminating with the rise of Islam.[85] Mediated through dress, fashion, and physical gestures, visible markers of difference set Muslims apart from others and publicly signaled their membership in the community of believers.[86] Some theologians, for example, anathematized Muslims for wearing a *zunnār,* a thick belt habitually worn by Christians—a penalty that applied to Muslims who did so in public, where it visibly signaled the rejection of Islam and the adoption of a new faith. The severity of the penalty reflects not only the symbolic value of this physical marker but also the socio-political value of the preservation of a distinct Muslim public.

This emphasis on physical appearance is anticipated by the imitation hadith, as this alternate translation makes clear: "Whoever *resembles* a people is one of them." Recall that *tashabbuh* can mean "resemblance," which primarily indicates likeness in physical appearance. But the association of *tashabbuh* with the visual realm is also conveyed by my original translation of imitation, which shares etymological roots with "image" through Latin (*imago*) and Proto-Indo-European (*aim*), and informs common portrayals of imitation as a surface-level or counterfeit copy. This emphasis inspires the bare reading of the hadith in which a person's identity is defined by looks alone. Image is indeed everything. Although *ʿulamāʾ* avoided a literal reading of the hadith, which anathematizes any Muslim who looks like a non-Muslim, they nonetheless placed immense value on looking different.

But Muslim difference needed not only to be seen but also to materialize through the other physical senses—sound, touch, taste, and smell. In other words, the obligation to be different became a means to cultivate Muslim aesthetic sensibilities—not in the Kantian sense of rationally contemplating the sublime and beautiful, but in the classical Aristotelian sense of experiencing the world through the physical senses (*aesthetikon*).[87] Muslim difference, after all, was not confined to the elite domain of fine art but comprehended the more expansive domain of everyday life. When the Prophet Muhammad was asked whether Muslims should live alongside idolaters, he replied: "Their fires shall not be visible to one another."[88] Signaling more than light and warmth, the vivid image of two separately lit fires is a visual metaphor for the physical and social distance believers should keep from unbelievers in order to safeguard an Islamic public sphere.[89] Inspired by such traditions, Muslim elites created a distinctively Islamic public sphere by defining the sensory landscape, from architectural styles to the acoustics of the call to prayer. But how did figures like Ibn Taymiyya and Ghazzī respond to carnivalesque disruptions to this sphere at festivals (*ʿīds*) and coffeehouses, which had the potential to overload the senses, overturn social hierarchies, and erase the lines that set Muslims apart? And how can a "sensitive" reading—one that draws our attention to the physical senses—refine our understanding of their multilayered discourses?

Existing within and through the body, the physical senses naturally draw our attention to the integral role of embodiment in expressing Muslim difference. Mauss's representation of imitation as a repertoire of *corporeal techniques*—movements, postures, gestures—can be extended to the practice of shunning imitation, of being different.[90] By framing imitation—and its obverse, difference—as embodied acts, "Whoever imitates a people becomes one of them" gains new meaning as an axiom that unites the physical body with the social body. Embodied acts of imitation, in other words, bring the imitator's physical body into the fold of the social body. To discipline the physical body then, as Mary Douglas argued in her classic study *Purity and Danger,* is to discipline the social body.[91] This book documents in colorful detail how Muslim religious authorities regulated the Muslim social body by means of the physical body.

But historians of Islam, especially early Islam, have underestimated the importance of embodied practices in shaping Muslim identity and solidarity. Scholars, then, must *embody* early Islamic history; they must put the body into their historical accounts of Islam, as this book does. If we set aside our modern Protestant-inspired expectations of what religion is supposed to be, we can better understand the role of the body in setting apart Muhammad's followers, "Muslims," from Jews, Christians, and others during the first centuries of Islam and beyond. Embodied practices, after all, are public; they are visible to others both within and beyond the community of believers. They are thus potent sites of analysis for scholars to better understand how Islam has been mediated in public life.

"I am conscious of the world," observed the French philosopher Maurice Merleau-Ponty, "through the medium of my body."[92] This insight suggests that the body functions as a porous boundary between the world outside and the self inside. But demystifying the relationship between these two apparently distinct zones has preoccupied thinkers across human cultures and societies. My approach is to move from the outside in, unveiling how Muslim thinkers endowed somatic practices of difference with symbolic meaning and value.

The ontological and epistemological relationships between exterior (*ẓāhir*) and interior (*bāṭin*), as *ʿulamāʾ* discourses on *tashabbuh* show, have profound implications for individual spiritual transformation and social solidarity.

Throughout Islamic history, *ʿulamāʾ* contemplated how the visible world reflects invisible spiritual truths. What are the external signs of spiritual-emotional states such as piety, sincerity, and love for God that reside deep within a person's soul (*nafs*) and heart (*qalb*)? Such questions were intertwined with Muslim anxieties over imitation's authenticity: how true is an imitation to the original? Is it a mere outward shell, a fake, or does it authentically duplicate the original in all its attributes, internal and external? The authenticity of imitation (and difference) figures into *ʿulamāʾ* discourses on Muslim spirituality and solidarity in a range of scenarios: the simple case of believers whose external behavior (*ẓāhir*) truly reflects their personal faith in Islam (*bāṭin*), and more complex cases of believers whose external behavior is not aligned with their faith—like those who bedazzle the public with their religious practice but are devoid of sincerity, like fool's gold, and others whose external demeanor and conduct appear unremarkable but who are illuminated from within.

IMITATIO MUHAMMADI

The quest for authenticity propelled the quest to canonize the hadiths, the treasury of the exemplary sayings and doings of Muhammad and the discursive building blocks of Muslim difference. A cadre of entrepreneurial religious scholars, the Partisans of Hadith, assembled these fragmentary texts into compilations that provided subsequent generations of Muslims with a comprehensive vision of the Prophet's model behavior (*sunna*).[93] But because the hadiths were compiled several generations after the Prophet's death, their authenticity was suspect: do the hadiths accurately represent what the Prophet Muhammad originally said and did? To establish their authenticity, the Partisans of Hadith provided every hadith with a set of credentials: a chain of transmitters that went back to the Prophet, like a diachronic game of telephone. Hadith transmission was itself mimetic, consisting of texts passed down over generations, copies that claimed to represent the Prophetic "original." But amid growing ideological divisions within the Muslim community, the Partisans of Hadith attempted to verify the authenticity of hadiths by meticulously evaluating the veracity of the transmitters themselves in order to assign each hadith a grade that ranged from fabricated to authentic.[94] As with any act of imitation, capturing the original text was elusive, but, in the view of these scholars, not impossible.[95]

The quest for authenticity became so central to the authority of hadith that it took precedence over the interpretation of the textual content (*matn*) of the hadith itself. With room to quarrel over both their authenticity and meaning, the hadiths became the main forum for interpretive disagreements among *ʿulamāʾ* across various schools of thought, sharpening sectarian differences between Sunnis and Shiʿis, who canonized their own distinct hadith collections. These divisions point to a deeper social function of hadith canonization: to define membership in the Muslim community along competing visions of orthodoxy and the Prophet's legacy. The canonization of hadith was thus marred by the political and theological schisms that fractured the early Muslim community from its birth.

We therefore must be very careful with how we use hadiths as historical sources. As a body of normative texts that portray a vision of what Islam ought to be, they do not provide a transparent window into the Islamic past; rather, they are portals into the Muslim social imagination and the collective memory of the Prophet's legacy. It was not uncommon for hadiths to polemically cast Others—Jews, Christians, pagans, Persians, Romans—according to a tinted lens of generalized stereotypes that reflected the local perceptions of their transmitters.

Historians of religion should nonetheless resist the urge to dismiss hadiths as mere intellectual abstractions detached from historical reality.[96] Such a blanket disavowal tacitly endorses a "semiotic ideology" embedded in modern Western Protestant Christianity that creates rigid (and artificial) dichotomies between belief and practice, texts and things, subject and object.[97] Muslim representations of the world, after all, are "materially located within it."[98] To deepen and complicate oversimplified representations of the Other in the hadith and accent the interplay of texts and things in the Islamic past, I emplace these discourses in concrete social contexts, drawing on historical evidence from Arabic chronicles, legal treatises, biographical dictionaries, literature, and material culture, which together elicit both continuities and contrasts between the ideals enshrined in the Muslim social imagination and the messier reality of Muslim social history.[99]

CHAPTER I

Turning Away from Christians and Jews?

Every community has a direction to which it turns.

—QURAN 2:148

According to Muhammad's cousin Ibn ʿAbbās, "The Messenger of God used to love to agree with the People of the Book when he was not commanded to do otherwise."[1] Here, Ibn ʿAbbās recalls a time when the Prophet intentionally modeled his behavior after Jewish and Christian practice—except when God commanded him not to do so. In the same tradition, Ibn ʿAbbās describes how the Prophet concretely applied this principle in everyday life, mentioning that he "let his hair fall down over his forehead" so that he outwardly resembled the People of the Book—as opposed to Arab pagans, who parted their hair. Reflecting the deep connection between physical appearance and social belonging, the Prophet's new hairstyle publicly displayed his affiliation to local Arab Jews and Christians. The logic of following this fashion seems clear: Jews and Christians were monotheists and pagans were not.

But this was not an isolated incident. According to another tradition, upon migrating from Mecca to Medina, Muhammad observed local Jews fasting the day of ʿĀshūrāʾ in celebration of Moses's victory over Pharaoh. In the spirit of rivalry, he then ordered his followers to fast as well, saying to the Jews, "We are closer to Moses than you."[2] In yet another, the Prophet would imitate Jews and Christians by standing up during their funeral processions.[3] And not least, the Quran (2:144) alludes to a honeymoon period when Muhammad and his followers would face Jerusalem during prayer—the most important Islamic daily ritual—in imitation of the Jews. All of these shared practices had potent symbolic value for elevating the early Muslim community's monotheistic credentials.

But Muslims not only copied Jews and Christians, they also assimilated many practices of pre-Islamic Arabia. In the brilliant treatise *The Conclusive Argument from God,* the towering eighteenth-century intellectual Shāh Walī Allāh of Delhi (d. 1762) enumerates some of these practices.[4] He states that, contrary to conventional wisdom, "the five pillars" that came to define the core rituals of Islam—divine unity, prayer, fasting, charity, and the pilgrimage to Mecca—were already in place in pre-Islamic Arabia before Islam. Beyond the domain of ritual, Muslims also came to embody pre-Islamic cultural values, such as hospitality and generosity. In sum, Shāh Walī Allāh observes that the Prophet retained "whatever remained of the true religion [of Abraham]" by defining how Muslims should worship and adopting morally upright norms that conformed to the values of Islam, while forbidding corrupt ones that did not.[5]

Walī Allāh's balanced analysis of Islam's relationship to its pre-Islamic past is unusual—given that Islamic tradition has accentuated how the first Muslims were *different.* To counter this accent on Islam's distinction, some historians have recently stressed what the first Muslims had in common with rival religious communities and proposed extended timelines for the crystallization of Muslims into a distinct religious community. In *Muhammad and the Believers,* Fred Donner argues that this evolutionary process lasted well into the seventh century—not before, but decades *after* the Prophet passed away. Donner draws attention to *the believers* in the book's title because the Quran uses that term (*muʾminūn,* s. *muʾmin*) far more often than *Muslim. Muʾmin,* in Donner's reading, emphasizes the affinities between Muslims, Christians, and Jews—who are all possessors of scripture (*ahl al-kitāb*)—more so than does *Muslim,* which is a distinct confessional identity set apart from Jews and Christians that, he argues, did not emerge until the reign of the Umayyad caliph ʿAbd al-Mālik b. Marwān (r. 685–705). Before this period, a broad interconfessional community consisting of Muslims, Christians, and Jews formed what Donner calls "the Believers' movement." Muslims came together with Jews and Christians, he argues, to oppose the sins of the world around them, from theft to adultery. The Quran also confirms the divine revelation of both Jewish and Christian scriptures, the Torah and Gospel, and interweaves the prophetic narratives of Jesus, Moses, and Noah into an extended history of communication between human and divine. Muslims even prayed in Christian churches. Donner concludes that "there is no reason to think that the Believers viewed themselves as constituting a new or separate religious confession."[6] Thus *Believer,* not *Muslim,* better describes the religious identity that prevailed during the first century of Islam.

The late historian of Islam Patricia Crone criticized Donner's history for its selective use of historical evidence.[7] Among the evidence Donner marginalizes are the hadiths—perhaps due to their questionable historicity and emphasis on Muslim difference. As a direct result of this dismissal, in my view, Donner also diminishes the pivotal role of the body in setting apart early Muslims from Jews and Christians—small physical gestures such as the cardinal direction of ritual prayer, the posture taken during funeral processions, and matters of grooming such as hairstyle. As mentioned above, however, some evidence in the hadiths in fact supports Donner's thesis that Muhammad's community modeled themselves after Jews and Christians—that a distinct Muslim community emerged from a gradual, evolutionary process. The main disagreement among historians of early Islam, however, lies in both the chronology of this process and how it was translated into everyday Muslim practice. I accord greater historical weight to the evidence contained in the hadiths and, by extension, to the role of the physical body in enhancing solidarity and defining membership in the early Muslim community. I view this evidence through the lens of René Girard's holistic theory of mimetic rivalry, which proposes a model of how imitation leads to rivalry and conflict. Muslim difference did not result in categorical opposition to Jews and Christians, but rather moderated between extremes—at once setting the believers apart and connecting them to the shared world around them. This narrative of Muslim difference aligns with evidence found in the Quran as well as material sources from the first decades of the seventh century. Although I am more interested in explaining *how* Muslim difference materialized into practice than in determining exactly *when* the event(s) took place, I defend the plausibility of the claim that Muslims began to perceive themselves as a distinct religious community while the Prophet was still alive—even as intercommunal boundaries continued to remain fluid.

MIMETIC RIVALRY

How does imitation lead to conflict, to difference? René Girard proposed that human beings learn to desire through imitation—that humans acquire their desires from others.[8] This *mimetic desire* for an object is thus mediated through a model—the one imitated, who possesses the desired object. This mediated relationship, argues Girard, creates a dynamic triangulation between imitator, object, and model—a theory that has striking parallels to the model of imitation proposed by the medieval Muslim theologian Ibn Taymiyya (see chapter 5). Girard explains, "The value of an object grows in proportion to the resistance met with in acquiring it. And the value of the model grows as the object's value grows."[9] A problem arises, however, when that object is rare or valuable, and a rivalry ensues between the imitator and model—a *mimetic rivalry:* "As rivalry becomes more acute, the rivals are more apt to forget about whatever objects are, in principle, the cause of the rivalry and instead to become more fascinated with one another. In effect, the rivalry is purified of any external stake and becomes a matter of pure rivalry and prestige. Each rival becomes for his counterpart the worshipped and despised model and obstacle, the one who must be at once beaten and assimilated."[10] As the *mimetic rivalry* between imitator and model intensifies, the value of the desired object decreases. The imitator eventually enters into a paradoxical relationship with the "worshipped and despised" model, whom he wants to both assimilate and overcome at once. Ultimately, the mimetic rivalry may spiral into a cycle of violence, where imitator and model come to mirror each other and once-differentiated rivals become undifferentiated "doubles."[11] The distinction between imitator and model thus collapses.

The "object" of mimetic rivalry, in Girard's theory, is not necessarily a material object; it can be an abstract idea or doctrine such as religion, God, or monotheism.

TURNING AWAY FROM JERUSALEM

Girard's mimetic theory helps to account for how early Muslims went from imitating their fellow monotheists—Jews and Christians—to becoming rivals seeking to differentiate themselves from them.[12] A common feature of the hadiths that describe instances when the Prophet imitated Judeo-Christian practice is that they are retrospective; although the Prophet originally wanted to be like Jews and Christians, he eventually stopped. The Prophet's policy of imitating the People of the Book was just a temporary phase.

This narrative arc appears to be grounded in the pivotal Quranic verse 2:144, which commanded Muhammad to change the direction to which he prayed from Jerusalem to Mecca, thus marking a literal and figurative turnaround for the Muslim community—one so symbolically potent that it likely inspired reversals in other areas of Muslim ritual and cultural life. The turn away from Jerusalem in ritual prayer may even be the single most pivotal gesture of collective Muslim distinction during Islam's formative period. Q 2:144 orders the Prophet to "turn your face toward the Holy Mosque," or the *ka ʿba* in Mecca, according to exegetes.[13] Two more times the Quran repeats, "Turn your face toward the Holy Mosque," in case Muhammad and his followers harbored any doubts. According to the Companion Ibn ʿUmar, Muslims responded immediately: "While some people were performing the early morning prayer at [the mosque of] Qubāʾ, a man came and said, 'Tonight, [verses of] the Quran have been revealed commanding the messenger of God to face the *kaʿba* [during prayer], so turn around and face it.' They were facing Jerusalem as they turned towards the *kaʿba*."[14] According to this testimony, the congregation did not wait until the next prayer to enact the command; they turned toward Mecca *while they were still performing* the morning prayer (figure 2). They literally turned away from Jerusalem.

In Q 2:144, the Prophet's face, *wajh,* is not only a metonym for the physical body but a surrogate for identity—connecting the exoteric to the esoteric.[15] Q 2:148 then justifies this command by panning from the individual person of Muhammad to the character and identity of human communities as a whole: "Every community has a direction [*wijhat^{un}*] to which it faces."[16] *Wijha,* translated here as "direction," shades into the semantic field of its linguistic relative, *wajh,* thus indicating that a community's physical orientation, which encompasses its repertoire of social practices, also reflects its moral orientation. Indeed, this Quranic verse reflects what may have been common knowledge among peoples living in the Near East. Historical narratives indicate that pre-Islamic Arabian monotheists, the *Ḥanīfs*, prayed toward the *kaʿba.*[17] Hadith reports of Jews praying toward Jerusalem are supported by the Torah, which suggests that Daniel faced Jerusalem when praying, and the Quran (10:87), which recounts that God commanded Moses and Aaron to "make your houses a direction [*qiblat^{an}*] to which men pray."[18] Some historians assert that Near Eastern Christians prayed toward the east; some even claim that Muslims initially followed that practice.[19]

The Quran has no illusions that everyone will turn around and follow Muhammad's new direction, fulfilling his expectations for a single united moral community, presaging instead a more likely result—interreligious conflict: "Yet if you should bring to those that have been given the Book every sign, they will not follow your direction; you are not a follower of their direction, neither are they followers of one another's direction" (Q 2:145). Neither will these differences be amicably accepted by Muhammad's rivals. Instead, the Quran predicts that they will revile him and his followers for their about-face: "The fools among the people will say: What has turned them from the direction they were facing in their prayer aforetime?" (Q 2:142). But who were

Figure 2. (*Top row, center*): illustration of the Mosque of the Two Qiblas (*Qiblatayn*). *Futūḥ al-ḥaramayn* (*Description of the Two Holy Cities*), by Muḥyī al-dīn Lārī, mid-sixteenth century. (Metropolitan Museum of Art, New York, no. 32.131, fol. 48r.)

these "fools"? The prolific Quran exegete and historian Ibn Jarīr al-Ṭabarī (d. 923) documents the plausible responses of Muhammad's rivals:

> The Hypocrites [*munāfiqūn*] said: "What is wrong with them? They faced one direction for a while, then they left it and faced another one?" The Muslims said, "If only we knew about our brothers who died while they prayed toward Jerusalem! Will God accept [these prior acts of devotion] from us and from them, or not?" The Jews said, "Muhammad missed the city of his ancestors—his birthplace; if he had held firm to our *qibla,* we would have wished him to be our master for whom we were waiting." The pagans [*mushrikūn*] from among the people of Mecca said, "Muhammad is confused about his religion so, through his *qibla,* he turned himself toward you [Meccans], knowing that you were upon firmer guidance than he was; so, perhaps, he will enter your religion [as well]."[20]

According to this portrayal, everyone was confused—even Muslims. Both the Meccan pagans and Medinan Hypocrites—fake Muslims who joined Muhammad's cause for political gain alone—accused Muhammad of "flip-flopping," a critique of politicians still common today.[21] While the pagans mock Muhammad, saying that he finally has come to his senses and will return to his ancestral religion, the Hypocrites accuse Muhammad of doing what they themselves often did: changing his mind. But Muhammad's true followers had other concerns. According to the earliest preserved Quran commentary, the exegesis of Muqātil b. Sulaymān (d. 767), a group of Jews asked the Muslims: "And what do you know [about the fate in the afterlife] concerning one of you who died [while having prayed toward] our *qibla?*"[22] This troubling question incited Muslim fears that their deceased relatives who had prayed toward Jerusalem but never toward Mecca were destined to be among the damned in the world to come. Given Muhammad's stress on preparing for life after death, both his opponents' prickly question and his followers' distressed response were not unreasonable. They both indicate the powerful social, political, and religious symbolism of the gesture to insiders and outsiders alike.

But of all the rival groups, in Ṭabarī's retelling, Medinan Jews responded most bitterly. Echoing the pagans, Jewish leaders accused Muhammad of returning to his ancestral tradition not because he was spiritually reborn but because he was just homesick. By impugning his motives, these rivals not only smear Muhammad but rob the physical gesture of its divine authority. The

Jews' second criticism—that they would have made Muhammad their prophet had he not turned away from Jerusalem toward Mecca—may indicate despair, although that scenario was becoming increasingly improbable. A third Jewish response narrated by Ṭabarī drips with scorn: "Muhammad and his companions did not know where their *qibla* was until we guided them to it."[23] Here, the Jews cope with the slow decline of their religious and political authority in Medina by reminding Muhammad of his humble origins and their (passing) glory. Collectively, the responses suggest that Medina's Jewish tribes interpreted the turn away from Jerusalem as a turn away from them—a culmination of deteriorating relations with Muhammad. They also suggest that the physical gesture of facing a new direction—and, indeed, the city of Jerusalem itself—was suffused with religious and political symbolism. In light of the symbolic crown the Quran and subsequent Muslim religious authorities placed upon this moment, a number of Western scholars going back over a century characterized the turn away from Jerusalem as "a break with the Jews."[24] Speaking of this "break," English Orientalist David S. Margoliouth presumed, "Mohammed had by this time resolved on their destruction."[25]

Did God's command to face Mecca correspond to what Muhammad wanted? Ṭabarī claims that even before the change of *qibla,* the Medinan Jews would taunt Muhammad: "He faces our *qibla* but opposes us in our religion."[26] Stating that Muhammad used to earnestly petition God to reorient the prayer to a new direction, the Quran implies that he indeed wanted to face Mecca. Perhaps he lost hope that the Medinan Jews would join him, or perhaps he longed to reestablish Mecca as the symbolic axis of communal worship. Whatever the reason, it is likely that he wanted a new direction for his community. Later generations of religious scholars from Ṭabarī to Ibn Taymiyya memorialized this event as a literal and metaphorical "turning point" in the Muslim community's relationship with Christians and Jews—shifting their social orientation from being similar to being different.[27] Turning toward Mecca, according to this narrative, established a new vision of selfhood for the Muslim community. Linking physical body to social body, the physical gesture of turning away embodied a new spirit of Muslim independence.

According to other hadith traditions, this new physical orientation also inspired a revaluation of sacred space. Mecca becomes the center of Islam—as indicated by hadiths that enumerate the *kaʿba*'s spiritual value: ritual prayer performed at the sacred precinct had one hundred thousand times more spiritual value than ritual prayer performed in a nonsacred space.[28] This spiritual math, in fact, applied to all of Mecca. The sanctity of the *kaʿba* thus flowed throughout the entire city, turning Mecca itself into an inviolable sanctuary and the foremost geographic symbol (*shiʿār*) of Islam.[29]

As a consequence of this new direction, not only did the Muslim community's geographic axis shift to Mecca, its historical axis shifted to Abraham. In the Quran, juxtaposed next to the command to face Mecca is the story of how Abraham and his son Ishmael established a holy sanctuary in Mecca. "Who would forsake the religion of Abraham except a fool?" the Quran (2:130) chides. By declaring explicitly that Abraham was neither Christian nor Jewish but a monotheist (*ḥanīf*), the Quran rejects rival claims upon his legacy.[30] Other verses critique Jewish and Christian claims to exclusive salvation and their efforts to persuade Muslims to leave their religion, paving the way for the Quran to lay claim to Abraham's legacy: "We have seen you turning your face toward heaven; now We will surely turn you to a direction that shall please you. Turn your face toward the Holy Mosque; and wherever you are, turn your faces toward it."[31] The performance of Islam's most important ritual, prayer, now requires that Muslims face the house that Abraham built.

The symbolic value of Mecca continued to grow in the following centuries—even beyond the domain of ritual prayer. In mosques, niches were carved into the walls facing Mecca to identify the direction of prayer, shaping Islamic architectural styles.[32] The *Ḥajj,* the fifth ritual pillar of Islam, requires all able-bodied Muslims to make a pilgrimage to Mecca at least once in their lifetime. Medieval pedagogical manuals urge students of religious knowledge to bless their intellectual pursuits by facing Mecca when studying.[33] Similarly, the living body of someone about to sleep and the dead body of someone about to be buried should be oriented toward Mecca.[34] By contrast, no one should ever urinate toward Mecca out of respect for its holiness.[35] In sum, Muslims should aspire to embody, and thus display, their distinctive religious orientation from cradle to grave. For this reason, beginning in the first Islamic century, Muslims began to call themselves "The People of the *Qibla.*"[36]

FROM STANDING TO SITTING

A cluster of hadith traditions follows this Quranic arc of transition from similarity to difference. According to the same account in which Ibn ʿAbbās observes that the Prophet originally conformed to Jewish and Christian norms, which included letting his hair hang down, he also mentions that "he began to part [his hair] afterwards." As with the direction of prayer, the Prophet ceased copying Jewish and Christian practice. In the narrations of this tradition collected by Bukhārī and Muslim, the two most authoritative compilations of Sunni hadith, Ibn ʿAbbās offers no explanation for this shift. He assumes the audience knows why.

If we emplot this anecdote within the grander narrative of the Prophet's biography, we see that it corresponds to both the gradual expansion of his authority and the crystallization of Islam into a distinctive brand of monotheism, which, in turn, precipitated a shift in Muslim rivalries and alliances with other religious communities; with the vanquishing of the pagan Arabs, Jews and Christians, originally allies, became Muhammad's new archrivals. The armed conflicts between Muhammad and the Jewish tribes of Medina as well as the Byzantine Empire, whose official religion was Christianity, would have expedited this transition.[37]

About two decades after the Prophet died, according to another tradition, the caliph ʿUmar (ʿUmar I, r. 634–44) completed this narrative circle by decreeing that Christian subjects in Damascus *not* part their hair in order to remain visibly distinct from Muslims, who did.[38] This mandate appears to confirm the testimony of Ibn ʿAbbās that the Prophet began to part his hair to look different from the People of the Book.[39] But now the caliph of a rapidly growing polity was in a position to legislate the behavior not only of Muslims but of non-Muslims as well. According to Muslim chroniclers, this distinctive hairstyle lasted through the beginning of the next century, when the Umayyad caliph ʿUmar b. ʿAbd al-ʿAzīz (ʿUmar II, r. 717–20) clipped the forelocks of some Christian Arabs from Najrān because they parted their hair like Muslims.[40] In fact, the clipped forelock became such a distinctive feature of non-Muslim minorities that the term *muqaṣṣaṣ,* one whose forelock has been clipped, became shorthand for non-Muslim subjects of the caliphate (*dhimmī*).[41] The shift in early Muslim hairstyles thus became a physical marker of the shift in religious rivalries, from paganism to monotheism, and a shift in the Prophet's orientation toward Jews and Christians from imitation to difference.

A similar pivot is seen with regard to the fast of ʿĀshūrāʾ, the tenth day of Muḥarram in the Islamic calendar, which some scholars have claimed is the Day of Atonement (Yom Kippur) in the Jewish calendar.[42] The Prophet originally ordered Muslims to fast, following Jewish custom, but, according to some traditions, withdrew this command once fasting during Ramadan was decreed. According to another tradition narrated by Ibn ʿAbbās, the Prophet vowed to observe ʿĀshūrāʾ on the ninth of Muḥarram instead of the tenth, as observed by the Jews, but died before fulfilling this vow.[43] In the version transmitted by Muslim, Ibn ʿAbbās does not offer an explanation for this date change.[44]

So then what happened? Early debates among Muslims over whether to stand or sit during funerals offer more clarity. While many traditions state that the Prophet stood in order to honor the funerals of non-Muslims, a small number say that he stopped, opting to sit instead, indicating that he changed his mind. Bukhārī, however, includes only traditions of the Prophet standing during funerals. In one instance, he stood to honor a deceased Jew and was questioned why he did so. He responded: "Was he not a human being?"[45] Apparently, Bukhārī did not believe that the traditions of the Prophet sitting down during funeral processions were credible. Muslim, however, did. He includes traditions of the Prophet standing but supplements them with traditions like this one: "The Prophet of God stood but then sat."[46] But none of the traditions collected by Muslim explain why.

Most jurists nonetheless concluded that the Prophet began to sit down as funeral processions passed by. Ibn Ḥanbal, a resident of Baghdad, included the following tradition in his *Musnad* collection on the authority of the Successor Abū Maʿmar, which clarifies the one transcribed by Muslim above: "We were with ʿAlī when a funeral procession passed him and people stood up for it. ʿAlī asked: Who gave you this ruling? So they replied: Abū Mūsā. ʿAlī said: The Messenger of God used to do this [stand] when he imitated [*yatashabbahu*] the People of the Book, but when he was prohibited from doing this he stopped."[47] In this tradition, ʿAlī explains that the Prophet stopped standing because he stopped imitating Jews and Christians, and he stopped imitating Jews and Christians because God commanded him to—perhaps alluding to the Quranic mandate to face Mecca (instead of Jerusalem) during prayer. This rationale resembles Ibn ʿAbbās's explanation of why the Prophet changed his hairstyle. What ʿAlī and Ibn ʿAbbās espouse is a theory of abrogation, or *naskh:* that a ruling on a given practice has changed (or should change) due to a change in circumstances (social, cultural, political, economic).[48] In light of such evidence, Ignaz Goldziher, over a century ago, boldly claimed that it was "unanimous that Muslims should not follow the customs of their coreligionists."[49]

Other traditions also conclude that the Prophet began to sit during funerals, but give alternative versions of how it came about. In one instance, the Prophet stood as a funeral procession was passing by. He was then informed by a Jew who was also present that standing during funeral processions was a distinctive Jewish custom. Alarmed, the Prophet abruptly ordered his followers to "be different from them [*khālifūhum*]," meaning the Jews, and sat down.[50] In this portrayal, the Prophet is initially unaware that Jews stood during funeral processions, but upon being informed of this custom, he promptly commands his followers to be different. Although this narrative never acknowledges a period in which the Prophet habitually imitated Judeo-Christian tradition, it does not eliminate that possibility, since this encounter could have taken place after God commanded Muhammad to be different.

Viewing the above traditions through the lens of Girard's mimetic framework helps to explain why Muslim emulation eventually gave way to differentiation. If we accept as historically plausible that the Prophet once parted his hair, stood during funeral processions, prayed toward Jerusalem, and fasted during ʿĀshūrāʾ—in direct imitation of Judeo-Christian practice—then these acts, in the aggregate, express a *mimetic desire* for the legacy of monotheism. But as the *mimetic rivalry* intensified between the upstart Muslims and these more established religious communities, conflict soon followed; these models of monotheism, once lauded, became "obstacles" who had to be "beaten"—as indicated by the traditions above that illustrate how the Prophet eventually stopped imitating the distinctive features of Judeo-Christian practice in Arabia.

MUDDLED MEMORIES

But the self-realization of the early Muslim community did not follow such a clear narrative arc. Notwithstanding the persuasiveness of Girard's explanatory model, succeeding generations of Muslims did not cease imitating others, whether they worshipped one God or many gods. Historians may justifiably question whether the symbolic value of these reversals had become apparent to Muhammad's contemporaries.

Contrasting narratives *within* Islamic sources suggest that the meaning and significance of the *qibla* remained fluid during the first century of Islam. One disputed fact was when the event took place. Estimates in hadiths range from sixteen months *before* the Prophet's emigration from Mecca to Medina to about two years *after* his emigration—meaning that the *qibla* change may have taken place in either Mecca or Medina.[51] There is also a vast difference between each city's social and political context. In Mecca, Muhammad had little, if any, interaction with Jews. But some skeptical historians go even further, questioning whether Muhammad had any interactions with Jews in

Medina, given that no material evidence apart from Islamic sources survives that attests to the existence of Medinan Jews or the type of Judaism they practiced.[52]

Adding to the confusion, Islamic traditions contain opposing narratives about where Muslims faced before turning to Mecca. Some traditions claim Muslims prayed toward Mecca, then Jerusalem, then once again toward Mecca.[53] Others claim that they prayed at the *kaʿba* in Mecca *while* facing Jerusalem.[54] And yet others suggest Muslims prayed in either cardinal direction.[55] Based on archeological evidence, historians have variously argued that Muslims prayed toward the east like Christians, the south like Jews, or the north toward Syria before finally choosing Mecca. Burial sites in Jordan and elsewhere indicate, for example, that some Muslim corpses were placed in the ground facing Jerusalem and others facing Mecca—although Robert Hoyland has convincingly argued that this inconsistency indicates confusion among early Muslims over how to *calculate* the direction of the *qibla,* not the direction itself.[56]

Conflicting narratives over the historical arc of the *qibla* change were echoed in contrasting portrayals of Jerusalem's religious sanctity. While some early hadith scholars compiled traditions into specialized collections dedicated exclusively to the "religious merits" (*faḍāʾil*) of Jerusalem, some traditions nonetheless claimed that nothing was sacred about the Jewish direction of prayer.[57] One disparaging tradition claims that the Jews prayed toward the Rock in Jerusalem only after God became angry with them and removed the ark from its presence; this narrative suggests the Rock itself was not holy.[58]

Although the "before and after" hadith traditions discussed above suggest that the decision to turn away from Jews and Christians was settled by the Prophet during his lifetime, we nonetheless have good reason to view these reversals with caution. First, there are many hadith traditions that do not conform to this narrative; some traditions claim, for instance, that ʿĀshūrāʾ was a pre-Islamic Arab practice that Muslims later assimilated, not a Jewish custom. As already discussed, most traditions that describe the Prophet's posture during funerals say that he stood, and there exist alternative versions of when and how Muhammad turned away from Jerusalem that do not conform to the standard narrative.

But among the most explicit acknowledgments in Islamic literary sources of ongoing inter-Muslim debate over interreligious boundaries is the disagreement between the prominent Companions ʿAlī and Abū Mūsā over whether to stand or sit during funeral processions. The eyewitness narrator of the tradition, Abū Maʿmar, was not a Companion but a Successor who lived in

Kufa, Iraq, indicating that the dispute takes place *after* the Prophet had passed away. Although Abū Mūsā, as governor of Iraq, was a wise Companion, ʿAlī, the Prophet's cousin, son-in-law, and caliph, was the "gate" to all knowledge.[59] It is unclear, based on this tradition alone, whether the two disagreed on principle or practice: was Abū Mūsā unaware that the Prophet wished to distinguish himself from Jews and Christians in general or, in the case of funeral processions, in particular? What is clear, however, is that two of the most venerable Companions disagreed on how to define the line between Muslims and non-Muslims, indicating that Muslim communal boundaries remained fluid decades after the Prophet had died.

When faced with such contrasting viewpoints between and within hadith traditions, it is perhaps understandable that Donner's historical account of early Islam leaves out this body of evidence altogether. Given the cumulative weight of these inconsistencies, the narrative that Muhammad turned away from Jerusalem due to "a break with the Jews" appears to unravel. Aziz Al-Azmeh thus concluded "that there was no such thing as a 'change' of the *qibla* from Jerusalem to Mecca. . . . The common assumption that this 'change' was a reaction to Muhammad's break with the Medinan Jews would need to be revised."[60] While acknowledging a shift, Fazlur Rahman argued that the new *qibla* was unrelated to Jews or Judaism since Muhammad could have disavowed the Jewish tribes while still facing Jerusalem; rather, "the real answer . . . is the centrality of the Meccan shrine to the religion of Islam."[61] Quran scholar Angelika Neuwirth also sees no evidence for this characterization and argues that it represents an "exilic longing" for the original homeland of Mecca—one that in fact mirrors the longing that the exiled Babylonian Jews experienced over a millennium before.[62] Put differently, in Neuwirth's intertextual reading, Muhammad's turn away from Jerusalem was in fact a turn *toward* the Jews.

I propose that instead of locking ourselves into a false binary choice of deciding whether the line distinguishing Muslims from Jews and Christians was either absolutely indeterminate or absolutely defined, we choose both. Facing a new direction in prayer was an act that at once assimilated Muhammad's followers to a preexisting late antique cultural idiom and set them apart from all others who faced different directions. Turning away from Jerusalem was neither intended to be, nor resulted in, a clean break with the Jews (or Christians), as many scholars across the East and West have traditionally presumed. The metaphor of a "break" carries implications of a definitive and permanent separation between Muhammad's community and the Jews, which

الیهود بو كون محمد بن عبد الله قریشولك جنكنه
چقدی كا بردوم ایلمك بیزه واجبدور یهودیلر
ایتدیلر بو كون سبت كونیدور نجه ایده لوم
مخیرق ایتدی لا سبت لكم یعنی سیزولك ایچون

is an exaggeration. Strictly speaking, the physical act of turning need not be a 180-degree about-face in the opposite direction, but can be a pivot toward a different direction that is nonetheless proximate to the old one. With this image in mind, we may presume instead that the line distinguishing Muslims from Jews and Christians became more defined but nonetheless remained indeterminate (figures 3 and 4).

There is thus no need to interpret the act of turning away from Jerusalem as symbolically monovalent. While the *qibla* change may express exilic longing and reverence for the *ka ʿba,* it is also likely that the very public and symbolically potent act of facing a new direction in ritual prayer would have been perceived by members of both Muhammad's community and rival communities as a powerful statement of self-determination—especially when viewed alongside the Prophet's first major military victory at Badr. It is understandable, even expected, that some members of Medina's Jewish tribes would have perceived Muhammad's sudden prosperity as a looming threat to their own political futures. The turn *toward* Mecca, after all, was at the same time a turn *away* from Jerusalem.

Among the most important indicators that the turn away from Jerusalem was neither intended to be nor resulted in a complete break from the Jews is the enduring status of Jerusalem in early Muslim historical memory. Although some historians suggest that the Umayyad caliph ʿAbd al-Mālik built the Dome of the Rock in Jerusalem to compete with Mecca as a pilgrimage site, Muslim religious authorities advanced a dominant narrative that resolved this tension by recognizing the sanctity of the al-Aqṣā mosque in Jerusalem but ranking it below that of the *ka ʿba.*[63] Prayer at the al-Aqṣā mosque, according to hadith, is valued at five hundred times more than an ordinary prayer but less than prayer at the *ka ʿba.*[64] Along with the holy mosques in Mecca and Medina, the al-Aqṣā mosque is ranked as one of only three pilgrimage destinations.[65] Whatever anxieties over Jewish influence remained, Muslims preserved the status of Jerusalem in their imaginations of sacred geography.

Figure 3 (*left*). Mukhayriq, in discussion with five Jewish confederates, agrees to fight with Muhammad in war (ca. 625). According to biographer Ibn Hishām, Mukhayriq did not convert to Islam. From *Siyar-i nabī* (*Life of the Prophet*), by Muṣtafā Ḍarīr. Illustrated ca. 1594–95. (New York Public Library, New York, Spencer Collection, vol. 3 [p. 118]. New York Public Library Digital Collections. Accessed March 30, 2020. http://digitalcollections.nypl.org/items/510d47da-616c-a3d9-e040-e00a18064a99.)

Figure 4. Muslims and Jews celebrate Fāṭima's wedding, which took place in 622 or 623. A sleeve of Fāṭima's cloak is shown to the rabbis, who marvel at its quality. Inside the chamber, four veiled Muslim women, Umm al-Ayman, Umm al-muʾminīn (ʿĀʾisha), Fāṭima, and Umm Salama (*seated right to left*), are engaged in lively conversation with nine unveiled Jewish women. Jews socialize outside wearing Ottoman-style red and black tarbushes. From *Siyar-i nabī* (*Life of the Prophet*), by Muṣtafā Ḍarīr. Illustrated ca. 1594–95. (Chester Beatty Library, Dublin, Turkish Collection, no. 419, vol. 4, fol. 44r.)

IN A MATERIAL WORLD

Some of the oldest artifacts of "Islamic" material culture suggest that some distinctive features of the early Muslim community emerged very early, while others developed later. Let us take, for example, the oldest tombstone ascribed to a Muslim, who was buried in al-Qarāfa, outside the garrison city of Fusṭāṭ, after the conquest of Egypt (figure 5).[66] How do we know that the tombstone belongs to a Muslim? One clue is the person's name, etched in Arabic: ʿAbd al-Raḥmān b. Khayr al-Ḥajrī. However, names were not always a reliable identity marker, as some Christians possessed "Muslim" names. There are, however, two more salient identifiers of his religious affiliation: the prefatory formula known as the *basmala,* "In the name of Allah, Merciful, Compassionate," and the deceased's death date, Jumādā II, AH 31/652 CE, calculated according to the Muslim lunar calendar. Leor Halevi observes that

Figure 5. The tombstone of ʿAbd al-Raḥmān b. Khayr al-Ḥajrī, AH 31/652 CE. From Hassan Mohammed El-Hawary, "The Most Ancient Islamic Monument Known Dated A.H. 31 (A.D. 652) from the Time of the Third Calif ʿUthman." *Journal of the Royal Asiatic Society of Great Britain & Ireland* 62, no. 2 (1930): plate 3. (Reproduced with permission of Cambridge University Press.)

because the tombstone lacks Quranic verses and salutations upon the Prophet Muhammad, features that came to distinctively mark subsequent Muslim graves, it "displayed no distinctively Islamic formulas."[67] Although Halevi is not wrong to point out the absence of these two notable "Islamic" features, I believe he overstates the case. If the tombstone of Ḥajrī did not exhibit any distinctively Islamic features, how would we know that he was almost certainly Muslim? It is thus important not to diminish the value of the religious markers that are present on this object.

Although not without precedents and parallels in other late antique Near Eastern religious traditions, the *basmala* is cited in the earliest extant Quran manuscripts, which date to the first half of the seventh century. While usually described by historians as Islam's earliest literary source, the Quran is at the same time indispensable *material* evidence of Muslim communal formation, a subject I will return to below.[68] Neuwirth reminds us that the *basmala* emerges early in the chronology of the Quran's revelation: "It must not be overlooked that from at least the middle Meccan period, the units of recitation, the suras themselves, take on the introduction *bi-smillāh al-raḥmān al-raḥīm,* 'In the name of God the compassionate, the merciful.'"[69] The *basmala*'s invocation in everyday life appears to have become so prevalent among the first generation of Muslims that not only was it transcribed onto the earliest Quran manuscripts and etched onto the earliest tombstones, it was also displayed on the earliest surviving Arabic papyrus (PERF 558), a receipt dating to Jumādā I, AH 22/March–April 643 CE, just a decade after the Prophet died in 632.[70] The *basmala*'s recurring presence among the earliest surviving artifacts of Islamic material culture suggests that it became a linguistic marker of belonging in the early Muslim community.

But as significant as the *basmala* was to the public display of Muslim identity, the inscription of the lunar year may, in fact, be the marker of greater communal significance to early Muslims. The calendar begins with the year of the Prophet Muhammad's emigration, or *hijra,* from Mecca to Medina in 622 CE. Medina is the city where the Prophet first established a single community of believers under his authority. Those who followed Muhammad from Mecca to Medina were known as the emigrants, or *muhājirūn,* a term attested by the Quran that designated their special spiritual and social status within the community of believers.[71] Some of the earliest non-Muslim sources to mention Muhammad's community, composed in Greek and Syriac during the middle of the seventh century, refer to Muhammad's community not as Muslims but as emigrants—*magaritai* (Greek) and *mhaggrāyē/mhaggrē* (Syriac)—signaling the importance of mobility and settlement to the formation of the Muslim community.[72]

By commemorating this event, the lunar calendar magnifies the value and meaning of the emigration, marking it as a new beginning for the Prophet. The physical immigration to a new place evolves into a socio-psychological immigration to a new way of imagining time, transforming the *hijra* into a chronotope, a marker of time/space. The calendar is thus appropriately referred to as the *hjirī* calendar.[73] The origins of the *hjirī* date nevertheless post-date Muhammad, having been established sometime between 636 and 639 by the second Caliph ʿUmar, who retroactively dated the calendar's first year to the year of Muhammad's emigration.[74] The same papyrus (PERF 558) that contains the earliest written version of the *basmala* also contains the earliest known reference to a *hjirī* date, AH 22, about five years after ʿUmar is said to have adopted the new calendar.[75]

As caliph, ʿUmar advanced a process of reshaping the Muslim community's imagination of time that the Prophet Muhammad had already begun. While the Prophet may not have instituted the *hjirī* dating system, he reportedly did shun the widespread pre-Islamic practice of intercalation (*al-nasīʾ*) and thus initiated a new way of calculating the calendar year after the conquest of Mecca in 622 that was distinct from existing Jewish lunisolar and Christian solar calendars. During his farewell pilgrimage, the Prophet publicly proclaimed, "Time has come full circle" (*inna al-zamān qad istadār*). In other words, the Prophet had taken the remarkable step of restoring time to "its original form, the day when God created the heavens and earth."[76] The new system of timekeeping ultimately produced a Muslim calendar that, in the estimation of Stephen Blake, "was radically different from those of contemporary Jews or Christians."[77]

With a bias toward seeking out conventional markers of religion, such as scripture, ritual, or creed, scholars of Islam can easily overlook the "religious" significance of quotidian practices, such as how a community tells time. But as Elisheva Carlebach has observed, a calendar is "one of the most crucial cultural monuments a society can create."[78] After all, a calendar synchronizes a community according to one schedule, creating solidarity among its members while setting them apart from others who follow a different schedule. By marking the significance of Muhammad's immigration to Medina, the *hjirī* calendar stands out, indexing not only Muslim solidarity but also the importance of community to Islam itself. "The ideological importance of the calendar is thus immense," concludes Sean Anthony. "It represents no less than a reorientation of human time-keeping around an event deemed so significant that it was placed at the axis of a community's historical consciousness."[79]

Given the calendar's pivotal role in positioning the Muslim community, it should not surprise us that the Quran's proclamation (9:36) of a new twelve-month lunar calendar follows a series of broadsides against other religious communities—idolaters and unbelievers, rabbis and monks, Christians and Jews (Q 9:28–35). The proclamation is then immediately followed by the bold endorsement "That is the right religion" (*al-dīn al-qayyim*)—an endorsement that frames the institution of the lunar calendar in unambiguously moral and religious terms.[80]

This brings us back to the question of drawing evidence from the Quran to document the historical formation of the early Muslim community. Angelika Neuwirth has advocated for a "diachronic reading" of the Quran that dynamically connects the scripture to its late antique historical context, including its religiously plural environment. Tracing Muslim communal formation across distinct stages, Neuwirth demonstrates how the lines between Muhammad's community and his religious opponents gradually sharpened, even if, with respect to Jews and Christians, they sometimes blurred. Key moments captured in the Quran include the "development of a structured prayer service" in the early and middle Meccan periods, intensifying "anti-pagan polemic" in the late Meccan period, and a new polyphony that now addresses "a confessionally mixed public" in the Medinan period.[81]

The sharpening polemics with the People of the Book, while complementing "inclusive" verses that connected Muhammad's community to them, nevertheless also hardened the lines that set these communities apart. The late Medinan chapter "The Banquet" (*al-mā ʾida*) criticizes Christians for affirming the divinity of Jesus (Q 5:72–3, 5:116) and the Children of Israel for distorting scripture (Q 5:13) and famously warns Muslims against forging alliances—sometimes read as friendships—with Jews and Christians (Q 5:38). Backed by divine imprimatur, the effects of these speech acts on the shape of the early Muslim community and their encounters with the People of the Book should not be underestimated. Through the cracked lens of this early material evidence, then, the fragmentary anecdotes portraying Muhammad's gradual shift toward communal difference through elemental but highly visible and public acts appear as plausible reconstructions of historical events.

EMBODYING EARLY ISLAMIC HISTORY

The problem with the question of when Islam became a distinct religion (or confession) is that the answer reflects back onto what the questioner means by "religion." "As this movement was not yet a 'religion' in the sense of a distinct confession," writes Donner in *Muhammad and the Believers,* "members of established monotheistic faiths could join it without necessarily giving up their identities as Jews and Christians."[82] For Donner, "The recognition of Muhammad as prophet was the decisive marker that distinguished Muslims from Christians, Jews, and all others."[83] He argues that the Umayyad caliph ʿAbd al-Mālik accomplished this feat in the 690s by employing new coinage that elevated Muhammad's stature with the addition of "Muhammad is his messenger" to the original declaration of faith (*shahāda*), "There is no deity except God," emphasizing the Quran and attacking the doctrine of the Trinity—features that sharply diverged from its Byzantine-inspired antecedents. Donner's conception of religion is thus primarily theological.[84] Halevi's conclusion regarding the lack of distinctively "Islamic" formulas on the earliest Muslim tombstone likewise fixates on the absence of scripture and prophecy.

These accounts reflect modern Protestant conceptions of religion that privilege creed and scripture above other domains such as quotidian practice—conceptions that inform their historical narratives of how Muslims fashioned a distinct religion set apart from Judaism and Christianity. But many scholars within the field of religious studies, with assistance from anthropologists, have come to recognize that embodied practices often play a greater role in defining religion—and setting apart religious communities—than do creed and scripture, and have advanced more dynamic theories of religion that take these insights into account.[85] Donner's chronology of how the "Believers' movement" became a religion, Islam, is thus a language game that semantically turns on his personal interpretation of what a religion is. Depending on how we define religion, then, we may mark the point at which Islam became a distinct religion at the critical moment ʿAbd al-Mālik struck new coins, ʿUmar instituted the use of a new calendar, or Muhammad turned away from Jerusalem in prayer.[86]

Together, the quotidian acts examined in this chapter—turning, standing, sitting, and hairstyling—begin to establish a distinctively Muslim aesthetic regime that draws our attention to the physical body. As these acts and other rituals such as the daily prayer (*ṣalāt*) illustrate, it was by means of the physical body that the Prophet defined the boundaries of the Muslim social body. Given the body's pivotal role in enhancing Muslim spiritual solidarity, I contend that we must put the body at the center of our historical narratives of how Islam blossomed into a distinct religion and how Muhammad's *qawm* materialized into a distinct religious community.

While our view of the past may indeed be blurred by the muddled accounts of Muhammad's behavior in the hadith narratives themselves, the very facts that narrators thought to transmit them and that collectors thought to preserve them tell us that these physical gestures were far from trivial. More skeptical historians may indeed dismiss them as fictional accounts projected back in time. But in my view, it is implausible that Muhammad's community members would invent an abstract system of telling time before having first begun to mark their physical bodies through distinctive rituals, gestures, and styles of dress. When taken together as a cluster, emplotted within the grander narrative arc of formative Islamic history, and framed within a "body-centric" anthropology of human behavior, these collective memories appear as plausible accounts of how these and analogous gestures became distinguishing markers that helped set apart the early Muslim community. In fact, it becomes difficult to imagine how Muhammad and his followers could *not* have at least begun to draw these lines of difference.

Although Muhammad and his followers may not have abruptly ceased imitating Jews and Christians altogether, as some of the traditions above suggest, it is nevertheless likely that lines distinguishing early "Muslims" from "non-Muslims" had begun to form very early—during the Prophet's lifetime, if we believe the testimony in the Quran and hadiths. This view, based primarily on Muslim sources, broadly aligns with that of Robert Hoyland, whose exhaustive survey of non-Muslim sources from the early Islamic period led him to conclude: "It is thus evident that the early Muslims did adhere to a cult that had definite practices and beliefs and was clearly distinct from other currently existing faiths."[87]

To be clear: this does not mean that all Muslims during the first centuries of Islam uniformly exhibited these distinctive markers. Jack Tannous has persuasively argued that most members of religious communities in the early Islamic Middle East were "simple believers."[88] Whether Christian or Muslim, they were not well educated in matters of religious doctrine and practice, prone to moral lapses, and thus likely doing many of the things that religious authorities were repeatedly telling them not to do—like interacting with and imitating the members of rival religious communities. In other words, interreligious boundaries between Muslims and others were continually transgressed in everyday life—regardless of what date we assign for the moment Islam transformed into a distinct religion. We must acknowledge that Muslim differentiation emerged alongside ongoing emulation and adaptation, and helped enable it. We thus find that after the early conquests, Muslim elites learned much about how to build and run an empire from former Byzantine and Sasanian bureaucrats, many of whom became administrators within the Islamic polity. The Umayyad caliphate drew heavily from Byzantine imperial culture, learning how to repair roads, collect tax revenues, issue coins, and build architectural monuments such as the Great Mosque of Damascus, while the Abbasids turned "toward the East," drawing heavily from Sasanian imperial norms, including the "mirror for princes" literature and the holiday celebrations of Nawrūz and Mihrajān.[89] After all, "The Prophet once put on a Byzantine robe [*al-jubba al-rūmiyya*]," observed one religious scholar, "and inquired no further."[90]

CHAPTER 2

From Narrative to Normative

I was sent [by God] on the eve of the Hour [to fight] with the sword until God is worshipped alone without any other partner ascribed to him.

—THE PROPHET MUHAMMAD

Another sign of the early Muslim community's growing ambivalence toward Jews and Christians is the semantic transformation of the Arabic term *tashabbuh* (imitation). Language and history, as the German historian Reinhart Koselleck points out, are intertwined: "It is language above all that decides about the potentialities of history *in actu*."[1] Although both the Hungarian Orientalist Ignaz Goldziher (d. 1921) and the late scholar of early Islam M. J. Kister (d. 2010) suggest that *tashabbuh* was always a negatively charged term, I argue that *tashabbuh* in fact gradually shifted from a neutral to a negatively charged term over time—a semantic shift that parallels the historical shift in the Prophet's orientation toward Jews and Christians.[2] *Tashabbuh,* ironically, came to signify its lexical opposite: a reprehensible type of imitation, or, in other words, an obligation to be *different.*

If we examine, for example, the earliest extant Arabic lexicon, *The Sourcebook* (*Kitāb al-ʿAyn*), attributed to the eighth-century South Arabian lexicographer Khalīl b. Aḥmad al-Farāhīdī (d. 791), we find that *tashabbuh* is most commonly employed as a neutral term.[3] Although Farāhīdī does not assign *tashabbuh* an independent entry, he nonetheless uses the word to define other words such as *tasalla,* imitation (*tashabbuh*) of one who drinks; *taraʾbala,* imitation (*tashabbuh*) of a tiger; and *tafatta,* imitation (*tashabbuh*) of a youth.[4] The one case in which it does carry a negative valence, however, occurs within a distinctively Islamic context—a saying attributed to the second caliph, ʿUmar

b. al-Khaṭṭāb: "Emigrate [*hājarū*] and don't just appear to emigrate [*tahajjarū*]! Or, make your emigration sincere for God and do not [just] outwardly imitate [*tashabbahū*] the emigrants."[5] Farāhīdī then adds, "Like you say, he appears forbearing, but he is not actually forbearing," indicating that *tashabbuh,* in this usage, is just an empty physical act devoid of true sincerity.[6]

But the evidence provided by Farāhīdī's lexicon is merely the point of departure for my analysis of *tashabbuh*'s early semantic field, which is best mapped through a rigorous analysis of the hadith tradition that best expresses the term's broad semantic range: "Whoever imitates [*tashabbaha*] a people becomes one of them"—the imitation hadith. To trace the evolution of the imitation hadith's meaning is, in a sense, to trace the evolution of the early Muslim community. At face value, the hadith is a neutral statement. Someone who imitates virtuous role models will become upright, while someone who imitates sinful role models will become corrupt. In a neutral reading, there is nothing inherently wrong with becoming "one of them"; the valence of the key term, *tashabbuh,* depends on the virtue of the role model.[7] How, then, did the imitation hadith progress from a narrative statement to a normative dictum—from a neutral axiom on the socializing effects of imitation to a negative censure against imitation?

Although the hadith "Whoever imitates a people becomes one of them" is, at face value, a neutral statement, how the Partisans of Hadith transmitted and classified this tradition in their compendia during the first centuries of Islam were not neutral events. These apparently "objective" processes in fact reflect how the Partisans of Hadith *subjectively* understood the hadith's meaning. A close study of the transmission and classification of the imitation hadith is thus pivotal to understanding how the semantic field of *tashabbuh* became so negatively charged. How hadith collectors transmitted and categorized hadiths according to subject matter illuminates the earliest Muslim interpretations of the imitation hadith before post-formative (after the tenth century) commentaries and compendia claimed authority over its meaning.

A HALL OF MIRRORS

To open a collection of hadiths is to enter a hall of mirrors. A single hadith, or tradition, may have multiple chains of transmission, which may include minor or major variations in the text (*matn*). Each of these variations in transmission is a different *narration* of the hadith.[8] And sometimes the distinction between these different narrations is ambiguous. Amid such textual fluidity, how does one know which narration to rely upon, let alone make sense of the hadith's meaning?

The ambiguity of the imitation hadith poses a number of challenges. Like the key term on which the tradition's meaning hinges, *tashabbuh,* the hadith can be read in many different ways. This ambiguity allowed religious authorities to steer their interpretations of the hadith in multiple directions aligned with their subjective worldviews, rhetorical objectives, and social circumstances. It has also been transmitted in multiple narrations, adding another layer of complexity to an already ambiguous text. I group these different narrations into two primary *versions:* a concise version—the one cited above—and a longer apocalyptic version:[9] "I was sent [by God] on the eve of the Hour [to fight] with the sword until God is worshipped alone without any other partner ascribed to him. My provision has been placed under the shadow of my spear, and abasement and contempt have been placed upon the one who disobeys my command. And whoever imitates a people becomes one of them."[10]

This narration is an apocalyptic call to jihad. By surrounding "Whoever imitates a people becomes one of them" with proclamations of conquest and empire, the apocalyptic narration illustrates how textual context can skew the imitation hadith's meaning away from neutrality. Setting an ominous tone, the narration begins with a reminder that Judgment Day looms. Mention of "the Hour"—a Quranic metonym for the climactic encounter between God and humanity—creates an imminent sense of urgency as the end times draw near. It then clarifies the role of the Prophet Muhammad, who is divinely authorized to proclaim God's unity with his sword drawn. The sword, the first of two weapons of war identified in the hadith, symbolically grants the Prophet worldly authority, evoking another well-known tradition: "Paradise lies beneath the shade of swords."[11] Another weapon of war, a spear, guarantees the Prophet sufficient provisions not just in the afterlife but here and now, via the spoils of war. Those who reject the Prophet's authority are destined to suffer "abasement and contempt [*ṣaghār*]." The word *ṣaghār* brings to mind Q 9:29, which urges Muslims to overcome the People of the Book until they are humbled and subdued (*ṣāghirūn*).[12] The battle lines now drawn, the Prophet finally proclaims, "Whoever imitates a people becomes one of them," a statement that, in this context, reinforces the opposition between believer and unbeliever, friend and enemy. Although several variants of this apocalyptic version exist, the version quoted above is the most widely transmitted, collected by Aḥmad b. Ḥanbal (d. 855) in his *Musnad.*[13] Only the concise version, however, was transmitted in one of the six most authentic collections of Sunni hadiths, the *Sunan* of Abū Dāwūd (d. 889).

The hadith's transmission network illustrates that it was widely circulated among Muslim traditionists; it can be found in both early and late collections of hadiths.[14] Both versions—the concise version and the apocalyptic version—can be traced back to the Companion ʿAbd Allāh b. ʿUmar (d. 692), although they were disseminated by other Companions as well.[15] A lesser-known narration of the concise version, however, attributes the statement to Ibn ʿUmar's father, the second caliph, ʿUmar b. al-Khaṭṭāb, not to the Prophet.[16]

There was some disagreement among hadith critics over the hadith's authenticity. Hadith critics ranked the authenticity of the imitation hadith's chain of transmission (*isnād*) along a spectrum, ranging from sound (*ṣaḥīḥ*) to weak (*ḍaʿīf*).[17] Ibn Ḥanbal classified the hadith's chain of transmission as weak, as did the Cairene hadith master Shams al-Dīn al-Sakhāwī (d. 1497).[18] But due to the supporting evidence provided by other chains, most critics, including Sakhāwī, raised their overall assessment of the hadith's authenticity to fair (*ḥasan/jayyid*) or sound (*ṣaḥīḥ*). Among premodern critics, Ibn Taymiyya, Ibn Ḥajar al-ʿAsqalānī (d. 1449), and Najm al-Dīn al-Ghazzī classified the hadith as fair, while Ibn Ḥibbān (d. 965), al-Ḥākim al-Naysābūrī (d. 1014), and Zayn al-Dīn al-ʿIrāqī (d. 1404) classified it as sound.[19] Among modern critics, former secretary to the Ottoman shaykh al-Islām, Muḥammad Zāhid al-Kawtharī (d. 1952), ranked the hadith as fair but elevated its authority due to its corroborating *isnād*s and social status within the Muslim community; Salafī hadith master Nāṣir al-Dīn al-Albānī (d. 1999) ranked the *isnād* as fair but the hadith as sound, while the late Syrian scholar Nūr al-Dīn ʿItr (d. 2020) elevated the *isnād*'s rank to sound (*ṣaḥīḥ li-ghayrihi*) due to the hadith's widespread circulation via other authorities.[20] Ultimately, the hadith's rhetorical power compensated for any lingering doubts over its authenticity.

TRANSMISSION NETWORKS FROM DAMASCUS TO BAGHDAD

Damascus became the capital of the Umayyad dynasty during the reign of Muʿāwiya (r. 661–80). It was from Damascus that the entrepreneurial Umayyad caliph ʿAbd al-Mālik issued his administrative reforms, whose impact on Islam, according to one historian, was second only to that of Muhammad himself.[21] The site of Islam's crystallization into an imperial religion, Damascus became a symbol of this new political and spiritual power.

The *isnāds* of the imitation hadith, coincidentally, pass through Damascus.[22] What role did this socio-political context play in the hadith's circulation? Religious actors, after all, are shaped by their social worlds. If circulated in Damascus during the first half of the eighth century, after ʿAbd al-Mālik's reforms, to what degree, then, does the imitation hadith express the transformation of Muslim collective self-representation from parochial tribe to religious confession—a community no longer defined primarily by kinship but by a cosmopolitan empire justified by faith in the One True God? How does this shift reflect a transition in Muslim communal self-consciousness, from a tribe (*qabīla*) defined by shared kinship relations to a cosmopolitan people (*qawm*) defined by faith in God and His Messenger?[23] And given that the hadith was transmitted from Damascus to Baghdad during the eighth century, following the transfer of the caliphate from the Umayyads to the Abbasids, to what extent does the content of the hadith also reflect the sectarian milieu created by the ideological fragmentation of the Muslim community into rival groups during the bloody seventh-century civil wars and the subsequent Abbasid revolt? These questions anticipate how the religious discourse inspired by the hadith defined Muslim encounters with both non-Muslims and fellow Muslims, especially in the city of Damascus, where religious difference often provoked political instability.

A less speculative line of inquiry involves documenting the transmission history of the imitation hadith (see figures 7–9 at end of this chapter). The two figures most responsible for circulating the hadith—whom I shall call the *primary circulators*—were Damascene.[24] ʿAbd al-Raḥmān b. Thawbān (d. 781–82) and the prominent jurist ʿAbd al-Raḥmān al-Awzāʿī (d. 774) knew one another.[25] They both learned the tradition from a highly respected Damascene, Ḥassān b. ʿAṭiyya (d. 737), who heard it from another Damascene, Abū al-Munīb al-Jurashī, whom some hadith critics impugned.[26] Together, these figures place the early circulation of the hadith in Damascus, undermining G.H.A. Juynboll's claim that the vocabulary of *tashabbuh* is Medinan.[27]

None of the authorities to whom Ibn Thawbān transmitted the hadith were Damascene, however. With the fall of the Umayyad dynasty, Ibn Thawbān moved to the Abbasid caliphate's new capital, Baghdad, where he transmitted the imitation hadith to four Iraqis, including Abū al-Naḍr (d. 820–22), a *secondary circulator.*[28] Abū al-Naḍr transmitted the hadith to five others, including Ibn Ḥanbal.[29] Strangely, Ibn Thawbān is said to have transmitted the hadith to only two Syrians.[30] The imitation hadith's Syrian *isnād* thus becomes Iraqi. All the early collectors who transmitted the imitation hadith via Ibn Thawbān did so through Iraqi authorities.[31] Moreover, Abū Dāwūd transmitted the concise version of the hadith in his *Sunan,* while the other early collectors transmitted the apocalyptic version, leaving us to wonder which version Ibn Thawbān circulated (and why).

Adding to the uncertainty, Ibn Ḥanbal based his critical evaluation of the imitation hadith's *isnād* on Ibn Thawbān's reputation for inaccuracy. Other hadith critics disputed his credibility and reliability as well.[32] It was because of the ambiguity surrounding Ibn Thawbān's status as a transmitter that many critics did not grade the hadith as sound (*ṣaḥīḥ*). And yet, critics considered narrations through Awzāʿī even less authentic due to other weak links in the *isnāds*.[33] Both Abū Dāwūd and Ibn Ḥanbal, compilers of the most authoritative collections that include the imitation hadith, transmit only from Ibn Thawbān.[34] My comparison between the narrations of Ibn Thawbān and Awzāʿī yields some minor differences in their textual contents (*matn*), but the analysis also demonstrates significant textual correspondences between different narrations of Awzāʿī, providing strong evidence that he circulated the hadith in Umayyad Damascus along with Ibn Thawbān.[35] This finding increases the likelihood that Ḥassān b. ʿAṭiyya transmitted the imitation hadith to both Ibn Thawbān and Awzāʿī in Damascus.[36]

The city of Damascus also connects the imitation hadith to the Pact of ʿUmar.[37] The historically disputed document attributed to ʿUmar b. al-Khaṭṭāb assembles a range of ordinances designed to regulate a religiously diverse public space by defining clear social boundaries between Damascus's Muslim minority and Christian majority.[38] In one of the ordinances, the newly conquered Christian subjects proclaim, "We shall not imitate [*lā natashabbahu*] Muslims in how they dress."[39] It may be no coincidence, then, that in Muslim collective memory, ʿAbd Allāh, the son of ʿUmar, is the main Companion who introduces the imitation hadith to Damascus sometime in the seventh century, when the Pact of ʿUmar is also said to have originated.[40] As already mentioned, one narration attributes the imitation hadith to the caliph ʿUmar himself.[41] Although the link between the circulation of the hadith and the political transformations of the early Islamic polity is tenuous, the figures involved in its transmission and the uncanny textual convergences with the Pact nevertheless strengthen its imperial overtones.[42]

THRESHOLDS OF MEANING

While plumbing the depths of a hadith's transmission history may demystify its origins, examining its collection and arrangement may illuminate its earliest interpretations. Collecting hadiths was not a value-free practice.[43] Like modern-day librarians, hadith collectors set out to systematically organize knowledge, defining Islamic society in the process.[44] And they did so not only by evaluating the epistemological value of hadiths, but also by producing taxonomies that hierarchically arranged hadiths into categories and subcategories according to shared attributes or affinities—an overlooked dimension of hadith studies.[45] Hadith collectors shaped the meanings of prophetic traditions through these taxonomies. The classification of hadiths, then, is a window not only into the collectors' Islamic worldview but also into how they understood a given hadith and how they wanted their readers to understand it.

Scholars organized hadiths in different ways, resulting in different types of collections: *muṣannafs*, in which hadiths are arranged according to legal categories; *musnads,* in which hadiths are arranged according to their transmitters; and *sunan* collections, the most popular type, in which both approaches are applied—a hadith is often repeated multiple times with different *isnāds*, in different linguistic forms, and under different chapters. Far from being redundant, a hadith mentioned under multiple subject headings reveals a range of possible interpretations. The subjective element of organizing hadiths into categories is underscored by the Arabic term *tarjama* (pl. *tarājim*). The word's technical meaning, a hadith collection's subject headings, overlaps with its general meaning, interpretation.[46] Even the subsections (*abwāb,* s. *bāb*) within a chapter (*kitāb*) are literally (and metaphorically) "doors," or, as Joel Blecher suggests, "thresholds" that unlock the meanings of a hadith.[47] Several Muslim commentators, classical and modern, devoted separate treatises to analyzing the subject headings in *Ṣaḥīḥ al-Bukhārī.*[48] "Bukhārī tried to win over readers to a certain partisan opinion in the headings and introductions of the chapters in his collection," observed Ignaz Goldziher.[49] Goldziher argued that Bukhārī arranged the subject headings of his collection first and added the hadiths later, a hypothesis supported by the absence of hadiths under some headings.[50] The subject headings may thus be considered the *Ṣaḥīḥ*'s "most important characteristic," for they usher readers into the process of interpretation.[51]

But the multivalence of hadith texts also played a critical role in the interpretative process. The ambiguity of the imitation hadith allowed collectors to shape its interpretation through classification. By assigning the hadith to specific subject headings and subheadings, collectors added context, which reduced the text's ambiguity. Nevertheless, no consensus among the Partisans of Hadith over how to classify the hadith emerged. Their divergent classifications reflect contrasting rhetorical objectives and ideological perspectives, anticipating the divergent interpretations of later Muslim hadith commentators.

The few academic studies of hadith categorization have followed Muslim commentators in focusing on the *Ṣaḥīḥ* of Bukhārī, while overlooking other canonical collections like the *Sunan* of Abū Dāwūd.[52] But the authoritative collection of Abū Dāwūd is the only one of The Sound Six (*al-ṣiḥāḥ al-sitta*), the six most authentic Sunni collections of hadiths, to include the imitation hadith (figure 6). A cosmopolitan journeyman, Abū Dāwūd traveled in search of knowledge from Sistān (modern-day eastern Iran and southwestern Afghanistan) to Egypt, Syria, Iraq, and the Hijaz.[53] He studied under some of the most prestigious scholars of his day, including the cornerstone of formative Sunnism, Aḥmad b. Ḥanbal. The breadth of his hadith collection, the *Sunan,* reflects his wide travels. It is also distinguished by its jurisprudential content. Viewed as a whole, the *Sunan* reflects Abū Dāwūd's theological and legal positions—shared with other Partisans of Hadith. Hadiths support his dogmatic positions on a range of divisive topics, from predestination and intercession to the piety of the righteous (*rāshidūn*) caliphs and the createdness of the Quran.

Abū Dāwūd's classification arguably was an expression of his polemical and sectarian milieu as well as his personal interpretations of hadiths.[54] He places the imitation hadith in the chapter on dress (*kitāb al-libās*) under the subsection on "Ostentatious Dress" (*Bāb fī libs al-shuhra*).[55] Many hadiths placed in this subsection moralize fashion, as this one does: "If anyone puts on ostentatious dress [*libās al-shuhra*], God will clothe him in a similar garment on the Day of Judgment."[56] Put another way, a believer should avoid deliberately attracting attention by flouting accepted sartorial norms; otherwise his fame may turn into infamy on the Day of Judgment.

Abū Dāwūd places the imitation hadith right after this hadith. This sequence, as well as the chapter heading itself, guides the reader to understand "Whoever imitates a people becomes one of them" in a particular way: a warning against sartorial nonconformity. Dressing like a foreigner is thus no small matter. It means that a person has turned away from his own people and become "one of them." Taking notice of Abū Dāwūd's categorization and arrangement of the imitation hadith helps decode his silent commentary on the moral and legal implications of dress for Muslim religious identity.[57]

The Yemeni compiler of traditions ʿAbd al-Razzāq of Ṣanʿāʾ (d. 826), whose topically arranged collection of hadiths (*muṣannaf*) is among the ear-

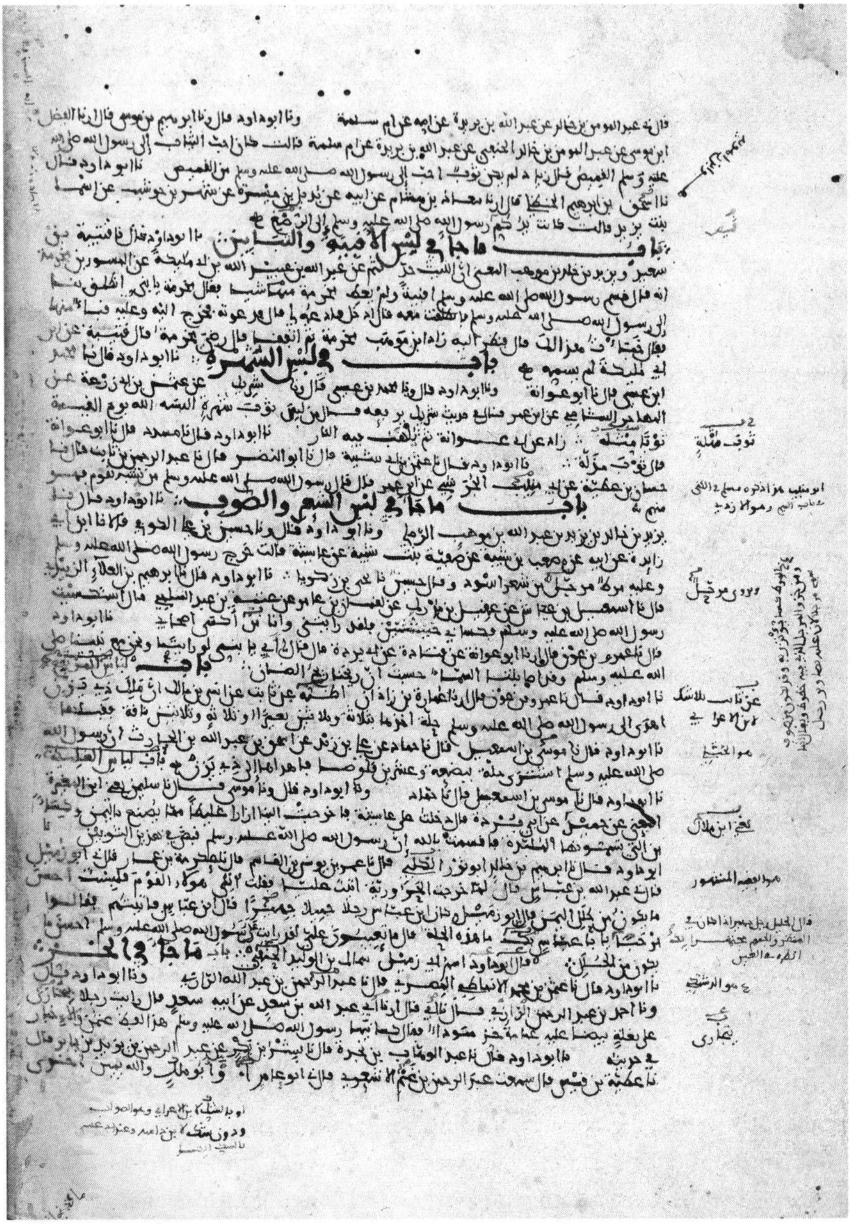

Figure 6. "Whoever imitates a people becomes one of them" (*man tashabbaha bi-qawm fa-huwa min-hum*), copied on lines 16–17 under the subsection on "Ostentatious Dress" (*Bāb fī libs al-shuhra*) in the chapter on dress (*kitāb al-libās*) in *Sunan Abī Dāwūd*. Completed 25 Ramadan 589/September 24, 1193, this manuscript of the *Sunan* is the first in a collection of texts composed by Abū Dāwūd. (Princeton University Library, Garrett Collection, no. 4999Yq, fol. 191b.)

liest to have survived, made a similar editorial decision.[58] Although ʿAbd al-Razzāq's narration of the imitation hadith lacks the textual authority of the traditions collected by Abū Dāwūd and other members of the *sunan* movement—it is a discontinuous (*mursal*) Companion tradition (*mawqūf*) traced back to ʿUmar b. al-Khaṭṭāb, not a continuous tradition traced back to the Prophet (*marfūʿ*)—his classification of the hadith deepens our understanding of how the first generations of Muslims understood and applied the imitation hadith to everyday life.[59]

ʿAbd al-Razzāq places the imitation hadith in "The Section on Cutting Hair from the Nape of the Neck and Asceticism" (*Bāb ḥalq al-qafā wa'l-zuhd*)—again drawing the reader's attention to dress.[60] At first glance, the title seems arbitrary, even whimsical: what is the connection between asceticism and trimming neck hair? The narrative context offers some answers. ʿUmar notices a man who had shaven the nape of his neck ostentatiously dressed in silk. Ready to command right and forbid wrong, ʿUmar warns him, "Whoever imitates a people becomes one of them." By scolding the man for looking like a foreigner, ʿUmar casts doubt on his Muslim identity while branding the acts of wearing silk and shaving the nape as foreign. Silk, which in copious amounts encoded ostentation and luxury, was a controversial topic among early Muslim religious authorities, who deemed it permissible for women but not men.[61] Shaving the nape of the neck, according to tradition, was a distinctively Zoroastrian fashion that Muslims should avoid.[62] ʿUmar's reaction is consistent with his biographical narratives, which portray him as an ascetic and statesman who orchestrated the territorial expansion of the caliphate beyond Arabia to Syria, Egypt, and Mesopotamia.[63] Numerous anecdotes boast that he wore tattered clothes and refused meat during famines, shunning the luxurious excesses that characterized courtly life in the rival Byzantine and Sasanian empires.[64] In Sunni tradition, ʿUmar represented a pious ideal of self-denial.

Aḥmad b. Ḥanbal was also portrayed as a pious exemplar and devout ascetic.[65] When asked about a man who shaves his nape, Ibn Ḥanbal allegedly replied, "Whoever imitates a people becomes one of them"—echoing ʿUmar's disapproval and strengthening the hadith's association with renunciation, physical appearance, and opposition to foreign cultural norms.[66] As literary figures, both ʿUmar and Ibn Ḥanbal represented ascetic rebuttals of the cultural and economic excesses of the caliphate. Although ʿAbd al-Razzāq and Abū Dāwūd locate the imitation hadith in distinct narratives, the anecdotes share a common ethical horizon that portrays the ostentatious styles of foreigners as incompatible with Islamic piety. Illustrating how fashion spreads through imitation, these narratives suggest that Muslim identity must be "dressed" appropriately in public.

Hadith collectors also placed the imitation hadith in sections on jihad. Explicit references to martial weapons in the apocalyptic narration linked the imitation hadith to war. ʿAbd Allāh b. al-Mubārak (d. 797), the itinerant Khurāsānī scholar-warrior-renunciant, includes the hadith in his *Kitāb al-Jihād,* the first such treatise of its kind.[67] Saʿīd b. Manṣūr (d. 841), a teacher of both Abū Dāwūd and Aḥmad b. Ḥanbal who migrated from Merv to Mecca, arranges it under the heading "One Who Says That Jihad Is Ongoing" (*Bāb man qāla al-jihād māḍin*).[68] The Iraqi hadith collector Ibn Abī Shayba, also one of Abū Dāwūd's teachers, includes two narrations of the hadith in his chapter on jihad.[69] The Egyptian Sunni theologian and Ḥanafī jurist Abū Jaʿfar al-Ṭaḥāwī (d. 933) includes it in a chapter on maintaining the abasement (*al-dhull*) of subjects by extracting the land tax (*kharāj*) through the proper harvesting of arable land—a context that highlights the economic dimension of the hadith's imperial message.[70]

This binary classification—jihad and dress—corresponds to the imitation hadith's two versions. It appears that the textual content of a hadith determined how collectors classified it. But collectors sometimes took more drastic measures to frame the meaning of hadiths. Instead of adapting their taxonomies to fit the hadiths, they sometimes edited hadith texts to fit their taxonomies. Some of the Prophet Muhammad's words were thus forgotten—lost in transmission—not by circumstance, but by choice. The willingness of hadith collectors to edit the Prophet's statements suggests that the categorization of hadiths was in some ways more significant than the hadiths themselves, for these categories underpinned their broader vision of Islam. It was thus possible for the compiler's "subjective" categories to drive the "objective" collection and transmission of hadiths.

An exemplar of this practice, Muḥammad al-Bukhārī (d. 870), produced both the most revered and, perhaps, the most polemical Sunni collection of hadiths.[71] In the chapter on jihad in his *Ṣaḥīḥ,* under the subheading "What Is Said Concerning Spears," he cites these familiar lines: "My provision has been placed under the shadow of my spear, and abasement and contempt have been placed on the one who disobeys my command."[72] This text is, of course, identical to the apocalyptic version of the imitation hadith—with the beginning and end ("I was sent on the eve of the Hour" and "Whoever imitates a people becomes one of them") truncated, courtesy of Bukhārī. The redaction reflects a deliberate editorial decision to focus on the topic of spears, a redaction that, as the commentator Ibn Ḥajar al-ʿAsqalānī explains, reveals Bukhārī's low opinion of the hadith's authenticity; aside from Ibn ʿUmar, Bukhārī omits the names of all other transmitters, two of whom are suspect.[73] Technically, the hadith is not part of the *Ṣaḥīḥ* collection of Bukhārī, who required, at a minimum, a *marfūʿ isnād,* a continuous unbroken chain of trustworthy transmitters traced back to the Prophet. This type of editing was not unusual for Bukhārī, who intermittently appends chainless, broken-chained, or unattributed reports to chapter titles and specific narrations of hadith as literary devices in order to advance a particular interpretation.

Nor was this type of editing unusual for Abū Dāwūd. According to the *isnād* of the imitation hadith in his *Sunan,* Abū Dāwūd heard it from the Baghdadi transmitter ʿUthmān b. Abī Shayba, brother of the hadith collector Abū Bakr b. Abī Shayba, who heard it from Abū al-Naḍr (see figures 7–9).[74] Abū Dāwūd's teacher, Aḥmad b. Ḥanbal, learned the hadith from Abū al-Naḍr directly. Yet, despite tracing their *isnād*s of the imitation hadith to Abū al-Naḍr, Abū Dāwūd and Aḥmad b. Ḥanbal each transmit two different versions of it in their respective collections—Abū Dāwūd the concise version, and Aḥmad b. Ḥanbal the apocalyptic version.[75] Why the difference?

The most plausible explanation is that Abū Dāwūd and Ibn Ḥanbal both heard the apocalyptic version, but Abū Dāwūd redacted everything except "Whoever imitates a people becomes one of them," while Ibn Ḥanbal faithfully transmitted it in full.[76] We know that the apocalyptic version appears in many other hadith collections apart from, and chronologically prior to, the *Musnad* of Aḥmad b. Ḥanbal. Had he whimsically added to the original text, creating what G.H.A. Juynboll would label a "composite" text, his version would have been sui generis to his collection.[77] Although it is possible that ʿUthmān b. Abī Shayba redacted the hadith, I am not aware of any evidence that indicates he habitually altered the textual content of hadiths. By contrast, in a separate epistle on his method of hadith collection written to Meccan scholars, Abū Dāwūd explains why he occasionally truncated a hadith: "Occasionally, I abbreviated a long hadith because if I wrote it out in full, some of those who hear it would neither know nor understand its legal subject matter."[78] It seems that extracting "Whoever imitates a people becomes one of them" made it easier for his students to understand the hadith's legal application to dress. For Abū Dāwūd, transmitting a hadith sometimes meant redaction, if doing so supported his normative vision of Islam.[79]

I can now attempt to answer the question I posed above: which version of the imitation hadith did Ibn Thawbān circulate in Damascus and Baghdad during the eighth century? Because Abū Dāwūd almost certainly redacted the tradition, we now know that all the compilers who collected the narration of the imitation hadith transmitted via Ibn Thawbān originally heard the apocalyptic version (figure 8). We can therefore deduce that Ibn Thawbān most likely circulated the apocalyptic version, not the concise version. This does not mean, however, that Abū Dāwūd was the first to proclaim "Whoever imitates a people becomes one of them" as an independent phrase. As discussed above, the Yemeni collector ʿAbd al-Razzāq transmits this statement in his early (first quarter of the ninth century) *Muṣannaf* collection. Abū Dāwūd was transmitting a saying that had already been in circulation for decades.[80]

That Abū Dāwūd deserves most of the credit for canonizing "Whoever imitates a people becomes one of them" as an independent axiom is an illustration of the bold editorial license that the Partisans of Hadith were ready to exercise in shaping Islam according to their vision of Sunni orthodoxy. Although veiled by an aura of objectivity, the practice of collecting hadiths involved subjective interpretation. The classification and transmission of hadiths, then, encode a complex process by which members of this intellectual community advanced their interpretation of religious orthodoxy and defined Muslim difference.

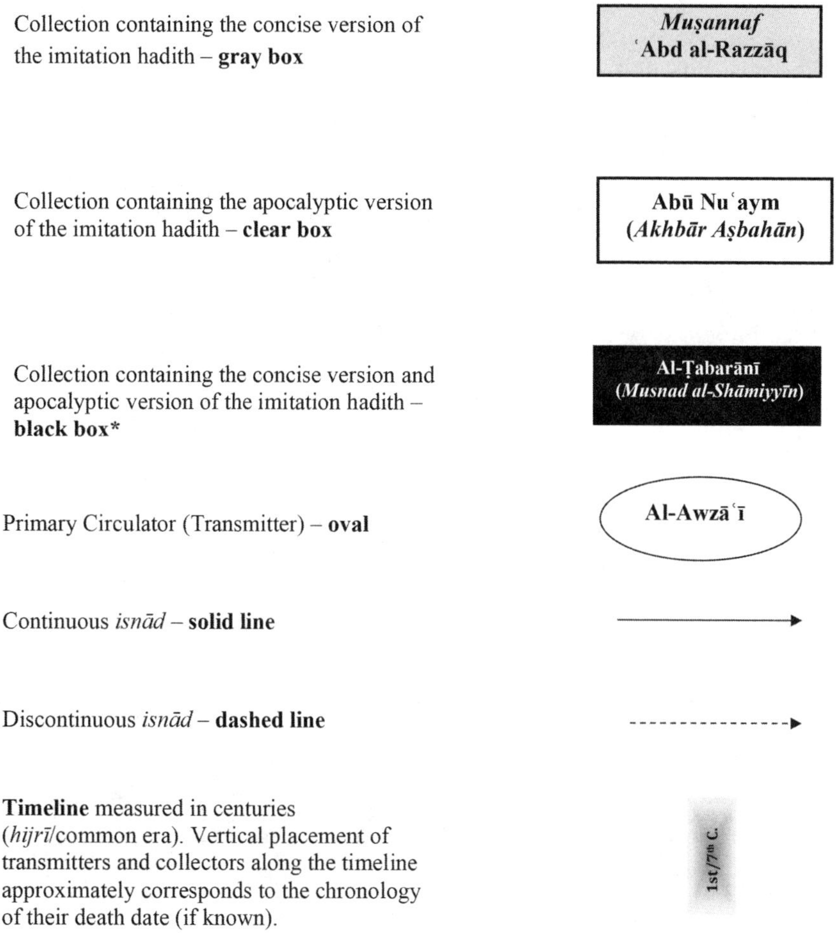
Collection containing the concise version of the imitation hadith – **gray box**
Muṣannaf ʿAbd al-Razzāq
Collection containing the apocalyptic version of the imitation hadith – **clear box**
Abū Nuʿaym (*Akhbār Aṣbahān*)
Collection containing the concise version and apocalyptic version of the imitation hadith – **black box***
Al-Ṭabarānī (*Musnad al-Shāmiyyīn*)
Primary Circulator (Transmitter) – **oval**
Al-Awzāʿī
Continuous *isnād* – **solid line**
Discontinuous *isnād* – **dashed line**
Timeline measured in centuries (*hijrī*/common era). Vertical placement of transmitters and collectors along the timeline approximately corresponds to the chronology of their death date (if known).
1st/7th C.

* *Musnad al-Shāmiyyīn* of al-Ṭabarānī contains two versions of the imitation hadith: the apocalyptic version (through Ibn ʿUmar) and the concise version (through Abū Hurayra). In Figure 8, the collection appears as a black box; in Figure 9, which displays the *isnād* network of Ibn ʿUmar, it appears in a clear box.

** The *isnād*s of the imitation hadith attributed to *Musnad Abī Yaʿlā* are found in al-Buṣayrī's *Itḥāf al-khiyara*.

Figure 7. Key to *isnād* maps (figures 8 and 9).

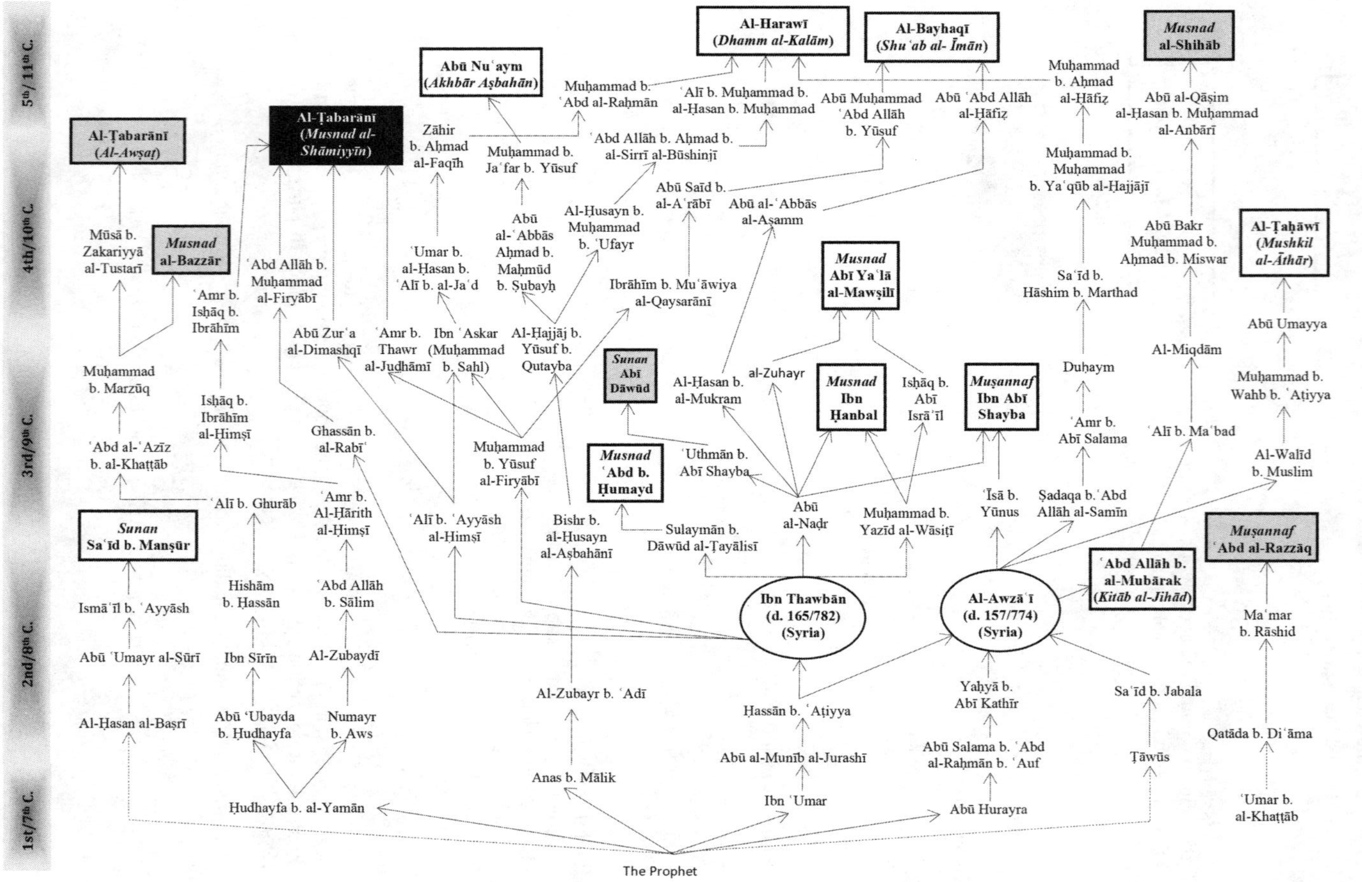

Figure 8. "Whoever imitates a people becomes one of them": transmission network (*isnād* map).

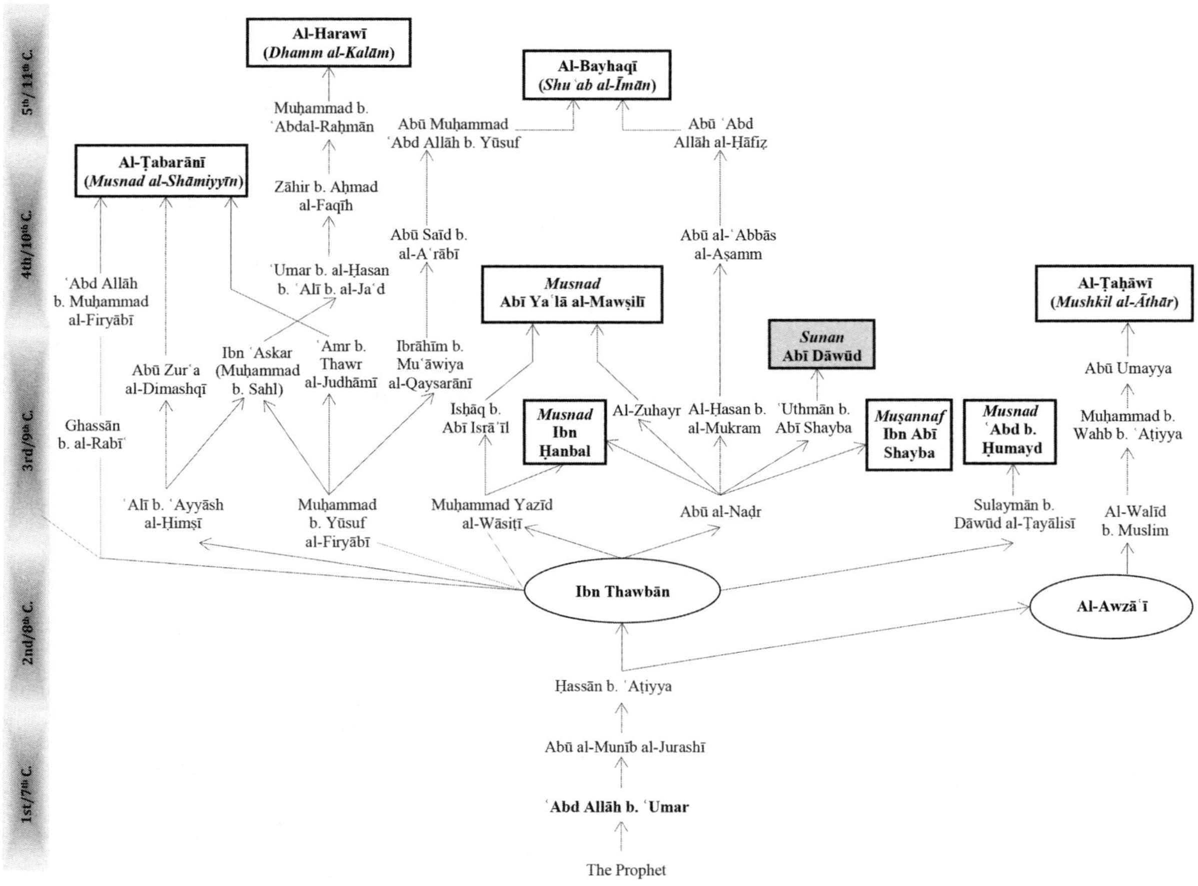

Figure 9. "Whoever imitates a people becomes one of them": ʿAbd Allāh b. ʿUmar transmission network (*isnād* map).

CHAPTER 3

Empire of Small Differences

> We have divided between them their livelihood in the present life and raised some of them above others in rank so that some of them may take others in servitude.
>
> —QURAN 43:32 (Arberry)

"ISLAM IS ABOVE, NOT BELOW"

Studies of Muslim interreligious relations conventionally view Muslim encounters with non-Muslims through a conceptual framework limited to religious identity, such as through the lens of "Abrahamic faiths," "Jewish-Muslim," or "Christian-Muslim" relations. While these studies are important, much can also be gained by framing Muslim interreligious relations within a wider field of social and political associations beyond religious identity. Instead of crudely citing scriptural texts such as Q 9:29 ("Fight non-Muslims [*dhimmī*s] until . . . they are humbled") to question whether Islam can "tolerate" non-Muslims, the holistic approach proposed here brings into view the grand cosmological vision of the Partisans of Hadith that illuminates *why* Muslim perceptions of other religions took the shape they did during the formative and early periods of Islam. This cosmological vision, what I call an imperial imaginary, also reveals unexpected *intersections* between Muslim religious and other categories of difference that otherwise go unnoticed with an exclusive focus on religious identity.

While the Partisans of Hadith defined clear lines between Muslims and non-Muslims, especially Jews, they also defined the lines between different groups of Muslims—between Sunnis and Shiʿis, men and women, Arabs and non-Arabs, free persons and slaves, young and old—and between humans and nonhumans, namely, animals and spirits, in order to bring forth a virtuous

Islamic society that conformed to the will of God. We may conclude, as Mary Douglas famously did in her study of sumptuary regulations in Leviticus, that "different classes of things shall not be confused."[1] Supporting this view, one enigmatic tradition associates liminality with the diabolic: "The Prophet forbade that a person sit in between sunlight and shade, saying, 'It is Satan's gathering [*majlis al-shayṭān*].'"[2] To avoid languishing in a morally ambiguous threshold space between light and darkness, cosmic symbols of good and evil, the true believer must make a clear distinction between the two, or else join the company of Satan, who resides in the unholy in-between, as a body out of place. In this cosmology, mixing categories, including classes of people, signals unholiness and impurity.

Nevertheless, it is reductionist and ahistorical to ascribe the value of these small differences to category distinctions alone. Doing so also fails to adequately explain the hierarchical nature of these differences. Although Christopher Melchert has characterized the Partisans of Hadith as a contractual community of "substantial equality," they still "ranked Muslims by the quality of their obedience [to God]," and thus "managed to accept a degree of hierarchy."[3] But in my exploration of hadith traditions against imitation, it becomes apparent that their morally driven impulse toward hierarchy was in fact stronger than most scholars have presumed. The Partisans of Hadith were difference-makers. A crucial function of the genre of hadith itself is to distinguish the Muslim community from rival groups. Despite the common ground shared between Muslims, Jews, and Christians, the Partisans of Hadith accentuated the differences between Muslims and their fellow monotheists. More broadly, they envisioned a society defined by hierarchical differences across key categories of identity: religion, ethnicity, gender, class, age, and the human. It was common for these categories of identity to intersect with and blur into one other—much as they do today.

The organization of society into hierarchical strata was a normal feature of political life in the late antique Near East. In the first centuries of Islam, Muslims paradoxically imitated the Byzantine and Sasanian manner of differentiating society into hierarchical strata, at once amplifying hierarchies inherited from pre-Islamic Arabia and undermining the egalitarian spirit of the Quran. They imported, for example, the Persian model of dividing society into elites (*al-khāṣṣa*) and commoners (*al-ʿāmma*). Ibn al-Muqaffaʿ (d. 756–57), the Umayyad and Abbasid secretary and translator of significant Persian treatises such as *The Testament of Ardashir* and *Kalila wa Dimna,* summarized the point of view that people should remain in their assigned places: "Each person has his station and [social] worth, and if he sticks to the station in which he finds himself, then he is likely to be content. . . . As a man's station has been determined for him since the beginning of time, he has no alternative but to be satisfied with it, whatever it is."[4] Muslim elites, with some exceptions, adopted this perspective.[5]

According to Jane Burbank and Frederick Cooper, the arrangement of society into hierarchical strata is a defining feature of empires, which they describe as "large political units, expansionist or with a memory of power extended over space, polities that maintain distinction and hierarchy as they incorporate new people."[6] All empires in history, in the authors' view, have met this criterion, from the Mongol and British Empires to the Byzantine and Islamic. Maintaining distinction, or difference, is thus both a prerequisite and a technique of empire. "Culturally and politically," observes one historian, "Islam and its empire was already implicit in late antiquity."[7]

Elite Muslim attempts to hierarchically arrange society reflect what I call an imperial imaginary—a social imaginary that aimed to maintain distinction and hierarchy.[8] This imaginary was not limited to the domain of government, but extended to the production of "religious" knowledge as well. As M. Qasim Zaman has argued, caliphs and scholars during the Abbasid period cultivated a relationship of cooperation and mutual accommodation.[9] The Abbasids, after all, patronized not only the translation of Greek philosophy into Arabic, but also the collection of hadiths to legitimize their political rule vis-à-vis Islam. Like government bureaucrats, hadith scholars also had a vested interest in maintaining and regulating differences—although with different motivations. While bureaucrats sought to maintain security and order in the Realm of Islam to retain political power, scholars pursued an upright spiritual and moral community that adhered to God's law—although these motivations were not always mutually exclusive, as the following tradition collected by Bukhārī suggests: "Islam is above, not below."[10] By forbidding non-Muslims to live in residences above Muslims, the Pact of ʿUmar and its commentators made clear that Muslims are not to be "looked down" upon.

In this chapter, I zoom out and take a bird's-eye view of the hadith traditions against imitation, reading them alongside the Pact of ʿUmar. By illuminating thematic convergences between canonical texts belonging to distinct literary genres and directed toward specific audiences, I demonstrate how religion and politics in early Islamic history were twins. In doing so, I show how Muslim religious discourses were mapped onto an imperial imaginary.

This imperial imaginary was meant to take shape in everyday life through the medium of small differences. These differences cut across ritual and everyday practice for, much like the lines between "religion" and "politics," no clear lines divided "religion" from "culture" during the formative period of Islam. But when seen through the lens of this grander political narrative, small differences become something of a misnomer; as a means to safeguard empire, small differences accrue great value, and thus no longer appear very small—a point I shall return to in this chapter's conclusion. First, let us explore how these "small" differences erupt unexpectedly in the strangest of situations and in the smallest of matters, leaving us to wonder, as Roberto Harari does: "How can a people so alike, united by language, tradition, and history end up confronting each other in situations that are so difficult to conceive of?"[11]

VOCABULARIES OF MUSLIM DIFFERENCE

Muslim vocabularies of difference diffused across both the literary and geographic landscapes of the early Islamic polity. As already mentioned, *tashabbuh* as reprehensible imitation is rarely found in Twelver Shiʿi hadith collections.[12] But the term appears in almost every Sunni hadith collection and was circulated in every major center of the Islamic polity by the eighth century: Kufa and Basra in Iraq; Ṣanʿāʾ, Yemen; Fusṭāṭ, Egypt; Damascus in Greater Syria; and Medina and Mecca in the Hijaz. Based on this *semantic geography,* we learn how widespread a distinctively proto–Sunni Muslim vocabulary of difference had already become.[13]

Nevertheless, my exploration extends beyond the term *tashabbuh* to include a network of related concepts that reflect how early Muslims imagined difference. Of course, language is a reflection—even if dim—of social practice. The following survey of traditions, then, offers a glimpse into the conversations and practices that defined the lines between different religious communities during the formative period of Islam.

The traditions are arranged by category of identity, such as religion, ethnicity, and gender, although the section on religious difference is further subdivided according to the type of practice (ritual, festivals, funerals, and the like). To maintain a panoramic view of these traditions, I do not comment extensively on their meaning and significance.

DO NOT IMITATE! / BE DIFFERENT!

One of the most fascinating discoveries that emerged from my exploration into the bewildering diversity of Prophetic sayings was how frequently exhortations to be different blurred into exhortations against imitating others. Many hadiths repeat certain commonplace phrases, or *topoi* (s. *topos*), on the obligation to be different, such as "Do not imitate" (*lā tashabbahū*), a command that circulated widely and applied to a broad range of practices associated with groups of diminished status.[14] A counterpoint to this negative command was the positive command "Be different" (*khālifū*), which represents the other side of the same rhetorical coin. Whether phrased in the form "Do not imitate!" or "Be different!" these topoi implicitly provided Muslims with a rationale and justification for performing, or not performing, a certain practice. Underscoring this close semantic relationship, some early biographers and hadith scholars arranged oral traditions employing these two topoi under a single heading, a textual juxtaposition that charged the term *tashabbuh* with a stronger negative value.[15] What may be considered the first treatise against imitation, written centuries later, is framed by its title as an obligation for Muslims to be different: *The Obligation of Following the Straight Path Is to Be Different [mukhālafat] from Those Damned to Hell.*

INTERRELIGIOUS DIFFERENCE

As already mentioned, most oral traditions against imitation in Sunni collections focus on religious identity, criticizing practices associated with specific religious communities. By contrast, I could not find a single hadith within the four canonical Twelver Shiʿi collections explicitly discouraging the imitation (*tashabbuh*) of non-Muslims.[16] The semantic distinction brings into relief the term's unique role in defining Sunni Muslim orthodoxy.

One Sunni tradition attributed to the Prophet Muhammad is exceptional for its blanket condemnation of imitating unbelievers, without qualification: "A Muslim should not support an unbeliever [*kāfir*], nor should he imitate [*yatashabbahu*] an unbeliever [*kāfir*]."[17] In a literal reading of this tradition, the Quranic term for unbeliever, *kāfir,* appears to include all non-Muslims—Jews, Christians, Zoroastrians, and pagans—suggesting that Muslims should shun imitating all non-Muslims as a general principle. Although not widely circulated, this tradition is nonetheless found in one of the oldest Arabic-Islamic papyrus codices in existence, a collection of traditions attributed to ʿAbd Allāh b. Wahb (d. 812), a prominent Egyptian student of the eponymous founder of the Mālikī legal school, Mālik b. Anas (d. 795).[18] This hadith diverges from the majority of traditions against imitation which, as we shall see, shun a specific practice associated with a specific group, such as the People of the Book.

People of the Book

Although many Quranic verses and hadith traditions express a positive attitude toward Judeo-Christian scripture and tradition, some traditions convey a critical outlook. Perhaps the most well-known tradition that warns Muslims against imitating the People of the Book is the hadith predicting that Muslims will follow Jews and Christians into a lizard's hole: "You will follow the ways of those nations who were before you, span by span and cubit by cubit, so much so that even if they entered a hole of a lizard you would follow them. We said, 'O Messenger of God, the Jews and Christians?' He replied, 'Who else?'"[19] Despite exhortations in numerous hadiths for Muslims to distinguish themselves from their monotheistic rivals, this tradition suggests that their fates are inevitably tied together. In fact, the Prophet presages that Muslims are destined to blindly follow Jews and Christians so closely that they would even follow them into a lizard's hole.

But another narration of this same tradition states that Muslims are destined to follow a different duo. In this alternate version, the Companions ask: "O Messenger of God! Do you mean by those [nations] the Persians and the Byzantines?" The Prophet again replies: "Who else can it be?" This divergence, though not unusual for hadiths, confused some hadith commentators. In an attempt to reconcile the two conflicting accounts, one appealed to historical demographics to argue that the hadiths refer to the same groups. He claimed that since many Jews inhabited Persia and many Christians inhabited Byzantium the hadiths did not contradict one another.[20] But, as we saw in chapter 1, ambiguity over who or what Muslims imitated was not unusual; it was a symptom of the blurry lines between Muslims and others during the formative stages of Islamic history.

But whether the hadiths refer to hybrid categories of Persian Jews and Byzantine Christians or to distinct categories of Jews, Christians, Byzantines, and Persians, the outcome for Muslims is the same: they fall into a lizard's hole. An undoubtedly negative image, the lizard hole signals a foreboding descent into darkness, a darkness in which Muslims will lose their way—and their distinction as a community guided by the light of God. Having recognized the apparent link between both narrations, Bukhārī juxtaposed them in a section of his canonical hadith collection titled, "Holding onto the Book [the Quran] and the *Sunna*."[21] Through Bukhārī's lens, these narrations were proof texts that future generations of Muslims must maintain their fidelity to the foundations of Islamic orthodoxy, the Quran and the *sunna*, to avoid losing their way like Jews and Christians. Orthodoxy, in other words, requires difference. Later commentators also read these hadiths through the lens of orthodoxy, predicting that Muslims would follow Jews and Christians into the lizard's hole by committing religious innovations and sinful transgressions.[22] As a result, this hadith was commonly invoked in both treatises against imitation and treatises against innovation (*bidʿa*), marking a key feature of their discursive function: to enforce Islamic orthodoxy.

Anxieties of Jewish Influence

Traditions against imitation suggest that, among unbelievers, Muslims are most likely to imitate the People of the Book, and among the People of the Book, they are most likely to imitate Jews. This perhaps explains why traditions against imitation gravitate toward them. While Muslim anxieties regarding Jewish influence arose due to a confluence of historical factors, one of those factors was likely the uncanny resemblance between the two rival communities—as acknowledged in a tradition by the Prophet himself: "How one night resembles the other," he said. "These Children of Israel—how we resemble them."[23]

In one account, some Muslims expressed their desire to hallow a tree, an act resembling a pagan ritual. In response, the Prophet sarcastically chides, "Both in your way and in your manner . . . you resemble the Children of Israel more than any other people. You follow their act in every way. But I am not sure. Are you worshipping the calf?"[24] The calf is an allusion to the "golden calf" worshipped by the Israelites, as mentioned in both the Hebrew Bible and the Quran.[25] Here, the Prophet criticizes this group of Muslims for imitating the Israelites, who themselves were punished for imitating idolaters.

A far greater number of traditions therefore command Muslims *not* to imitate Jews than to imitate them. Both Goldziher and Kister noticed that hadith traditions warn Muslims against emulating Jews more than any other group—an observation that corresponds to historical narratives of intensifying Jewish-Muslim conflict in Medina and the frequency of references to Moses and the Israelites in the Quran.[26] As Goldziher notes, the Prophet often called upon believers not to imitate Jews in either ritual or everyday life, which obliged

Muslims to observe a number of small differences—to clean their armpits, dye their hair, sit down during funeral processions, cover the faces of the deceased, and pray while shod—a controversial topic that Kister dwells on at length—as well as not to hoard goods or wrap oneself in a single garment when praying.[27]

One tradition instructing men how to treat women during menstruation suggests that the Jewish tribes in Medina did not take this rejection well. According to this tradition, the Prophet ordered Muslims to avoid following the local Jewish custom of sequestering women in separate quarters during their menses, instead encouraging them to continue cohabiting with their spouses while avoiding sexual intercourse. In response, one Jewish figure exclaimed, "This man [Muhammad] only does the opposite of what we do!"—expressing frustration at what might have been perceived as a sign of his community's loss of status in Muhammad's eyes.[28]

Ritual

There are many traditions that differentiate Muslims through ritual, given that ritual plays an important social function in defining, binding, and setting apart religious communities. Most focus on distinguishing Muslim from Judeo-Christian rituals, especially prayer and fasting. In one tradition, the Prophet expresses disdain for praying in niches, or small narrow spaces, because Christians did so.[29] Most traditions, however, comment on Jewish ritual practices:

> Pray in your shoes, and do not imitate [*lā tashabbahū*] the Jews![30]
>
> Be different from [*khālifū*] the Jews! They neither pray in their sandals nor in their leather socks.[31]
>
> ʿUmar b. al-Khaṭṭāb saw a man pray wrapped up in a cloak [*multaḥif*[an] *bihi*] so he said, "Do not imitate the Jews. If anyone of you can only find a single garment [*thobe*], let him make a waist-wrap [*izār*] with it."[32]
>
> She [the Prophet's wife ʿĀʾisha] disliked that one place one's hands over the belly button [*al-ikhtisār*] while standing during ritual prayer—saying: "Do not imitate the Jews."[33]
>
> God is good and He loves goodness. A clean person loves cleanliness. A generous person loves generosity. A benefactor loves beneficence. So clean—I think he said—your armpits and do not imitate the Jews.[34]

While some of these traditions encourage Muslims to observe appropriate dress during ritual prayer, others urge its proper performance. All nonetheless consist of minor adjustments involving the physical body.

Everyday Practice

Because mimesis usually took place in public spaces, where encounters between members of different communities were most common, many traditions exhort Muslims to distinguish themselves not only through ritual but also through everyday practice.

One of the first ways, besides dress, of identifying a person's communal affiliation is through his or her style of greeting others. Although Muslims developed a distinctive way of greeting one another verbally—"Peace be upon you" (*al-salām ʿalaykum*) in some locales—they also tried to cultivate a distinctive visual gesture to accompany the verbal greeting. The shrewd general who helped lead the conquest of Egypt, ʿAmr b. al-Āṣ (d. 663), transmitted to his son, who transmitted to his son, the following tradition on the proper etiquette of greeting other Muslims: "One who imitates others is not one of us. So do not imitate Christians and Jews. The Jews greet each other using their fingers and the Christians greet each other using their palms."[35] The two Egyptian religious authorities who transmitted this tradition, Layth b. Saʿd (d. 791) and ʿAbd-Allāh b. Lahīʾa (d. 790), suggest that religious communities in eighth-century Egypt had cultivated their own distinctive styles of greeting. Once belonging to the Byzantine Empire, Egypt contained significant populations of Jews and Christians, including Christian Arabs who could initially pass as Muslim Arabs.[36] To deter assimilation, the first Arab Muslims were confined to garrison cities and were discouraged from moving to the countryside, while Christian Arabs were prohibited from dressing like Muslims.[37] The command for Egyptian Muslims to adopt their distinctive style of greeting one another is consistent with these early historical accounts.

This tradition is also significant because of how it is phrased. The syntax of the declaration "One who imitates others is not one of us" echoes that of the imitation hadith: "Whoever imitates a people becomes one of them."[38] Both statements express a politics of belonging, distinguishing between insiders and outsiders, although the former takes on a definitively negative connotation. While some commentators dismissed the admonition due to its potentially spurious chain of transmission, others expanded its prescriptive scope beyond greeting into a general admonition against imitating Christians and Jews.[39]

Among the public sites that posed the greatest risk for reprehensible practices of imitation were the carnivalesque spaces known as *ʿīd*s, which encompassed festivals, holiday celebrations, and ceremonies. To the masses, whether Muslim or non-Muslim, *ʿīd*s provided some recreational fun, but to religious elites, they carried the danger of spiritual, moral, and political corruption, as the caliph ʿUmar warns: "Whoever settles in foreign lands, celebrates their holidays—Nawrūz and Mihrajān—and imitates them [*yatashabbahu*] until he dies, will be resurrected with them on the Day of Judgment."[40] With the expansion of the caliphate into non-Arab territory, it became more common for Muslims to relocate to foreign lands, including territory once belonging to the Sasanian Empire, where they might be tempted to assimilate and adopt the customs of the native population. The tradition warns these migrant Muslims against resembling the natives, mentioning the Persian holidays of Nawrūz and Mihrajān, which inhabitants of the Sasanian Empire would have celebrated. To celebrate these holidays along with non-Muslims, according to the tradition, signaled that Muslims had assimilated into a foreign culture and become "one of them"—a change in communal identity that would be revealed on the Day of Judgment when they would be resurrected with them instead of with the Muslim community. As I discuss in chapter 5, this tradition helped script the discourses of religious reformers who criticized Muslim participation in unsanctioned festivals and holidays.

Like *ʿīd* festivals, funerals publicly marked a community. Funeral processions in early Islamic society were public performances of social distinction.[41] Muslims not only debated whether to sit or stand during funeral processions, as discussed in chapter 1, they also discussed other ways of distinguishing their funeral processions from those of Jews and Christians. According to one tradition that spread from Mecca to Iraq in the middle of the eighth century, the Prophet said: "Cover the faces of your dead and do not imitate the Jews."[42] Claiming that the faces of corpses remain exposed to the public during Jewish funeral processions, the hadith calls upon Muslims to do the opposite.

According to another tradition, transmitted on the authority of Kufan religious authorities, a Companion once saw an incense burner lit at a funeral and then intentionally broke it, justifying his inflammatory action with the admonition "Do not imitate the People of the Book!"[43]

What binds together the above traditions against imitation, whether they encompass the fields of ritual or everyday practice, is that they apply to practices that are visible in public spaces to both Muslims and non-Muslims. If these practices were invisible, or unnoticeable to the public eye, then Muslims would fail to set themselves apart by either acting upon or shunning them. As already discussed, the semantic field of the term *tashabbuh* prefigures this emphasis on outward appearance, as does Abū Dāwūd's categorization of the imitation hadith in a section on dress. We thus find many hadith traditions that seek to define Muslim physical appearance by regulating the community's sartorial code, such as footwear, headgear, and hairstyle.[44]

As already discussed, some traditions urge Muslims to distinguish their footwear, an important status symbol in late antiquity as it is today. The Bible and the Quran both mention that Moses removed his shoes upon entering holy ground on Mount Sinai where he first spoke to God—an act that may have become a part of Medinan Jewish ritual. Piecing together the information conveyed by hadith traditions, M. J. Kister has narrated how Muslims originally followed Muhammad's command to oppose Jewish ritual and pray in mosques while shod, but eventually reversed course after the Prophet's death and began to remove their shoes to keep the prayer area in mosques clean—despite its correspondence to Jewish practice.[45]

But footgear provided Muslims opportunities for distinction even beyond the mosque. According to one anecdote, the jurist Ibn Ḥanbal espied a pair of Sindhi sandals, which had become fashionable in Abbasid Baghdad, on someone's doorstep. After inquiring about their owner, he expressed his disapproval of their style: "He is imitating [*yatashabbahu*] royalty [*awlād al-mulūk*]."[46] Ibn Ḥanbal's condemnation suggests that pious Muslims should avoid the ostentatious styles of wealthy and powerful government bureaucrats lest they become corrupt like them.

Moving up from the feet to the head, numerous hadiths instruct Muslims to distinguish themselves through their headgear and hairstyle, which I examine in greater detail in the following chapter. The importance that hadith traditions placed on these two features of a Muslim's sartorial code can be explained, in part, by their close proximity to a person's face, which is usually how someone's identity is first determined. Here, I cite the most influential of these traditions: "The difference between us [Muslims] and the pagans is the turbans wrapped around the *qalansuwa*s."[47] The *qalansuwa* was a type of hat worn by Sasanian elites as well as Arabs. Because Arabs in pre-Islamic Arabia wore turbans as well, the Prophet encourages Muslims to blend both styles to create a new distinct Muslim style of wearing headgear.

Besides the issue of parting the hair, discussed in chapter 1, a cluster of hadiths command Muslims to distinctively style their beards by either growing them out or dyeing them:

> Be different from [*khālifū*] the pagans [*mushrikīn*]! Grow the beard and trim the moustache.[48]

> Dye your gray hair and do not imitate [*lā tashabbahū*] Christians and Jews![49]

> Verily, the Jews and Christians do not dye their hair, so be different from them![50]

> O gathering of Helpers, dye your hair red and yellow, and be different from the People of the Book![51]

While dying beards differentiated Muslims from Jews and Christians, growing beards differentiated them from pagans. Muslim beards therefore entangled multiple differences at once (see chapter 4).

SECTARIANISM

A close study of Islamic discourses on religious difference reveals that the lines dividing Muslims from non-Muslims occasionally intersected with the lines dividing Muslims from other Muslims. To establish the ideal Muslim community, Sunni Partisans of Hadith were charged with defining correct Islamic belief and practice, or orthodoxy, which required that they clearly distinguish not only between Muslims and non-Muslims but also between their "orthodox" Muslim community and "heterodox" Muslim communities.[52]

One widely transmitted and influential apocalyptic tradition illustrates how *inter*religious conflicts feed into *intra*religious conflicts, predicting that Muslims will imitate Jews and Christians by splitting into numerous sects: "The Jews split into seventy-one sects. One is in heaven and seventy are in hell. The Christians split into seventy-two sects. One is in heaven and seventy-one are in hell. By Him in whose hands is Muhammad's soul my community will split into seventy-three sects. One will be in heaven and the rest will be in hell. It was said to Muhammad, who are they? He replied: The majority [*jamāʿa*]."[53] Despite predicting that some Jews and Christians will enter heaven—which is a remarkable pronouncement in itself—the hadith ultimately serves as a warning to Muslims. Reflecting the civil strife that befell

Muslims during the first centuries of Islam, this apocalyptic tradition predicts that Muslims will split into seventy-three sects, "outdoing" even Jews and Christians.

There are multiple variants of this tradition.[54] Some narrations compare Muslims to Jews only, excluding Christians altogether. Other narrations differ on the number of sects—seventy-one or seventy-two. Other narrations omit the key detail that all but one sect will be damned. One "tolerant" narration in fact claims the opposite—that all but one sect will be saved.[55] In many treatises on Islamic theology, this tradition is cited in tandem with the hadith predicting that Muslims would follow Jews and Christians into a lizard hole due to their shared relevance to Islamic orthodoxy. Muslim sectarianism was, arguably, the natural outcome of a well-defined religious ideology; as it became clearer to the Partisans of Hadith what correct Islam was, it became clearer to them what correct Islam was not.

ETHNIC DIFFERENCE

Because being Muslim often overlapped with being Arab and being non-Muslim often overlapped with being non-Arab during the first decades of Islam, some hadith traditions coded Muslim religious difference through Arab ethnic difference from non-Arabs. Illustrating the literal and figurative entanglements of religious and ethnic identity, one tradition urges Muslim men, "Grow your beards and do not imitate the non-Arabs [*aʿājim*]."[56] Here, the label of "non-Arabs" is used in place of references to religious identity, such as "People of the Book" or "Jews and Christians," which are more commonly found in hadiths on growing the beard. Such linguistic slips suggest that the significance of "Muslim" as an identity marker during these early stages of Muslim history remained fluid and undefined, and that the distinction between Arab and non-Arab may even have prevailed over the distinction between Muslim and non-Muslim as a way to define communal boundaries.

Another way in which the Partisans of Hadith coded Muslim religious difference through ethnic difference was by distinguishing between Arabs of greater and lesser status. In yet another tradition on the subject of hairstyle, ʿAbd-Allāh b. ʿUmar reported that he heard his father, ʿUmar, say: "Whoever braids his hair should shave after coming out of the sanctified state of pilgrimage [*iḥrām*]. Do not imitate the [pagan Arab] practice of braiding your hair with gum [*talbīd*]."[57] Having criticized a pre-Islamic pagan Arab custom of braiding hair with gum during pilgrimage to the sacred precinct (*ka ʿba*), ʿUmar encourages Muslims to shave their hair instead.

Other hadiths differentiate urban settled Arabs from nomadic desert Arabs, the Bedouin. Displaying a bias against these Bedouins, some hadiths criticize them for trying to tailor Islam to suit their nomadic lifestyle by redefining the times of ritual prayer.[58] "Do not let the Bedouins overcome you with regard to the name of the sunset prayer [*maghrib*], which they call night prayer [*ʿishāʾ*]."[59]

GENDER AND SEXUAL DIFFERENCE

Social intermixing in public spaces blurred lines between men and women, inciting anxieties among the Partisans of Hadith, who considered it their moral duty to preserve sexual difference. Upholding the integrity of the Muslim social body, then, required disciplining the gendered physical body. According to one tradition that circulated widely in Iraq during the mid- to late eighth century: "The Messenger of God cursed men who imitate women [*mutashabbihīn*] and women who imitate men [*mutashabbihāt*]."[60] Although the hadith treats both sexes equally, chastising both men and women who resemble one another, it nonetheless upholds a hierarchical relationship between the sexes. According to a tradition transmitted by Shiʿi collectors, the sixth Imam, Jaʿfar al-Ṣādiq (d. 765), criticized a man who habitually dressed in long garments using gendered language: "I really detest that he resembles [*yatashabbahu*] women."[61]

With the exception of ʿĀʾisha, who led an army into battle just decades after her husband, the Prophet, passed away, female political leaders were neither common nor encouraged in early Islamic society (or in late antiquity generally). Amid the Quran's spiritual empowerment of women, Muslim religious authorities, mostly men, limited women's participation in public life in order to maintain visible distinctions between men and women. Nevertheless, in court life and in the harem, eunuchs, who blurred distinctions between male and female, played an important role as go-betweens and entertainers. Although the scope of the hadith's condemnation of imitation between men and women is unrestricted, religious authorities commonly employed the tradition to enforce sartorial differences between the sexes, a gloss that followed Deuteronomy 22:5: "There shall not be a man's gear on a woman, nor shall a man wear a woman's garment, for whoever does all these is an abhorrence of the Lord your God."[62]

CLASS AND STATUS DISTINCTIONS

Beyond the identity markers of religious, ethnic, and gender affiliation, social status in early Islam was determined by a number of other factors, including tribal lineage, wealth, eloquence, progeny, age, and the distinction between free person and slave. There are *tashabbuh*-related traditions that enforce distinctions between the latter two markers. According to one of these traditions, "The best of your youth emulate [*yatashabbahu*] your elders and the worst of your elders emulate your youth."[63] Proclaiming that young people ought to model their behavior after their elders—but not vice versa—this hadith is among the few that invest the term *tashabbuh* with a positive connotation. Young people should acknowledge the wisdom that elders have gained from their life experiences, while elders should refrain from demeaning themselves by emulating the behavior of young people, who have yet to mature spiritually, morally, and intellectually. Although this tradition defends hierarchical distinctions between young and old, some pietists, such as Abū Ṭālib al-Makkī (d. 996), subverted its apparent meaning by turning hadith commentary into a biting social critique of the stodgy conservatism of older generations that arrogantly disparage youth and their ways.[64]

In pre-Islamic Arabia, and the late antique Near East more broadly, slavery was assumed to be a normal feature of everyday life. The Quran inherited this worldview. Muhammad himself owned slaves; he may even have married one.[65] Although both the Quran and hadiths encourage Muslims not only to treat slaves with respect but to set them free, the Partisans of Hadith did not question the validity of the basic social distinction between free person and slave, requiring that their status be publicly visible, as implied by the following tradition: "ʿUmar saw a slave woman who veiled her hair. He struck her and told her: 'Do not imitate free women [*lā tashabbahī bi'l-ḥarāʾir*]!'"[66] This tradition, which I discuss further in the next chapter, indicates that wearing a headscarf was an act not simply of religious piety but of class distinction, namely, between free woman and slave woman. In this context, the most virtuous act for a slave woman was *not* to wear a headscarf and falsely resemble a free woman.

THE HUMAN-ANIMAL BOUNDARY

The line dividing nature from culture in the early Muslim social imagination was less defined than it is today. Humans and animals intermingled frequently in premodern Muslim societies before the transformations of modernity altered this relationship.[67] It is thus no coincidence that the Quran mentions several animals familiar to its late antique audience—camels, horses, cattle, mules, donkeys, sheep, monkeys, dogs, pigs, snakes, worms, ants, bees, spiders, mosquitoes, and flies—humanizing them in several ways: they speak their own languages, form their own communities (*umam*), and are even capable of receiving divine revelation.[68] One Muslim thinker even believed that God sent animals prophets to guide them on the straight path![69] Nevertheless, the Quran assigns humanity the responsibility of being God's steward on earth, placing animals at its service.[70] Some hadiths thus reinforce the boundary between human and animal by calling upon Muslims to avoid resembling certain beasts, like the camel: "When one of you prostrates [in prayer], he should not kneel like a camel, but should place his hands [onto the ground] before his knees."[71] A camel, by contrast, places its knees on the ground first—the incorrect technique during ritual prayer, according to this tradition.

Other traditions stigmatize human resemblance of animals outside the domain of ritual, such as this amusing tradition about a man mimicking a donkey: "He [the Prophet] passed by a group gathered around a man who was making them laugh. So he asked, 'What is this?' They replied, 'A man mimicking [*yatashabbahu*] a donkey and making his friends laugh.' So he responded, 'Glory be to God, no one will believe this! God had perfected his image; now he transforms him into the image of a donkey!'"[72] Although the Prophet joins in the lighthearted fun and cracks a joke, he nonetheless implies that the man mimicking a donkey is demeaning himself. After all, "God had perfected his image."

RESEMBLING SATAN

While God may have created humanity in His image, the figure known as Satan, according to biblical and Quranic narratives, refused to bow down in deference to this new creature. This first encounter between Satan and human is said to have taken place in a realm where a clear distinction between heaven and earth was yet undefined—human, angel, and jinn inhabited a single realm. But even on earth, according to this cosmology, interactions between humans and spirits abounded, ensuring that the boundary between terrestrial and spirit worlds remained porous. But because Satan is a fallen jinn, a shape-shifting spirit created from fire who vowed to lead humanity astray, according to most Islamic accounts, Muslims are warned against resembling him, even in something as small as table manners: “Do not eat with your left hand, for the devil eats and drinks with his left hand.”[73]

But while Muslims may successfully avoid resembling Satan, Satan may still resemble them. According to another tradition, Satan is able to assume the likeness of any human being except the Prophet: “He who has seen me in his sleep has seen me, for Satan cannot simulate my form [*lā yatashabbahu bī*].”[74] In this hadith, the Prophet reassures his followers that whoever sees him in a dream has truly seen him because Satan cannot assume his likeness. In another account, which depicts an apocalyptic scene appropriate for a horror movie, Satan’s minions transfigure (*yatashabbahūna*) into zombies and haunt the living by posing as their family members: “Do you know me? I am your brother and your father.”[75] While these traditions may indeed be fantastic, they nonetheless depict a world in which humans and spirits interact.

So what can we conclude from this exploration of traditions against imitation of all kinds? First, it confirms earlier studies that argued traditions against imitating other religious groups focused disproportionately on Jews. Second, it demonstrates that this Islamic vocabulary mediated a range of differences beyond religion, including gender, ethnicity, status, class, age, and the human—which attributes a much grander cosmological and moral ambition to the Partisans of Hadith than the subjugation of non-Muslims, that is, the establishment of a virtuous and *hierarchical* Islamic society. Third, it illustrates that most of these traditions do not call for a wholesale rejection of another group’s practices—religious or otherwise—but, more subtly, for the embodiment of *small differences* that would enable Muslims to stand out from the crowd. And finally, the social hierarchies endorsed by these traditions reflect an imperial imaginary, thus inviting comparisons to other “Islamic” texts, such as the Pact of ʿUmar, an administrative “document” that governed the public behavior of non-Muslim subjects living under Muslim rule (*dhimmīs*).

THE PACT OF ʿUMAR

The Pact of ʿUmar is among the earliest attempts by Muslim state authorities to regulate a religiously plural public space—the conquered city of Damascus, according to most accounts. Attributed to the second caliph, ʿUmar b. al-Khaṭṭāb, the pact assembled polyglot ordinances limiting non-Muslim imitation of Muslim religious and cultural practices in urban Damascus. The ordinances pertain to four main areas of public life: (1) dress; (2) public display of religious markers; (3) social/communal segregation; and (4) security and respect for Muslims (see table 1). Together, these ordinances advanced a new Islamic imperial narrative that suppressed the architectural and material symbols of Byzantine-Christian power.

The Pact of ʿUmar was an ocular-centric mandate; a majority of its ordinances focus on transforming the visual landscape of newly conquered Damascus. The pact prohibits Damascene Christians from building homes higher than those of Muslims; building new churches and renovating old ones; and displaying holy books, ceremonial lights, and crosses. Among its central purposes, then, is to define clear social boundaries between the new Muslim minority and the native Christian majority.

Many ordinances echo prescriptions against imitation found in the hadiths, such as those pertaining to the physical appearance of Christian residents:

> We shall not imitate [*lā natashabbahu*] Muslims in their dress, such as with the *qalansuwa,* the turban, footwear, or parting the hair.
>
> We shall dress in our traditional fashion wherever we may be and we shall bind the zunnār around our waists.
>
> We shall clip the forelocks of our heads.[76]

These ordinances appear to extend the obligations imposed upon Muslims in the hadiths to non-Muslims, who must also set themselves apart through headgear, footwear, and hairstyle.

Another set of ordinances appear to extend the hadith-based prohibition on Muslim participation in foreign *ʿīd*s to non-Muslims as well, who are called upon to limit the public impact of their religious celebrations and funeral processions:

> We shall not come near them during our funeral processions [or bury the dead among the Muslims].
>
> We shall not go outside on Palm Sunday or Easter, nor shall we raise our voices in our funeral processions.
>
> We shall not hold public religious ceremonies.

How should we conceptualize the mutual concern over religious difference in these two distinct source texts—one "religious," the other "political"? How

TABLE 1. THE PACT OF ʿUMAR (ARRANGED BY THEME)

Type of prohibition	Regulation
Dress/fashion	We shall clip the forelocks of our heads.
	We shall not attempt to resemble (*tashabbuh*) Muslims in any way with regard to their dress, as, for example, with the *qalansuwa,* the turban, footwear, or parting the hair.
	We shall dress in our traditional fashion wherever we may be and we shall bind the *zunnār* around our waists.
	We shall not ride on saddles.
Public display of religious markers	We shall not build new churches, monasteries, or monk cells, nor shall we repair any of them that have fallen into ruin or that are located in the quarters of Muslims.
	We shall not hold public religious ceremonies.
	We shall not display our crosses or our books anywhere in the roads or markets of the Muslims.
	We shall only beat our clappers (drums) in our churches very quietly.
	We shall not raise our voices in our church services, nor in the presence of Muslims.
	We shall not go outside on Palm Sunday or Easter, nor shall we raise our voices in our funeral processions.
	We shall not display lights in any of the roads of the Muslims or in their marketplaces.
Social segregation	We shall not teach our children the Quran.
	We shall not seek to proselytize to anyone.
	We shall not engrave Arabic inscriptions on our seals.
	We shall not speak as they do, nor shall we adopt their names (*kunyas*).
	We shall not come near them during our funeral processions (or bury the dead among the Muslims).
Security and respect for Muslims	We shall not wear swords or bear weapons of any kind, or even carry them on our person.
	We shall not sell alcoholic beverages to Muslims.
	We shall not give shelter in our churches and homes to spies.
	We shall provide three days' food and lodging to Muslim travelers.
	We shall keep our gate wide open for travelers.

Type of prohibition	Regulation
	We shall not prevent our kin from embracing Islam if they so desire.
	We shall show deference to Muslims and shall rise from our seats when they wish to sit.
	We shall not take slaves who have been allotted to Muslims.
	We shall not build our homes higher than theirs.

common was it for a polity in late antiquity to govern public displays of religious difference?

The muddied origins of the pact's ordinances, which scholars have debated, may offer some answers. Both Mark Cohen and Milka Levy-Rubin propose that the pact drew upon Byzantine regulations. Cohen argues that the literary form of the Pact of ʿUmar contains the elements of a decree, indicating that the conquered Christians played an important role in formulating the ordinances, many of which were likely rooted in Christian Byzantine norms existing prior to the Muslim conquest. Levy-Rubin, on the other hand, argues that the ordinances governing dress and hairstyle reflect the "Sasanian ideal of an immobile hierarchic society, where each estate is clearly discernible through its dress and paraphernalia."[77] Downplaying the pact's correspondence with *tashabbuh* hadith traditions, she emphasizes the correspondence between Persian social norms and the pact.

Like Cohen and Levi-Ruben, Albrecht Noth emphasizes continuity over rupture, arguing that the pact displays uncanny resemblances to other early treaties, indicating that its content was drawn from the existing practices of the conquered. Although Muslims possessed greater political and military power than their subject populations, Noth reasons, they were nonetheless a numerical minority amid a non-Muslim majority, a difference magnified by their lack of cultural prestige relative to their subjects, who were steeped in the high cultures of Byzantine and Sasanian civilization.[78] If we expand the conception of power implicit in Ibn Khaldūn's observation that the weak imitate the strong to include culture, then we can understand how Muslim authorities would have shunned assimilation by setting themselves apart from their non-Muslim subjects. Noth thus concludes, pace Levi-Ruben, that hadith traditions against imitation are a "confirmation" of the pact's early genesis and indigenous origins.[79] What binds together these two source-texts is thus a shared interest in defining sharp differences between Muslims and non-Muslims in public life.

Yet, as Levy-Rubin astutely notes while downplaying their historical correspondence, the hadiths and the pact are rhetorically distinguished by their audiences: the Pact seeks to limit Christian imitation of Muslims, while the hadiths seek to limit Muslim imitation of Christians.[80] Put differently, the two types of normative texts represent two different kinds of authority; that is, whereas the pact invokes state authority to regulate non-Muslim behavior, the hadiths call upon religious authority to regulate Muslim behavior. Although this distinction is important to keep in mind, it is nevertheless peripheral, in my view, and does not undermine Noth's conclusion regarding the texts' historical and literary correspondence. The distinct audiences of these texts may simply reflect a gradual expansion in the scope of Muslim governance, which first encompassed Muslims only, but eventually came to include non-Muslims as the caliphate extended its territorial borders.[81]

How the Pact of ʿUmar approaches interreligious relations is very different from how the document commonly called the Constitution of Medina (*ṣaḥīfat al-umma*) does.[82] Said to have been forged just after Muhammad migrated from Mecca to Medina, this document is a compact governing political, economic, and legal relations between the Prophet and the city's Arab tribes, which included the Jews. Most historians agree that the version(s) we have today likely originates from a very early period, in part because the document's portrayal of interreligious boundaries is so fluid.[83] Although Jews were permitted to follow their own respective religion (*dīn*), they were nonetheless included with "Muslims" as members of "a single community [*umma wāḥida*] to the exclusion of others."[84] They were all believers.[85]

What, then, accounts for the difference in how the Constitution of Medina and the Pact of ʿUmar approach Muslim relations with non-Muslims? The answer, in sum, is power. The contrast between how each document defines interreligious relations is reflected in the transformation in communal power relations. Whereas the Constitution of Medina reflects a moment when the Muslim community was weak, politically and militarily, the Pact of ʿUmar is an expression of a new era when the community was ascendant—as the caliphate began to realize its imperial ambitions. The constitution's orientation toward interreligious relations thus appears to correspond to the period in which Muhammad was still intentionally emulating Judeo-Christian tradition, before he was ordered to follow a new direction. In the Constitution of Medina, Muslims and Jews are bound together in symmetrical power relations, as indicated by the term *believer.* In the pact, however, Muslims and Christians are distinguished by asymmetrical power relations whereby Muslims have authority over Christians. As a result, the pact coercively disciplines and marks the bodies of non-Muslims in a way that the constitution does not (and cannot). In sum, while the constitution brings different religious communities together, the pact keeps them apart. The Pact of ʿUmar thus presages (or reflects?) an imperial logic of difference.

The impulse of Muslim elites to set themselves apart was grounded in the imperial imaginary of the late antique Near East—as indicated by late seventh-century Christian canon laws. There is little evidence to genetically link the canon laws to the ordinances in the pact, but their existence suggests that the content of the pact was not historically out of sync with the seventh century, as some historians have claimed. In fact, both sets of prescriptions govern the everyday encounters between different religious communities through a common legal idiom, suggesting that they each drew upon a shared late antique cultural heritage. The canon laws were issued at the Council in Trullo, which was convened in Constantinople in 692, but later rejected by the pope.[86] Consider canon XI, which reveals Christian anxieties over intermingling with Jews: "Let no one in the priestly order nor any layman eat the unleavened bread of the Jews, nor have any familiar intercourse with them, nor summon them in illness, nor receive medicines from them, nor bathe with them; but if anyone shall take in hand to do so, if he is a cleric, let him be deposed, but if a layman let him be cut off."[87] Other canons from this council decree that priests shall avoid horse races and theater performances, as well as meat cooked in a church; that neither layperson nor cleric shall play dice, hunt, leap over fires during the new moon, or plait their hair; and that students of law shall not adopt gentile customs or roll in the dust.[88]

Frequent references to the Pact of ʿUmar in Islamic literature—administrative manuals, legal treatises and responsa, hadith collections, historical chronicles, and interfaith polemics—reflect how Muslim religious authorities turned it into an ideal template for conceiving interreligious relations.[89] Consider, for example, the eighth-century legal text *The Treatise on Taxation* (*Kitāb al-Kharāj*), written by the prominent Ḥanafī jurist Abū Yūsuf (d. 798), who served as chief judge of Baghdad during the legendary reign of the Abbasid caliph Hārūn al-Rashīd (r. 786–809). Abū Yūsuf's treatise was more than a tax manual. It addressed a wide range of topics pertaining to the political economy of the Islamic state, including Muslim relations with non-Muslim subjects (*dhimmīs*)—from rulings on marrying Zoroastrian women to regulations governing non-Muslim dress.[90]

In a section of the treatise on imposing visible markers of distinction upon non-Muslims, Abū Yūsuf refers to the relevant ordinances from the Pact of ʿUmar: "No one should be permitted to imitate and resemble [*yatashabbahu*] Muslims in their dress, riding beast, and general appearance. They should be subdued by placing around their waists their special belts—such as a thick cord tied around the waist of each one of them. Their conical hats should be quilted; they should hang two wooden balls resembling pomegranates from the rear of their saddles; they should wear double-thonged sandals, and not wear shoes like Muslim shoes; their women are prohibited from riding on saddles."[91] The obligations for non-Muslim subjects to adopt distinct headgear, footgear, belts, and saddles all resemble regulations stipulated in the pact. Abū Yūsuf's rationale for enforcing these regulations is likewise the same: "so that their dress is distinguished from Muslim dress."[92] Abū Yūsuf's other rulings also conform to what is stipulated in the pact, including bans on non-Muslims renovating places of worship, displaying crosses in public, and selling wine and pork to Muslims.[93] Appearing as they do in an administrative treatise on taxation, these legal rulings are evidence of how hierarchical conceptions of religious difference had begun to define Muslim ideals of Islamic governance.

The pact became so influential within Islamic jurisprudence that it inspired a distinct genre of Islamic legal treatises that defined how non-Muslim subjects ought to be governed (*aḥkām ahl al-dhimma*).[94] Briefly considering how these treatises harmonized the Pact of ʿUmar with scholarly discourses on reprehensible imitation brings into relief the pact's place within the normative universe of Islam. In the finest example of this genre, the Mamluk-era polymath Ibn al-Qayyim al-Jawziyya (d. 1350) devotes a substantial portion of his treatise *Aḥkām ahl al-dhimma* to the ordinances.[95] To explain, for example, why non-Muslims must adopt visible markers of distinction (*ghiyār*), Ibn al-Qayyim quotes from the now lost treatise on the pact (ca. tenth/eleventh century) of Shāfiʿī jurist Abū al-Qāsim al-Lālakāʾī (d. 1027):

> Clear evidence for the legal obligation of enforcing visible markers of distinction upon non-Muslim subjects is found in the Prophet's statement (peace and blessings be upon him), "Whoever imitates a people becomes one of them." It means (God willing) that Muslims ought to

> emulate other Muslims in their distinctive style of dress so they can be identified as Muslims, while unbelievers ought to emulate other unbelievers in their distinctive style of dress so they can be identified as unbelievers. Unbelievers must therefore be compelled to resemble members of their own religious community so that Muslims may identify them through their dress.[96]

Lālakāʾī reads the imitation hadith through the lens of the Pact of ʿUmar, contending that all citizens of *dār al-Islām* must outwardly conform to the religious communities they belong to so that their religious affiliations are made public. In Lālakāʾī's view, the apocalyptic narration of the hadith is "the tradition that is most germane to the matter of religious distinction [*ghiyār*] and nearest to it in both theory and application." The Prophet's threat that "abasement and contempt have been placed upon the one who disobeys my command" is read by Lālakāʾī as a divine sanction for the subjugation of unbelievers, "who are abased through their sartorial distinction from Muslims whom God [by contrast] has elevated in rank." The sartorial markers imposed upon unbelievers are thus a "distinctive sign of abasement [*simat al-hawān*] upon them."[97]

This outlook is shared by the Punjabi Ḥanafī jurist ʿUmar b. Muḥammad al-Sunāmī (d. 1300–24), who cites the imitation hadith to explain why the market inspector (*muḥtasib*) must police the boundary between believer and unbeliever in the public sphere: "The unbeliever is abased whereas the Muslim is exalted . . . if they were to resemble us then we would come to resemble them as well, and external resemblance enables social amity and concord. However, [the Prophet issued] a grave warning against our emulating them: he (peace be upon him) said, 'Whoever imitates a people becomes one of them.'"[98] It was the responsibility of the market inspector to bring the everyday conduct of the inhabitants of *dār al-Islām* into line with the ideals of Islamic governance, including unruly Muslims and non-Muslims who promiscuously crossed religious lines.[99] By tying the Pact of ʿUmar to the imitation hadith, both Lālakāʾī and Sunāmī harmonize discourses that originally represented distinct domains of authority, tightening the link between religion and statecraft.[100] In this imperial imaginary, hierarchies of Muslim distinction constitute a key feature of public life in *dār al-Islām.*

Sunāmī's simple yet profound insight that mimesis is reciprocal demystifies the hierarchical logic behind this imperial imaginary: "If they were to resemble us then we would come to resemble them." Put differently, "If they become like us, then we become like them." Mimesis, in other words, erases the line between believer and unbeliever. Sunāmī helps explain why state and religious authority within the Realm of Islam had common cause in maintaining this line. While the pact as an extension of state authority circumscribed non-Muslim behavior and the discourses against reprehensible imitation as an extension of religious authority circumscribed Muslim behavior, the dialogical nature of confessional identity transformed these distinct forms of authority into complements—like matching pieces of a puzzle.

The close alignment between religious and state authority is also manifested through the occasional correspondence between the caliph's imperial policies and the literary production of the *ʿulamāʾ*. How vigilantly the market inspector actually policed the boundary between believer and unbeliever remains suspect, given that caliphs and sultans across Islamic history intermittently issued imperial decrees inspired by the pact that imposed sartorial regulations upon *dhimmī*s, from the Abbasids (ninth century) and Fatimids (tenth/eleventh century) to the Ayyubids (twelfth/thirteenth century), Mamluks (fourteenth century), and Ottomans (sixteenth century).[101] During the Mamluk and Ottoman periods, imperial decrees preventing non-Muslims from resembling Muslims were complemented by the composition of religious treatises forbidding Muslims from resembling non-Muslims.

THE GREAT VALUE OF SMALL DIFFERENCES

Rather than view hadith traditions against imitating Jews and Christians in isolation, in this chapter I have looked at them *in relation to* other texts; first, in relation to other categories of difference—Arab and non-Arab, men and women, old and young, free person and slave, human and nonhuman (animal/devil)—within the body of hadiths; and second, in relation to the administrative document known as the Pact of ʿUmar. From this panoramic view of Muslim difference, we see convergences between these texts that are otherwise invisible. As a whole, these textual convergences reflect what I call an imperial imaginary, a social imaginary common to religious and political elites in which the ideal Islamic society is hierarchically stratified.

As mediators, then, of an Islamic imperial imaginary, these differences may have been small in scale but nonetheless great in *value*. These small differences were (and in many cases remain) meaningful and important to Muslims and, arguably, to non-Muslims who perceived them. Although Freud's theory of small differences is a powerful model for explaining why differences between entities otherwise similar to one another appear, at first blush, insignificant, we must nonetheless refine the application of the descriptor "small" to their scale alone. So while the magnitude of these differences remained small, their value, by contrast, was often great.

But why was the scale of these differences often so small? That is, why didn't their magnitude assume greater proportions? To answer this question, we need to recall Freud's observation that "small" differences take shape between people who are otherwise alike. In Medina, Muslims and Jews were part of a single Arab culture—as was the community of Muslims, stratified across lines of gender, ethnicity, and status. As Muhammad's successors expanded the territorial sovereignty of the *umma* beyond Arabia, the spaces of encounter with foreigners also expanded. To stand out from the crowd, Muslims needed to publicly display their small differences, which, as I show in the next chapter, semiotically transformed those differences into potent symbols.

CHAPTER 4

The Symbolic Power of Muslim Difference

Whoever honors the symbols of God does so from a pious heart.

—QURAN 22:32

As anybody who saw the beard from the crowd or on TV will tell you . . . its blackness seemed to drown all thought . . . as it curled into and over and around itself. It seemed to evade definition somehow. For its top side was its underside its right side was its left side and its inside was its outside.

—STEPHEN COLLINS, *The Gigantic Beard That Was Evil*

The great value of small differences to early Muslims derived not only from the imperial hierarchies they upheld but also from social and cultural meanings they embedded. But to understand the magnitude of this value, and to elicit the manifold social and cultural meanings these differences carried, this chapter pivots from the panoramic view of hadith traditions in the previous chapter to a focused analysis of a small cluster of traditions that draw practices of Muslim difference into close view. From this vantage point, we can observe how everyday practices became potent symbols of Muslim difference, and better apprehend why they mattered.

Because all human beings, past and present, invest the world with meaning through symbols, the great scholar of religion Mircea Eliade called our species *homo symbolicus.*[1] Muslim thinkers, too, saw a world filled with meaning, inspired by the Quran, which describes the cosmos (and itself) as filled with signs (*āyāt*) of God's presence. The existence of a cosmological symphony does not imply that human beings are passive observers of these signs, but rather that they actively create meaning in the world. Human beings are meaning-makers, stewards entrusted with filling the world with signs of their presence—their difference. Religious scholars thus circumscribed the discursive zone of Muslim difference by means of a key Arabic term: *shiʿār* (pl. *shaʿāʾir*), a distinctive symbol, sign, or marker. The multivalent term can also be traced back to the Quran: "Whoever honors the symbols [*shaʿāʾir*] of God does so from a pious heart" (Q 22:32). Displaying reverence for the symbols of God, the verse suggests, is a sign of true faith and, more broadly, constitutes an essential part of religion.

But while the Quran ties this concept to the divine realm, religious scholars applied it to the earthly realm of quotidian life. In this semiotic imaginary, everyday practices, "religious" or otherwise, accrue abundant value and meaning. Symbols, observed anthropologist Clifford Geertz, mediate culture.[2] For Muslim scholars, symbols (*shaʿāʾir*) defined an individual's place within a community, and a community's place within a culture. Every community, by definition, possesses its own repertoire of distinctive markers and symbols. And it is these symbols that do the powerful work of setting apart one community from another in public life.

But symbols are not just pure abstractions. Symbols are embedded in the material world, as the gritty array of lexical meanings also carried by the Arabic term *shiʿār* illustrate—a flag, a battle cry, a geographic landmark, a ritual, or even the rag used by a menstruating woman to stop the flow of blood. The Quran (2:158, 22:36), for example, names the camels sacrificed in God's name and the landmarks of Ṣafā and Marwa visited by pilgrims during the Hajj pilgrimage the "symbols of God" (*shaʿāʾir Allāh*). The heterogeneous semantic field of *shiʿār* may thus encompass embodied practices, material objects, or physical spaces that become charged with symbolic value.

The entanglement between symbols and the material world they represent is also captured by the etymologically related terms *mashāʿir* (s. *mashʿar*), the five physical senses—hearing, sight, smell, taste, touch—and *shaʿr*, hair. Reflecting the socio-symbolic value of physical appearance, *shaʿr* would become a *shiʿār*, a distinctive marker that set Muslims apart, while *mashāʿir* mediated these markers in public life.

The potent term *shiʿār*, then, offers a conceptual template for understanding how the symbols of Muslim difference materialized into everyday practice. Realizing that the symbols that enforce the social boundaries of a community can paradoxically also unravel those same boundaries, leading to social disorder and cultural contamination, Muslim religious and state authorities exerted themselves to define the meanings of these symbols in public life. They transformed a cluster of everyday practices into potent symbols of difference invested with meaning and value that cultivated a distinct style (*ziyy*) of being in the world.

But to understand the symbolic value and meaning of these markers of Muslim difference we must pay close attention to the precise forms they took, which encompass sartorial codes, physical gestures, and sensory perceptions. Distinctive sartorial and gestural styles are highly visible practices that shape a group's public image. The importance that human beings throughout history, including Muslim communities, have placed on gestural and sartorial codes reflect the outsized importance of physical appearance to group identity and solidarity. For Muslims to be different, they had to look different. It also speaks to the broader importance of vision, and sensory perception more generally, for the expression and recognition of social differences. Although most acts of Muslim difference are visual, they materialize through all the physical senses, especially hearing. Together, the physical senses connect and orient the human body to the physical landscapes around it, defining what constitutes the public sphere.[3]

In what follows, I introduce and in some cases revisit a series of traditions that charged a repertoire of embodied practices with symbolic meaning; they include growing and dyeing the beard, wearing turbans and headscarves, summoning Muslims to prayer, wiping over leather socks, prostrating before God, and consuming food with the left hand. Because the meanings that symbols encode are dynamic and fluid, embedded within contexts—social, cultural, political, and historical—I read these traditions alongside an array of other literary and documentary sources that restore some of this context, including commentaries, legal treatises, historical chronicles, biographical dictionaries, and material culture. From this vantage point, we can see how practices designed to set Muslims apart draw on preexisting cultural idioms that paradoxically connect them to the peoples around them. My objective, then, is to discern the cluster of meanings reflected on the surfaces of these practices, employing a semiotic approach that showcases Muslim meaning-making.

BEARDS OF DISTINCTION

What I call a person's *sartorial code* encompasses styles of both dress and hair and is simultaneously visible, material, and symbolic.[4] It functions as a second layer of skin that beautifies and protects the physical body, mediating its relationship to the social body.[5] Fashion, in its many forms, is prone to "prestigious imitation," the desire to emulate and look like high-status members of society, and is thus easily transmitted across cultural boundaries.[6] "The truth is that fashion follows the tastes of the Muslim community's upper-class," observed an Egyptian periodical nearly a century ago. "There is no doubt that a small group of people who are early adopters of new styles are then followed by the masses."[7] Due to their capacity to both bind together and set apart members of society, sartorial codes embed an assemblage of symbolic meanings and values. The symbolic meanings of dress and hair are multilayered, like identity, weaving together religious difference with political, gender, ethnicity, and status differences. A rich site for mapping Muslim difference, the sartorial code is a prism through which markers of identity dynamically intersect.

A universal marker of social and cultural belonging, hairstyle is a significant part of a person's sartorial code. Easily copied, hairstyle spreads across communities and societies, becoming knotted with symbolism and meaning—as the Arabic word for hair, *sha ʿr, s*uggests. Because hair is a prominent and visible feature of the body, near the face, it may also be a powerful status symbol, as in the case of Muslim beards.[8]

More than a highly visible extension of a person's physiognomy, the beard is a metaphor for the manifold meanings it can convey. Ungroomed, the beard becomes an unwieldy tangled mass of hair, an unruly and volatile signifier of cultural meaning. In the late antique and medieval Near East, it was standard practice for Jewish, Christian, and Muslim men to grow distinctively styled beards.[9] A well-groomed beard became part of the Prophet's *sunna,* a signal of both masculine and religious difference. As subsequent generations of religious scholars defined the shape, size, and color of the ideal Muslim beard, they implicitly defined its meanings as well.[10]

Although the Quran is silent on the matter of styling beards, a number of hadiths exhort believing men to grow them:

> Cut the moustaches and grow your beards. Be different from the Magians [*khālifū al-majūs*].[11]

> Be different from the idolaters [*khālifū al-mushrikīn*]; trim your moustaches and grow out your beards.[12]

The effective cause for the Prophetic command is to be different from the "idolaters," identified by Muslim commentators as Magians (not pagan Arabs), the Persian Zoroastrian priestly class. This reading is supported by another tradition, which describes a strange encounter between the Prophet Muhammad and two nearly clean-shaven Persian men: "Abū Hurayra reported that the ruler of Yemen, appointed by the Persian emperor Kisrā (Khosrow II [d. 628]), sent two envoys to the Messenger. They entered upon him clean-shaven except for their moustaches, which they had grown out. Disliking their appearance, he [the Prophet] turned his face away and said, 'Woe be to you, who told you to do this [shave off their facial hair except for the moustache]?' They replied: 'Our lord [Kisrā] did!' The Messenger responded: 'But my Lord commanded me to grow my beard and trim my moustache.'"[13] In an unusually candid gesture, the Prophet turns away from his guests, displaying his disgust at their appearance. Although primarily a marker of Persian ethnonational identity, the envoys' distinctive hairstyle bundles together a group of identity markers across ethnicity, class, gender, and religion. Within this heterogeneous semiotic field, the Prophet's opposition to being clean-shaven except for the moustache takes on a much deeper significance: his rejection of Persian-Zoroastrian imperial authority and affirmation of Arab-Islamic authority, as represented in the figures of Kisrā and Allah. With the collapse of the Sasanian Empire and conversion of many Zoroastrians to Islam, however, the symbolic value of long beards transcended the provincial Arab-Persian rivalry and became a global marker of Muslim difference.

Leading by example, the Prophet allegedly possessed a "copious beard" (*kāna kaththa al-liḥya*)—as did other paragons of Muslim piety, including the first four caliphs.[14] 'Alī's beard was reportedly so big that it spanned the distance between his two shoulders (*mala'at mā fī bayna al-mankabayn*). The Prophet Aaron's beard was supposedly even bigger, reaching down to his chest.[15] Muslim obsession with beard size inspired, in the words of Baghdadi Sufi and Ḥanbalī jurist Abū Ṭālib al-Makkī, "a strange interpretation" of Quran 35:1: "He increases His creation in whatever way He pleases [*yazīdu fī al-khalq mā yashā'*]," which shifted its reference point from the celestial to the terrestrial sphere; instead of God bestowing angels with any number of wings, the verse's mainstream interpretation, He increases *the size of a beard* in whatever way He pleases.[16] Growing a long beard, according to other hadith traditions, is part of true religion (*fiṭra*).[17] And according to all the Islamic legal schools, growing the beard is more than a voluntary meritorious act (*sunna*)—it is an obligation. To shave the beard, even to trim it, according to some schools of law, is disdained—although, in the view of the founding jurists of the Ḥanafī school, "There is no problem in shortening the beard as long as it does not resemble those of the pagans."[18]

But even more than the masculine virtue of strength, a fully grown and well-groomed beard represented Muslim ideals of masculine beauty. The Prophet's wife ʿĀʾisha reportedly said, "All praise belongs to the One who beautified men with beards."[19] The Sufi jurist Ghazālī, paraphrasing Makkī, opined, "Beards are the ornaments of men [*zīnat al-rajul*] . . . the perfection of creation [*tamām al-khalq*]," and "by means of it, men are distinguished from women."[20] These aesthetic appraisals of facial hair were anticipated (and likely informed) by Judeo-Christian tradition: "The beard signifies strong men," wrote St. Augustine of Hippo (d. 430), "the beard signifies young, vigorous, active, quick men. When we therefore describe such men, we say that a man is bearded."[21] By the early eighth century, the Arabs had instituted the punishment of shaving off the beards of Egyptian Christian and Jewish men who transgressed the law to strip them of their masculinity.[22]

But if Jews and Christians also grew their beards, how did Muslims set their beards apart? Inspired by a cluster of widely circulated hadiths—"Dye your gray hair and do not imitate the Jews and Christians"; "The Jews and Christians do not dye [their beards], so be different from them!"—many early Muslims dyed their beards distinctive hues to stand out from the monotheist crowd.[23] They coordinated the distinctive hues of their beards with their attire, including robes, turbans, and shoes, to create a unique visual language of Islam. Compared to other sartorial attributes such as pattern and material, color is easily identified. In fact, according to the Quran, color is a mark of the sacred: "Such is God's coloring: and who is better than God at coloring?" (Q 2:138).

G.H.A. Juynboll speculates that early Muslims invested this issue with significance because they adopted the foreign custom of applying henna, a specific dyeing agent.[24] But this materialist reading diminishes the beard's significance as a symbolic marker of difference. The absence of dye on the beards of Jewish and Christian men was not intended to be a symbolic marker of communal distinction. But the Prophet transforms the practice of dyeing beards into a symbolic marker of Muslim difference by instructing his followers to do so. This teaching signals the significance of beards to the early Muslim community's sense of solidarity. In most cases, the Prophet instructs Muslims to shun symbolic practices of rival communities that are already in circulation, not create ones anew (for example, Jews are known to stand up during funerals, so Muslims should do the opposite and sit down).

Given that these hadiths were both unambiguous and widely known, we would not expect Muslims to disagree on the virtue of dyeing beards. Yet they did. So while Muslims came to a consensus on the virtue of growing beards, they disagreed on the virtue of dyeing them. There are a few reasons for this dispute. First, while it was widely known that the Prophet Muhammad grew out his beard, it was unclear whether he dyed it.[25] If the earliest generations of Muslims could not establish that the Prophet himself dyed his beard, how could they mandate the practice, or even encourage it? They also debated the correct manner of dyeing beards, including which substances and colors to use.[26] For example, some jurists permitted black dye, if used for a specific purpose, while others banned it completely, based on anecdotes like this one: "The Prophet saw a man with black hair whom he had seen the day before with white hair. The Prophet asked, 'Who are you?' The man replied, 'I am so and so.' He said: 'No, you are Satan.'"[27] Through his insult, the Prophet associates the falsification of bodily form with the diabolic.

But black was not the only color that could deceive. The chronic misuse of white dye brought into relief inter-generational rivalries between young Muslims who dyed their beards white to look old and wise, and old-timers who plucked out their white hairs to look forever young—both sinful acts according to Abū Ṭālib al-Makkī.[28] Makkī also criticized the habit of using bright red or yellow dye to draw public attention.[29] In the eighth and ninth centuries, effeminate men and hermaphrodites (*mukhannathūn*) commonly dyed their hair eccentric colors.[30] Other impious Muslims may have been doing the same, threatening to recast the dyes' pious signification among religious authorities. In sum, for the outward practice of dyeing beards to be virtuous, a Muslim's motives had to be pure.

And so dyeing beards not only differentiated Muslims from non-Muslims but distinguished Muslims from other Muslims. Dye literally colored the political and ideological divisions between hadith scholars.[31] Although each of the first four caliphs possessed fully grown beards, the biographer Ibn Saʿd (d. 844–45) mentions that the first two caliphs, Abū Bakr and ʿUmar, dyed their beards, while ʿAlī did not, anticipating sectarian divisions between Sunnis and Shiʿis.[32] Later generations of Muslims therefore came to their own conclusions about whether or not to dye their beards.

TURBANS AND HEADSCARVES

Like hairstyle, headgear is an extension of a person's physiognomy, and thus may become a crucial marker of social identity. Along with Jews, Persians, and pre-Islamic Arabs in the late antique Near East, Muslims used protective headgear, although they ultimately devised their own distinct style.

Creativity is not merely the act of bringing something into existence from nonexistence. Creativity is also the synthetic act of putting together things that already exist into new combinations. The style of headgear that came to define the Muslim man originated in this way, a creative fusion of two preexisting types of headgear: the *qalansuwa* and the turban. Worn by Sasanian elites, the *qalansuwa* came in two distinct sizes and styles, regular and tall.[33] The Persian fashion had spread to Arabia, so that eminent Muslim figures such as the Prophet Muhammad and the third caliph, ʿUthmān (r. 644–56), wore regular-sized *qalansuwa*s.[34] But the hat's foreign origins did not deter the architects of the Pact of ʿUmar from banning non-Muslims from wearing the *qalansuwa* to make it an exclusively Muslim style.[35] Muslim attitudes toward the tall *qalansuwa* were more conflicted. According to the Abbasid litterateur Jāḥiẓ (d. 868–69), Muslims originally shunned tall *qalansuwa*s, which were worn during Sasanian court ceremonies.[36] After the Umayyads rose to power, however, the caliph and other Muslims of noble rank began to adopt Sasanian courtly styles like the tall *qalansuwa,* eventually forgetting its foreign associations with the excesses of pre-Islamic Persian culture.

According to archaeological evidence from the Achaemenid period, Persians wore turbans as well.[37] The ancient historian Herodotus hypothesized that they did so because they had weak skulls. Nevertheless, the Prophet Muhammad perceived the turban not as a Persian style but as an Arab one, reportedly proclaiming, "Turbans are the crowns of the Arabs."[38] Muhammad himself regularly wore a turban—a sartorial habit that became part of his *sunna* and helped transform an Arab cultural norm into a Muslim religious norm.[39] A millennium later, the philosopher John Locke would refer to the Muslim world as the "turbanned nations."[40]

But because Muslims adopted styles of headgear that were in vogue among foreigners and unbelievers, they were inspired to distinguish their hats from the crowd, lest their identity be mistaken. However, instead of creating an entirely new style of headgear that was radically different from anything currently worn, they synthesized existing styles into something unique: "The difference between us [Muslims] and the idolaters," Muhammad declared, "is the turban wrapped around the *qalansuwa.*"[41] Zoroastrians may have worn turbans and *qalansuwa*s, but they did not wear them together. They allegedly wore turbans with the crowns of their heads exposed. To set themselves apart, Muslims did not need to categorically reject these styles; it was sufficient to enact a small difference and wrap their turban around a *qalansuwa,* transforming their headgear into something that was at once similar to and different from existing styles.

But some Muslims may have felt that this difference was too minor; the Pact of ʿUmar took the more dramatic step of banning non-Muslims from wearing turbans as well as the *qalansuwa*. This ban, however, appears to have been short-lived. Non-Muslim subjects (*dhimmīs*) of the caliphate continued to wear turbans, blurring the lines between conqueror and conquered. Subsequent caliphs experimented with a new approach to setting apart *dhimmīs* by means of headgear: instead of banning Jewish and Christian men from wearing turbans, caliphs issued sartorial decrees that *required* them to wear distinctively colored turbans. The Abbasid caliph Mutawakkil (r. 847–61) decreed that Jews and Christians wear honey-colored turbans in contrast to the blue and black turbans worn by Muslims.[42] Not to be outdone, the Fatimid caliph Ḥākim (r. 996–1020) decreed that Jews and Christians wear black turbans, transforming the color black from a prestigious symbol of Abbasid Muslim power into a humiliating symbol of non-Muslim subjection.[43] The Mamluk Sultans had a brighter outlook; they issued a color-coded decree that outfitted Jews with yellow turbans, Christians with blue turbans, and Samaritans with red turbans.[44] Similarly, the Ottoman sultans mandated black hats for Jews and red hats for Christians; only Muslims were permitted to wear turbans.[45]

Turban colors symbolized not only distinctions between Muslims and non-Muslims but also between different kinds of Muslims. Shiʿi Muslims interpreted the Prophet's gesture of placing a black turban upon the head of ʿAlī at the sacred site of Ghadīr Khumm as a spiritual and political symbol of succession.[46] The Abbasid caliphate appropriated the color black, requiring ʿAlī's sympathizers, the ʿAlids, to display loyalty by wearing black turbans. Even the angels who fought with Muhammad's army at the battle of Badr are said to have worn white, yellow, green, and red turbans as badges of celestial distinction.[47]

Early generations of Muslims attached great social prestige to the turban, as the following encounter, narrated by the biographer Ibn Saʿd, illustrates. One day, a man of modest means saw ʿIkrima (d. 723), the client (*mawlā*) of the distinguished Companion Ibn ʿAbbās, wearing a tattered turban. Seeing an opportunity to assist a stranger in need, the man offered to replace ʿIkrima's tattered turban with a new one. But to his surprise, ʿIkrima pompously rejected the gift: "We only accept [gifts] from elites [*al-umarāʾ*]."[48] ʿIkrima, in other words, felt it was beneath him to accept a gift from the man due to his noble status as a client of Ibn ʿAbbās. Through this public display of his status, ʿIkrima signaled that a gift's value is derived not from its material worth alone, but also from the social status of its giver. Offended, the man curtly responds with a Quranic verse (75:14): "Indeed, man will be a clear witness against himself." Overturning the social hierarchy, the commoner teaches ʿIkrima, an elite, an important spiritual lesson: that piety and good deeds, not social status, are the true measure of a person's worth. Through this anecdote, we learn that the turban had come to mark Muslim social status by the first Islamic century. Over time, as caliphs, professional guilds, and mystical groups adopted their own distinctive turbans, the symbolism of the headgear continued to multiply in value, much like the layers of fabric that comprised the turban itself.

When women began to wear turban-like dresses, Quran exegetes responded by listing turbans, along with beards, as markers of men's natural superiority over women.[49] In defense of the turban as a distinct marker of masculinity, Ibn Taymiyya authored a fatwa forbidding women from wearing large turbans.[50] "The turbans that these women wear are without doubt forbidden." Paraphrasing a hadith, he opined, "They resemble the humps of the Bactrian camel [*asnimat al-bukht*]."[51] A century earlier, the Ḥanbalī jurist Ibn Qudāma (d. 1223) issued a ruling that permitted believing men to wipe over their turbans during ablution, but not believing women, reasoning that they should not be cross-dressing anyway.[52] Cross-dressing meant crossing gendered social boundaries, which could lead to social disorder, or *fitna*. "The most severe trial [*fitna*] I have left behind me for the men of my community," the Prophet warned, "is [the trial of] women."[53] Citing this hadith in his fatwa, Ibn Taymiyya warned that *fitna* could have drastic political consequences: "It is submission to women that brings corruption to kingship and empire."[54]

Most Muslim women, however, covered their hair with a headscarf, not a turban. Wearing a headscarf was a late antique social norm among Greeks, Romans, Jews, and Assyrians that indexed class distinctions and cultural meanings.[55] Not only did the veil differentiate women from men, it distinguished between classes of women—although quite differently from how it does so today.

A cryptic anecdote involving the caliph ʿUmar, transmitted on the authority of the Companion Anas b. Mālik, illustrates how the headscarf marked different classes of women during the formative period of Islam.[56] "ʿUmar espied a slave woman who belonged to us but had veiled her hair [*mutaqanniʿa*]. He struck her and told her: 'Do not imitate free women [*lā tushbihī bi'l-ḥarāʾir*]!'"[57] Demonstrating whether this event actually happened is less important than recognizing that it could have. According to Anas, ʿUmar reprimands a slave woman belonging to him who had veiled her hair. In what appears to be a severe reaction (to a contemporary viewer, at least), he strikes her and orders her not to resemble free women.[58] This response seems strange to us because we commonly perceive the veil as a virtuous symbol of modesty and a religious marker of difference between Muslim and non-Muslim women. We thus expect that ʿUmar would in fact have wanted the slave woman to cover more of her body. But in the seventh century, the headscarf signified more than just modesty. It was a display of nobility, of being a free woman. ʿUmar thus reprimanded the slave woman for hiding more than her hair. By veiling and posing as a free woman, she was hiding her inferior status as a slave woman. But when ʿUmar erotically exposes her hair, he exposes the truth of her social status. The circulation of similar anecdotes among early Muslim traditionists suggests that such encounters were not unusual.[59]

Caliphs during Islam's formative period may have required slaves and free women to display visible marks of their inferior status as official policy. Slaves received half the entitlements (but also half the punishments) of free persons. But in order for these laws to be applied properly, Muslim authorities needed first to distinguish slave from free person, and the presence or absence of a headscarf was an easy way to identify a woman's legal status. In the above encounter, ʿUmar exposes the slave woman's hair in public, disregarding its potential to incite male sexual desire or to undermine the expression of female modesty in the public sphere. According to classical Muslim jurists, hair is part of a free woman's *ʿawra,* the legally defined area that must be covered in public.[60] The headscarf, in this encounter, is a means to enforce social boundaries between slave women and free women, not between men and women. This portrayal of the application and social function of veiling is very different from its modern application in Islamic law, which portrays the headscarf as mandatory for *all women* who have reached maturity.[61] From the late classical period (tenth–fourteenth centuries) onwards, although most Muslim jurists permitted slave women to appear in public without headscarves, based on ʿUmar's alleged preference for this sartorial distinction, they increasingly stressed the headscarf's semiotic role in deterring sexual temptation (*fitna*).[62]

During the formative period of Islam, however, only urban middle- and upper-class women wore headscarves in mixed-gendered public spaces. "The veil served not merely to mark the upper classes," Leila Ahmed observes, "but, more fundamentally, to differentiate between 'respectable' women and those who were publicly available."[63] In the Quran, the Prophet's wives are enjoined to sequester themselves behind a curtain (*purda*) when unrelated male visitors enter the home, at once asserting that they were both not like men and "not like other women."[64] Early Muslims thus perceived the headscarf as a prestigious marker of class distinction.[65]

As ʿUmar's command to not imitate free women suggests, wearing a headscarf is, in fact, easy to imitate. Anas's slave woman donned a veil in order to be treated with the respect and nobility of a free woman. She wanted to become "one of them." Slave women, after all, were treated like material objects. During the Abbasid period, a Muslim man might purchase "a house, furniture, concubines, and other objects" when he received his inheritance.[66] Thus, "woman, and slave, and object for sexual use came close to being indistinguishably fused."[67] ʿUmar's act of physically striking the slave woman symbolically inscribes patriarchal control on her body.

MUSLIM SOUNDSCAPES

Although a majority of the public markers of Muslim difference, such as dress, are occular-centric, demonstrating a bias toward sight, some of the most salient markers of Muslim difference are mediated through sound. What we hear, after all, is often more intrusive than what we see. Sound can become noise. Early generations of Muslims thus paid close attention to the potential of sound to disrupt physical and social boundaries. "In Muslim piety," observes William Graham, "the written word of its scripture has always been secondary to a strong tradition of oral transmission and aural presence of scripture that far surpasses that of Judaic or Christian usage."[68] The Quran, after all, is a recitation—an oral performance that is said to have caused some people to swoon, and even die of shock.[69] The Arabic word *al-samʿ*, literally "hearing," became a synonym for divine revelation and a metonym for the Quran itself. The authority of the hadith, too, depended upon the authenticity of its oral transmission. Recalling the muddled origin narratives of the *adhān,* then, underscores the important role of aurality in defining Muslim difference.[70]

The *adhān,* the distinctive Muslim summons to ritual prayer, became a fundamental aesthetic expression of Islam. According to one early oral tradition: "The *adhān* is the marker [*shiʿār*] of faith [in Islam]."[71] ʿ*Ulamāʾ* imagined the *adhān* as a key symbol that acoustically projected Islam's difference from other religions across great distances and, more concretely, empowered the human voice to inspire Muslims to perform prayer, the most important

TABLE 2. THE *ADHĀN* (SUNNI)

Allāhu akbar! (× 4)	God is great!
Ashhadu an lā ilaha illā Allāh! (× 2)	I bear witness that there is no god but God!
Ashhadu anna Muḥammad rasūl Allāh! (× 2)	I bear witness that Muhammad is the Messenger of God!
Ḥayya ʿalā al-ṣalāt! (× 2)	Come to prayer!
Ḥayya ʿalā al-falāḥ! (× 2)	Come to success!
al-Ṣalāt khayr min al-nawm! (× 2 before sunrise)	Prayer is better than sleep!
Allāhu akbar! (× 2)	God is great!
Lā ilaha illā Allāh! (× 1)	There is no god but God!

ritual obligation in Islam. To non-Muslim subjects of the caliphate, however, the *adhān* may have been perceived as a daily acoustic reminder of Muslim political sovereignty.

Amid both Muslim interreligious and intrareligious rivalries, the formula of the *adhān* evolved over time (table 2). Sunni Muslims, for example, credit the caliph ʿUmar with suggesting that the summons to prayer should occur through the medium of the human voice, and with inserting the phrase "Prayer is better than sleep!"—as shown in the following tradition.[72] "When the Muslims arrived in Medina, they used to congregate for prayer, but would guess its [proper] time. In those days, the practice of calling the *adhān* for prayer had not yet been introduced. One day, they discussed the issue of the call to prayer. Some people suggested the use of a knocker [*nāqūs*] like the Christians, others proposed a trumpet like the horn used by the Jews, but ʿUmar was the first to suggest that a man should call [the people] for the prayer; so the Messenger of God ordered Bilāl to get up and call the *adhān* for prayer."[73]

There are, of course, alternative narratives. Another hadith tradition claims that Jews lit a fire to call people to prayer while Christians used a knocker.[74] The Mamluk Egyptian commentator Ibn Ḥajar al-ʿAsqalānī reconciles these divergent traditions by explaining how each religious community publicly announced ritual worship in its own distinctive way: Christians struck knockers, Jews blew horns, and Zoroastrians lit fires.[75] According to most historians, the *adhān* developed gradually, assuming multiple forms across time and place, which helps explain the variations among the Islamic schools of jurisprudence.[76] Some early twentieth-century Orientalists have suggested that the *adhān* actually derived from the Christian mass or Jewish Tephillah (prayer).[77]

Although the acoustic competition inspired Muslims to establish their own call to prayer, it also provoked them to suppress other sounds that might clash with theirs. We thus find that Muslim religious authorities complained about ringing bells. Pre-Islamic Arabs hung bells around animals in order to defend against the evil eye, which struck the wrong theological note regarding God's omnipotence. This superstitious noise offended pious Muslim sensibilities.[78] One hadith condemns bells as "musical instruments of the devil."[79] Another equally pejorative tradition warns, "The angels do not accompany any group with whom there is a dog or a bell."[80] Muslim commentators explain that these condemnations did not arise due to Christian noise polluting the Prophet Muhammad's ears. Church bells, which had originated in Europe, are not mentioned in the Muslim East until the ninth century.[81] Ibn Ḥajar notes that Christians living in Muslim lands began ringing bells in order to publicly call the community to prayer.[82] As European church bells moved east these traditions—and the bell itself—rang in new meanings; bells became a key symbolic marker of Christianity in public life. Unsurprisingly, Ibn Ḥajar condemns the practice of ringing bells due to their Christian associations.

Yet not all Muslims complied with such proscriptions. Some historians claim that, as a token of peace and goodwill, the Abbasid caliph Hārūn al-Rashīd presented Charlemagne with an organ, an instrument used in churches since the age of Constantine.[83] Although religious sounds sometimes clashed, reverberating with the differences that divided communities, they occasionally produced harmonies that could dissolve those same differences.

Religious sounds thus had political implications—for both Muslim interreligious and intrareligious relations. Sunni and Shiʿi Muslims each claimed their own distinctive *adhān* and crafted a unique historical narrative to authorize their version. Twelver Shiʿis argued that the Angel Gabriel revealed the *adhān* directly to the Prophet with heavenly authorization from the divine, without the human interference of any Companion—a striking contrast to the Sunni narrative. Twelver Shiʿis also claim that ʿUmar is a central figure in the narrative, but as the villain, not the hero. They blame ʿUmar for altering the *adhān* from its divinely sanctioned original, claiming that he fraudulently struck the phrase *Ḥayya ʿalā khayr al-ʿamal!* ("Come to the best deed!") from the formula because it would incite Muslims to leave the public duty of jihad and absorb themselves in private prayer instead. Giving credence to the

Shiʿi version of events, the earliest Sunni legal texts also mention this phrase, suggesting that Sunnis debated this issue among themselves. None other than ʿUmar's son, Ibn ʿUmar, occasionally recited *Ḥayya ʿalā khayr al-ʿamal!* as part of the *adhān.*[84] Shiʿis also rejected the addition of the phrase "Prayer is better than sleep" as a heretical innovation of ʿUmar's, but added "ʿAlī is the friend of God" to audibly declare their difference from Sunnis and allegiance to ʿAlī, the rightful successor to the Prophet.[85] Although Twelver Shiʿi *ʿulamāʾ* did not officially authorize the latter addition to the *adhān,* most could not denounce its practice, fearing they might be condemned for harboring Sunni sympathies.[86]

These inter-Muslim quarrels over a single utterance swelled and hardened into symbols of sectarian difference that blurred the line between religion and politics in post-formative Islamic history. When the phrase "*Ḥayya ʿalā khayr al-ʿamal!*" was first publicly declared in Sunni-ruled lands, residents knew immediately that a Shiʿi government had taken power. This happened when the Buyids conquered Baghdad, the Fatimids took control of Cairo in 970, and the Qarmatians claimed Damascus in 971.[87] Likewise, its removal from the *adhān* meant that Sunnis had reclaimed power, such as in 1055–56, when the Sunni Seljuks expelled the Shiʿi Buyids from Baghdad; in 1078, when the Seljuks took over Damascus; and in 1171, when the champion of Sunnism Saladin conquered the Shiʿi Fatimids and established the Ayyubid dynasty in Egypt.[88] Saladin's restoration of the Sunni *adhān,* explains the preeminent medieval historian of Egypt Maqrīzī (d. 1442), "erased the distinguishing marker [*shiʿār*] of the [Fatimid] Dynasty."[89]

WIPING OVER LEATHER SOCKS

Complementing sartorial codes, physical gestures translate Muslim difference into everyday life. Gestures are embodied acts that express a thought or a feeling, whether intentional or unintentional, secret or public.[90] And like sartorial codes, physical gestures are charged sites of meaning—as demonstrated today by controversies over American football players refusing to stand for the national anthem and Muslim students in Switzerland refusing to shake hands with female teachers.[91] Although biology is essential to understanding how gestures work, one must look to culture to see what they mean. "To know why he [a person] does not make a certain gesture and does make a certain other gesture," Marcel Mauss observes, "neither the physiology nor the psychology of motor symmetry is enough, it is also necessary to know the traditions which impose it."[92] Gestures, in other words, have a history, and are thus sites of collective memory.

Another visible, though unlikely, marker that divided Sunni and Shiʿi Muslims was the proper performance of ritual washing (*wuḍūʾ*), whose procedure is described plainly in the Quran: "When you rise to pray wash your faces and your hands up to the elbows and wipe your heads and your feet up to the ankles" (Q 5:6). On a casual reading of the verse, there appears little to disagree about. Nevertheless, Muslim exegetes and jurists discovered several ambiguities that resulted in extensive debates, including on topics not explicitly mentioned in the verse.[93] The stakes of this debate were high because ritual washing is a prerequisite to ritual prayer. One seemingly minor topic in particular became a flashpoint of disputes between Sunnis and Shiʿis: does the gesture of wiping over leather socks (*masḥ ʿalā al-khuffayn*) fulfill the divine command to wipe or wash "your feet up to the ankles?" Or does it invalidate the ritual washing because one must wipe or wash over bare feet only? The disagreement represents another case in which footgear became a marker of social distinction.

The dispute was not merely academic. Wiping over footgear became one of the preeminent physical gestures distinguishing Sunnis from Shiʿis in early Islam, eventually becoming a point of religious creed. It thus counts among the clearest examples of how social practice can shape religious belief. To better understand why this minor gesture provoked a major disagreement, we first must recall that, in normal circumstances, ritual prayer is invalid without the proper performance of ablution. To reject the obligation of prayer is equivalent to apostasy, according to some Muslim theologians.[94] The dispute also became a hermeneutical test case for measuring the authority of the Quran against that of the hadith. Both Sunnis and Shiʿis needed to determine how much hermeneutical weight to give hadiths if they contradicted or added to the Quran. Nevertheless, the significance of the gesture cannot be reduced to hermeneutics.

Sunnis permitted the practice of wiping over footgear; Shiʿis did not. During ablution, Sunnis required that both feet be washed, but if leather socks were worn over the feet, they required that only the socks be wiped. Still, Sunni jurists debated among themselves the proper technique of wiping over leather socks—whether to swipe the hand across the top of the sock, underneath its sole, or both.[95] By contrast, Shiʿi jurists required that both feet be wiped with a wet hand, not washed. They did not allow wiping over leather socks at all.

The sectarian disagreements simmering beneath the surface of this gesture eventually hardened into religious dogma. Not only was Islamic dogma a statement of cognitive belief, but it also reflected the community's embodied practices, including gestures and dress.[96] The declaration that wiping over leather socks is permissible can be found in the earliest Sunni statements of creed, which defined core beliefs such as the attributes of God, resurrection of the dead, and the nature of prophecy, and minor beliefs such as the permissibility of drinking the controversial intoxicant *nabīdh*.[97] The earliest surviving work of Sunni creed, *The Greater Knowledge* (*al-Fiqh al-Akbar*), attributed to Abū Ḥanīfa (d. 750), states that "wiping over leather socks is *sunna*."[98] The later Sunni creeds of Ṭaḥāwī (d. 933) and Nasafī (d. 1142) upheld this position: "We approve of wiping over leather socks on a journey or in residence."[99] Explaining the rationale for including this minor issue, Taftazānī (d. 1390), a Persian commentator on Nasafī's creed, wrote that this gesture achieved the grander objective of visibly distinguishing Sunnis from religious innovators—Twelver Shiʿis, Ismāʿīlīs and the Khawārij—who rejected it.[100] It was not Quran hermeneutics that determined the creedal significance of the gesture, but the Muslim social landscape.

What is remarkable is that, according to Sunnis, wiping over the socks is not even an obligation; a Sunni needed only to affirm that the gesture is permissible in order to clearly establish that he was not Shiʿi. A Sunni could die never having wiped over his socks but still remain Sunni; what mattered is that he simply *believed* that it is lawful to do so. Emphasizing this point, Taftazānī hyperbolically warned: "I fear unbelief for the one who does not believe that wiping over socks is permissible."[101] Sunnis nevertheless wondered if it was better to wash the bare feet, as prescribed in the Quran, or to wipe over leather socks, as prescribed in the books of creed. Some (Ḥanbalīs) said it was better to wipe over the socks if a person was motivated by the intention to be different from religious innovators, that is, Shiʿis.[102] Others said it was better to wash the feet, as long as a person believed that wiping over footgear was permissible.[103]

Shiʿis also framed the gesture of wiping over the socks as a matter of dogma. Mirroring Sunni theologians, the sixth Shiʿi Imam, Jaʿfar al-Ṣādiq, lists *not* wiping over leather socks among seven criteria for a Muslim to be a true believer (*muʾmin*).[104] He also includes the silent gesture in his short list of acts that a Shiʿi cannot do under any circumstances—even under duress: "Precautionary dissimulation [*taqiyya*] is my religion and religion of my fathers, except in three actions: drinking intoxicants; wiping over leather socks; and not pronouncing the *basmala* loudly [in prayer]."[105]

Protective dissimulation (*taqiyya*), as discussed earlier, is a distinctive principle of Shiʿism that encompasses a repertoire of gestures. When dissimulating, Shiʿis attempt to hide their true religious identity to avoid danger or harm. That Imam Jaʿfar prohibits the small gesture of wiping over footgear even under duress demonstrates the symbolic power it carried as well as the importance of preserving differences between Shiʿi and Sunni. Other religious authorities were less strict, however, permitting Shiʿis to wipe over their footgear "under duress and in circumstances where there is a threat to life from an enemy, wild beasts or extreme cold."[106]

What did these creedal statements mean for Muslim identity? Biographical entries on two socially liminal Muslim figures from eighth-century Iraq illustrate how attitudes toward wiping over footgear could play a pivotal role in defining religious identity. One figure was a traditionist from the Iraqi city of Kufa, Sālim b. Abī Ḥafṣa (d. 755), who disavowed the first three caliphs like a Shiʿi, but wiped over his socks like a Sunni.[107] Hard to categorize, he was nevertheless embraced by Sunnis and demonized by Shiʿis. It did not seem to matter that he held a core belief common to most Shiʿis because he practiced like Sunnis. Another liminal figure, the Kufan traditionist Mūsā b. ʿUthmān, suffered a similar fate.[108] He transmitted the following statement: "The Quran invalidates wiping over the socks [*sabaqa al-kitāb masḥ ʿalā al-khuffayn*]."[109] His apparent rejection of the gesture's validity led to his infamy among Sunnis.[110] In posterity's assessment of both liminal figures, gesture trumped creed. By the first half of the eighth century, wiping over leather socks had come to distinguish Iraqi proto-Sunnis from proto-Shiʿis and was among the first visible signs of the sectarian divisions that were yet to come.[111]

PECKING LIKE A ROOSTER

Learning how to pray meant learning the corporeal techniques of ritual prayer—how to stand, bow, sit, and prostrate. When teaching his followers how to pray, the Prophet Muhammad occasionally drew analogies to the behavior of animals—as models *not* to follow: "The Prophet prohibited us from three things: pecking like a rooster, sitting like a dog, and turning around like a fox."[112] Because the transmitter omits the context of the Prophet's advice, the reader may assume that he is admonishing believers against mimicking animals in general. But the Prophet is in fact describing the specific physical gestures and postures to avoid during ritual prayer by drawing analogies to the behavior of creatures well known among his community. When prostrating,

Figure 10. Mounted on a camel, a man kills a dragon with a lance in *Kitāb al-Bulhān* (*Book of Wonders*), ca. fourteenth–fifteenth century. (Bodleian Library, University of Oxford, Arabic Manuscripts and Maps collection, no. Or. 133, fol. 33b.)

the believer should do so at a measured pace to avoid resembling a rooster pecking at the ground.[113] When sitting down, the believer should place his rear on one or both of his feet to avoid resembling a dog, which places its rear on the ground while extending its paws forward.[114] And throughout the prayer, the believer should keep his eyes downcast, focused on the ground immediately before him, to avoid resembling a fox, which turns its head left and right rapidly.

When teaching, the Prophet drew comparisons to other animals as well. Despite the Arabs' love for camels (figure 10), the Prophet said: "When one of you prostrates [in prayer], he should not kneel like a camel, but should place his hands [onto the ground] before his knees."[115] When a camel kneels onto the ground from a standing position, it places its hind knees onto the ground before lowering the rest of its body. But the Prophet instructs Muslims to do the opposite; when prostrating, believers should place their hands on the ground before their knees. Not all Muslim jurists follow the literal instructions of this hadith, however. Ḥanafī and Shāfiʿī jurists dismiss it, preferring that one prostrate by first placing the knees on the ground, then the hands—just like a camel. Not wanting to take sides, Ibn Taymiyya validates both opinions: "Praying in both ways is permissible, according to the consensus of the scholars. If a person wants to go down knees first or hands first, his prayer is valid in either case, according to the consensus of the scholars." Another scholar concludes that Islamic scripture endorses "being different from all animals in the techniques of ritual prayer."[116]

The Prophet once again actualizes Muslim difference by connecting his followers to the social landscape around them, which includes the animal kingdom. Humans and animals, in his view, inhabited a single ecosystem. He effectively employs zoological idioms as a rhetorical strategy to reach an audience who habitually interacted with animals. These and other traditions suggest that the presence of nonhumans helped believers define what it meant to be Muslim—and human. Most early Muslims lived in agrarian societies where nature and culture blended into each other. The pre-Islamic Arab brigand and poet Shanfarā spoke of the blurry lines between human and animal in verse:

> I have in place of you other kin:
> The wolf, unwearying runner,
> The darting sand leopard,
> The bristle-necked hyena.

These are my clan. They don't reveal
A secret given in trust,
And they don't abandon a man
For his crimes.[117]

Shanfarā finds more intimacy with the wolf, leopard, and hyena than he does with fellow humans. Having found true belonging within the animal kingdom, Shanfarā deepens his connection to the beasts around him. He slowly assimilates their attributes and behaviors until the line between human and animal dissolves and he miraculously transforms into a white-footed mountain goat.[118] In his monumental encyclopedia *al-Ḥayawān,* Jāḥiẓ comments on humanity's uncanny ability to become like the animals: "He [man] displays the fury of the camel, the swiftness of the lion, the treacherousness of the wolf, the cunning of the fox, the cowardice of the nightingale, the parsimony of the ant, the industry of the termite, the generosity of the cock, the sociability of the dog, and the navigational skill of the pigeon."[119] Human beings are able to acquire the qualities of animals, whether these be virtue or vice. Humanity, in sum, is the microcosm.[120]

Following Jāḥiẓ, other scholars acknowledged the possibility of interspecies socialization, the capacity for social interaction and adaptation across the line separating one species from another. Like humans, animals are social creatures: "There is no animal on earth nor bird flying with two wings, but are peoples [*umam*] like you" (Q 6:38). The shared capacity for community among humans and animals meant that bonds of intimacy could form between them as well. Jāḥiẓ views human beings as a species of animal that transforms, and is transformed, through interactions with different species. Ibn Taymiyya and Najm al-Dīn al-Ghazzī each view human-animal relations through the lens of mimicry, as expressed in the Prophet's maxim "Whoever imitates a people becomes one of them."[121] Like Jāḥiẓ, Ibn Taymiyya believes that human beings acquire the cardinal virtues and vices possessed by animals: camel herders become prideful like camels, sheepherders become humble like sheep, and dog owners become like their dogs. But he also argues that animals adopt virtues from their human owners. Camels, sheep, and dogs become more virtuous, adopting the qualities of the humans they interact with, showing greater affection and love and less hostility and hatred. The moral outcomes from these human-animal interactions are uneven. Animals, in Ibn Taymiyya's zoological imagination, are more likely to acquire noble virtues from these interactions than humans, who are more likely to acquire vices.

Despite their shared capacity for community, Ibn Taymiyya held fast to the conviction that humans are ontologically superior to animals. He rationalizes this hierarchy in an entertaining fatwa criticizing human mimicry of animals—a habit that appears to have been surprisingly common in Mamluk Damascus. He contends that mimicking animals by "barking like a dog" or "braying like an ass" corrupts human nature (*fasād al-fiṭra*).[122] Drawing a line connecting the hierarchies governing human society to those governing the natural world, he claims that animals are intrinsically inferior to humans, just as non-Arabs, Bedouin Arabs, and the People of the Book are intrinsically inferior to (Arab) Muslims.[123] Animals remain inferior, explains Ibn Taymiyya, even though they share primal habits with human beings such as eating, drinking, and mating. If humans are to shun imitating lower-status members of their own species, then on what basis can they justify imitating animals, whose status is even lower? Islamic scripture, he argues, supports this position. Q 7:179, for example, states, "We have destined to hell many jinn and men; they have hearts, but they do not understand with them; they have eyes, but they do not see with them; and they have ears, but they do not hear with them. They are like cattle. In fact, they are even more misguided. They are heedless." People who aimlessly wander through life with dulled spiritual senses are no better than cattle. Ibn Taymiyya thus concludes that mimicking animals is morally reprehensible in itself, although its reprehensibility is commensurate with the moral value of the qualities being mimicked. Citing the hadith "The Messenger of God cursed men who imitate women and women who imitate men," he disparages all forms of hybridity between different classes of creatures.[124]

THE DEVIL'S LEFT HAND

Islamic tradition personified the devil—a jinn, according to most accounts—attributing to him human motivations and behaviors, including distinctive gestures. One of these traditions describes the distinctive way in which the devil consumes food and drink: "When any of you eat, then let him eat with his right hand and let him drink with his right hand, because Satan eats with his left hand and drinks with his left hand."[125] Here, the Prophet teaches his community the proper technique of eating and drinking. Food, as David Freidenreich observes, is "a powerful medium for the expression and transmission of culture, and more specifically, of communal identity."[126] Traditions thus abound that instruct Muslims not only how to prepare food but also how to consume it. Muslim scholars compiled these traditions into manuals on the etiquette of eating, which describe how to sit properly, how to eat with one's hands, which utensils to use, and how to invoke God before and after eating to prevent the devil from partaking in the meal.[127]

In the hadith, Satan plays a similar role to the animals in the traditions on prayer discussed above—as anti-models that Muslims should not follow. According to Ḥanafī jurists, emulating the devil is detested (*makrūh*) in daily habits such as eating and drinking—unless there is good cause to do so.[128] Still, commentators wondered if Satan, a noncorporeal spirit demon, physically eats and drinks with his left hand or if he merely simulates the act.

What is so satanic about using the left hand? Beyond instructing believers on the proper etiquettes of eating, the hadith taps into a greater moral and symbolic cosmology that privileges right over left. This cosmic dualism is staged dramatically in the Quran as a flash-forward to the eschaton, in which humanity is sorted into two groups, the saved and the damned:

> Those on the right; what of those on the right?
> Among thornless lote trees
> And clustered plantains
> And spreading shade
> And water gushing
> And fruit in plenty
> Neither out of reach nor yet forbidden
> And raised couches . . .
>
> And those on the left: what of those on the left?
> In scorching wind and scalding water,
> And shadow of black smoke
> Neither cool nor refreshing
>
> (Q 56:27–34, 41–44)

The contrast drawn between the two groups could not be starker. "Those on the right" are promised everlasting bliss, while "those on the left" are condemned to perpetual misery. But, as the Prophet's exhortation to eat with the right hand suggests, believers should signal their predilection for the "right" side through their comportment here and now. Several traditions illustrate how the Prophet translated this cosmology into a repertoire of quotidian practices. One tradition, collected by Imam Muslim (d. 875), imposes a blanket prohibition on using the left hand: "Do not take up anything with that [left hand]

and do not give anything with that."[129] According to another tradition transmitted on the authority of ʿĀʾisha, "The Prophet used to love to start doing things from the right side whenever possible . . . in performing ablution, putting on his shoes, and combing his hair."[130] When healing a sick person, he would rub his right hand over the afflicted part of the body while supplicating God.[131] As already mentioned, whether going to sleep or entering the grave, Muslim bodies were to face right, toward Mecca. When two believers pray together, the follower should stand to the right of the imam, not the left.[132] At a communal meal, the person sitting to the right, not the left, should eat and drink first.[133] By contrast, one ought to touch one's private parts or cleanse oneself with the left hand.[134]

Distinguishing between right and left sides also distinguished between sacred and profane spaces. When entering a sacred space like a mosque, one leads with the right foot; when leaving, one leads with the left foot.[135] But when entering a polluted space such as a bathroom, the sequence is reversed: one enters with the left foot and exits with the right foot.[136] And so, Muslims came to associate the right side with what is right, the left side with what is wrong.

Muslims shared this cosmology with other religious and philosophical traditions of the late antique Near East. Like the Quran, the Bible sorts resurrected bodies into two groups (right and left), marking them as either saved or damned.[137] Like Muslims, Jews put on their right shoe before their left.[138] Also like Muslims, the Greek philosopher Pythagoras (d. ca. 500 BCE) believed that one should enter a sacred place with the right foot and leave with the left.[139] As early Muslims set themselves apart from Satan, they aligned themselves with the religious and philosophical traditions of antiquity.

CONCLUSION

The traditions examined in this chapter deepen our understanding of how Muslim difference works. The value of small differences arose not only from the imperial hierarchies they upheld but also from the cultural contexts in which they emerged. Our glimpses into these cultural contexts illuminate how small differences become charged with symbolic meaning and value. By moving from the outside in, we see that symbolic markers, *shiʿār*, do not float in an empty void but grow out of material forms—sartorial codes, physical gestures, and sensory perceptions—that define a distinctively Islamic public sphere.

These forms, intended to set Muslims apart, paradoxically connected them to the social world around them. Through the appropriation of existing ritual and cultural idioms, the Prophet defined community through public markers that mirrored those of rival communities. Rather than invent a style of headgear completely unlike those worn by others, the Prophet urged his followers to blend styles already in fashion, the turban and *qalansuwa,* into a unique Muslim style; rather than abandon the widespread custom of growing facial hair, he urged Muslim men to grow and dye their beards while trimming the moustache; and instead of abandoning public calls to worship together because Jews and Christians already did so, the Prophet instituted a public call to worship that employed the human voice instead of musical instruments. The Prophet's exhortations that Muslims avoid resembling nonhumans in their everyday comportment likewise reflected a preexisting social imaginary in which humans, animals, and demons inhabited a single cosmic ecosystem. These cases all suggest that the Prophet and his followers intended to build group solidarity around a kind of difference that shunned sharp oppositions and was firmly rooted in late antique cultural norms.

We are now in a position to explore how subsequent generations of religious authorities synthesized these fragmented traditions and anecdotes into a coherent Islamic discourse of difference.

CHAPTER 5

Ibn Taymiyya and the Innovation of Imitation

Invention, using the term most broadly, and imitation, are the two legs, so to call them, on which the human race historically has walked.

—WILLIAM JAMES

Perhaps no figure in the history of Islam polarizes Muslims today more than Ibn Taymiyya (d. 1328). Reviled by opponents as a precursor to modern-day extremism and heralded by devotees as a fierce defender of Islam as it was originally practiced, Ibn Taymiyya was, and remains, one of the most controversial figures in the history of Islamic scholarship.[1] One of his contemporaries, the traveler Ibn Baṭṭūṭa (d. 1367–78), went as far as to claim that he had a "screw loose" (*fī ʿaqlihi shayʾan*—literally, "something in his mind").[2] It was not only his support of unpopular religious opinions but also his tactless manner of doing so that gained him enemies, as the following criticism leveled against him by his own student, Shams al-Dīn al-Dhahabī (d. 1348), illustrates: "How long will you see the speck in your brother's eye but fail to see the plank in your own? How long will you flatter yourself, your bluster, and your own viewpoints, while reviling religious scholars and seeking to expose the weaknesses of others?"[3] Many other prominent figures within and beyond his close circle, however, attested to his brilliance, piety, magnanimity, and courage, which earned him the sobriquet the Shaykh of Islam.

A stark contrast to the archetypical remote scholastic, Ibn Taymiyya was an engaged and outspoken public intellectual, ready to confront laypeople and authorities alike, as attested by his nine court trials and six prison sentences. In one memorable incident, he espied two people playing backgammon and kicked over the board in disapproval—always ready to command what is right and forbid what is wrong.[4] But Ibn Taymiyya made his enduring contribution to Islam through his scholarship.

The impressive list of polemical treatises he composed includes seven against Christianity alone, as well as several directed against Muslim ideological rivals, including speculative theologians, Greek logicians, Shiʿis, and Sufis.[5] The urgency of defending Islam against these ideological threats was heightened by the existential geopolitical threat to the Mamluk Sultanate posed by the Mongol menace looming in the horizon. Ibn Taymiyya likely believed that things were on the verge of falling apart, and as a fearless scholar-activist with boundless energy, he refused to stand on the sidelines. Defending the borders of Islam from the "enemy" became the center of his scholarship.

Ibn Taymiyya composed the most influential and, to my knowledge, the first treatise against imitation: *The Obligation of Following the Straight Path Is to Be Different from Those Damned to Hell* (*Iqtiḍāʾ al-ṣirāṭ al-mustaqīm mukhālafat aṣḥāb al-jaḥīm*). Weaving together a range of disciplines across ritual, psychoanalysis, sociology, popular culture, politics, theology, ethics, and law, the treatise's bold thesis is that being different from Jews, Christians, and other rival communities is an essential Islamic doctrine and a universal religious principle. Yet existing scholarship has overlooked Ibn Taymiyya's elaborate critique of blind imitation, paying attention instead to his denunciations of unsanctioned festivals and religious innovations (*bidʿa*).[6]

The Obligation of Following the Straight Path resides at a critical juncture between Islamic discourses on difference and Mamluk social history. It is the first treatise to compile and interpret the hadith traditions on Muslim difference, transforming *tashabbuh* from a diffuse concept into a coherent Islamic discourse. Having read these traditions as signposts that map the transformation of Muslim difference during the early period of Islam, I now follow this transformation to an entirely different historical context several centuries after those traditions were first compiled. How did the outlook on Muslim difference change?

Among the most noteworthy features of Ibn Taymiyya's critique is the manner in which he uses shariʿa-based terminology and modes of reasoning to mobilize *tashabbuh* into a potent legal discourse applicable to a range of everyday practices, including Muslim participation in unsanctioned festivals. As part of this discursive scaffolding, Ibn Taymiyya creatively ties together imitation and innovation, conventionally imagined as distinct concepts, into a unified Islamic discourse that reveals their complementarity. It becomes apparent that Ibn Taymiyya's discourse against imitation is a discourse of power, intended to safeguard the collective good of the Muslim community vis-à-vis rivals within and beyond the Mamluk Sultanate.

When reading a polemical treatise composed by a confrontational figure who obliges Muslims to be different while repeatedly disparaging the Other, we might expect to encounter a crudely oppositional discourse. A close reading of *The Obligation of Following the Straight Path* reveals, however, that this is not the case. Ibn Taymiyya's theorization of Muslim difference is unexpectedly supple, moderated through notions of the Muslim *umma* as a middle community and grounded in a psycho-spiritual model of intent that resists categorical oppositions.

TURNING DAMASCUS UPSIDE DOWN

How did the *ka'ba,* originally a sanctuary built by Abraham for the exclusive worship of the One True God, become the fountainhead of idolatry in Arabia? This origin story, first told by the eighth-century biographer Ibn Isḥāq (d. 776), is retold by Ibn Taymiyya in *The Obligation of Following the Straight Path.*[7] Decades before the Prophet Muhammad was born, the story goes, an entrepreneurial Arab named 'Amr b. Luḥayy traveled from his home in Mecca to Syria and returned with some idols, which he then placed in the *ka'ba,* summoning his brethren to worship them. The new trend soon caught on. The Meccans began to worship these idols until paganism replaced monotheism—first instituted in Arabia by Abraham, according to Islamic tradition—as the dominant religion of Mecca. 'Amr b. Luḥayy became known among Muslim theologians as the notorious figure who turned Mecca into a pagan city and the *ka'ba* into a pagan shrine. The punishment for such a crime was eternal perdition, as foretold by the Prophet based on a gruesome vision: "I saw 'Amr b. Luḥayy in hell carrying his intestines." In his retelling, Ibn Taymiyya lays blame for the Arabian origin of Islam's most egregious sin, idolatry, on Ibn Luḥayy's imitation (*tashabbuh*) of Syrian foreigners. But for Ibn Taymiyya, the peril of imitation still remained a clear and present danger one millennium later in his adopted home of Damascus.

As a geographic and cultural crossroads linked by trade routes to the Mediterranean, Central Asia, the Indian Ocean, and Arabia, the ancient city of Damascus was a cosmopolitan metropolis pregnant with dangerous foreign beliefs and practices.[8] At the time, the city was governed by the Mamluk Sultanate, whose sovereignty encompassed Syria, Egypt, and the Hijaz. But at the turn of the fourteenth century, the future of the Mamluks was in peril, as the Mongols looked to add the sultanate to their series of conquests in *dār al-Islām,* which included Baghdad, the capital of the Abbasid caliphate, in 1258. Never before had the Sunni Muslim community been without a caliph to lead them.[9] The Mongols had historical ties to the Crusaders and Christianity through a Franko-Mongol alliance that lasted until their public conversion to Islam in 1295—a conversion Ibn Taymiyya rejected in a fatwa that declared them fake Muslims. When the Mongols invaded Damascus in 1300, Ibn Taymiyya defended the city, fighting jihad and negotiating the return of Muslim, Jewish, and Christian prisoners.[10] That same year he traveled to the Syrian Lebanese mountains to fight jihad against Nuṣaybī and Druze Shiʿi Muslims suspected of collaborating with the Mongols. In total, the Mongol-Mamluk conflict lasted more than sixty years, ending with a peace treaty in 1323, five years before Ibn Taymiyya passed away in prison.

The political disorder incited by the foreign Mongol threat was symbolized at the local level by the social disorder that characterized unsanctioned *ʿīd*s—public commemorative gatherings including holiday celebrations, pilgrimage rites, ceremonies, and funeral processions.[11] A central feature of public life in the sultanate, *ʿīd*s take place when any one of three dimensions—space, time, or social practice—is delimited and particularized, according to Ibn Taymiyya's broad definition of the term.[12] "Every nation has its own unique *ʿīd,*" said the Prophet Muhammad.[13] *ʿĪd*s are thus key markers of communal belonging and identity. Communities in the sultanate marked *ʿīd*s to honor specific holidays, whose public spectacles, in turn, marked those same communities: Christians celebrated Easter, Christmas, and Maundy Thursday; Muslims of all kinds celebrated *ʿīd al-fiṭr* and *ʿīd al-aḍḥā,* while Sufis celebrated the Prophet's birthday at the *mawlid* and Shiʿis honored Ḥusayn's martyrdom during ʿĀshūrāʾ; Egyptians celebrated Nawrūz—a festival marking the Coptic new year. Jews, on the other hand, celebrated their holidays out of public view.[14]

The perceived threat posed by these gatherings to established social hierarchies and identities provoked boundary panic among many *ʿulamāʾ*. Although *ʿīd*s were distinguishing markers of specific communities, whether Muslim, Christian, or Jewish, they also brought different people together, blurring social distinctions between Muslims and non-Muslims, men and women, Sunnis and Shiʿis, Arabs and non-Arabs, rich and poor, adults and children, free persons and slaves, and even the living and the dead. This social mixing resulted in what Mikhail Bakhtin called *carnivalistic mesalliances,* wherein things that are hierarchically distinct in normal circumstances are united: "Carnival brings together, unifies, weds, and combines the sacred with the profane, the lofty with the low, the great with the insignificant, the wise with the stupid."[15] During Nawrūz, for example, it was customary for a "thinly bearded" replica of the procession's emir to be mocked by crowds, for students to beat their teachers, and for men to dress like women. Like medieval carnivals, *ʿīd*s turned conventional social hierarchies upside down. Thus, for many *ʿulamāʾ*, *ʿīd*s were dangerous sites of mimetic contagion and social upheaval that needed to be quarantined.

Ongoing tensions at home and abroad strained interreligious relations within the sultanate's provinces. Although Muslims went from a ruling minority to the ruling majority after seven centuries in Damascus, state and religious authorities felt threatened by non-Muslims who had integrated into medieval Muslim society.[16] According to historian Mark Cohen, "The *dhimmīs*' ubiquitous presence in Arab ruling circles involved them in the business of state in ways unimaginable for Jews in Christian North Europe. It gave them influence and honor and imparted to the minority communities to which they belonged a feeling of embeddedness in the larger society."[17] Softening boundaries between the Mamluk Sultanate's Muslim majority and its non-Muslim minority (*dhimmīs*) intensified Ibn Taymiyya's anxieties that Christians and Jews might be collaborating secretly with foreign enemies to undermine the Islamic state, which cast them under a cloud of suspicion. In 1301, soon after the temporary Mongol occupation of Damascus in 1300, the sultanate revived the application of the Pact of ʿUmar in order to contain the perceived *dhimmī* threat.[18] The color-coded regulations on dress mandated that *dhimmī* men be visibly distinguished through turbans of different colors: blue for Christians, yellow for Jews, and red for Samaritans. Muslim men, by contrast, continued to wear white turbans.[19] Christian, Jewish, and Samaritan women were required to wear blue, yellow, and red wraps (*izār*), respectively. Christians, specifically, were required to wear a distinctive belt (*zunnār*).[20] The decree also forbade *dhimmī*s from building houses higher than those of Muslims, riding on horses, and working in administrative positions.[21]

Complementing these state decrees, *ʿulamāʾ* composed treatises that condemned the participation of Jews and Christians in public life.[22] For example, Taqī al-Dīn al-Subkī (d. 1355), a rival of Ibn Taymiyya who served as head judge in Damascus for sixteen years, composed works on the regulation of building, repairing, and renovating non-Muslim houses of worship.[23]

However, in 1309, the Mamluk sultan al-Nāṣir Muḥammad b. Qalāwūn

(d. 1341) considered rescinding the decree governing *dhimmī* dress. None other than Ibn Taymiyya, then staying in Cairo, paid the sultan a visit, knelt down deferentially, and implored him not to do so.[24] Around this time—sometime before 1315–16, according to Jon Hoover—Ibn Taymiyya was also busy translating his political activism into a religious treatise against imitating unbelievers.[25]

THE LIMITS OF FRIENDSHIP

In *The Obligation of Following the Straight Path,* Ibn Taymiyya's main objective is to demonstrate that Muslims must be different from unbelievers—as a general rule. *Tashabbuh,* in other words, is not a peripheral teaching but a fundamental doctrine of Islam. While jurists prior to Ibn Taymiyya had condemned specific forms of reprehensible imitation, none had proclaimed a wholesale ban on imitating unbelievers as Ibn Taymiyya does here. By supporting his theory of Muslim difference with evidence from a wide array of primary sources—Quranic verses, hadiths, and legal opinions—Ibn Taymiyya transforms *tashabbuh* from a diffuse concept into a coherent Islamic discourse. While his occasional references to treatises (now lost) on Muslim-*dhimmī* relations, such as *Aḥkām ahl al-dhimma* of Ḥanbalī scholar Abū Yaʿlā b. al-Farrāʾ (d. 1066) and *Shurūṭ ahl al-dhimma* of Abū al-Shaykh al-Iṣbahānī (d. 979), suggest a long-standing concern among jurists with setting apart Muslims in public life, these treatises nonetheless focus on the enabling role of non-Muslims in reaching this aspiration.[26] In *The Obligation of Following the Straight Path,* however, Ibn Taymiyya's gaze remains sharply focused on the claims that Islam makes upon Muslims. He contends that when the Prophet ordered Muslims, "Be different!" he intended this command to be general and absolute, not limited to the specific practice of dyeing the beard.[27] Ibn Taymiyya reasons that Muslims who believe that being different (*mukhālafa*) is inherently good will be safeguarded from lapsing into blindly copying non-Muslims and their deviant ways.

Perhaps the best way to enter the treatise is through Ibn Taymiyya's distinctive reading of the imitation hadith "Whoever imitates a people becomes one of them" (figure 11). He starts with a broad outlook on the hadith's legal and theological consequences: "This hadith, at the very least, prohibits *tashabbuh;* a literal reading [of this hadith], however, implies that *tashabbuh* is heresy [*kufr*]."[28] Imitation, in other words, is a serious matter whose worst outcome is anathema. To frame his interpretation of the hadith, Ibn Taymiyya reads it alongside two other scriptural texts whose main subject is also belonging.

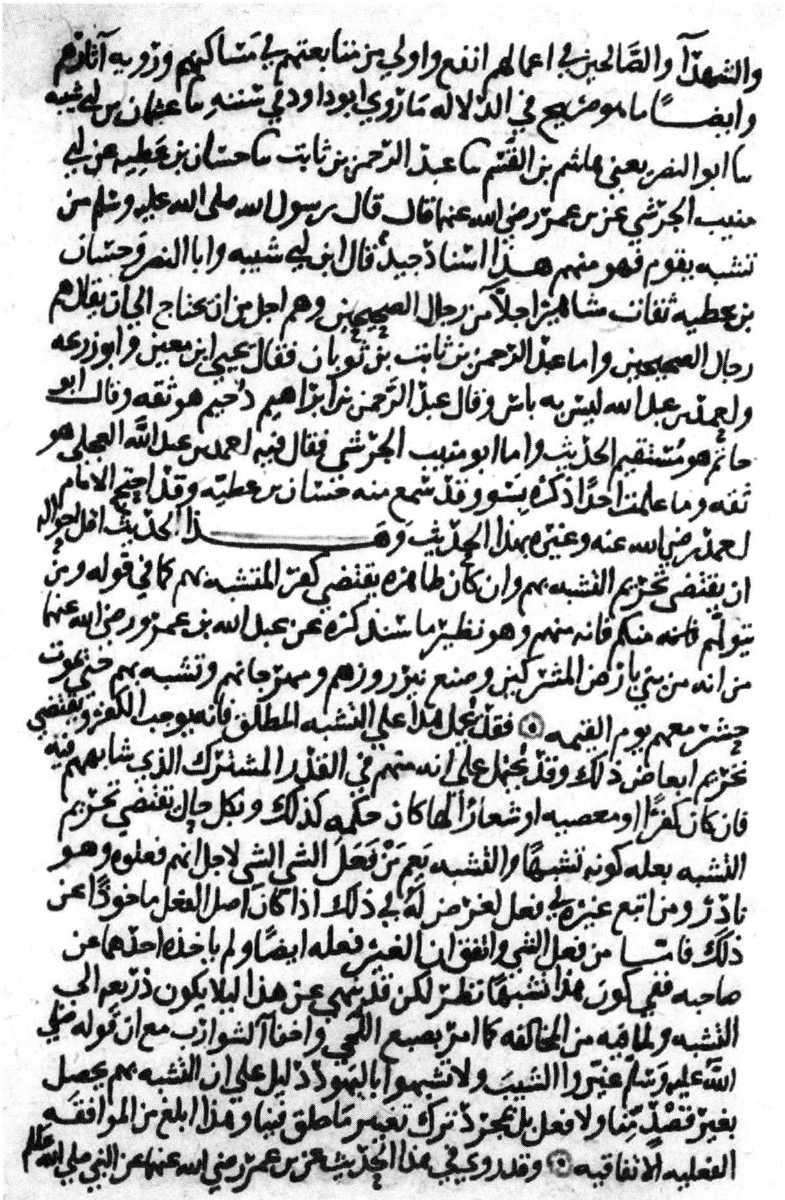

Figure 11. Ibn Taymiyya's commentary on "Whoever imitates a people becomes one of them" in *Iqtiḍa al-ṣirāṭ al-mustaqīm* (*The Obligation of Following the Straight Path*), ca. fifteenth–seventeenth century. (Princeton University, Garrett Collection, no. 3889Y, fol. 28v.)

Exegetes conventionally explained the meaning of the Quran through the interpretive lens of hadiths (*tafsīr bi'l-maʾthūr*), but Ibn Taymiyya reverses this exegetical norm by explaining the meaning of the imitation hadith through one of the Quran's most polemical verses (Q 5:51): "Whoever among you befriends them [*yatawallahum*] becomes one of them."[29] But this verse is a conditional statement whose meaning is ambiguous and needs further explanation, like the imitation hadith.[30] To define the scope of the imitation hadith's interpretation more precisely, Ibn Taymiyya reaches for a second text, another hadith: "Whoever settles among idolaters in their lands, celebrates Nawrūz and Mihrajān [with them], and imitates [*yatashabbahu*] them until he dies, will be resurrected with them on the Day of Judgment."[31]

This tradition is more explicit, defining both the types of acts that constitute reprehensible imitation and the eschatological consequences that take place; it warns that anyone who settles permanently in a foreign (non-Muslim and non-Arab) land and assimilates into its culture will be excluded from the Muslim community in this world and in the world to come. Ibn Taymiyya sees two possible legal outcomes of this hadith: either that a believer is guilty of complete and total assimilation (*tashabbuh*) and has become an infidel or that the severity of the punishment should align with the degree of imitation.

Tashabbuh, in other words, cannot be reduced to a binary opposition between similarity and difference; it inhabits varying levels of intensity. Based on this insight, Ibn Taymiyya constructs a typology that divides *tashabbuh* into three kinds. The first type is the rare situation of pure social conformity: someone who does something "just because others [foreigners] do it."[32] The second type, far more common, occurs when someone appropriates a practice from foreigners but acts out of self-interest, *not* because others do it. The third type, also common, takes place when someone does not intend to emulate a foreign community but nonetheless behaves in a way that coincidentally aligns with the ritual and cultural norms of that community. Though unintentional, this behavior is potentially unlawful because it may lead to *tashabbuh.* All three types of reprehensible imitation are sinful, Ibn Taymiyya insists, for the simple reason that they are reprehensible forms of imitation. The act of imitating foreigners—whether non-Muslim or non-Arab—is wrong in itself.

Appearing within the Chapter of the Banquet (*sūrat al-māʾida*), Q 5:51 addresses the controversial subject of befriending unbelievers, particularly Jews and Christians. The verse, in full, reads: "O believers, do not take Jews and Christians as friends [*awliyāʾ*]; they are friends of each other. Whoever among you befriends them becomes one of them. God does not guide wrongdoers." If believers cannot befriend Jews and Christians, who are their true friends? A subsequent verse (Q 5:55) provides an answer: "Your friend is only God, and His Messenger, and the believers." Without further textual or social context, these verses not only express a tense religious rivalry, they also advance a nativist narrative of inclusion and exclusion in which believers befriend only fellow believers and disavow everyone else. To befriend Jews and Christians, by contrast, is to belong with them and not with the believers. Advocating a form of social boycott, Q 5:51 at once brings the members of Muhammad's community together and sets them apart.

Through the tinted lens of these polemical Quranic verses, the neutral valence of the imitation hadith is obscured. A brief comparison between the linguistic features of the imitation hadith and Q 5:51 supports this conclusion. Both texts propose that social interaction beyond the boundaries of one's community can alter a believer's sense of belonging—as signaled by the shared phrase "becomes one of them." In a neutral reading of the imitation hadith, this shift in belonging is morally ambiguous—either negative or positive, depending on the moral valence of the referent "them." But in Q 5:51, this shift is categorically negative, following the moral valence of "them," who are identified as hostile Jews and Christians. By juxtaposing these texts, Ibn Taymiyya transmits the negative charge of Q 5:51 onto the imitation hadith, eliminating its positive valence.

There is a second key difference between the two texts: the term *tashabbuh* is absent from Q 5:51 (and the entire Quran, for that matter).[33] Instead, the verse invokes a sociological term with a similar morphology but different meaning, *yatawallahum.*[34] A linguistic relative of the term *awliyāʾ*, *yatawallahum* is the act of turning toward someone for friendship, protection, or intimacy.[35] If Jews and Christians are not "friends," then are they merely "acquaintances" or, much worse, "enemies"? This is more than a question about the limits of Muslim solidarity. The very notion of politics itself, according to the German political philosopher Carl Schmitt, may be distilled into a basic distinction between friend and enemy.[36] Ibn Taymiyya's reading thus politicizes the imitation hadith, and the discourse of *tashabbuh,* by sharpening the hadith's ambiguous distinction between self and other into a clear opposition between friend and enemy.

Deepening the connection between the two texts, Ibn Taymiyya argues that both imitation and friendship share an emotional core. Imitation, like friendship, indexes someone's admiration and affection for another person or group.[37] Indeed, it is difficult to imagine scenarios in which people emulate models they detest. With imitation, however, affection usually leads to a hierarchical relationship between imitator and model that elevates the model above the imitator. Although imitation of spiritual exemplars such as the Prophet Muhammad is praiseworthy, it becomes reprehensible, in Ibn Taymiyya's view, when it undermines the hierarchies that support the ideal Islamic social order. When believers imitate unbelievers, they (consciously or unconsciously) esteem them—inverting the ideal social order in which "Islam is above, not below." By emulating those who, in Ibn Taymiyya's worldview, are spiritually and morally inferior, such misguided believers inevitably become weak in their faith. They should rather focus their emulation on the first, and best, generations of Muslims, the *salaf,* who are the true spiritual heirs of the Prophet.

Cultivating strong emotional ties with the wrong people may have serious theological outcomes. As such, Ibn Taymiyya concludes, "Whoever loves an infidel is not a believer."[38] This gloss intensifies the theological implications of the imitation hadith: intentional imitation, if born of sincere affection and reverence for unbelievers and disdain for believers (Muslims), may lead to apostasy. This position upheld by Ibn Taymiyya is in fact less strict than the alternative position held by Ḥanafī jurists—that unintentional imitation may also lead to apostasy.[39] I am not aware of any theologians prior to Ibn Taymiyya who elaborated in as great detail the conditions for the application of this ruling.[40]

This, of course, is not the only possible reading of the imitation hadith, or of Q 5:51. Ibn Taymiyya conveniently omits a cluster of important Quranic verses (60:8–9) that put a fence around Q 5:51, stating that shunning amicable relations with Jews and Christians is an exceptional case, not a general rule: "God does not forbid you concerning those who neither fight nor drive you out of your homes from dealing kindly and justly with them; God certainly loves those who are just. God only forbids you from befriending those who fight you in religion, drive you out from your homes, and support [others] in driving you out."[41] Put simply, the only people Muslims should not befriend are those who physically attack them. Everyone else, including Jews and Christians, should be dealt with "kindly and justly." Without this textual refinement, Q 5:51 becomes a blunt object that, in the exegetical handiwork of Ibn Taymiyya, flattens the imitation hadith into an admonition against *tashabbuh.*

Although Ibn Taymiyya was preceded by other jurists who read the hadith as a dictum against imitating non-Muslims, such as Abū Yaʿlā b. al-Farrāʾ, whom he cites, and Lālakāʾī, who goes unmentioned, his gloss became influential.[42] Eminent scholars like Munāwī (d. 1621) of Ottoman Cairo, as well as Ibn Taymiyya's prominent students Ibn al-Qayyim al-Jawziyya and Shams al-Dīn al-Dhahabī, all read the imitation hadith through the scriptural lens of Q 5:51.[43]

THE GOLDEN MEAN

Ibn Taymiyya's cautious outlook on imitation is grounded in a negative view of unbelievers: "The act of imitating unbelievers [*al-tashabbuh bi'l-kāfirīn*] lies at the root of the effacement of God's religion and His laws."[44] In his view of the past, Islam ushered in a period of enlightenment and progress after *jāhiliyya,* a derogatory term connoting the ignorance and backwardness of pre-Islamic Arabia that Ibn Taymiyya expands to encompass Judaism, Christianity, Zoroastrianism, and paganism as well.[45] Unbelievers are thus incapable of being spiritually and morally upright: "It cannot be imagined that any of their deeds can ever be perfect . . . everything in them is harmful or deficient . . . infidelity is like a malady of the heart or even worse."[46]

But the two non-Muslim communities that exerted the greatest influence on Damascene Muslims were fellow monotheists, Jews and Christians. Ibn Taymiyya views both communities through a polemical reading of the opening chapter of the Quran (*sūrat al-fātiḥa*) that positions Muslims between Christian excesses and Jewish shortcomings. While Christians "have lost their way" by deifying Christ and mortifying the flesh through extreme monastic practices, Jews "have incurred God's wrath" by altering scripture and refusing to share their religious wisdom with others.[47] Muslims, by contrast, comprise the "middle community" (*umma wasaṭa*), which exhibits the virtue of the golden mean.

This dim outlook on unbelievers, however, does not imply that Muslims are required to do the exact opposite of what they do. Drawing inspiration from the Prophet's *sunna* as well as from the Quran-based doctrine of the mean, he concludes that everyday Muslim practices may share essential features with those of non-Muslims as long as they are distinguished through minor details, bringing to mind Sigmund Freud's theory of "small differences." To explain his point, Ibn Taymiyya discusses the case of Islamic regulations on menstruating women.[48] According to a hadith, the Prophet Muhammad distinguished how Muslims treated menstruating women from how Jews did. Whereas Arab Jews sequestered menstruating women into separate quarters, banning any sort of physical intimacy with them, the Prophet permitted menstruating women to share physical spaces with their husbands but not to pray or have sex. When the Medinan Jews learned of this ruling, they expressed their disapproval, seeding doubt in the mind of one of the Prophet's Companions about the veracity of the ruling. Seeking reassurance, the Companion questioned the Prophet, "Should we not cohabit with them [menstruating women]?"[49] But the Prophet became upset at having been second-guessed. Realizing his poor etiquette, the Companion gifted the Prophet milk as a gesture of peace. The gesture worked, and the Prophet calmed down.

In his commentary on this tradition, Ibn Taymiyya explains that the Prophet did not command Muslims to do the exact opposite of what the Jews do, abandoning regulations on menstruating women altogether. That would be tantamount to imitating Christians, who dispensed with such norms. Instead, Muslims followed a middle path that set themselves apart from both Jews and Christians by enacting small differences that enabled Muslims to be both similar and different at the same time.

CORRUPT MUSLIMS

Polemics, by their nature, stress differences—which are often exaggerated through the polemicists' mutual denigration of one another. Sometimes this denigration takes the shape of smearing the opponent by drawing comparisons to other stigmatized groups. In *The Obligation of Following the Straight Path,* Ibn Taymiyya cautions his readers that the spiritual diseases of non-Muslims can, and do, infect Muslims through imitation: "A [Muslim] man, despite virtue, learning and piety, may still have something of the traits called pagan, Jewish and Christian."[50] In fact, throughout the treatise, Ibn Taymiyya deflects his criticisms of non-Muslims onto Muslims themselves. He criticizes Damascene Muslim men, in particular, for fracturing into sectarian groups, deviating from correct religious interpretation, concealing knowledge for personal gain, uncritically imitating religious leaders, participating in the cult of saints, and—worst of all—slavishly succumbing to their womenfolk. *The Obligation of Following the Straight Path* is thus also a critique of contemporary Muslim practice.

Ibn Taymiyya was alarmed by the gradual weakening of the Muslim community due to sectarian fragmentation. Drawing from the vocabulary of the Quran, Ibn Taymiyya tars the heterogeneous cluster of deviant Muslims—Sufis, philosophers, speculative theologians, Greek logicians, wannabe jurists, and Shiʿi subgroups—with the derogatory label *ahl al-ahwāʾ,* those who follow their base desires and lose their way.[51] When people's desires overcome their rational and spiritual faculties, in this view, they deform into corrupt ideas and practices that transgress the boundaries of orthodoxy.[52] Perhaps because, as René Girard suggests, desire is mimetic—it is acquired from and may spread to other humans—Ibn Taymiyya believed these groups needed to be tamed. He accused the Shiʿis of being "the most lying and polytheistic of those groups who follow their base desires [*ahl al-ahwāʾ*]," urging Sunnis to visibly set themselves apart from them by wearing signet rings on their left hand instead of their right.[53] In his fierce polemic against Twelver Shiʿis, Ibn Taymiyya signals their distance from true Islam by lumping them with non-Muslims (Christians and Jews).[54] Although he was sympathetic to many forms of Sufism, and may even have been a Sufi himself, he nonetheless fiercely attacked features that he believed deviated from orthodox Islam.[55]

In *The Obligation of Following the Straight Path,* Ibn Taymiyya transfers his disdain for unbelievers onto non-Arabs, stating that he composed the treatise to demonstrate the "vices of the People of the Book and non-Arabs."[56] His appeal for Muslim difference is thus more precisely an appeal for *Arab* Muslim difference. It was the reprehensible imitation of both non-Muslims and non-Arabs, in his opinion, that led to the greatest catastrophe in recent memory, the fall of the caliphate: "When the imitation on the one hand of the Jews and Christians and on the other of non-Arabs such as the Byzantines and Persians became rampant among the eastern kings, who thereby violated the tenets of Islam and thus plunged into doing things that displeased God and His Prophet, God brought these infidel Turks."[57] Knowledge that the office of the caliph, historically an Arab descendent of the Quraysh tribe, was eliminated by the non-Arab "infidel Turks," the Mongols, must have fueled Ibn Taymiyya's xenophobia. The Mongols' ignorance of Arabic was matched by their ignorance of Islam. For local Christian and Muslim minorities to collaborate with Mongol foreigners to bring down the Mamluk Sultanate was a great betrayal to the *umma.*

Arabs, in Ibn Taymiyya's imagination, are morally superior to non-Arabs: "Arabs are more inclined to good works than any other people. They are closer to generosity, sagacity, courage, loyalty and other such praiseworthy moral qualities."[58] Non-Arabs should emulate Arabs, learning Arabic in the process. Arab Muslims, however, should speak Arabic and "not learn the gibberish [*raṭāna*] of the non-Arabs."[59] "When the shariʿa prohibited Muslims from imitating non-Arabs, it meant to include all old or new practices of the non-Arab unbelievers and also those of the non-Arab Muslims which were not in vogue among the early converts."[60] The subgroup of non-Arab Muslims worthy of emulation is thus very small: the *salaf.* Otherwise, the distinctive practices of non-Arab believers, like those of non-Arab unbelievers, contaminate pure Islam.

Ibn Taymiyya's Arab chauvinism, however, did not outstrip his meritocratic outlook on piety: "A [non-Arab] Abyssinian [slave] may be more distinguished in the eyes of God than [an Arab] Qurayshī [noble]."[61] Perhaps Ibn Taymiyya recalled that he himself was of non-Arab Kurdish origin.

SHARIʿA-BASED REASONING

Although the canonical collections of hadiths offer a glimpse at how the Partisans of Hadith envisioned Muslim difference, subsequent generations of scholars still had to determine how to interpret these traditions. How should believers understand the statement, attributed to the Prophet—"Grow out your beards!"—as a binding command or an enthusiastic recommendation? If it is read as a command, does it apply in all times and all places, or only in specific situations? Do other hadiths attribute to the Prophet a different opinion? If so, which tradition should take precedence, or should a reconciliation between the two be attempted? More fundamentally, how is a beard defined, and what is the minimum length necessary to fulfill the meaning of "grow out"? These are the types of questions that Muslim jurists asked when determining how to interpret and apply the Prophet's teachings.

Drawn from the hadiths, Muslim interpretations of the scope and application of *tashabbuh* evolved into a discourse rooted in Islamic law, or a shariʿa-based discourse. By the eleventh century, authoritative legal compendia representing all Sunni law schools—even the Literalist (*Ẓāhirī*) school—held opinions that censured imitation, suggesting an undeclared consensus among jurists on its blameworthy status by at least this time.[62] A contemporary of Ibn Taymiyya who anonymously composed a treatise against employing non-Muslims (*al-Qawl al-mukhtār*) concludes that the comprehensiveness of the Pact of ʿUmar's stipulations governing non-Muslim behavior "necessitates a scholarly consensus among Muslims [*ijmāʿ al-Muslimīn*] that believers be visibly distinguished from unbelievers and that they cease imitating them."[63] Nevertheless, the potential legal outcomes governing *tashabbuh* were not limited to a binary choice of lawful versus forbidden, but followed a finely tuned spectrum of legal possibilities designed to govern the complexity of human actions and motivations.

Throughout *The Obligation of Following the Straight Path,* Ibn Taymiyya draws on established shariʿa-based forms of reasoning to discursively scaffold the hadith traditions on Muslim difference. This enables him to treat the subject with nuance, taking into consideration degrees of severity and the diversity of human situations: "The shariʿa makes it obligatory to appear different from them [non-Muslims] and sometimes makes it obligatory for them to appear different from us, such as in the case of dress and related matters. In other situations, the practice is simply recommended [*mustaḥabb*], as in dyeing the beard and praying with shoes . . . and yet in other situations, imitating them is detested [*makrūh*], as in praying during sunset and breaking one's fast belatedly."[64] To determine these legal outcomes, Ibn Taymiyya draws from a normative typology—accepted by most Sunni schools of law—in which human acts are assigned one of five rulings: illicit (*ḥarām*), detested (*makrūh*), licit (*mubāḥ*), recommended (*mustaḥabb*), and obligatory (*farḍ* or *wājib*).[65] These outcomes encompass both positive and negative rulings: acts that Muslims should or must do, and acts that Muslims should not or must not do. And the legal rulings governing *tashabbuh,* as summarized by Ibn Taymiyya above, include both: some acts of imitation, such as praying during sunset (like idolaters), are detested (*makrūh*), while other acts, such as praying with shoes on (to be different from Jews), are recommended (*mustaḥabb*).

Because some acts carried greater spiritual and religious weight than others, the shariʿa did not require that Muslims shun imitation in every situation. Imam al-Shāfiʿī allegedly declared, "We do not prohibit imitation [*tashabbuh*] of them [Jews and Christians] in all situations; we eat like they eat."[66] When jurists lacked direct scriptural evidence to prohibit a practice, they settled on the lesser ruling of declaring that practice detested. For instance, Ibn Ḥanbal ruled that wearing Sindhi sandals, a custom not mentioned in either the Quran or the hadiths, was detested, not forbidden.[67] With some exceptions, jurists also agreed that imitation in nonritual matters was detested, not forbidden.[68] However, when an act of *tashabbuh* overlapped with a sinful act, jurists often ruled the act unlawful, such as praying during sunrise and sunset, which resembled the grave sin of idolatry.[69] In general, Islamic law gave Muslims some room to define the scope of imitation for themselves. Determining whether an act of imitation was reprehensible was thus subjective; jurists from different legal schools, and even within the same school, often held different opinions on a single issue, such as whether it was necessary to cover the face of a corpse with a garment to be different from the Jews.

Although jurists often had differences of opinion, they nonetheless relied on a set of methodological principles (*usūl al-fiqh*) that systematized their legal reasoning. The most authoritative of these principles is rooted in Islamic scripture, the Quran and hadiths. Other methodological principles, however, are marginally related to scripture (or unrelated to scripture altogether). In what follows, I discuss the relevance of a principle from this latter group to the legal application of *tashabbuh.* Called "blocking the means to the illicit [*sadd al-dharīʿa*]," this legal principle resembles what Anglo-American jurists call "the camel's nose dilemma."

THE CAMEL'S NOSE DILEMMA

In ordinary speech, the phrase "slippery slope" usually refers to the dire consequences or imminent disaster that may result from a specific action or choice. In logic, it describes the fallacy that one decision will necessarily lead to a particular result in a deterministic fashion; it assumes that precedence dictates the future. Contemporary legal scholars have dubbed this issue the camel's nose dilemma.[70] The label gets its name from a colorful (fictional) anecdote that also explains the problem. One day a curious camel poked its nose into a tent inhabited by a Bedouin Arab. At first, the Bedouin paid little attention to the camel. But slowly, more and more of the camel's body entered the tent, until eventually the entire the camel had entered the tent—creating an uncomfortably close encounter between the camel and the Bedouin, who was now forced to share his tent with the uninvited guest. The moral of the story is that the seemingly harmless entry of the camel's nose marked the first cause in an inevitable, but unexpected and undesirable, chain of causes and effects. One should not belittle seemingly harmless events when they arise but preemptively stop them from leading to bigger problems.

The camel's nose rationale is commonly invoked by jurists across cultures. Implying a pessimistic decent into the illicit, this rationale is also an outlet for jurists to express their anxieties about a specific issue. Because a jurist *perceives* the danger in a specific practice, he forbids it—even if a harmful outcome never results. As one contemporary legal scholar observes, this form of rationality does not permit for an ethical ledge along the slippery slope; there is no middle ground.[71]

The Islamic legal principle of blocking the means to the illicit (*sadd al-dharīʿa*) was employed by just two of the four Sunni schools of jurisprudence: the Ḥanbalī and Mālikī.[72] To defend the legitimacy of this form of reasoning in Islamic law, Ibn Taymiyya's dedicated student, the Ḥanbalī jurist Ibn al-Qayyim al-Jawziyya, zealously adduced ninety-nine examples of this principle's application under the heading "Proofs on Prohibiting One Who Does What Leads to the Forbidden Although It [that act] Is Permissible in and of Itself."[73] Of the examples given, cases involving *tashabbuh* arise frequently—nearly 10 percent of the total number—and comprise both familiar and unfamiliar practices: praying during sunrise and sunset, praying without footgear, dressing like unbelievers, and speaking openly about sexual indiscretions. As Ibn al-Qayyim explains, it is necessary to avoid these practices, despite their inherent permissibility, due to the harm that may follow.

Through these examples, Ibn al-Qayyim seeks to prove that scripture itself, the hadiths, provides the basis for this legal principle. Consider the hadith "Dye your gray hair, and do not imitate the Jews."[74] Here, the Prophet explicitly justifies why Muslims should dye their hair: to avoid resembling Jews. Reprehensible imitation (*tashabbuh*) is the detrimental outcome that the Prophet is trying to prevent. Because this hadith provides the rationale for the ruling, jurists did not have to extrapolate a reason (*ʿilla*) to explain why Muslims should dye their hair.[75] In other situations, however, the reasoning behind a legal ruling was unclear. Jurists had to build a case that a practice constituted an instance of reprehensible imitation, as Ibn Taymiyya does with regard to Muslim participation in unsanctioned festivals.

THE POWER OF INTENTION

By arguing that the intent behind imitation—not the act itself—is the key variable that determines whether or not a Muslim commits apostasy (*kufr*), Ibn Taymiyya demonstrates that a believer's "subjective" intention has greater ontological significance than the "objective" act. As Raquel Ukeles has shown, this tension becomes evident in Ibn Taymiyya's discussion on celebrating the Prophet's birthday (*mawlid*). Despite his staunch opposition to the *mawlid* as both a reprehensible innovation (*bidʿa*) and reprehensible imitation (*tashabbuh*) of Christmas without any basis in the Quran or *sunna,* he still believes that some Muslim participants can obtain a "great reward" in the world to come.[76] It comes down to their intention, comprehended in affective terms; if believers participate in a *mawlid* out of genuine love for the Prophet Muhammad, then they may in fact be "rewarded" by God in the afterlife, despite having committed a sin! As the Prophet Muhammad famously said, "Acts are defined by their intentions."[77] It is important to keep in mind, however, that

Ibn Taymiyya limits this dispensation to two kinds of believers: simple believers who are unaware that *mawlid*s are sinful and weak believers whose faith is so feeble that they may otherwise commit bigger sins.[78] For such believers, the spiritual benefits of attending a *mawlid* exceed the drawbacks. Believers who should know better are not granted such dispensations.

Through this shariʿa-based cost-benefit analysis, Ibn Taymiyya resolves a tension between the external laws (*ẓāhir*) that define normative Islam and the internal emotional and spiritual states (*bāṭin*) that define the piety of true believers. Sometimes outward appearances are poor reflections of a true believer's subjective experience. Outwardly sinful acts that deserve divine chastisement can, in Ibn Taymiyya's view, lead to divine pleasure under specific conditions—enabling the subjective truth of the believer to triumph over the objective truth of the law. However, the purity of a true believer's intent will only become known in the world to come (*ākhira*), "when all that is hidden in the hearts will be exposed" (Q 100:10).

THE COLLECTIVE GOOD

There are situations, Ibn Taymiyya acknowledged, when Muslims imitating non-Muslims is not only permissible but even good. How Ibn Taymiyya addressed the unique situation of Muslims living abroad as minorities is yet another example of how he employed shariʿa-based forms of reasoning to nimbly address a diverse range of human circumstances by creating exceptions to the general rule.

Muslim jurists divided the world into three kinds of territory: territory governed by Muslims (*dār al-Islām*), territory in which Muslims were at war (*dār al-ḥarb*), and territory governed by non-Muslims (*dār al-kufr*). A main variable that distinguished these different territories was power—defined across political, economic, social, cultural, and religious lines. How could Muslims abroad compensate for their deficit in power relative to Muslims at home? As already discussed, Muslim religious difference during Islam's formative period intensified with the acquisition of political power. Ibn Taymiyya draws on this historical narrative to explain how Muslims living abroad should be ready to acculturate and assimilate in order to pass as non-Muslims:

> If a Muslim resides in a war zone [*dār al-ḥarb*] or in territory governed by non-Muslims [*dār al-kufr*], he is not obligated to appear different from its people (non-Muslims) in their outward conduct due to the

> potential harm that may befall him. In fact, it may be commendable or even binding upon a Muslim to participate occasionally [with non-Muslims] in their public affairs if it fulfills a religious objective [*maṣlaḥa dīniyya*]. This includes summoning them to Islam; exposing their internal affairs in order to inform the Muslims about them; or stopping their attempts to harm Muslims, and other similar objectives [*maqāṣid*]. However, in Muslim territory, in which God has exalted his religion, debased unbelievers, and imposed upon them the poll tax, Muslim difference is required. If it becomes clear that the correct religious policy with respect to similarity and difference changes with time and place, then the truth of these hadith traditions does so too.[79]

Ibn Taymiyya again employs a shariʿa-based calculative form of reasoning that weighs the benefits and drawbacks of specific outcomes to determine the course of action that advances the collective good of the Muslim community. His most significant point is that the shariʿa-based requirement to appear different from non-Muslims is suspended if a believer resides in foreign territory due to the potential harm of being identified as Muslim. Ibn Taymiyya assumes Muslims are more vulnerable living as minorities abroad than as a majority at home. At home, in a position of strength, Muslims are obligated to publicly enact their difference. But abroad, in a position of weakness, they are not. In these situations, power is the crucial variable defining when *tashabbuh* is necessary or not.

Clarifying his position, Ibn Taymiyya insists that assimilation and acculturation (*tashabbuh*) are not only permissible in this situation but may in fact be recommended (*mustaḥabb*) or even binding (*farḍ/wājib*), "if it fulfills a religious objective." These objectives include spying, spreading Islam, or preventing unbelievers from hatching a plot against the Muslims. These options parallel what one might encounter in a modern spy novel, indicating the degree of Ibn Taymiyya's concern for the collective welfare of the Muslim community—at once a "religious" and "political" matter.[80] It thus becomes apparent that the type of pragmatic calculations that define the field of politics also defined shariʿa-based reasoning.[81] Indeed, as Ibn Taymiyya writes elsewhere, the shariʿa "came for the purpose of promoting the collective good [*maṣlaḥa*] and bringing this to completion, as well as averting or limiting harm, giving consideration to the best of what is good and the least of what is evil."[82] He adds, "It becomes clear, then, that evil may be tolerated under two conditions: (1) where doing so averts a greater evil that cannot be averted otherwise;

and (2) where tolerating evil secures a greater benefit than not doing so, and there is no other way to secure this benefit."[83] The most fundamental objective of the shariʿa, then, is to seek benefit, and the most fundamental way to seek benefit is to avoid harm. In comparison to Ghazālī, whose robust conception of the collective good (*maṣlaḥa*) was defined by several criteria, Ibn Taymiyya's minimalist conception enables a style of legal reasoning that Felicitas Opwis describes as "more inclusive."[84] The small "evil" of *tashabbuh* thus helps to realize the greater good and avert the greater harm, an outcome that empowers the Muslim community. In this scenario, *tashabbuh* turns from a sinful practice to a pious deed.

SHARIʿA AND SYMBOL

Ibn Taymiyya insists that Muslims preserve their difference by refusing to adopt the distinctive markers (*shiʿār*) of foreign communities: "The real reason why a Muslim is forbidden to participate with unbelievers in their festivities is that such practices are distinctive markers and symbols [*shiʿār*] of unbelievers."[85] The legal scope of Muslim difference, that is, the zone of what the shariʿa defines as reprehensible imitation, is a semiotic landscape. Predecessors and contemporaries from Ibn Ḥanbal to Ibn al-Qayyim shared Ibn Taymiyya's semiotic imaginary, admonishing believers to shun the distinctive markers of unbelievers. Concerning Muslim participation in the burial rites of non-Muslims, Ibn Ḥanbal ruled that Muslims may dig a grave for a Jew or Christian but not construct a sarcophagus for a Zoroastrian. Ibn Taymiyya explains that Ibn Ḥanbal was not biased against Zoroastrians but perceived the sarcophagus as one of the "distinctive markers [*khaṣāʾiṣ*] of the false Zoroastrian religion."[86] There is nothing distinctive about burial in a grave, however, since the custom is common to Muslims, Christians, and Jews. Muslims who dig graves or partake in any practice that is not a distinctive marker of a foreign community are not committing a sin. Within this socio-semiotic framework, symbols not only define what counts as reprehensible imitation but set limits on how the shariʿa regulates Muslim difference.

But symbols also add an element of unpredictability to the law. How, for example, should Muslims view symbolic practices that diffuse beyond the community from which they originate and are no longer distinctive? Ibn Taymiyya offers an "originalist" response to this question: Muslims are forbidden from copying practices that originate from a foreign community, even if they have spread to other communities.[87] Because it was common for Muslims to unknowingly copy practices that originated from unbelievers, Ibn Taymiyya fixes the identity of a practice at its origins. There, frozen in time, the practice becomes attached to the community that originated it—whether Muslim or non-Muslim. But if it can be determined that a practice does not have foreign origins, Muslims may share in that practice without committing a sin.

Conversely, what happens if the roles are reversed, and non-Muslims imitate Muslims? Ibn Taymiyya considers this hypothetical scenario as well. In his view, non-Muslims may adopt Muslim customs as long as they do not appropriate the sartorial styles (and other related markers) distinctive to Muslims—as decreed by the sultan. Within this social imaginary, the definition of Muslim difference is not the exclusive province of religious authorities but trickles down from the apex of the Realm's political hierarchy. Muslims are not required to further distinguish themselves from non-Muslims in public. Muslim men, for example, do not need to shave off their beards if non-Muslim men begin to grow out their beards. Muslims are the originators, not the imitators.

There are some markers of difference, however, that become extinct. Ibn al-Qayyim agreed with Ibn Taymiyya that non-Muslims should not appropriate cultural markers that are distinct to Muslims. However, he disagreed with Lālakāʾī's view that non-Muslims are prohibited from wearing the color yellow because it was customary for the Prophet and his followers to do so.[88] Ibn al-Qayyim reasoned that not all sartorial distinctions are alike. Some forms of dress are forbidden to non-Muslims due to their inherent prestige and nobility, while others are forbidden simply because they set non-Muslims apart from Muslims. While the first type of prohibition is always enforced, the second is contingent upon time and place. According to Ibn al-Qayyim, the meaning of the color yellow had changed in the Mamluk Sultanate. He contends that the style of dressing in yellow attire had diffused across religious boundaries, evolving into a non-Muslim cultural norm. The symbolic value of the color yellow, he asserts, had likewise transformed into a sartorial marker of unbelief (*shiʿār al-kufr*). Because there was nothing inherently prestigious about the color yellow, it no longer made sense to forbid non-Muslims from wearing it—especially when it had become a sign that enhanced Muslim difference.

Power dynamics thus lie at the root of Ibn Taymiyya's and Ibn al-Qayyim's opposition to Muslim cultural appropriation. Power, real and imagined, is often mediated through symbols, and symbols mediate communal identity in public life. In Ibn Taymiyya's view, to adopt the distinctive markers of unbelievers is to exalt them and debase Muslims—turning the ideal Islamic social order upside down. For this reason, he prohibits Muslims from selling drums, flags, and banners either the day of or in physical proximity to Jewish and Christian festivals—the objects themselves are permissible to sell, but they symbolically empower Jews and Christians on their holidays.[89]

Symbols are thus multivalent, carrying both positive value and negative value; some symbolic markers strengthen Islam and moral uprightness, while others strengthen unbelief and moral corruption. Although Ibn Taymiyya generally discourages Muslims from appropriating the distinctive markers of unbelievers, he makes exceptions for Muslims to enhance the distinguishing markers (*shiʿār*) of Jews and Christians in some situations. In line with the sultan's decrees enforcing the sartorial distinction of non-Muslim subjects, Ibn Taymiyya permits Muslims to sell Jews and Christians outfits that visibly distinguish them in public (*thiyāb al-ghiyār*).[90] These *shiʿār* do not empower but debase unbelievers—while enhancing Muslim difference and the social prestige of Muslims in public life. In Ibn Taymiyya's view, it was essential for Muslim authorities to regulate *shiʿār* in a manner that placed Muslims in a position of strength relative to their rivals.

THE INNOVATION OF IMITATION

The classical psychologist of religion William James called invention and imitation "the two legs . . . on which the human race historically has walked."[91] But as the guardians of Islam, *ʿulamāʾ* were trained to view imitation and invention (or innovation) with skepticism—as powerful social forces that need to be regulated in order to safeguard the boundaries of Muslim community and Islamic orthodoxy (especially the Prophet's *sunna*). Although medieval jurists placed unsanctioned innovation (*bidʿa*) and imitation (*tashabbuh*) under the domain of the shariʿa, Ibn Taymiyya was the first to illustrate their discursive symbiosis, integrating both concepts into his legal reasoning: "All the proof texts adduced from the Quran, *sunna,* and consensus opinion of the early Muslim community [*ijmaʿ*] that indicate innovation is reprehensible and foul—whether declared forbidden or [less severely] that it be avoided—encompass [the issue of Muslims] resembling [non-Muslims], and thus combine both factors: they are recent innovations and [derive from the] imitation of unbelievers. . . . So when both factors *converge* in a single act they become two independent legal causes for judging the act foul and forbidden."[92] Here Ibn Taymiyya considers the legal import of a hypothetical act that is both a reprehensible innovation and reprehensible imitation. More specifically, it is a practice that originated from the imitation of non-Muslims and leads to a religious innovation.[93] In this schema, imitation is portrayed as the gateway through which innovations infect Muslim behavior.

That the practice merits two distinct shariʿa-based rationales for its prohibition strengthens the weight of the legal ruling. "Imitation is in general forbidden, even if the first generations of Muslims [*salaf*] attempted it, and so is innovation, even if the unbelievers did not resort to it."[94] In other words, imitation is still wrong, even if there is precedent for it among the first and most authoritative generations of Muslims; and innovation is still wrong, even if it originated from Muslims and not from non-Muslims. Both reprehensible imitation and innovation are thus wrong in themselves, no matter who does it. In Ibn Taymiyya's legal schema, both shariʿa-based concepts work independently to define the boundaries of Islamic orthodoxy.

Within the normative universe of Islam, *bidʿa* and *tashabbuh* have much in common; they are both boundary-regulating concepts that stigmatize practices that lack authentic precedent in Islam. They share scriptural evidence, such as the "seventy-three sects" and "lizard hole" hadiths discussed earlier, for their normative authority. They also apply to a shared field of Muslim practices, including ritual practices such as prayer, tomb visitations, and funeral processions, and cultural practices such as festivals, dress, and gendered interactions. Like *tashabbuh, bidʿa* is intertwined with the legal principle of blocking the means to the illicit (*sadd al-dharīʿa*) which, as discussed above, aims to prevent harm.[95] One key difference, however, is that the discourse on innovation matured much sooner than its counterpart; the first treatises against innovation were composed in the ninth century, several centuries before Ibn Taymiyya's treatise.[96]

Unsanctioned *ʿīd*s, in Ibn Taymiyya's view, are dangerous spaces teeming with innovation and imitation in their most insidious forms. Believers are likely to engage in all types of rituals and practices that mimic the distinctive markers of unbelievers. The Christian holiday of Maundy Thursday, in particular, provoked vitriolic responses from many *ʿulamāʾ*, including Ibn Taymiyya. Tied to the agricultural calendar and change of seasons, the holiday signified rebirth, coinciding with the end of the Lent fast that culminated with Easter. On this day, specially prepared lentils or rice with milk and clarified butter piqued the taste buds of Muslim participants, male and female. They would have inhaled the pleasant aroma emitted by these festive foods. In fact, due to the culinary significance of this day, Maundy Thursday was dubbed "Rice Thursday" in Syria and "Lentil Thursday" in Egypt.[97] Contributing to the holiday's visual spectacle, participants would light incense, dye clothes, paint eggs, draw images of snakes and scorpions, and display crosses and banners. They would hear the strike of their mini copper drums and feel new sensations as they bathed in olive water. They would also socialize and physically rub up against non-Muslims and members of the opposite sex. On this day, "a man cannot walk in the markets without difficulty because of the crowds of women," gripes the Egyptian jurist Ibn al-Ḥājj (d. 1336). Fearing the spiritual contamination resulting from this physical contact, he moralizes, "There is no good for a man who crowds along with them."[98] The entire sensorium was excited during this festive occasion. For purists like Ibn Taymiyya, this holiday was nothing less than "despicable."[99] In *The Obligation of Following the Straight Path,* he warns: "A Muslim must refrain from riding in the same boat that Christians had boarded en route to their festival sites, lest he too may become the recipient of divine wrath befalling the Christians on account of their polytheistic behavior [*shirk*]."[100]

Other kinds of *ʿīds* assaulted the senses as well. At the Nawrūz celebration of the Coptic new year in Egypt, miscreants sprayed unsuspecting victims with water bottles.[101] At funerals, the piercing screams of wailers, sobbing mourners, the scent of incense or the stench of a corpse, and the spectacle of a crowded procession in the night guided by fire and light created a solemn but sensational public event that brought the living in contact with the dead. During a visitation to a saint's tomb, pilgrims may taste sweets, inhale the scent of perfumed pillars, listen to chants of supplication and religious song, and witness crowds circumambulating the tomb, which they may kiss and rub for spiritual blessings. Critics like Ibn Taymiyya became irate at tomb visitors who beseeched a dead corpse for assistance instead of God.

This blatant *tashabbuh* makes Muslim participation in such festivals reprehensible at best, and illicit at worst. But "all new festivals," even those that "do not involve imitating the People of the Book," Ibn Taymiyya contends, "are still bad."[102] He believes that any festival not already sanctioned in Islam can lead to reprehensible innovations, following a slow descent into the illicit that was anticipated by the Prophet himself, who announced: "The worst things are inventions. Every invention is an innovation. Every innovation leads astray. And every stray deed leads to the hellfire."[103] Often recited in the prelude to a Friday sermon, this well-known hadith warns against the dangers of innovation. Based on this and other evidence, Ibn Taymiyya concludes that all innovations are bad, dismissing Muslim scholars who claim there is such a thing as a "good innovation."[104] Inventing new rituals, practices, and norms morally corrupts Muslims, individually and collectively. Over time, innovations diffuse across the Muslim community, infecting greater numbers of people, until they become habits that are difficult to root out. Innovations spread through imitation. In sum, there are two independent shariʿa-based rationales—*tashabbuh* and *bidʿa*—to justify the prohibition of *ʿīds*.[105]

Academic and Muslim religious scholars alike have drawn attention to the opposition between *bidʿa* and *sunna* in defining Islamic orthodoxy. But here I propose that Islamic orthodoxy is better conceived as a triangulation between *sunna, bidʿa,* and *tashabbuh* in which religious authorities like Ibn Taymiyya seek to discipline Muslim innovation (*bidʿa*) and imitation (*tashabbuh*) in order to safeguard the authority of the Prophet's normative conduct (*sunna*). This was, indeed, a great burden, as indicated by the following supplication of Dhahabī: "O Turner of the hearts! Inspire us to follow the *sunna* of your Prophet and save us from innovation and imitation."[106]

EMULATING IBN TAYMIYYA

Measured by the number of treatises, premodern and modern, that cite it, *The Obligation of Following the Straight Path* is the most influential treatise against imitation ever written. Ibn Taymiyya's cohort of protégés followed their teacher by composing treatises that stressed the importance of defining clear lines between Muslims and non-Muslims in public life. Ibn al-Qayyim al-Jawziyya composed the first comprehensive treatise on the laws governing non-Muslim subjects living in an Islamic state (*dhimmīs*).[107] The anonymous Ḥanbalī author of *The Chosen View concerning the Prohibition of Preferring Unbelievers* cites several of Ibn Taymiyya's legal opinions concerning *dhimmīs* to strengthen his case against employing non-Muslims.[108] Shams al-Dīn al-Dhahabī, a distinguished and prolific scholar, most famous for his works on prosopography, hadith, and biography, composed a compact, focused treatise against imitation that recasts key features of Ibn Taymiyya's argument (without ever mentioning it) in abbreviated form: *The Despicable Imitation of the People of Thursday: Rejecting the Imitation of Pagans* (*Tashabbuh al-khasīs bi-ahl al-khamīs fī radd al-tashabbuh biʾl-mushrikīn*).[109] Dhahabī shares Ibn Taymiyya's semiotic imaginary of difference in which symbols play a crucial role in policing religious boundaries. He admonishes Muslims against manifesting and exalting the distinguishing markers of Christians and Jews by imitating them. Through imitation, these symbolic markers are publicly displayed on physical bodies and mediated through material objects that blur the line between believer and unbeliever. Like Ibn Taymiyya, Dhahabī adduces proof texts against imitation from the hadiths and links the vices of imitation and innovation as twin evils that undermine the *sunna* to condemn Muslim participation at unsanctioned *ʿīds*, focusing on Maundy Thursday (as indicated by the title): "What evil is greater than joining Jews and Christians in their celebrations . . . while they do not join or imitate us in our celebrations!"[110] Disgusted by Muslim mimicry of Christians at these festivals, Dhahabī criticizes seemingly harmless holiday rituals such as baking flat loaves of bread, painting eggs, dyeing hair, wearing special attire, burning incense, and hanging crosses made of tar. For good measure, Dhahabī censures Good Friday, Christmas, and Nawrūz as well.

Perhaps inspired by his preaching activities, Dhahabī keeps his message concise and simple to appeal to the common Muslim by focusing on scripture and avoiding the complex legal discussions that characterized his teacher's treatise.[111] "Whoever imitates a people becomes one of them" is repeated like a poetic refrain from beginning to end. However, in seeking clarity of expression, Dhahabī sacrifices conceptual nuance by diminishing the relevance of intention to *tashabbuh;* no matter how noble a believer's intention may be, a prohibited act of imitation remains prohibited—a hard-line legal position that Ibn Taymiyya had softened in *The Obligation of Following the Straight Path.*[112]

CONCLUSION

"Danger lies in transitional states," Mary Douglas observed, "simply because transition is neither one state nor the next, it is undefinable. The person who must pass from one to another is himself in danger and emanates danger to others."[113] Ibn Taymiyya was attuned to the dangers, real and imagined, brought on by the social and political transformations affecting the Mamluk Sultanate at the turn of the fourteenth century. The scholar-activist exerted himself to maximize the welfare of the Muslim community, complementing his direct involvement in the sultanate's political and military affairs, by composing religious treatises against the forces and figures that threatened to harm the collective body of Muslims.

Given Ibn Taymiyya's ongoing efforts to recover the original Islam of the first Muslims, the *salaf,* it is perhaps appropriate that he opposed all forms of inauthentic imitation that threatened to bury this sacred past. But unlike modern-day Salafis who seek to access this past unmediated by later tradition,

Ibn Taymiyya liberally employed shariʿa-based reasoning to translate the original Islam of the *salaf* into a new form that befit his present. He transformed the concept of *tashabbuh* into a shariʿa-based discourse designed to safeguard the boundaries of Islamic orthodoxy. This discourse binds together a diverse set of concepts, forms of reasoning, and literary genres that are mediated through both history (Islamic scripture and tradition) and the present (the social and political life of the Mamluk Sultanate) to construct a normative way of knowing and being in the world. Ibn Taymiyya pulled many shariʿa-based levers to demonstrate that being different is indeed an Islamic obligation—from arguing that it advanced the common good (*maṣlaḥa*) of the Muslim community to forbidding Muslim cultural appropriation of foreign symbols (*shiʿār*) to illustrating that imitation (*tashabbuh*) and innovation (*bidʿa*) are symbiotic concepts that each function as independent legal grounds (*ʿilla*) for prohibiting a practice. Taken together, these forms of reasoning reveal that Ibn Taymiyya's discourse of difference is a discourse of power, designed to position Muslims a degree above their rivals.

CHAPTER 6

"A person belongs with the one he loves"

> If you are not among the virtuous, imitate them,
> For imitating the virtuous leads to success.
>
> —POPULAR SUFI COUPLET

I was taught this couplet (in Arabic) by a shaykh of the Shādhilī Sufi order during field research in Aleppo, Syria. It is a distinctively Sufi gloss on the hadith "Whoever imitates a people becomes one of them," which, in this context, contrasts how jurists normally read it—as a stern admonition to oppose sinful unbelievers. Instead, the tradition becomes an encouraging homily for the pursuit of spiritual excellence. A seeker who aspires to join the spiritual elect should begin by outwardly emulating their behavior until they are socialized into embodying their piety from within. This versified gloss on the imitation hadith signals how *tashabbuh* entered into the expansive Sufi vocabulary on spiritual transformation.

Building on Arin Shawkat Salamah-Qudsi's important study of *tashabbuh* among Sufi communities in twelfth- and thirteenth-century Baghdad, in this chapter, I draw attention to some novel conceptions of imitation in these sources that have until now been ignored—most notable among them, the figure named the "Imitator of the Imitator." Unlike the Partisans of Hadith portrayed in earlier chapters who invoke the vocabulary of *tashabbuh* to define the social boundaries of the Muslim community, the Sufi figures discussed here draw upon the same language to expand the social boundaries of their spiritual communities.

IMITATION AS SELF-CULTIVATION

From the tenth century onward, Sufis identified imitation as a technology of self-cultivation. "The beautification of the self [*taḥallī*] is achieved through imitation [*tashabbuh*] of the Sufi in both word and deed," declared Abū Naṣr al-Sarrāj of Ṭūs (d. 988), author of the canonical manual of Sufi terminology *The Book of Flashes* (*Kitāb al-Luma'*).[1] Convinced that humans, by nature, are "bred to imitate and follow," the "Proof of Islam," Abū Ḥāmid al-Ghazālī (d. 1111), urges believers to reach the lofty spiritual ranks of the angels by copying their rituals: in circumambulating the *ka'ba* during the Hajj pilgrimage, for example, believers mirror the angels, who are circumambulating their own *ka'ba* in the heavens.[2] But even in the mundane course of daily life—when getting pulled into an argument with someone, for example—believers should embrace the better angels of their nature:

> Let him [a believer] reflect upon the ugliness of anger's appearance when it emerges by recalling the [ugly] appearance of another angry person. Let him reflect upon the ugliness of anger within himself and the resemblance of its possessor to a vicious dog or an ordinary beast, and [by contrast] the resemblance of the forbearing one who controls his temper to the prophets, gnostics, scholars, and wise folk. Then, let him choose between imitating [*tashabbuh*] the habits of dogs, wild beasts, and the vilest of people, and imitating [*tashabbuh*] the habits of scholars and prophets so that his ego-self inclines to the love of following the latter . . . if any sound judgment from his intellect remains with him.[3]

Ghazālī draws a sharp contrast between the physical appearance of the forbearing believer and the angry believer. Appealing to readers' aesthetic sensibilities, he invites them to contemplate the ugly appearance of anger as manifested in a rabid dog and its visual contrast to the noble countenances of the prophets and gnostics who subdue their anger. Readers must choose between these models of behavior.[4] In highlighting the connection between the virtue and vice of forbearance and anger and their contrasting physical manifestations, Ghazālī illustrates how imitation is a holistic form of self-cultivation that encompasses both a person's external and internal attributes.

But other Sufis saw in imitation the potential to deceive. The Persian mystic Alī b. 'Uthmān al-Hujwīrī (d. 1072–77) flips Sarrāj's definition, writing that Sufi adepts must distinguish true Sufis from those who just look like them: "*Taḥallī,* then, is to imitate people without really acting like them. Those who seem to be what they are not will soon be put to shame, and their secret character will be revealed."[5] The Sufi biographer ʿAbd al-Raḥmān al-Sulamī (d. 1021) of Nishapur offered similar counsel to beginners: "In our times, the rational person must understand the basic principles of Sufism and the spiritual path of its true adherents so that he can distinguish between those who just imitate them [*mutashabbihūn*], dress like them, or look like them, and thus avoid becoming one of these false Sufis."[6] Exoteric and esoteric practice, these warnings imply, need not always cohere. Imitation, in other words, may not lead to true spiritual realization, but instead project a false and superficial image.

THE SUHRAWARDĪ SCHOOL

A version of the couplet quoted in the epigraph was composed in the twelfth century by the "Illuminationist" theosopher Shihāb al-Dīn Yaḥya al-Suhrawardī (d. 1191), said to have been executed for heresy at just thirty-six years old.[7] But it was two of his countrymen from the northwestern Iranian town of Suhraward, Abū Najīb al-Suhrawardī (d. 1168) and his nephew Shihāb al-Dīn Abū Ḥafṣ ʿUmar al-Suhrawardī (d. 1234), who developed *tashabbuh* into a distinctive Sufi concept.

In a concise but influential manual, *The Etiquette of Spiritual Aspirants* (*Ādāb al-murīdīn*), Abū Najīb illuminated the many degrees of imitation that take place in a Sufi community, from surface-level copying to authentic self-transformation.[8] He therefore urges beginners in his eponymous Sufi community—*mutashabbihūn,* or "Sufi Imitators"—to do more than just look like the community's truly committed Sufis: "When the Prophet said, 'Whoever imitates a people becomes one of them,' he meant the assumption of their way of life, not of their dress. He also said, 'Whoever imitates a group in his style of speech and dress while his practices do not cohere with his appearance is accursed by God, the angels, and all humans.'"[9] Sufi imitators should not be content to merely conform, but should strive to transform their whole selves. Encompassing inside and outside, this holistic transformation spans their physical appearance and moral character.

Realizing, however, that some beginners excel while others lag behind, Abū Najīb distinguishes between ranks of Sufi imitators: "He who adheres to the dispensation and accepts the rules that govern them is one of the 'True Imitators' [*min al-mutashabbihīn al-ṣādiqīn*], about whom the Prophet said,

'Whoever imitates a people becomes one of them' and 'Whoever increases their numbers is one of them.'"[10] No one before Abū Najīb had developed this concept in detail.[11] He distinguishes between authentic and inauthentic forms of imitation. A true Sufi imitator—as opposed to the unnamed fake Sufi imitator—follows the devotional practices mandated by the Sufi master, which include performing ritual worship, shunning forbidden practices, and relinquishing worldly possessions.[12] By following these practices, the True Imitator fulfills the minimum requirements for belonging to the Suhrawardī Sufi community and becoming "one of them." Abū Najīb enumerated these minimum requirements to include Sufi Imitators who did not perform the spiritual exercises that more committed aspirants performed into the social orbit of the Sufi community.[13] Without this category of membership, the Sufi community's stringent regulations would have alienated beginning aspirants who wanted to belong but who lacked the ambition of its committed members. Abū Najīb's interpretation of the imitation hadith—in contrast to jurisprudential glosses—stresses inclusion over exclusion.

THE IMITATOR OF THE IMITATOR

Abū Ḥafṣ ʿUmar al-Suhrawardī formalized and elaborated the spiritual ranks conceived by his uncle, Abū Najīb, and constructed a Sufi lodge (*ribāṭ*) along the Tigris River that helped bring the Suhrawardī Sufi order (*ṭarīqa*) to prominence.[14] In his treatise on Sufi etiquette, *The Perceivers of Gnosis* (*ʿAwārif al-maʿārif*), Abū Ḥafṣ elaborates on his uncle's teachings regarding the Sufi Imitator's role in the spiritual community, pushing the boundaries of inclusive membership even further.

Even those who failed to qualify as "True Imitators" found a place in Abū Ḥafṣ's spiritual community, which was organized hierarchically according to three socio-spiritual ranks: the "[True] Sufi," the "Would-be Sufi" (*mutaṣawwif*), and the "Sufi Imitator" (*mutashabbih*), a category his uncle considered the lowest-ranking member of the community.

But from the rank of Sufi Imitator emerges a new rank—what Abū Ḥafṣ calls the "Imitator of the Imitator":

> As for the True Imitator . . . he advances to the rank of the Would-be Sufi, one who observes himself and meditates over his relationship to God and his creation. Next, he advances to the rank of Sufi, one who witnesses God. As for the one who neither advances to the state of the

> Would-be Sufi or the Sufi through imitation, nor aspires even to inculcate the fundamentals of their spiritual objectives, and is rather committed only to outward imitation of the superficial aspects of dress and of sharing a common style and appearance, and is devoid of their inward characteristics and attributes, he is not a Sufi Imitator [*mutashabbih bi'l-ṣūfiyya*] because he does not mimic them by entering into their beginnings. He is therefore an Imitator of the Imitator [*mutashabbih bi'l-mutashabbih*]. He connects to the community solely through his dress. Despite that, they [the Sufis] comprise a community whose associates will not be reduced to misery.[15]

In this hierarchy, the True Imitator (*al-mutashabbih al-ḥaqīqī*) does not remain at the margins of the Suhrawardī Sufi community forever. By enjoying the companionship of higher-ranking Sufis, he may soar to the loftiest spiritual ranks of the community, becoming a Would-be Sufi and finally a True Sufi. But one whose imitation is inferior is, in the words of Abū Ḥafṣ, an "Imitator of the Imitator"—a Sufi in appearance only. If the True Imitator lingers at the outer edges of the Sufi community, the Imitator of the Imitator is even further removed from the center.

Nevertheless, Abū Ḥafṣ includes Imitators of the Imitators in the Suhrawardī community—members that his uncle did not acknowledge. His use of terminology plays an important role in signaling their participation. A cruder label for these lukewarm participants, such as "false imitator," would have hardened boundaries around the community and signaled that they did not belong. But Abū Ḥafṣ softens the boundaries dividing insiders and outsiders, indicating that connecting to the community through dress alone is sufficient; the Imitator of the Imitator is blessed by their company and, in the words of a famous hadith, "will not be reduced to misery."[16] Imitation, then, socialized these beginners into a more pious disposition—an extension of the principle of companionship, or *ṣuḥba,* which was central to Sufi discourse and social life.[17] Abū Ḥafṣ's robust conception of *tashabbuh,* in the estimation of Salamah-Qudsi, helped create "a popular system open to one and all" that was, at the same time, "an alternative to the hierarchical structure of Abbasid society" in which "the institutionalized Sufi centers were supported by potential waves of adherents from all social sectors and educational levels."[18]

The emphasis on dress and appearance in the category of the Imitator of the Imitator, then, was intended to create solidarity between members of the Suhrawardī Sufi community—not to turn people away. In the Sufi spiritual imagination, dress possesses transformative power.[19] It indexes a correspondence between the spiritual and physical, esoteric and exoteric. Beginning in the ninth century, Sufi shaykhs such as Abū Ḥafṣ bestowed cloaks (*khirqas*) upon their followers to visually signal both their spiritual and social rank in the community.[20] Citing Aḥmad al-Ghazālī (d. 1126), an Iranian Sufi and lesser-known brother of the more scholastic Abū Ḥāmid al-Ghazālī, Abū Ḥafṣ sheds light on the transformative power of Sufi style: "If we invest him [the novice] with the cloak so that he resembles [*yatashabbahu*] the community of Sufis and dresses in their style it will draw him nearer to their gatherings and to the blessing derived from their company. By observing the spiritual states and inward attributes he will grow to love their spiritual path, and through that love, he will attain a portion of their spiritual states."[21]

Joining the exoteric to the esoteric, Aḥmad al-Ghazālī explains how looking like a Sufi slowly draws adepts into their social world, transforming their spiritual and emotional states. Based on this teaching, Abū Ḥafṣ believed that even the Sufi Imitator should receive a cloak to aid his transformation into a True Sufi. In fact, he defines two kinds of cloaks to publicly distinguish two ranks of membership: the cloak of discipleship (*irāda*) for True Sufis and the cloak of blessing (*tabarruk*) for Sufi Imitators.[22] The practice of bestowing cloaks of blessing was a material expression of Abū Ḥafṣ's boundary-expanding concept of the Imitator of the Imitator. In one instance, he gifted a cloak of blessing to a ruler, urging him to join the Suhrawardī Sufi community.[23] This invitation complemented his other efforts to encourage potential Sufi Imitators to pursue the spiritual path and expand his community's circle of members.[24]

Ultimately, however, a Sufi Imitator's place in the Suhrawardī Sufi order was not defined by a piece of cloth but by deeply felt emotion, that is, true love. In *The Perceivers of Gnosis,* Abū Ḥafṣ narrates a famous hadith on the authority of his uncle in which a man approaches the Prophet and asks, "When is the Day of Judgment?" But instead of answering the question, the Prophet deflects the question back to him: "What have you prepared for it?" The person replies that he is poorly prepared, having failed to perform an abundance of good deeds or acts of devotion. Unable to boast of his deeds, he can recall only one virtue he possesses and proclaims, "I love God and his Messenger." To this confession, the Prophet famously responds, "A person belongs with the one he loves."[25] In his gloss on this tradition, Abū Ḥafṣ defines the Sufi Imitator as "one who chooses to imitate the Sufis and not others due to nothing other than his love for them. Despite his shortcomings in comparison to their religious performance, he is on par with them because of his desire and love."[26] A sincere and deep emotional attachment to his spiritual community compensates for the Sufi Imitator's shortcomings in devotion. Within the community of Sufis, then, love is the great equalizer. But what sets apart this kind of affection from all others is its spiritual origins. Arising from the mutual attraction of kindred spirits (*arwāḥ*), this love—unlike transient worldly love—lasts forever.[27]

CHAPTER 7

Escaping the Devil's Lair

GHAZZĪ BETWEEN SPIRIT AND LAW

Love is conformity.

—POPULAR SUFI APHORISM

I imagine our age as a destitute invalid,
When every sparrow becomes a vulture.

—NAJM AL-DĪN AL-GHAZZĪ, *The Virtue of Awakening*

"His book is unprecedented."[1] This was how Muḥibbī (d. 1699), the preeminent biographer of Sufi jurist, hadith master, and litterateur Najm al-Dīn al-Ghazzī described his monumental treatise, *The Virtue of Awakening to What Has Been Transmitted about Imitation* (*Ḥusn al-tanabbuh li-mā warada fī al-tashabbuh*). An exhaustive compendium of knowledge, *The Virtue of Awakening* is a weighty tome that spans twelve volumes in the published edition. Considering its imposing physical size and vast intellectual scope, the treatise may be classified as an encyclopedia—an encyclopedia of imitation that, as Muḥibbī rightly points out, is sui generis in the history of Islam.[2] The magnum opus is a testament to the Damascene scholar's dedication; he spent nearly forty years, almost half his life, writing, editing, and perfecting it (figure 12). The treatise alone supports the recent work of historians who have recast the historiographical narrative of seventeenth-century Arab Muslim intellectual life from stagnation and decline to creativity and progress.[3] The most comprehensive Islamic treatise on imitation ever written, *The Virtue of Awakening* showcases the ability of Ghazzī—and his contemporaries—to synthesize the knowledge of the past to produce new historical frames of reference.

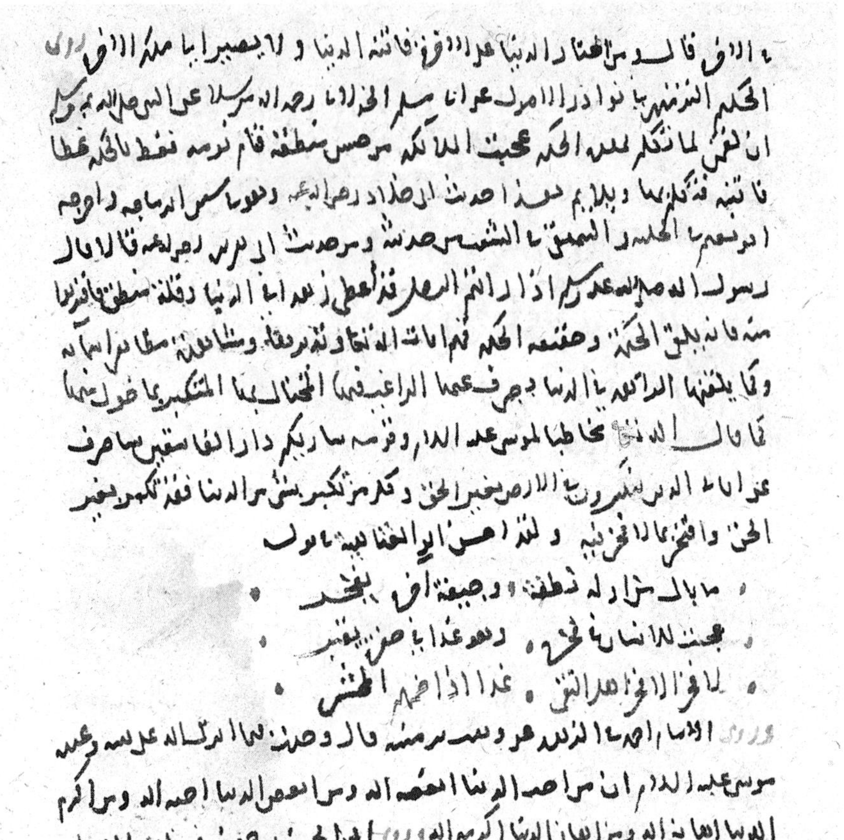

Figure 12. Ghazzī's handwritten colophon, with signature and date of completion, from volume 3 of *The Virtue of Awakening* (*Ḥusn al-tanabbuh*), February 13, 1626. (Chester Beatty Library, Dublin, Arabic 3216, vol. 3, fol. 279v.)

The Virtue of Awakening is inflected by Ghazzī's Sufi sensibilities. Although almost all treatises on imitation, past and present, confined their ethical scope to the prohibition of vice, content to explore imitation's darker side, Ghazzī's treatise breaks the mold, exploring the virtues of imitation as well. Properly speaking, then, the text is both a treatise *against* imitation and a treatise *for* imitation. It brings marginalized Sufi perspectives that portray *tashabbuh* as a positive and holistic form of self-cultivation to the center.

But Ghazzī was also a jurist in the Shāfiʿī school. His double identity as both Sufi and jurist is reflected in the treatise's synthesis of esoteric and exoteric language. Ghazzī opens *The Virtue of Awakening* with a profound commentary on "Whoever imitates a people becomes one of them," proposing a robust theory of belonging that seeds an elaborate vision of the ideal Islamic social order. *The Virtue of Awakening* may in fact be viewed as a monumental commentary on this single tradition. While most religious scholars came to read the hadith as a warning for believers to be different from unbelievers, as already discussed, Ghazzī is among the few who saw both sides. Ghazzī portrays imitation as a bipolar phenomenon that could lead to good or bad consequences for believers. At the level of the individual, imitation could corrupt or illuminate the believer's soul, and at the level of the collective, it could bind or unravel the Muslim community. Given that Ghazzī embraces the full spectrum of human moral and spiritual possibility, we should not be surprised that tensions emerge between Sufi and legal modes of reasoning in *The Virtue of Awakening*.

These tensions become apparent in Ghazzī's examination of imitation. Building on his Sufi predecessors, he argues that imitation is true and lasting only when motivated by deep affection—love. Love is what defines whether or not someone belongs to a community—how a person truly becomes "one of them." As the Prophet said, "A person belongs with the one he loves."[4] But if love alone ultimately defines communal membership, one must consider the limit case of a person who claims to love God and the Prophet Muhammad but nonetheless fails to perform the most essential rituals of Islam. Does such a person still belong to the community of believers? An affirmative response appears to render the elaborate architecture of Islamic law superfluous. As both a Sufi who values the centrality of love to Islamic spiritual life and a jurist who values obedience to God's laws, Ghazzī struggles to balance these conflicting epistemic sensibilities: Is love alone sufficient to determine membership in a religious community or must good works follow? Is it even ontologically possible to isolate human affects from acts?

Ghazzī's interdisciplinary approach in *The Virtue of Awakening* reflects a well-defined Islamic humanistic tradition. His rich discourse draws from the entire repertoire of Islamic religious disciplines—hadith, law, Quranic exegesis, theology—and cuts across the "secular" disciplines of ethics, history, psychology, sociology, natural science, literature, poetry, and philology, blurring, in the process, conceptual dichotomies between Sufism and Shariʿa, esoteric and exoteric, individual and collective. Ghazzī's ability to bridge spirit and law is reminiscent of Iraqi Sufi jurist Abū Ḥāmid al-Ghazālī, whose magnum opus, *The Revival of the Religious Disciplines,* is regarded as one of the greatest intellectual achievements of classical Sunni Islamic thought.[5] The interdisciplinary scope of Ghazzī's treatise mirrors the scope of imitation itself, which configures nearly every field of human experience.

It is through the prism of this intellectual framework that Ghazzī illuminates the multivalence of human identity, weaving Muslim religious life into a variegated and complex social world. Although most treatises against imitation concentrate nearly exclusively on religious identity, *The Virtue of Awakening*—following the collections of hadiths—embeds religious identity within a broader landscape of identity that spans ethnicity, gender, status, ability, and age. Relations between men and women, Arabs and non-Arabs, free persons and slaves, rich and poor, scholars and commoners, and humans and non-humans (angels, devils, and animals) are included in the treatise. Religious identity, after all, is not the only dimension that determines a Muslim's moral possibilities.

Yet despite the originality and breadth of its subject matter, *The Virtue of Awakening* has gone virtually unnoticed by modern scholars, Muslim and non-Muslim alike.[6] No serious study of this treatise exists in a European language, aside from some passing mentions; even references to it in Islamic scholarship are rare. *The Virtue of Awakening* suffers the dubious distinction of being one of the most underappreciated works of religious scholarship in the history of Islam.

In this long-overdue study, I showcase how Ghazzī's contrapuntal sensibilities as both Sufi and jurist produce a creative, rich, and nuanced discourse on imitation at two junctures in his treatise: at the outset, where he elaborates a robust theory of belonging, and in a fatwa, composed in verse, on attending coffeehouses. But before examining these specific topics at close range, let us first look at the treatise from a distance. The following sketch of its structure and contents affords us a panoramic view that allows us to see how the work's apparently unrelated parts fit together into a coherent whole.

AWAKENING TO THE POWER OF IMITATION

The Virtue of Awakening is held together by a fundamental opposition that underpins the two antipodes of human moral possibility: good and evil. This dichotomy frames the basic structure of Ghazzī's magisterial treatise, which is divided into two types of imitation: good and bad. The association of *tashabbuh* with good expands the term's semantic field beyond a homogeneous association with moral reprehensibility, reflecting the author's attempt at an objective and balanced analysis of the subject matter.

But this binary framework is merely the first-order classification of knowledge in the treatise. Ghazzī's second-order categories indicate that he did not view human behavior through the lens of crude oppositions or absolutes. His moral appraisal of human behavior is in fact heterogeneous, residing along a graduated spectrum of good and evil. This spectrum is expressed through Ghazzī's subcategorization of good imitation and bad imitation into social categories or groups. These groups are then defined by their distinguishing moral attributes that qualify them as either worthy or unworthy of emulation.

As already mentioned, this social taxonomy expresses Ghazzī's vision of an ideal moral order, an order that spans the cosmos. This taxonomy is inspired by the social categories described in both the Quran and the collections of ninth- and tenth-century hadith scholars. One thus sees parallels between the social categories found in these two sources of Islamic revelation and *The Virtue of Awakening*. This "scriptural" framework differentiates Ghazzī's treatise from previous encyclopedic ventures, which were guided by a specific discipline, such as history, or a topic, such as animals, or, in the opposite vein, attempted to include all available knowledge. Ghazzī's organizational framework does not resemble that of the Mamluk Egyptian historian Nuwayrī (d. 1333), for example, who arranged his encyclopedia according to a different organizing principle that was not bound to scripture: cosmos, earth, plants, animals, humans, and history. Through this contrast, one may thus discern the primary audience that Ghazzī was attempting to reach: the Muslim scholarly elite, Arab and Rumi, within the Ottoman Empire. Put differently, *The Virtue of Awakening* anchors Ghazzī's vision of orthodox Islam in the social technology of imitation.

Part 1, on praiseworthy imitation, begins with a chapter on angels, who perform many of the same mundane daily tasks that humans do: they pray, repent, colorfully style their dress, and even brush their "teeth" with a toothstick. Ghazzī then turns his attention to human beings, with four chapters that follow a Quranic social taxonomy (Q 4:69) of exemplars: pious folk (*ṣāliḥīn*), martyrs (*shuhadā'*), true servants (*ṣiddiqīn*), and prophets (*anbiyā'*). Qualities of the pious include virtues such as gratitude, patience, generosity, and exemplary conduct in ritual, belief, and other matters. True servants, as modeled by the Companion Abū Bakr, possess four essential attributes: renunciation of the world, unwavering belief in divine decree, honesty in all affairs, and consistency in upholding these virtues. Prophets embody similar virtues to those of the pious but do so more holistically.

Part 2, on blameworthy imitation, is more extensive (about 60 percent of the treatise's content) and is arranged into three primary groups: Satan, unbelievers, and transgressors (*fasaqa*). These groups are further divided into subgroups. Unbelievers fall into a number of subcategories: damned communities (such as those of Noah and Pharoah), Jews and Christians, pagans, non-Arabs, and hypocrites (*munāfiqūn*). The category of transgressors, which catalogues different types of wayward Muslims, is subdivided into two main groups: religious innovators (from a Sunni perspective) and non-innovators. To map the sectarian landscape of religious innovators, Ghazzī, like Muslim heresiographers of the past, followed the blueprint of the well-known "seventy-three sects" hadith discussed earlier, naming non-Sunni "heterodox" sects such as the Qādiriyya, Murji'a, Khawārij, and Shi'a.

The category of non-innovators includes a number of groups not inherently corrupt, including children, the insane, and the unlettered, but that nonetheless are unworthy of imitation due to their inferior social status, according to Ghazzī and like-minded elites. Their counterparts—adults, the sane, and the *'ulamā'*—however, are worthy of imitation due to their superior social status. So children *should* imitate adults, but adults should not imitate children; the insane *should* imitate the sane, but the sane should not imitate the insane; and the unlettered *should* imitate the *'ulamā'*, but *'ulamā'* should not imitate the unlettered. In each of these pairs, one member is the spiritual and moral exemplar for the other.

But other categories of non-innovators, such as women, slaves, the poor, and Bedouin Arabs, ought to maintain a different mimetic relationship with their counterparts. Although these non-innovators are hierarchically inferior to their counterparts—men, free persons, the rich, settled Arabs—they should nonetheless remain socially distinct from them. Put differently, they should neither imitate nor be imitated, that is, men and women, free persons and slaves, rich and poor, and Bedouin and settled Arabs should not imitate each other.

The final, unexpectedly long section on animals (nearly two volumes of the printed edition) is an outlier.[7] This category, unlike the others, is divided into both praiseworthy and blameworthy imitation, where some animals deserve emulation and others do not. Some animals, including select species of birds, insects, and four-legged animals, receive praise for their exemplary behavior. These habits include waking up early for prayer like a rooster, longing for one's homeland like an eagle, revering the *ʿulamāʾ* like speechless animals, being productively useful like a bee, and being nimble like a gazelle. By contrast, dogs and other species of animals are criticized for their poor etiquette. Some of these blameworthy traits include becoming obsessed with the material world like a monkey, sniffing gluttonously before eating food like a dog, overworking like an ant, usurping someone else's property like a snake, and rejecting acts of generosity like a donkey. Throughout *The Virtue of Awakening*, Ghazzī often draws analogies to the habits of lowly animals when criticizing a blameworthy human trait, implying that such behaviors are expressions of a person's animal soul that has yet to evolve.

As Elias Muhanna has observed, encyclopedic works like *The Virtue of Awakening* are "antiquarian"; they transmit and preserve the inherited wisdom of a civilization.[8] Ghazzī transmits information found in earlier Arabic compilatory texts. In one instance, Ghazzī describes the monkey's lustful habit of performing fellatio on itself, on the authority of a Mamluk-era treatise on animals. In another, he describes the dog's habit of showing respect to men of high status while barking at men of lowly status, a detail found in Mamluk-era encyclopedias as well. It was not necessarily the presence of new information that made compilatory works like *The Virtue of Awakening* "original," Muhanna observes; it was the creation of new connections between disparate domains of knowledge, much of which was already known, that distinguished them.[9]

Why does Ghazzī arrange *The Virtue of Awakening* in this order? Ghazzī does not disclose the reasoning behind his arrangement of *The Virtue of Awakening* until its conclusion. The treatise begins with angels and ends with animals, Ghazzī explains, because these creatures represent the two antipodes of human moral possibility: it is through imitation that a human may attain the lofty rank of the angels or may descend to the lowly rank of the beasts. For similar reasons, Ghazzī juxtaposes the sections on divine and satanic attributes in the middle of the treatise to signal that a spiritual aspirant who fails to adopt godly attributes is destined to become "Satan's companion."[10] Ghazzī ends *The Virtue of Awakening* with a homily on seeking forgiveness to remind the reader that the main purpose of the treatise is to chart a spiritual path to redemption.

The sources of *The Virtue of Awakening* are many. Ghazzī draws from the genres of creed, Quranic exegesis, collections of hadiths and their commentaries, legal treatises and responsa, historical chronicles, biographical dictionaries, Arabic lexicons, treatises on ethics and Sufism, and compendia on animals and miscellany. Based on the quantity of works cited, he draws most from members of his school—Jalāl al-Dīn al-Ṣuyūṭī (d. 1505), Sharaf al-Dīn al-Nawawī (d. 1277), and Ghazālī—but he also draws from the Ḥanbalī scholars Ibn al-Jawzī (d. 1201) and Ibn Abī Dunya (d. 894), the Sufi Ibn ʿArabī (d. 1240), and works composed by his father, Badr al-Dīn al-Ghazzī (d. 1577), and grandfather, Raḍī al-Dīn al-Ghazzī (d. 1529). His copious references to prominent Sufi figures such as Abū al-Qāsim al-Qushayrī (d. 1072), Ḥārith al-Muḥāsibī (d. 857), Sahl al-Tustarī (d. 896), and Ghazālī demonstrate that Ghazzī was deeply immersed in a Sufi spiritual and intellectual genealogy.

A close reading of the treatise indicates that Ghazzī harbored anxieties over Ibn Taymiyya's influence. Although Ghazzī borrows much from *The Obligation of Following the Straight Path* without attribution, he retains a critical stance toward his Damascene predecessor, reiterating the criticisms of scholars like Ṣuyūṭī, who accuses Ibn Taymiyya of theological anthropomorphism.[11] Ghazzī also criticizes his controversial legal opinion that a marriage is not dissolved if a husband makes three pronouncements of divorce in a single enunciation—an opinion that dissented from long-established precedent.[12]

These theological and legal differences are also reflected in the authors' different approaches to *tashabbuh;* each composed his treatise for different reasons and for different audiences. Seeking to contribute something entirely novel to Islamic scholarship, Ghazzī employs a sober rhetorical style that appeals to an academic audience of scholars, whereas Ibn Taymiyya employs a forceful and polemical style of argumentation to deter Muslims from participating in unsanctioned festivals (*ʿīds*). Ultimately, *The Virtue of Awakening* and *The Obligation of the Straight Path* are two very different treatises.

But why the tepid reception? Perhaps the most compelling explanation is that *The Virtue of Awakening* is too long; Ghazzī's inclusion of all available knowledge on imitation may have undermined the treatise's accessibility. *The Obligation of the Straight Path,* which can fit into a single published volume today, gained more traction, especially in modern times. It mattered little that, by comparison, *The Virtue of Awakening* comprehends far more knowledge.[13] That the treatise defied easy categorization into one of the conventional (and thus recognizable) Islamic disciplines, such as law (*fiqh*), theology (*kalam*), hadith, or Quranic exegesis (*tafsīr*), may have also lessened its appeal to a broader audience.

GHAZZĪ BETWEEN TEXT AND CONTEXT

Why did Ghazzī spend nearly forty years writing and revising a treatise on imitation? To understand Ghazzī's ambitions, and the conditions that inspired them, we need to know something of his life and times. According to Muḥibbī, a contemporary whose biography is based on Ghazzī's autobiographical accounts, he was born in 1570 into a family of religious scholars who originated from Gaza in Palestine and eventually migrated to Damascus (figure 13).[14] His father, Badr al-Dīn al-Ghazzī, the prominent chief Shāfiʿī judge of Damascus, initiated Najm al-Dīn and his brothers into the city's cosmopolitan religious culture. In his autobiographical account, Ghazzī credits his father for kindling his interest in piety and learning at a very young age:

> I grew up in the care and protection of my father until I reached seven years of age. I would read to him small sections from the Quran, and was with him on *ʿīd al-fiṭr* the year he passed away. One day I said to him: "O Father, I want to read to you from the beginning of chapter 'The Cow' [*al-Baqara*]." He replied: "Do you know how to read it?" I replied: "Yes." He said, "Bring me a copy of the Quran." So I brought him a copy and read to him. . . . So, that day, he gifted me four silver coins to get me excited. He then instructed me to fast the month of Ramadan, though I was just six years old. He gave me a silver coin for each day [I fasted], until I fasted a majority of the month. That kindled my interest and was good pedagogy on his part. The following year, the year he passed away, I fasted every day, except just one or two days.[15]

After his father died, Ghazzī continued his religious education. Ghazzī studied with teachers from Damascus as well as other Ottoman centers of learning, such as Aleppo, Mecca, and Egypt. His curriculum blended the knowledge traditions of Sufism and shariʿa. Ghazzī was initiated into the Qādirī Sufi order and studied both Shāfiʿī and Ḥanafī jurisprudence, composing legal responsa for thirty-five years (1616–51) until he died. This extensive training earned him the privilege of teaching the public at the Umayyad mosque, under the hallowed cupola of the eagle (*qubbat al-nasr*), for twenty-seven years. His

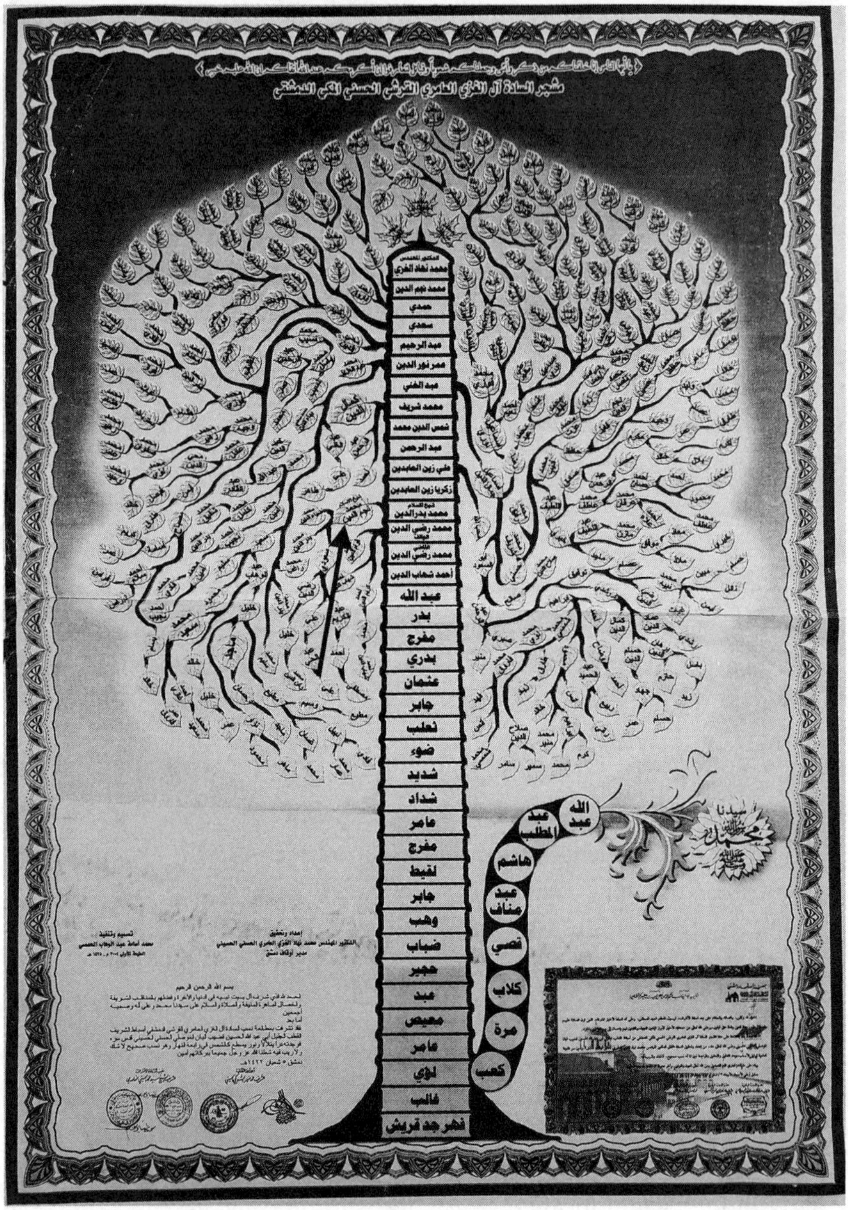

Figure 13. Ghazzī family tree. The arrow points to Najm al-Dīn.
(Courtesy of the Ghazzī family, Damascus.)

students included adherents from all four Sunni schools of law—Shāfiʿī, Ḥanafī, Ḥanbalī, and Mālikī. While controversy did not appear to follow Ghazzī as it did Ibn Taymiyya, he nonetheless became involved in some public disputes concerning his academic career with fellow *ʿulamāʾ*.[16]

Ghazzī was a prolific author. He composed approximately fifty works, fewer than half of which survive, on a wide range of subjects including grammar, rhetoric, poetry, jurisprudence, medicine, Sufism, ethics, hadith, Quranic exegesis, history, and travel.[17] As was customary among *ʿulamāʾ* of his time, his writings encompass a variety of literary forms—commentaries, supercommentaries, verifications, abridgements, and rhyming prose. While he excelled as a scholar of hadith, he is known today for his biographies of Muslim notables living in Ottoman Arab lands during the sixteenth and early seventeenth centuries.[18]

Ghazzī stayed aloof from politics, despite the increasing involvement of religious scholars in government during the sixteenth century. "The gradual affiliation of scholars with the government," argues Abdurrahman Atçıl, "was a development that was perhaps unprecedented in Islamic history."[19] They worked in the scribal, financial, judicial, and military sectors of the Ottoman administration. In fact, establishing a centralized bureaucracy, Atçıl claims, was one of the key distinguishing features of early modern empires.[20] However, in contrast to Ibn Taymiyya, who had the ear of the Mamluk sultan, Ghazzī was busy composing treatises *against* political participation, such as *Preventing the Brothers from Approaching the Sultan* (*Zajar al-ikhwān ʿan ityān al-sulṭān*), a versified form (*naẓm*) of a treatise authored by the Egyptian Shāfiʿī jurist Ṣuyūṭī that warns against the seduction of power: "Guard against kings and sultans according to the measure of [their] strength and power / for the hellfire touches the one who relies on them while the one who arrives at their doorsteps is seduced."[21]

The more political power involved, the higher the spiritual stakes become, for once someone has entered the sultan's orbit, it is very difficult to escape corruption. In another set of verses, Ghazzī—rephrasing Ṣuyūṭī—urges religious scholars, as trustees of the Prophet Muhammad, to be especially cautious:

The jurists—they are exalted in rank and are the trustees of the Messenger
Unless they mix with the sultans or unless they lose themselves in worldly matters, for they are the *ʿulamāʾ*
So they must be suspicious and cautious, and they must withdraw, then remain apart

If they are people of good faith and fulfill their promise to the messengers
And how can those who betray the messengers of our Lord while they are venerated *not* be suspected?[22]

Because he urged the *ʿulamāʾ* to stay far away from the halls of power, we may assume that Ghazzī was not merely indifferent but hostile to political life. However, his actual behavior reveals a more moderate and nuanced outlook. By granting permission to Ottoman officials to lead a belated funeral prayer (*ṣalāt al-ghāʾib*) for the deceased Ottoman sultan Ahmed I (d. 1617) at the Umayyad mosque on January 11, 1618, Ghazzī publicly acknowledged the officials' authority and the sultan's legitimacy. He also cultivated relationships with administrative officials, seeking to achieve mutually beneficial interests such as ridding society of corruption and oppressive taxes.[23] So, although Ghazzī remained deeply suspicious of direct involvement in political affairs, he was not outrightly hostile, maintaining a pragmatic outlook on the potential convergences between religion and politics.

The Ottoman Empire at the turn of the seventeenth century had fallen into a state of crisis that some thought would lead to its collapse.[24] A currency inflation catastrophe, population swells, peasant lawlessness, rebellions, climate change, rising power of the janissaries, and millenarian fever precipitated a sense of insecurity and anxiety among Ottoman religious and state authorities over the social, political, and economic well-being of the realm.[25] In their efforts to restore order to a disintegrating empire, these authorities "transformed crisis into a novel form of political analysis" that idealized the past as a golden age and framed the present as a period of decline.[26] "I imagine our age as a destitute invalid," complains Ghazzī, "when every sparrow becomes a vulture."[27] In this dim view of Ottoman society, collective morality is so impoverished and systemic corruption is so widespread that even a harmless person transforms into a harmful predator who preys on the weak and poor.

Ghazzī's pessimism was fueled, in part, by the ongoing presence of foreign rule in Arab lands. Although the Ottomans displaced the Mamluks as sovereigns of the central Arab Islamic provinces, from an Arab point of view they were still foreign Turks—even if they espoused Sunni Islam. Arabs called the Ottomans Arwām (s. al-Rūm), an ambiguous but derogatory term once used to describe the Christian Romans that underscored their otherness.[28] The ongoing tensions resulting from Arab-Turkish ethnic differences occasionally bubbled to the surface in Ghazzī's writings when Arabs were portrayed as superior to non-Arabs.

Ibn Taymiyya shared these views, as did other Ottoman Arab scholars. During a bitter dispute with a rival Turkish scholar, ʿAbd al-Ghanī al-Nābulusī (d. 1731), a Damascene Sufi jurist who counted Ghazzī among his first teachers, reminds the Turkish "boor" of the superiority of "the Arab mind"—quoting Ghazzī at length from *The Virtue of Awakening:* "There is no doubt that the Arabs' logic is better, their expression clearer, and their language the most perfect in eloquence and the ability to differentiate [between nuances]. . . . The Arab mind is the most perfect, since language is the expression of one's understanding. Therefore, the Arab mind has no need of training by the formal apparatus called the science of logic in order to understand ideas and sciences and to protect it from error, unlike the minds of the non-Arabs."[29]

The keenness of Arab minds is perhaps matched only by their noble character, which, in Ghazzī's view, "is more inclined than others to gentleness, forgiveness, tolerance, generosity, courage, loyalty, and other noble qualities."[30] Nevertheless, his ethnic pride did not blind him to the virtuous traits of non-Arabs, such as the "Rumi" chief jurisconsult (*şeyhülislam*) Ebuʾs-suʿud (d. 1574), whom Ghazzī eulogized: "I have not seen among the *mawālī* of Rum someone more intelligent or more eager to learn than he."[31]

A different type of inter-Muslim tension emerged along the geographic frontier between the Ottoman and Safavid Empires. The Ottoman state tried to accommodate its Shiʿi Muslim subjects, but religious authorities like Ebuʾs-suʿud singled out the Qizilbash supporters of the Safavid shahs for opprobrium due to their distinctive Shiʿi creed and practice.[32] The competition between the imperial rivals for territorial sovereignty over eastern Anatolia, the Caucasus, and Iraq erupted into a series of military conflicts (1532–55, 1578–90, 1603–18, 1623–39) that sharpened the Ottoman state's Sunni identity.[33]

Ongoing inter-Muslim conflict overlapped with protracted conflict between the Ottoman and Austrian-Habsburg Empires, which exposed longstanding Muslim-Christian rivalries. In the battle of Keresztes (Haçova), which took place in 1596 during the Long Turkish War (1593–1606), the Ottoman army put the Habsburg army to flight after initially facing a rout. Seyyid Lokman's illustrated history (figure 14) captures this reversal in fortune, depicting Ottoman soldiers on foot, camelback, and horseback in hot pursuit of terrified Hungarian soldiers, distinguished by their black attire, as they retreat from battle. Other representations of the battle portray a swift decent into mayhem, as civilians enter into the fray. In one miniature, a brave but foolish Ottoman cook strikes a sword-wielding Austrian soldier with a pot in the heat of battle.[34] But as Palmira Brummett observes, artists could represent the

Figure 14. *The Battle of Haçova (Keresztes) in Hungary in 1596. When the Ottomans Vanquished the Hapsburg Forces.* From Seyyid Lokman's history of Mehmed III's campaign in Hungary. (The David Collection, Copenhagen, No. 10/2000, fols. 17v, 18r. Photographer: Pernille Klemp.)

battle according to the image they wanted to portray. One Austrian artist allegedly depicted a scene of the courageous Habsburgs terrifying the Ottomans at Keresztes—a graphic denial of Christian defeat.[35]

How would these military conflicts on the borders of Europe configure Muslim interreligious relations within the borders of the Ottoman Empire, where a visible minority presence of Jewish and Christian subjects remained? In 1569, one year before Ghazzī's birth, Christians and Jews may have comprised greater than 20 percent of the population of Damascus.[36] The Ottoman Empire's Jewish population continued to expand with the emigration of exiled Jews from Spain and Portugal.[37] In Istanbul, Venetian Christians traded with Muslims at markets in the Jerrahpasha district, indicating that interreligious encounters within the empire were not always defined by conflict.[38]

Given this conviviality, it was common for Jews and Christians to adopt Muslim cultural practices such as styles of dress. In the second half of the sixteenth century, Jews imitated Turkish Muslim dress in all aspects but color.[39] Jewish and Christian men grew beards and women wore headscarves. Even non-Muslim elites in eastern European countries such as Poland emulated Ottoman sartorial styles. Their external resemblance reached such a degree that during the 1683 Ottoman siege of Vienna, some Polish soldiers attached straw sprigs to their headgear in order to distinguish themselves from their Turkish enemies![40] However, the potential for role reversal was also possible, as depicted in figure 15. In this illustration of an early seventeenth-century poem by ʿAṭāʾī (d. 1621), Ṭayyib and Ṭāhir, young Ottomans on their way to Egypt to become dervishes, are captured by Christians, but soon fall in love with their captors and eventually adopt their European style of dress as their affection propels them across boundaries of religion and gender.

Such social boundary crossing incited anxieties over mimesis among religious and political authorities alike. Exercising his imperial prerogative, Sultan Murad III (r. 1574–95) revived the sartorial restrictions on Christians and Jews. Seeking to deter non-Muslim elites from imitating the prestigious dress of Muslim elites, the first of these decrees, or *firmans,* issued in 1577, prohibited Jews and Christians from wearing silk and sandals colored red or white.[41] A second decree in 1579 ordered that Jews and Christians replace their turban with conical hats: red for Jews and black for Christians.[42] But the most punitive of these decrees was issued when Murad III heard that a Jewish lady had publicly flaunted her social status with ornaments and jewelry on the streets of Constantinople; the sultan impulsively mandated the extermination of all the empire's Jews. One wonders what might have happened if an influential

Figure 15. Ṭayyib (*standing before canopy, rightmost*) and Ṭāhir (*seated under canopy, rightmost*) in European attire at a party with their Christian captors (rescuers?). In *Hamse* (*Quintet*), composed by ʿAṭāʾī (d. 1621), illustrated by Heyrullah Heyri Çavuszade, 1721. (The Walters Art Museum, Baltimore, no. W.666, fol. 138r.)

Ashkenazi Jewish couple, Murad's grand vizier, and his own mother had not intervened, persuading him to rescind the decree.[43]

But dress was just one of many material objects that culturally mediated Muslim encounters with non-Muslims. Another object was the alarm clock. It had become customary for European ambassadors to gift the Ottoman court with alarm clocks, a recent invention coveted by fashionable Turkish Europhiles.[44] A critic of this trend, Ghazzī complains that these alarm clocks sonically transmitted Christian sounds across European borders into Muslim lands, displacing Muslim sounds like the *adhān*.[45] Impersonal mechanical alarms, Ghazzī feared, would silence the *adhān*'s live voices, the iconic sound of Muslim difference. At the same time they were importing European objects, Muslims were unwittingly assimilating European culture, erasing the distinctive features of Islamic civilization in the process.

Part of the *adhān*'s symbolic value derives from its power to define a space as Islamic. Physical spaces, like physical objects, mediated interreligious encounters in Ottoman Damascus as they did in Mamluk Damascus. Both eras were plagued by the spread of new disruptive social spaces. While Mamluk Damascus was afflicted by the spread of unsanctioned *ʿīds*—festivals, funerals, and tomb visitations—Ottoman Damascus was beset by the spread of coffeehouses, an institution that had diffused throughout Ottoman lands during the sixteenth century. Both social spaces brought together people belonging to different religions, classes, and cultures, dissolving the lines of difference that commonly separated these groups from one another. Like Ibn Taymiyya, Ghazzī was alarmed by the level of cultural sharedness Muslims, Christians, and Jews experienced in these spaces, fearing it might lead to brazen public displays of moral corruption and social disorder.

It is against this historical background that Ghazzī composed *The Virtue of Awakening*, as well as fatwas on coffeehouses, tobacco, and hashish. "The text is expressive of wider socio-economic transformations," one Ottoman cultural historian reminds us. "It is indicative of specific cultural phenomena and is invested with meanings that need to be decoded."[46] But as Ghazzī's monumental treatise also demonstrates, a literary text is composed of a greater discursive context that needs to be decoded. Muslim thinkers throughout Islamic history often drew on the rich spiritual and intellectual heritage of the past to address the pressing challenges of the present. As discussed above, compiling an encyclopedic work was historically a scholastic enterprise that drew upon a repertoire of antiquarian figures, concepts, and sources from past tradition.[47] *The Virtue of Awakening* draws on the Islamic past in order to speak to the Ottoman present.

GHAZZĪ'S UNIVERSAL THEORY OF BELONGING

Amid the vanishing lines of social difference within the realm, Ghazzī resolved to bring discursive clarity to the meaning of group belonging. Presenting a critical engagement with Islamic scripture, Ghazzī commences *The Virtue of Awakening* with an elaborate gloss on the imitation hadith that evolves into a universal theory of human belonging. "One who imitates a people belongs with them," he explains, "because his imitation of them indicates both love and contentment with their moral dispositions and social conventions."[48] Although Ghazzī shares with Ibn Taymiyya the keen observation that imitation is an indicator of affection, Ghazzī's mode of discourse is more exploratory than polemical.

Instead of reading the imitation hadith through the hostile scriptural lens of Q 5:51, Ghazzī does so through a neutral lens of Sufi aphorisms on the nature of love. Imitation, he insists, engenders deep affection. Citing several prominent Sufis—Abū al-Qāsim al-Qushayrī, Ḥārith al-Muḥāsibī, and Sahl al-Tustarī—Ghazzī observes, "Love is conformity."[49] "This is a true statement," elaborates Ghazzī, "because when a human being loves someone, he loves all his habits and virtues. And when he loves all his attributes, he becomes inspired to acquire them and be defined by them."[50] Love is what inspires someone to become like another person and to be associated with him, inwardly and outwardly. On the other hand, the opposite vector is equally true: the more a person comes to emulate and resemble another, the deeper the love and affection between them. Imitation and love exist in a dialectical relationship.

Love is thus essential to understanding what it means to truly belong to any human community. Echoing Suhrawardī, Ghazzī cites the well-known Prophetic hadith "A person belongs with the one he loves" to underscore this point.[51] He also cites the Greek sage Euclid by way of the Persian heresiographer Shahrastānī (d. 1153) to explain how love between two strangers can blossom: "Whoever wants what he loves to become what you love should love what you love; if you both share a single love you will achieve harmony in other areas."[52] Put differently, mutual love grows over time when it is mediated by shared objects of affection.

But what is the origin of this love? Ghazzī insists that the mutual affection shared by human beings on earth has primordial roots, transcending space and time. In this cosmology, human and spirit worlds overlap. Drawing on Suhrawardī, Ghazzī describes how spirits (*arwāḥ*) intermingle in the primordial spirit world before being clothed in human form on earth, where they reunite and reactivate their primordial love.[53] In this sense, "love is a divine affair."[54] This divine imprint ensures that the spirits of true lovers remain intimately connected "even when their physical bodies are far apart."[55] True love transcends the body. But "if their bodies come together one day," Ghazzī informs us, "these meanings will become apparent to them through their appearance, imitation, companionship, and conformity."[56] This kind of love is true and lasting because it springs from divine love, in contrast to love that is false and fleeting, which springs from unbelief (*kufr*). Whether grounded in belief or unbelief, communities are fashioned in the primordial spirit world before coming together on earth.

After their mortal deaths, these same communities will then be resurrected in the eschaton. Communities that were first formed in the spirit world, then reunited on earth, will once again be reunited in the world to come, an event foretold by the Prophet Muhammad: "Whoever loves a people, God will resurrect him in his group."[57] Echoing the Prophet, Ghazzī adds the following apocalyptic gloss to the imitation hadith: "Whoever adopts the ways of a people and loves them becomes one of them and belongs with them in this life and the next."[58] A person's community in this world will become his community in the world to come.

Not all modes of emulation, however, engender such lasting love and communal belonging. Because some forms of imitation are clearly inauthentic, Ghazzī distinguishes between two essential types of *tashabbuh:* true imitation and superficial imitation. True belonging, he believes, is grounded in deeply felt emotions: "When someone conforms to all the behaviors and moral qualities that define a specific community, he becomes one of them and belongs with them, without any doubt, because his love enables him to acquire all their attributes, and mirror all their spiritual states, which then propel him to the highest ranks of love. So how can he not belong with them!" To truly follow and, ultimately, become like another person or belong to another community, one must have a strong connection to them (*nisba ilayhim*).[59] This sense of belonging, Ghazzī recognizes, is strengthened by other feelings besides love, such as contentment, admiration, and attraction, which bind individuals to their community.[60] It is this deep affection that inspires a person to emulate someone else's character, habits, and spiritual states—a holistic mimesis that defines true *tashabbuh.* This is a point also made by his Sufi predecessors.

By contrast, superficial imitation is limited to surface-level behavior and affectation. A surface-level imitator only seeks to debate (*munāẓara*), disgrace (*muʿāraḍa*), or poke fun at others—not become like them. According to Ghazzī, this form of emulation signals hostility and enmity, not affection; it is purely external (*ṣūra ẓāhira*) and is not an expression of belonging.[61] To adore only what someone else does, but not the actual person, does not lead to true spiritual and social transformation because it lacks deep affection. True imitation—and true belonging—is felt internally and displayed externally.

Imitation, then, exists in varying intensities. Ghazzī imagines mimesis as a fluid spectrum between the poles of similarity (*muwāfaqa*) and difference (*mukhālafa*).[62] He distills this heterogeneous spectrum of social interaction into three distinct conditions: (1) absolute assimilation (similarity); (2) absolute opposition (difference); and (3) a mixture of similarity and difference. According to Ghazzī, absolute assimilation leads to full communal membership where imitators truly "belong with them," while absolute opposition does not (even if the nonconformists claim, falsely, to love them).[63] One who completely assimilates into a community expresses the highest degree of love (*maḥabba*) for its members, as indicated by Q 3:31 with respect to loving the Prophet: "If you love God, then follow me [Muhammad] and God will then love you." One who sincerely loves the Prophet Muhammad conforms to his behavior in its totality, and earns the honor of becoming God's beloved (*ḥabīb Allāh*). "Following God's beloved proves he truly loves God," explains Ghazzī, "so he too becomes God's beloved."[64]

The socio-spiritual status of believers stuck between conformity and nonconformity is more ambiguous, however, and depends upon the presence (or absence) of love in their hearts for the community.[65] If their hearts are full of faithful adoration, then their interior spiritual state compensates for periodic lapses and safeguards their membership in their community.

There are, of course, other factors besides spiritually inspired emotions like love that define communal membership. Another key factor identified by Ghazzī is religious creed. Ghazzī's perspectives on this dimension lay bare his Sunni theological and Shāfiʿī legal orientation. He endeavors to set limits on the modes of imitation and belonging that are possible between believers and unbelievers in order to safeguard Islamic orthodoxy.

Religious difference—the difference between believer and unbeliever—erects an insurmountable wall between friend and enemy.[66]

> For all hostilities, there is hope of friendship
> Except the hostility of one who shuns your religion.[67]

It is not possible for an unbeliever, regardless of faith, to belong to a community of believers. The true enemy, Ghazzī asserts, "is one who opposes you in religion [*dīn*]."[68] Because "every enemy desires that it be loved," Muslims living among unbelievers are in danger not only of cultivating strong affections for them but, due to the magnetic pull of imitation, becoming one of them. This is a disgraceful outcome, according to Ghazzī, because "loving sinful people is [itself] sinful."[69] If Muslims are outnumbered by unbelievers, they will likely be treated with scorn and disdain, and "a Muslim should never demean himself."[70] For these reasons, Muslims should live among fellow believers, not unbelievers. The Prophet warned, "Whoever adds to a community's population is one of them."[71] However, Ghazzī grants exceptions to spies or those who want to relocate to Muslim territory but cannot due to physical, political, or economic obstacles.[72] Ghazzī's cost-benefit analysis resembles the form of the legal reasoning employed by Ibn Taymiyya, who granted similar exceptions to Muslims living in non-Muslim territories.

Ghazzī's attitude toward Jews and Christians is likewise uncompromising, despite their monotheistic credentials. Loving (*mawadda*) Jews and Christians (*dhimmīs*) is forbidden; even conversing with them at length or being cheerful around them is detested.[73] Although Jews and Christians, like Muslims, expressed their belief in and love for their prophets, Ghazzī dismisses these claims of loyalty on the grounds that they, unlike Muslims, turned away from them.[74] On this matter, Ghazzī declares, the Prophet Muhammad was clear: "Whoever shuns my way does not belong with me."[75] Ghazzī concludes that Jews and Christians discredited themselves by not practicing what they preached. Consistent disobedience to God and His messengers, according to Ghazzī, "is a sign that [one's] love is not true."[76] Community and orthodoxy are intertwined.

But this is not Ghazzī's final word on the matter. He appears to be torn. Despite his theological convictions, his spiritual and ethical sensibilities compel him to retreat from this strict conclusion. Do not all human beings—even the most devout Muslim believers—disobey God on some occasions? Do lapses that are unintentional, resulting from incapacity, weakness, or lack of willpower, carry the same moral value as intentional acts of defiance? Ghazzī concludes that spiritual perfection is not a criterion for membership in the community of believers. Even believers whose worship consistently falls short of the prophetic ideal have good cause to be optimistic—a compassionate view that Ghazzī expresses in poetic verse:

Whoever aspires to reach the farthest station,
On Resurrection Day despite his shortcomings in devotion,

Let him make sincere his love for the Master of Creation, the Chosen One,
For "A person belongs with the one he loves."[77]

These verses express Ghazzī's alacrity to reassure all believers of the power of love to erase sins and join them with the Prophet in the world to come. His message echoes the socially inclusive efforts of Abū Ḥafṣ al-Suhrawardī to bring spiritual novices into the fold of his Sufi community. Indeed, "A person belongs with the one he loves." By concluding with this punch line, Ghazzī reminds the reader once again that love defines true belonging in Islam. Even the most wretched of believers should not fall into spiritual despair as long as their hearts are filled with divine love. On this point, Ghazzī recounts a brief dialogue between God and Satan, on the authority of the eighth-century historian Wahb b. Munabbih:

> SATAN. Your servants love you and disobey you, but they hate me and obey me.
> GOD. I have forgiven them due to their love for me despite their disobeying me, and I have forgiven them for obeying you since they hated you.[78]

Ultimately, deeply felt emotion—not physical practice—defines the ontology of the true believer. A believer's love for Allah triumphs over a lifetime of misdeeds.

THE DEVIL'S LAIR

Nonetheless, setting limits on disobedience continued to preoccupy Ottoman jurists, who debated the vices and virtues of new social habits such as imbibing coffee, smoking tobacco, and mingling at coffeehouses.[79] The rise of these new forms of pleasure produced new forms of sociability that threatened to disrupt established social distinctions and hierarchies and exacerbated perceptions of turbulence and instability among religious elites.[80] Ghazzī himself produced legal responsa (*fatwas*) on coffee, tobacco, and hashish, substances that enjoyed wide usage not only in his native city of Damascus but across the Ottoman Empire.

Paging through Ghazzī's biographical dictionary of sixteenth-century notables, one is struck by the frequent references to coffee.[81] The earliest sources for coffee can be traced back to Yemen and Ethiopia in the late fifteenth century. Coffee drinking and coffeehouses soon spread to Mecca and Cairo, Damascus and Aleppo, and eventually arrived at the imperial capital, Istanbul, in the sixteenth century.[82] The monetary economy that evolved around coffee included the establishment of new guilds of coffee sellers, coffee roasters, and owners of coffeehouses. According to Ghazzī, a Yemeni named Abū Bakr al-ʿAydarūsī first made coffee licit among religious scholars in the latter half of the sixteenth century.[83] Sufis who stayed awake during the late-night hours performing acts of devotion were among the first to extol the miraculous effects of coffee. However, as some religious scholars compared coffee and its yet undetermined effects to the intoxication of alcohol, it did not become legalized in other regions of the Muslim world until the first half of the seventeenth century.[84] During this period of controversy, many associated the habit of drinking coffee, especially in coffeehouses, with larger themes of social critique, debauchery, and decline.

Nobel Prize laureate Orhan Pamuk satirizes pious anxieties over coffee through the voice of a fictional preacher in the historical novel *My Name Is Red,* which takes place in the court of Sultan Murad III in 1591:

> Ah, my devoted believers! The drinking of coffee is an absolute sin! Our Glorious Prophet did not partake of coffee because he knew it dulled the intellect, caused ulcers, hernia and sterility; he understood that coffee was nothing but the Devil's ruse. Coffeehouses are places where pleasure-seekers and wealthy gadabouts sit knee-to-knee, involving themselves in all sorts of vulgar behavior; in fact, even before the dervish houses are closed, coffeehouses ought to be banned. Do the poor have enough money to drink coffee? Men frequent these places, become besotted with coffee and lose control of their mental faculties to the point that they actually listen to and believe what dogs and mongrels have to say.[85]

The preacher's coffeehouse sermon is brimming with satire and irony—mostly due to his muddled sense of time and place. In his ahistorical and inaccurate retelling of the Islamic past, the Prophet avoided coffee because it was unhealthy. But Muslims did not begin consuming coffee until the sixteenth century, nearly a millennium after the Prophet lived, so he (obviously) could not have condemned it because he was unaware of its existence! Betraying his lack of spatial awareness, the preacher delivers his sermon against coffee and coffeehouses *inside* a coffeehouse—precisely where he should not be. The audience can only assume that this preacher is himself one of the "pleasure seekers" and "mongrels" who has lost control of his "mental faculties" and deserves to be ignored.

Although today we may find Pamuk's caricature of the preacher amusing, to early modern *ʿulamāʾ*, drinking coffee was no laughing matter. In the sixteenth century, when coffee drinking was still novel, they associated the drink with a wide range of social ills—not unlike Pamuk's preacher above.

In his biographical dictionary of sixteenth-century notables, Ghazzī praises Ebuʾs-suʿud for issuing a fatwa against drinking coffee when it was still a disputed topic among *ʿulamāʾ*.[86] When Ebuʾs-suʿud was asked if it was licit for someone to drink coffee for health benefits—"to aid concentration and digestion"—he replied, "How can anyone consume this reprehensible [substance], which dissolute men drink when engaged in games and debauchery?"[87] In fact, Ebuʾs-suʿud inspired the Ottoman sultan Sulayman I to ban coffeehouses. When asked about judges who did nothing about "ruffians" who refused to comply with the law, Ebuʾs-suʿud maintained his hard-line opinion: "Judges who neglect to deter them should be dismissed."[88]

By Ghazzī's time, coffeehouses had spread across Damascus, and *ʿulamāʾ* appeared to have settled on a middle position. When an unnamed petitioner, likely an ordinary but literate and devout Muslim living in Damascus, sought Ghazzī's opinion on the legal status of drinking coffee, he responded with a fatwa, in verse (figure 16):

Oh petitioner who comes to us hoping
That we will permit him to drink coffee.

Coffee is not unlawful.
It does not cause the person dizziness,

Except he who frequents coffeehouses.
In them, coffee becomes the nullifier of honor,

Where a person sees beardless youths, musical instruments, and backgammon,
Everything that causes diversion or leads to diversion . . .

All of this contradicts the way delimited
By the Chosen One and leads away from it.

So avoid it and leave the folk who invite you to it
No matter how persuasive their call.

Do not obey them even if they desire of you but one step
So that you obey the Accursed One in every step.

If you wish to drink coffee, even one sip,
You will desire one thousand more.

So let coffee remain in the midst of your home so that
You do not mix its purity with the cause of foolishness.[89]

Ghazzī explains that "coffee is not unlawful" because it does not cause its consumer to become dizzy. Coffee, in other words, neither intoxicates like wine nor harms the body like illicit drugs—eliminating the Islamic legal justification for its outright prohibition. Although Ghazzī could have concluded the fatwa there, he proceeds to the related but different issue of idling in coffeehouses, where coffee miraculously transforms from a harmless beverage into "the nullifier of honor."

Ghazzī's disdain for coffeehouses echoes some of the sentiments expressed by Pamuk's preacher. Like the preacher, Ghazzī claims that the repertoire of immoral practices associated with coffeehouses opposes the Prophet's exemplary conduct. Like the preacher, Ghazzī warns that coffee is part of Satan's ruse to lure unsuspecting believers into a web of sin. And like the preacher, Ghazzī warns against mingling with lowly folk in the coffeehouse.

Unlike the preacher, however, Ghazzī avoids the temptation of falling into absolutes. Coffee itself is not the problem, according to Ghazzī; it is rather where and with whom a person drinks coffee. A specific social practice gains cultural meaning and moral value within a network of other social practices that are located within a particular space. Put simply, it is the spatial and social context that matters. Drinking coffee is thus only a problem inside coffeehouses. The intimate relationship between coffee and the place in which it was consumed is also reflected in linguistic convention. One of the indigenous words for coffeehouse was *qahwa,* which is the name of coffee itself. The perception of the coffeehouse as a space of moral reprehensibility inevitably tainted the reputation of the drink. So, although a colorful range of practices may have characterized social life in the coffeehouse, it was still coffee, as both symbol and substance, that defined, and was defined by, the space.[90]

Ghazzī's anxieties over the coffeehouse also stem from its doubleness, its capacity to blur the line between public and private. In *The Virtue of Awakening,* Ghazzī discusses the coffeehouse in a subsection titled "On Loitering in the Marketplaces," indicating that he imagined the coffeehouse not in isolation but *in relation to* commercial life. Drawing from hadith, Ghazzī perceives the marketplace, and by extension the coffeehouse, as Satan's house of worship. "The coffeehouse is the devil's lair," Ghazzī writes, "because it is a market that is actually a house, or a house that is actually a market."[91] The coffee-*house,* as its English name suggests, juxtaposed the contrasting spaces

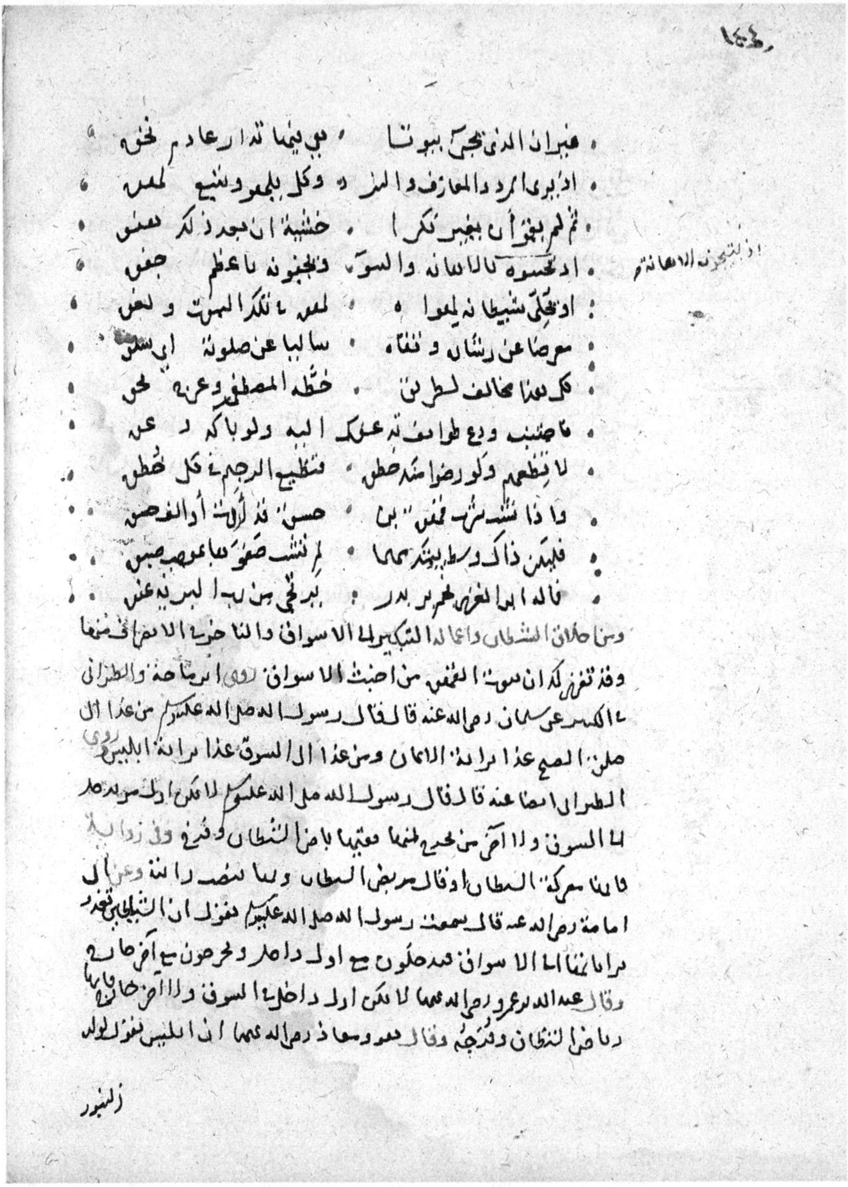

Figure 16. Ghazzī's handwritten fatwa (begins on p. 177) on drinking coffee from *The Virtue of Awakening* (*Ḥusn al-tanabbuh*), February 13, 1626. (Chester Beatty Library, Dublin, Arabic 3216, vol. 3, fols. 62r–62v.)

بيت الفقر

عقد باطل او كذب او غش او غبن لاحد المتعاقدين فيتشمت ويعرض لخطيئة الدم
وروى الترمذي وصححه عن قيس بن ابي غرزة رضي الله عنه قال مر علينا رسول الله
ونحن نسمى السماسرة فقال يا معشر التجار ان الشيطان والاثم يحضران البيع
فشوبوا بيعكم بالصدقة دون مسامحة. النهي عن البيع في المسجد وروى الترمذي
والحاكم وصححاه عن عثمان بن كعب رضي الله عنه قال قال رسول الله صلى الله عليه وسلم
اذا رايتم من يبيع او يبتاع في المسجد فقولوا لا اربح الله تجارتك واذا رايتم
من ينشد فيه ضالة فقولوا لا رد الله عليك. التنبيه الثاني ان السوق
ماوى الشيطان لانه سوقه سعى لنا او ستة سعى لسوق بل لوا فيه الاسواق
لان اللغط والمعاصي التي تصدر فيه اكثر مما يصدر عن غيره من الاسواق ولانه محل
مستقذر ويبغضه الله بالرحمة اليسيرة وحسبنه بالبين وقد علمت ان الكل تكرار يصدر
نحو ماوى الشيطان واستقذار من جهة المنكرات المتتابعة مما دابة النفس
الدنية كما انذار النفس المتكبرة وبذلك تنقلب حرمة بعد ما كانت مباحة ومن
الامراء على النظر الى المرد المتبعين باحسن من تبعل النساء. وبعض الذكور عامهم
لطلب زمرة المناجين منهم واكل الحشيشة والامرين بحضرة الطبيعة عن ما
من المسكرات والمخدرات والاكباب على الات اللهو واستماعها واللعب
بالنرد والطاب وغيرها واللغو والرفث والخوض في الباطل والغيبة والنميمة
والكذب والاكاذيب والمضحكات والمواعدة على السوء وغير ذلك مما لا يشك
في انه من اعظم الحرام الا ان يكون محمودا في الجملة وقد اجبت عن سؤال الصورة

• ايها الفاضل الذي جمع العلم • وحاز التقى فاصبح قدوة •
• افتنا انت بعد تمهيد حلال • ام حرام على الورى منه حظه •

فقال

• ايها السائل الذي جاء يرجو • عندنا ان يبين منه حكمه •
• حكمه الحق لا نكون حراما • انما لا تفيد في النفس نشوة •

of market and home, creating a new kind of space altogether, a heterotopic space.[92] Heterotopia, Michel Foucault proposed, is "capable of juxtaposing in a single real place several spaces, several sites that are in themselves incompatible."[93] Ghazzī and like-minded *ʿulamāʾ* perceived coffeehouses as socially disorienting spaces defined by multiplicity. According to one Ottoman historian, coffeehouses were "spaces with connections to the neighbourhood, home and market that made them at once familiar but contemporaneously novel in the way that men could gather within them as spaces of layered functionality and a multitude of ambiences."[94] Scrambling the familiar and novel, public and private, transformed the coffeehouse into a new kind of space altogether—a "devil's lair." This heterotopic space incubated satanic imitation across social classes, blurring the differences between them. As discussed in chapter 3, Muslims characterized diabolic gestures as ambiguous and contradictory, as perpetually in-between. For Ghazzī, in-betweenness, and the social disorder it inspired, became a defining feature of the coffeehouse.

But how did the coffeehouse erase this line between home and market? The problem was that the coffeehouse had become a unique space where the conventional rules governing public decorum did not apply.[95] It also meant that God's law, as the *ʿulamāʾ* saw it, could be easily transgressed. Ghazzī enumerates some of the sinful practices that took place in coffeehouses, such as playing backgammon and musical instruments, consorting with beardless youths, smoking hashish, consuming opium, and engaging in idle talk. *ʿUlamāʾ* considered these habits, if unchecked, as *lahw,* or unnecessary diversions from the ideal Muslim way of life.[96] Coffee, though itself licit, nevertheless became entangled in a web of sinful practices that cast a negative value on the drink among *ʿulamāʾ*.[97] The consumption of intoxicating substances such as tobacco, opium, and hashish became entwined with the spread of coffee drinking and helped produce a new sociability that revolved around pleasure.[98] Ghazzī believed that smoking induced slovenliness, a characteristic that he associated with non-Muslims, and composed a separate treatise prohibiting the use of cannabis.[99] It was the coffeehouse that provided a space for these addictive substances to be consumed together.

A repertoire of embodied practices thus both came to define and was defined by the coffeehouse. Embodied practice, according to Henri Lefebvre, "produces itself in spaces and also produces that space," suggesting that there is a dialectical relationship between a human body and the space it inhabits.[100] This relationship, in turn, is mediated by the physical senses: sight, hearing, touch, taste, and smell. Like the *ʿīd*s vehemently opposed by Ibn

Taymiyya, the coffeehouse stimulated all five senses. Pleasure-seekers might gaze at handsome youths, listen to music and gossip, rub up against the riff-raff of Ottoman society, drink coffee (of course), and inhale thick fumes of tobacco smoke. By warning believers against committing these illicit practices in his fatwa, Ghazzī attempts to safeguard Muslim sense and sensibility from the corrupting effects of the coffeehouse.

But if coffee did not alter the mind, as did wine, why does Ghazzī warn, "If you wish to drink coffee, even one sip / You will desire one thousand more"? A popular saying on display at several Ottoman coffeehouses offers a clue: "The heart desires neither coffee nor a coffee house. The heart desires conversation. Coffee is simply an excuse."[101] So coffee itself was not the problem, rather that it served as a pretext for people to come together, to cultivate old friendships and meet new people. It was not that people could not socialize elsewhere—in the home or at the mosque and market—but that they socialized differently at the coffeehouse; they had fun. "There was no place where you could enjoy yourself so much," wrote the Ottoman Bosnian historian İbrahim Peçevi (d. 1650). "It became impossible to find a seat."[102] The social pleasures of the coffeehouse became so intoxicating that, according to scholar, historian, and bibliographer Kâtib Çelebi (d. 1657), "working for one's living fell into disfavor."[103] More problematic for the *ʿulamāʾ*, however, was that people also became distracted from prayer: "Nobody went any more to the mosques."[104] It was thus not a physical addiction to coffee that compelled folks to drink more and more, but a social addiction to good company.

But in the view of Ghazzī and other critics, good company at coffeehouses too often mixed with bad company. Coffeehouses scrambled social distinctions—undermining what I have argued is Ghazzī's main objective in composing *The Virtue of Awakening*. Elite and commoner, rich and poor, sat around the same table drinking, smoking, and laughing together. "Dismissed officials, judges, medrese [*sic*] teachers and the unemployed and idle . . . and even imams, muezzins, blue-robed religious figures, and ordinary people," observes Peçevi, "became addicted to the coffee house."[105] The British traveler Charles White also took note of the mixing of class and rank at Ottoman coffeehouses, describing them as "the solace of the rich and the principal sustenance of the poor."[106] Ottoman bureaucrat Muṣṭafā ʿĀlī (d. 1600) observed that the poor were "content with coffee as a liquid and roasted coffee-beans and one or two dry biscuits as solid food."[107] Although Ghazzī recounts that his father, Badr al-Dīn, would host daily meals during Ramadan attended by both the rich and poor, unfettered class mixing was viewed by Ottoman elites as a source of corruption.[108] On some occasions, according to Çelebi, the social mixture at coffeehouses became volatile, leading to violence: "The people, from prince to beggar, amused themselves with knifing one another."[109] As Ghazzī mentions, coffeehouses disrupted sexual boundaries as well; beardless youths were in full view of the penetrating male gaze, although illicit sexual relations should be confined to the private sphere. To ensure that the line between private and public spheres remained clear, Ghazzī permitted coffee consumption only when detached from the disruptive semi-public space of the coffeehouse—safe within the well-defined boundaries of the private home.

In a period of unprecedented crisis at the turn of the seventeenth century, coffee and coffeehouses became a metonym for the upheaval and disorder that religious and political elites aimed to prevent. Likes religious scholars, Ottoman government bureaucrats were troubled by the social life of coffeehouses—although their motives and methods of intervention were different. Archival records indicate that government spies frequented coffeehouses to eavesdrop on the conversations of potential troublemakers.[110] Surveillance of coffeehouses became so common that Ottoman officials coined the term "state talk" to describe the rumor-mongering that occurred there.[111] They feared suspects might incite civil unrest, undermining the security and stability of the Ottoman state. Their anxieties were not born of irrational paranoia. Many uprisings against the Ottoman sultan, some of which originated from within the government itself, began in coffeehouses.[112] The janissaries, an elite guard within the Ottoman army, built their own coffeehouses, which were distinguished by an emblem hung over the entrance and painted on the walls.[113] Linking space to body, this emblem was also tattooed onto the janissaries' upper arms, visible to the public. Although intended to forge group solidarity, these coffeehouses became incubators of sedition. To thwart a janissary uprising, Osman II (r. 1618–22) took the drastic step of shutting down their coffeehouses, a poor calculation that ultimately led to his imprisonment and death.[114] Yet Sultan Murad IV (r. 1623–40) acted even more aggressively, banning coffeehouses, along with the sale and consumption of wine, opium, and tobacco, in 1633, two weeks after a great fire destroyed nearly 20 percent of the city.[115] The conflagration visually symbolized the chaos that had been slowly burning inside the coffeehouses. Whether done to prevent another fire, undermine another potential janissary uprising, or reaffirm social hierarchies leveled by the coffeehouses, the ban sought to restore order in the imperial capital. Nevertheless, hundreds were executed for disregarding the law, according to Çelebi, who recognized the futility of prohibiting addictive substances like coffee, tobacco, and wine. Prohibiting a custom that is "second nature" only compounds the problem because, in Çelebi's words, "men desire what is forbidden."[116] So the prohibition was eventually revoked and coffeehouses reopened (although they had never closed outside Istanbul).[117] By the seventeenth century, coffeehouses had become a part of Ottoman everyday life that could not be undone.

POEISIS

Buried deep within *The Virtue of Awakening,* in the section on imitating the devil under the subheading "Dressing Like Someone Else to Disguise One's Identity," Ghazzī transmits a strange story about Satan's attempt to impersonate Jesus.[118] One day, Satan visits the home of an unsuspecting Christian monk. He knocks on the door and proclaims, "Receive me, for I am Jesus!" Skeptical that Jesus has returned to earth in this form, the monk tartly replies, "If you are Jesus, then I have no need of you. Did you not command that we devote our time to worship, and did you not warn us to prepare for the Day of Judgment? Leave and take care of your affair." Outwitted by the monk, who sees through his ruse, Satan departs.

In his commentary on the encounter, Ghazzī takes us from the magically real to the ordinary—from an anecdote about satanic deception to the apparently unrelated task of debt collection. Ghazzī describes a scene where a debt collector visits the home of an insolvent debtor seeking to reclaim his money. The debt collector knocks on the door and the debtor asks, "Who is it?" The debt collector responds, "I am so and so," changing his name in order to conceal his true identity. Ghazzī explains that the debt collector (and those who imitate him) commits a satanic deception by disguising his identity just to enrich himself at the expense of someone else. Here a reader may wonder: is Ghazzī taking aim at corrupt state-administered tax-collection practices?

While Ghazzī avoids mentioning actual events or people, he may nonetheless have obliquely delivered a sharp critique of widespread government corruption and exploitation. Although Ghazzī kept aloof from direct political activism, through his scholarship he creatively interprets the Islamic past to shape the contemporary moral and social well-being of the Muslim present, voicing his opinion on new cultural developments such as the consumption of pleasure-inducing substances—coffee, tobacco, and cannabis.

But Ghazzī's quest to restore order amid crisis and corruption did not turn him into a curmudgeon whose view of Islamic orthodoxy was limited to stark oppositions between lawful and prohibited. Ghazzī's normative commitment to the letter of the law was balanced by his Sufi sensibilities, which remained bound to the spirit of the law. Although he remained within the boundaries of orthodox Sunni Islam, and the Shāfiʿī *madhhab* in particular, he also had to consider scenarios when orthodoxy broke down, such as the limit case of the disobedient Muslim who loves God, where outward appearances fail to reflect inner truth. At such moments, formal legal reasoning gives way to poeisis, what Ebrahim Moosa describes as "the craft of imagination and inventive making and creating."[119] By means of this "making," Ghazzī's mind crossed vast historical and discursive horizons: past and present, legal and mystical, imagined and real. Although Ghazzī's nuanced discourses on mimesis and coffee cannot be easily summarized, we may nonetheless conclude that, on the whole, they bend toward expansion and inclusion, not restriction and exclusion.

Ghazzī's poeisis is most clearly expressed through his poetry. Verse is the most effective literary form to capture the ontology of emotion, with all its mood swings. Through poetry, Ghazzī brings coherence to the contradictions that characterize everyday human experience. He explains, in verse, how the disobedient Muslim is absolved through his love of God—how emotion transcends ritual failure—despite arguing that adhering to orthodoxy is essential to being a good Muslim. He also explains, in verse, why drinking coffee is okay at home but not in the coffeehouse. These contradictory viewpoints coexisted in Ghazzī's mind. Coffee is both lawful and unlawful; the disobedient Muslim is both outcast and exemplar. And indeed, if we zoom out and view *The Virtue of Awakening* from afar, we perceive not a monovalent treatise against imitation but a multivalent composition that explores imitation as a complex process of human becoming and belonging, with all its ambiguities and contradictions. Ghazzī thus avoids being narrowly confined within a binary logic of absolutes, opting instead to inhabit a world of *adjacent contradictions*—a way of thinking (and being) that Kâtib Çelebi considered a virtue: "Some may ask, can one thing be simultaneously indifferent, disapproved, and forbidden? Is this not self-contradictory? The answer is that it is possible, with a change of aspect and viewpoint. For example, while it is permissible to eat baklava, it is forbidden to do so when one is sated, as this is harmful."[120]

CHAPTER 8

Can Muslims Wear European Hats?

To one who observes the changes in fashion, it appears to follow no order, proceeding in a way that resembles chaos.

—*AL-HILĀL,* December 1925

What kind of *tashabbuh* is more evident than [for Muslims] to dress in outfits distinctive to non-Muslims and to increase their multitudes by visibly manifesting the external features of their community?

—MUḤAMMAD ZĀHID AL-KAWTHARĪ

On October 28, 1903, the grand mufti of Egypt and vanguard of Islamic modernism Muḥammad ʿAbduh (d. 1905) responded to a petition from Transvaal, South Africa, regarding three disputed topics: eating meat slaughtered by Christians; wearing European hats for practical purposes, like conducting business with non-Muslims or being shielded from the sun on hot summer days; and followers of the Shāfiʿī school of law praying behind imams who adhere to the Ḥanafī school of law during *ʿīd* holidays.[1] ʿAbduh permitted all three practices, unleashing a tide of controversy within and beyond Egypt, across all sectors of Muslim society, that continued long after his death in 1905. It was "perhaps the best known of ʿAbduh's fatwas," according to Charles Adams; and in Jakob Skovgaard-Petersen's bold estimation: "No fatwa had ever been the object of such a heated debate in the history of Islam."[2]

The prospect of Muslims eating meat slaughtered by Christians was the single most controversial ruling of the fatwa, provoking visceral disgust among ʿAbduh's opponents. But it was the sight of Muslims wearing European hats that threatened to refashion Islamic aesthetic and cultural sensibilities. Headgear, as already discussed, enhances a person's visage, the main locus of personal identity. It is no wonder, then, that cultures across human history have attached great value to this sartorial object. But to decode the meanings of symbolically charged objects like headgear requires that they be viewed within their historical and cultural contexts. Sartorial styles, we have seen, are cultural forms that elude fixed origins and meanings because they are easily imitated and repurposed, crossing cultural, political, and confessional boundaries with ease. The case of Muslims adopting European hats is no exception. As the transmission of the European hat blurred the lines between Muslim and European, native and foreign, religion and culture, interior faith and exterior practice, a diverse group of Muslim gatekeepers were inspired to redraw those lines.

In the early nineteenth century, the Ottoman Empire, whose territorial sovereignty extended to Egypt, adopted the red felt cap known as the tarbush (or fez) as a national symbol of progress. It did not matter that the origins of the headgear were, in fact, foreign. Decades later, with the British occupation of Egypt, the symbolic capital of dress, and the tarbush cap in particular, took on new cultural and political meanings within the country. "For the first time," asserts Wilson Chacko Jacob, "the very essence of Egyptian identity was at stake."[3] The prospect of a European hat replacing the tarbush, among the most potent symbols of Egyptian identity, was deeply unsettling for many Muslims.

In the following decades, religious scholars from across the Muslim world—Egypt, India, Turkey, Syria, and Saudi Arabia—responded directly (and indirectly) to the fatwa; while some supported it, using *ijtihād* (independent reasoning) to defend ʿAbduh's position on Islamic legal grounds, many criticized it, arguing that the trend of Muslims wearing European hats not only violated *taqlīd* (conformity to Islamic legal precedent) but was a public and visible sign of Western political and cultural hegemony and Muslim geopolitical weakness that culminated in the fall of the caliphate in 1924. The fatwa, then, brought into relief Muslim anxieties over the seismic transformations reshaping Islamic civilization in colonial modernity.

It is not a coincidence that during this tumultuous period, the quantity of treatises against imitation composed by *ʿulamāʾ* swelled, spreading across the continents of Europe, Asia, and Africa, including the nations of Turkey, Austria, India, Indonesia, Nigeria, Syria, Morocco, and Egypt.[4] Many of these treatises erupted from the cauldron of political conflict, from the Spanish-Moroccan War and civil strife in Nigeria to the British colonization of India and the creation of a secular republic in Turkey. The importance of maintaining a distinctively Muslim physical appearance is a recurring theme.

A graduate of the renowned Islamic seminary Azhar, Muḥammad ʿAbduh was an ambitious reformer who shot up through the bureaucratic ranks of the Egyptian government, reaching the post of grand mufti in 1899. ʿAbduh wished to restore Muslim civilization to its past glory by adopting European norms whose roots, he believed, belonged to Islam, and by breaking entrenched habits, such as *taqlīd,* that enervated the religion's ability to thrive amid the fast-paced changes of modernity. But as an outspoken public intellectual with close ties to the British who was also sharply critical of the *ʿulamāʾ*, he invited suspicion as to where his true loyalties lay. The print media that ʿAbduh so effectively used to establish his public image as a reformer was also manipulated by his opponents to tarnish it. Just as the person of ʿAbduh was portrayed at once as a stooge of the British and a fearless defender of Islam, his fatwa on wearing European hats was read as both a sign of capitulation to non-Muslims and a visionary form of legal pragmatism designed to strategically elevate Muslims to a position of strength.

Although some excellent studies have examined reactions to the Transvaal fatwa within the Egyptian media, most have overlooked the fatwa's significance within the broader Islamic discourse on *tashabbuh.* In this chapter, I emplace the fatwa within a longer history of inter-Muslim debates around wearing European headgear spanning nearly a century—from its antecedents in the reformist writings of a Tunisian-French Muslim thinker who has been largely forgotten to its afterlife in the bitter debates between ʿAbduh's reformist defenders and conservative detractors during the first half of the twentieth century, roughly the period in which Egypt was under British control.

These legal debates over Muslim headgear lay bare competing imaginaries over the proper configuration of religion—and Islam—in Muslim public life. Although some historians of Islam have resisted translating the Arabic term *dīn* as "religion" due to the distinct genealogies of these terms, I defend this translation due to a shared characterization of religion/*dīn* as a distinct sphere of human activity among modern European thinkers and Muslim reformists alike.[5] The characterization of *dīn* as a distinct domain has a long history among Muslims. In the ninth century, ʿAlī b. Rabban al-Ṭabarī (d. 870) composed a polemical treatise that distinguished between *dīn* and *dawla,* religion and the state, although he and many of his successors argued that Islam bound these domains together. Debates over the relationship of *dīn* to politics evolved in modernity with the rise of the nation-state. Some Egyptian reformists adopted European ideas concerning the sharp division of religion and politics through the prism of Islam. In the treatise *Islam and the Foundations of Political Power,* Oxford- and Azhar-educated jurist ʿAlī ʿAbd al-Rāziq (d. 1966) argued for separating Islam from politics, based on the controversial claim that the Prophet Muhammad was a religious teacher, not a political leader.[6] Most reformist thinkers, including ʿAbduh, did not seek to divorce religion from the state, however, but to redefine its relationship to public life so that Muslims could flourish in a rapidly changing world. In fact, as Junaid Quadri has demonstrated, even conservative jurists were not immune to these transformations.[7] Nevertheless, as opponents to the European hat show, many Muslim intellectuals during the first half of the twentieth century resisted these attempts to reconfigure religion. By documenting these internal Muslim debates, I not only show how Muslims came to define a distinctively modern Islam, I add to the history of how "Islam *became* a religion in the modern sense of the term" (emphasis mine).[8]

FOREIGN HATS IN A FOREIGN LAND

Nearly six thousand kilometers south of Egypt, the South African republic of Transvaal was a new British colony when ʿAbduh issued his fatwa. In Transvaal, the Muslims of Malay and Indian descent who assimilated, that is, who dressed like Europeans, were treated like Europeans. "Even more than in Egypt or India," observes Leor Halevi, "hats in this part of the world functioned as liminal markers of social, racial, and professional identity."[9] Having lived abroad in exile for several years, ʿAbduh was in fact well acquainted with the unique challenges of being a religious minority in a foreign country, and he appears to sympathize with their situation, as indicated by his accommodative response in the fatwa: "The wearing of a hat [*al-burnayṭa*], if the one who wears it does not intend thereby to leave Islam and enter another religion, is not to be considered as constituting the wearer an unbeliever; and if wearing it is to meet some need, such as to protect from the sun or prevent some undesirable result or to make possible some advantage, it has likewise not been considered as 'disliked' because the idea of conformity [*tashabbuh*] to another religion has disappeared entirely."[10] According to ʿAbduh's fatwa, merely wearing a European-style hat does not turn a believer into an unbeliever, as long as the intent behind the sartorial gesture is not "to leave Islam and enter another religion." Here ʿAbduh follows a line of reasoning parallel to that of Ibn Taymiyya in *The Obligation of Following the Straight Path,* who stressed the importance of motive in determining the legal status of *tashabbuh* within the shariʿa: a believer who wears a European-style hat but does not intend to exit Islam thus remains a believer and does not become an apostate.[11]

Next, he evaluates the act's legal status in the shariʿa—whether it is lawful, unlawful, recommended, detested, or required. ʿAbduh's line of reasoning once again mirrors that of Ibn Taymiyya regarding the legal status of *tashabbuh* among Muslim minorities living abroad. Following a legal pragmatism that a less reform-minded mufti would have shunned, ʿAbduh invokes the principle of public interest to circumvent the application of this doctrine. According to ʿAbduh, wearing the hat in order to fulfill a practical need—whether to avoid harm or to obtain a benefit—invalidates the legal grounds for judging the act detestable (*makrūh*), or, by extension, unlawful. In other words, prohibiting the act on the basis that it constitutes reprehensible imitation of unbelievers does not apply. It is therefore lawful, and may even be praiseworthy, for Muslims in Transvaal to wear a European-style hat due to the collective benefits of doing so.

Classical jurists had established a long-standing precedent of appealing to public interest (*maṣlaḥa*) or necessity (*ḍarūra*) to circumvent established legal norms, and reformist thinkers like ʿAbduh made abundant use of such hermeneutical tools.[12] Among the features that set apart European-style hats—such as the trilby, bowler/derby, and the beret—from the fez was the brim, which projected out from the hat's bottom and shielded one's face from the sun. ʿAbduh suggests that wearing brimmed hats to avoid sunburn or exposure to direct sunlight is healthy for the body. This position was supported decades later by the Egyptian Medical Association, which claimed that European-style hats were more healthful for the head and eyes than the tarbush.[13] Classical jurists ranked the preservation of life among the five fundamental objectives (*maqāṣid*) of the shariʿa.[14] An additional benefit of Muslims adopting local styles of headgear concerns economic prosperity. If Muslims in Transvaal lost business due to local customer biases against foreigners who refused to adopt indigenous styles of dress, that too constituted legitimate grounds for wearing the hat. Economic prosperity was a precondition for the collective welfare of a vulnerable Muslim minority living in a majority non-Muslim country. In sum, ʿAbduh's fatwa made it easier for Muslims living in foreign lands to conform and assimilate.

"GOD DOES NOT LOOK AT YOUR PHYSICAL APPEARANCE"

But Muslim intellectuals had already been debating the limits of assimilating European cultural norms in the decades preceding ʿAbduh's "liberal" fatwa. In 1862, Sulaymān b. ʿAlī al-Ḥarāʾirī (d. 1877), a Tunisian scholar of applied sciences living in Paris, published a brief treatise on the question of Muslims wearing French brimmed hats: *Responses to Those Confused about [the Legal Status of] the Christian Hat* (*Ajwibat al-ḥayārā ʿalā al-qalansuwat al-naṣārā*).[15] Some foreign Muslim students living in Paris, he writes, complained that French natives would stop and stare at them in astonishment due to their strange outfits and lack of headgear; others claimed that the hat protected their eyes during the country's cold winters; and yet others claimed that wearing the hat would result in grave theological and legal consequences, turning them into infidels and nullifying their marriages. Upon returning to their home country, they would be obligated to restate the testimony of faith (*shahāda*) and remarry their spouses. But Ḥarāʾirī dismissed these alarmist positions, arguing that the shariʿa interdiction on imitating non-Muslims applied exclusively to religious practices, not to neutral practices like wearing a French-style hat. He concluded that no evidence from either scripture or the authoritative opinions of the early Muslims supported its prohibition. Ḥarāʾirī's liberal view was consistent with his broader political outlook, in which he promotes Muslim cooperation with the French. As his pioneering Arabic translation of a classic primer on French grammar indicates, he wanted to build bridges, not walls, between the two cultures.[16]

While Ḥarāʾirī's progressive opinion did not meet the level of resistance that ʿAbduh's fatwa did, it nonetheless alarmed some *ʿulamāʾ*, who believed that a pseudo-scholar was encroaching upon their divinely sanctioned pastoral role. Chief jurisconsult (mufti) of the Mālikī school at Azhar, who also hailed from North Africa, Muḥammad ʿIlīsh (d. 1882), responded with a blistering refutation that contended Ḥarāʾirī's opinion had no basis in the shariʿa.[17] Identity is at the core of his critique. "This man is an unknown [*majhūl*] who is blind to his deficiencies so that he deluded himself into believing that he is a member of the *ʿulamāʾ* and thus transgressed the boundaries of the shariʿa [*kharaja ʿan ḥadd al-sharīʿa*]." True believers, especially when speaking in God's name, should know their limits. A refrain repeated throughout the refutation (with minor variations in wording) warns against the moral corruption that could infect the public if this essential rule is ignored: "O clever people, you marvel at someone who is blind to his vice; so, driven by his ego, he calls to people and spreads his vice until it becomes widespread." In ʿIlīsh's view, Ḥarāʾirī was the quintessential example of the blind leading the blind.

Employing shariʿa-based terminology, ʿIlīsh argues that wearing the hat (*qalansuwa*) is prohibited by the binding consensus of the Muslim community (*ijma*ʿ) because it is distinctive to Christians, and wearing it signals the intention to honor this symbol, which is utterly disgraceful for the Muslim. Disingenuously claiming that it protects the eyes during cold weather is a false pretext. Muslims should be more worried about being unable to perform the most important ritual act in Islam: prayer. A brimmed hat hinders the believer from prostrating on the ground, a prerequisite for a valid performance of the ritual prayer.

But how important are matters of physical appearance in Islam? Ḥarāʾirī claims that adopting the external cultural forms (*tashabbuh fī al-ṣūra*) of another people is harmless, citing a well-known hadith in which the Prophet proclaims: "God does not look at your physical appearance or your wealth, but looks at what is inside your hearts and what you do."[18] Surely, then, God will not chastise a believer on the Day of Reckoning for wearing a brimmed hat. But this is a disgraceful reading of the hadith, according to ʿIlīsh. He accuses Ḥarāʾirī of misunderstanding the Prophet's statement, which refers to someone who feigns good appearances in order to hide the ugliness inside, not to someone who transgresses the bounds of the shariʿa and sins openly. Ḥarāʾirī, in ʿIlīsh's view, diminishes the importance of physical appearance and, more generally, a person's public image in the shariʿa.

ʿIlīsh's critical view of the French hat is intertwined with his spatial imaginary of Europe and its people, which sharply contrasted Ḥarāʾirī's. Europe, for ʿIlīsh, was "enemy territory," and he feared that Muslims would eventually join the enemy if they stayed there long enough.[19] To dress like infidels is "one of the most disgraceful acts [*ashnaʿ al-faḍāʾi*]," and traveling abroad for the sake of earning a living "discredits the testimony of faith" because Muslims can learn nothing of value from Christians, who are ignorant of the shariʿa and the linguistic competence in Arabic needed to understand it. Whatever else they might learn abroad is superfluous. "Most of their sciences derive from weaving, smithing, and cupping, which are the lowliest trades among Muslims."[20]

A teacher of ʿAbduh, Muḥammad ʿIlīsh was one of the most influential voices and prominent figures at Azhar in the second half of the nineteenth century. Although both figures supported the ʿUrabi revolt, for which ʿAbduh was later exiled, their visions of reform were grounded in divergent outlooks on the Islamic tradition.[21] ʿIlīsh perceived *taqlīd* as a stabilizing force that connected believers to a continuous unbroken tradition of scholarship, safeguarded the *ʿulamā*ʾ's prominent role as the gatekeepers to Islamic orthodoxy, and upheld the rule of law by producing consistent rulings that unified the

Muslim community.[22] But reformers like ʿAbduh perceived the social unity enforced by *taqlīd* as uniformity, consistency in legal rulings as stagnation (*jumūd*), and connection to a single school of law as disconnection from revealed scripture (Quran and hadiths).[23] ʿAbduh's disregard for *taqlīd* had already become apparent while he was a student at Azhar, where his relationship with his teacher ʿIlīsh soured. ʿIlīsh publicly reprimanded ʿAbduh for teaching a theological text that most scholars, let alone students, are unqualified to teach. When questioned by ʿIlīsh if he preferred the (heterodox) Muʿtazilī theological school over the (orthodox) Ashʿarī one, ʿAbduh boldly replied: "If I were to abandon Ashʿarī *taqlīd* then why would I practice *taqlīd* of the Muʿtazilī? Rather I would abandon *taqlīd* altogether and use only the evidence."[24] Offended at ʿAbduh's audacity, ʿIlīsh's students promptly grabbed his turban from his head as others mocked him.[25] ʿIlīsh also ensured that ʿAbduh received a second-rank instead of a first-rank degree upon graduating Azhar (although he was awarded an honorary first-rank degree twenty-six years later).[26] ʿIlīsh's suppression of ʿAbduh's reformist impulses at Azhar as well as his fierce refutation of Ḥarāʾirī presaged the conservative *ʿulamā*ʾ's hostility to the Transvaal fatwa decades later.

Nevertheless, the reformist outlook on adopting European cultural norms continued to gain momentum. In 1898, the inaugural year of the reformist journal *The Lighthouse* (*al-Manār*), Muḥammad Rashīd Riḍā (d. 1935), its founder and ʿAbduh's close associate, expressed a benign attitude toward Muslims adopting foreign headgear.[27] Following a utilitarian line of reasoning characteristic of reformist legal argumentation, Riḍā defends the practice of Muslims imitating non-Muslims (that is, Europeans) when it strategically benefits the community of believers; these include matters of political economy such as strengthening the nation's defense and increasing its wealth.[28] In Riḍā's view, Muslims must not be content to remain consumers of foreign goods but must also learn how to be producers. In the past, Muslims used to borrow liberally from other civilizations, but would refine those practices so that they conformed to Islamic ethical and cultural standards. Citing several variations of the famous prophetic tradition "Wisdom is the lost camel of the true believer," he argues that it is wrong to oppose everything foreigners (Europeans) do just because they are different, without regard to the impact on the collective interests of the Muslim community. Imitation in this context is not merely permissible, but may even be necessary, according to the shariʿa. Alternatively, it is better for Muslims to discard foreign practices that are inconsequential to the community, but if they cannot avoid adopting them, they should at least block out their foreign origins from their minds. Of course, Muslims should avoid foreign practices that are harmful altogether. For Riḍā, foreign dress fits into the category of being either inconsequential or harmful, depending on the situation. Although the mass adoption of opulent dress like silk and other luxury goods softens a civilization, leading to its eventual downfall, the Prophet still wore foreign headgear, like the Persian-styled *ṭaylasān* shawl that resembled what some Arab Jews wore over their heads, indicating that adopting foreign sartorial styles is permissible in itself. Riḍā had already laid the groundwork for ʿAbduh's fatwa.

Debates on Muslim relations with Europe eventually moved beyond the elite circles of religious authorities to the mainstream Egyptian print media, which had acquired a powerful role in shaping public opinion at the turn of the twentieth century. On November 9, 1899, the Egyptian journalist Muḥammad al-Muwayliḥī (d. 1930) criticized Egyptian imitation of foreigners in a fictional serial about British-occupied Cairo published in his father's Cairene newspaper, *The Lamp of the East* (*Miṣbāḥ al-Sharq*): "They imitate foreigners, but only in trivial and undesirable ways that incite their lusts, false ostentation and phony tinsel—the kinds of thing that only result in bodily disease and wasted money. But, when it comes to beneficial aspects of civilization they're not merely ignorant of them, they even disparage them. In summary, one may say that the way Egyptians have adopted the habits of Western civilization is analogous to a sieve that retains all the worthless waste and lets through the useful things with any value."[29] Somehow, the serial's narrator complains, Egyptian Muslims adopted the bad habits of Western civilization, absorbing "all the worthless waste" while failing to absorb the attributes that enabled it to flourish.

Seven months later, on June 8, 1900, Muwayliḥī's serial returned to this issue, stating that misguided imitation had corrupted Egyptian society: "The root cause lay in *the way* Easterners were imitating [*taqlīd*] Western civilization. . . . They have only picked the thorns off the fruit tree and tasted the bitter fruit."[30] A dialogue within that issue expresses the characters' confusion over why Easterners continued to be image obsessed:

> (FRIEND). People have failed to distinguish what suits them from what does not, and have not discriminated between the authentic and the phony. Quite the opposite, they have contented themselves with useless superficialities and utter trivialities. In so doing, they have abandoned all

> national norms and firmly rooted principles. . . . We're destroying our own house with our own hands.
> (PASHA). I can't understand why peoples of the East have chosen to adopt the useless aspects of civilization rather than its true essence, the surface rather than the core. They seem to confine their attention to the shell rather than the pith, whereas in earlier times they were of all peoples the most steeped in civilization and culture.[31]

Looking back with nostalgia at how "peoples of the East" were once "the most steeped in civilization and culture," the characters in the dialogue, Pasha and the Friend, lament how they now imitate the most superficial and inauthentic features of Western civilization instead of the core principles and values that enabled it to flourish. But what "useless superficialities and utter trivialities" were they referring to? According to the Pasha, Egyptians were drawn to Europe's image as expressed through the outward behavior of its people, their "postures, clothes, way of life, gestures, and repose." They were, in other words, obsessed with *embodying* European modernity.[32] Given the paper's wide readership within and beyond Cairo, many Egyptian intellectuals likely shared Muwayliḥī's criticism of the ongoing Muslim fascination with replicating Europe's image.

THE FINE LINE BETWEEN RELIGION AND CULTURE

The Egyptian print media also played an important role in turning ʿAbduh's fatwa into a national controversy. While periodicals such as *al-Ahrām* and *al-Waṭan* supported ʿAbduh, others lampooned him. Supported by conspirators from within the circles of the khedive, *ʿulamāʾ*, and the sultan who distrusted ʿAbduh, various papers advanced a campaign to smear his reputation and limit his influence in the years leading up to the fatwa, portraying him as a Europhile, British pawn, and heretic. While Muḥammad al-Muwayliḥī viewed ʿAbduh as a mentor, having assisted him with the publication of *al-ʿUrwā al-wuthqā* in Paris, his father, Ibrāhīm al-Muwayliḥī, held a different view: in 1901, he publicly censured ʿAbduh in *The Lamp of the East* for his ties with the British, concluding that his nebulous religious and political loyalties disqualified him from retaining the post of grand mufti.[33] The following year, *Humarat al-Munyati* published a scandalous photo of ʿAbduh taken during a visit to Europe in which, surrounded by four women and their male chaperone, he leans against a fence, smiling. The paper's editor was sentenced to three months in prison for disgracing the office of grand mufti, but the stain on ʿAbduh's reputation remained.

The Transvaal fatwa provided ʿAbduh's enemies with yet another opportunity to discredit him. They purchased a copy of the fatwa from the petitioner in Transvaal and published it in the Egyptian newspaper *al-Ẓāhir* on December 19, 1903, under the title "How Can That Be Declared Lawful That Which God Has Declared Unlawful?"[34] The subsequent ten issues of the newspaper criticized the fatwa as well. Expressing anxieties that this fatwa signaled the Westernization of Egypt, on January 12, 1904, another paper published a satirical cartoon depicting ʿAbduh holding the waist of a scantily clad European woman as a dog licks his leg, rendering him ritually impure—a representation of what they imagined ʿAbduh might be doing during one of his jaunts to Europe.[35] Adding to his Europeanization, the paper mockingly addresses ʿAbduh as "Al-Mister" instead of the conventional Arab address of *al-Sayyid.* Ironically, the same papers that ridiculed Egyptians for their mimetic fixation on Europe's image were themselves obsessed with ʿAbduh's image.

Another great irony of lampooning ʿAbduh for mimicry of the West (*taghrīb*) was that, as already discussed, he loathed imitation. It was the system of education in the Muslim world that needed reform, above all. The *ʿulamāʾ*, in his view, had failed the community of believers. Their stubborn refusal to embrace new knowledge and adapt their pedagogical styles had led Muslim civilization to stagnation and decline. Seminaries like Azhar were plagued by the disease of *taqlīd,* blind imitation of a leaden tradition that weighed down the inquiring mind of the believer. The mimetic reliance on the dry scholasticism of later commentators in the educational curriculum, ʿAbduh believed, needed to give way to a direct engagement with the original texts of the Quran and *sunna* to liberate Muslim minds and unleash the transformative power of independent critical thinking and reasoning (*ijtihād*) that could revitalize Islamic civilization from within.

Unsurprisingly, religious scholars who objected to ʿAbduh's bold reformist agenda composed refutations of the fatwa. In 1904, an Egyptian Azhari jurist, Yūsuf Shalabī al-Shubrā al-Shāfiʿī, published a treatise that criticized ʿAbduh's fatwa on procedural grounds.[36] As the grand mufti of Egypt, ʿAbduh was obliged to issue rulings that conformed to the Ḥanafī school of jurisprudence. But ʿAbduh breached protocol, Shalabī argued, by issuing a fatwa that deviated from the Ḥanafī school's authoritative position. As a follower of the school (*muqallid*), he ought to issue a legal opinion based on the most authoritative opinion within the school (*ṣaḥīḥ*), not a weak or disclaimed opinion. Shalabī's argument can be distilled into one main point: in the Ḥanafī school, the core issue regarding foreign dress is not the question of intent—whether or not a Muslim wants to leave Islam and enter a new religion—but the question of necessity, whether wearing a hat qualifies as a genuine need. If it cannot be established that wearing a European-style hat is a true necessity, then doing so is unbelief (*kufr*), regardless of intent. A person who believes in the truth of the Prophet's message (*taṣdīq*) and has no desire to leave Islam (*khurūj*) may still perform an act that indicates unbelief (*ʿalāmāt al-kufr*).

But other scholars rushed to ʿAbduh's defense.[37] Muḥammad Rashīd Riḍā published an article in *The Lighthouse* on the fatwa, referring to ʿAbduh not by name but indirectly as "the scholar" (*al-ʿālim*).[38] He claims that most Muslims, viewing the adoption of European headgear as a disgrace to the religion of Islam (*al-dīn al-Islāmī*), had been closely following the news about the Transvaal fatwa. A key legal distinction, in Riḍā's view, is whether to categorize the adoption of foreign headgear as a religious (*dīniyya*) practice or a local cultural norm (*ʿādiyya*). Classical jurists formally recognized the customary practices (*ʿurf/ʿāda*) of a society as a source of law in order to assimilate local norms into the shariʿa.[39] Whereas religious norms like ritual prayer are fixed, local cultural norms change with time and place. Riḍā argues that the opponents of the fatwa incorrectly categorize wearing headgear among religious matters (*al-mushkilāt al-dīniyya*) due to their "paltry knowledge of Islamic law and lack of attention to the Prophet's *sunna* and the history of the Muslim community."[40] But he—and by extension ʿAbduh—sees the matter of headgear as a local cultural norm; although it is blameworthy for Egyptians to visit Europe and wear the native hat, they have not sinned and do not deserve God's chastisement. This reclassification of the Muslim adoption of the brimmed hat narrows the scope of religion (*dīn*) from the traditional conception held by the fatwa's conservative opponents. Classifying the adoption of foreign headgear as a cultural rather than a religious matter also means that this issue falls outside the scope of both the "claims of God" and the "claims of men," the two fundamental categories of law encompassed by the shariʿa.[41] The original practice of the first generations of Muslims, he argues, supports this view. The Prophet and his Companions adopted the sartorial styles of their people not out of obedience to a divine commandment but in response to the local climate. Choice of dress is thus mainly a product of historical and cultural context: "The preference of dressing one way over another conforms to changes in time and place."[42]

Imitation (*tashabbuh*) is forbidden within the shariʿa in religious matters (*umūr al-dīniyya*/*umūr al-dīn*) alone. When questioned about the permissibility of using a gong at the mosque to call Muslims to prayer, or of Muslim printers engraving crosses on copper plates, Riḍā issued fatwas forbidding these practices because of their uncomfortably close resemblance to Christian religious rituals and symbols.[43] "As for worldly matters [*umūr dunyawiyya*] such as food and dress, being different [from non-Muslims] is not necessary; rather, people coming together through cultural practices unites them and eliminates the discord [*tanāfur*] that blinds every group to the good qualities of the other. And when mutual discord is eliminated, then truth prevails over falsehood."[44] By placing sartorial practices that are disconnected from ritual matters outside the zone of religion, Riḍā effectively expands the domain of culture, as well as the range of foreign practices that Muslims are free to adopt.

Riḍā concludes his defense by distinguishing between the socio-political circumstances of Muslims living in Egypt and Transvaal: it is not in the collective interest (*maṣlaḥa*) of Egyptian Muslims to wear the European-style hat, he argues, because they aspire to gain independence from British rule; but it is in the collective interest of Muslims living in Transvaal to do so because, as religious minorities, they are incapable of seizing political power from the Christian majority. The decision to wear a European-style hat is, in other words, a pragmatic calculation, dependent upon the socio-political status of the local Muslim community. Riḍā's reasoning indicates how colonialism, and the disparity in power between Muslims and Europe, shaped reformist interpretations of Islamic law.

On March 18, 1904, Riḍā issued a fatwa in response to a similar matter: whether "Islam is a matter of appearance," that is, whether American or British converts to Islam are required to give up their native dress, including European-style hats, and adopt distinctive Muslim dress.[45] Riḍā took a bolder stance on the issue than he had just three months before. "Those who argue that wearing Christian-style hats is contrary to Islam know no more about Islam than an ordinary cobbler." Adopting the radically anti-essentialist stance of a historicist, he goes so far as to question the very notion of "Islamic" dress: "Muslims never adopted one single uniform during any period. So how can we tell which of their customs was the proper Islamic form of dress and which was the form of dress used by unbelievers and apostates?" Because Muslim fashion was constantly in flux, changing with time and place, crossing confessional lines, it is impossible to assign the marker of "Islamic" to a specific style of dress. The scriptural basis for the position is likewise weak, he contends. Not only is the authenticity of the imitation hadith uncertain, its meaning is unrelated to sartorial matters. "Merely putting on the clothes worn by brave warriors, or by generous wealthy people, does not make a person a member of such a group." One must rather adopt the distinctive attributes of a people to truly belong with them, as illustrated by the well-known Sufi couplet

> Imitate the virtuous, if you are not among them,
> For imitating the virtuous leads to success.[46]

Islam is not a matter of appearance. New Muslims are therefore free to dress as they did before their conversion to Islam.

Joining Riḍā, a group of Azhari scholars representing the four Sunni schools of jurisprudence published a brief treatise, *Irshād al-umma,* in support of ʿAbduh's opinions.[47] They concurred with ʿAbduh that intent was the most critical factor in determining the theological consequences of wearing a European hat, arguing that faith, which is an internal matter of the heart, cannot be negated by dress alone, which is an external matter. As long as a believer neither intends to emulate (*tashabbuh*) unbelievers nor signals approval (*istiḥsān*) of their religion, but wears the hat for utilitarian purposes—to either attain a benefit (*maṣlaḥa*) or prevent harm—he is not sinful. The group of scholars did, however, offer a key elaboration: "Wearing the European hat was never a distinguishing marker [*shiʿār*] of their *dīn,* nor was the hat unique to them. Rather, it is part of their national [*qawmī*] dress."[48]

The gloss's conceptual distinction between *dīn* and *qawm* is significant. It diverges from the evident meaning of the canonical hadith "Whoever imitates a people [*qawm*] becomes one of them," which indicates that when someone changes his *qawm,* the community to which he belongs, he changes his *dīn* as well. Here the usage of *dīn* closely parallels modern imaginaries of "religion" as a distinct domain set apart from the nation. Distinguishing *qawm* from *dīn,* nation from religion, in modern Islamic legal reasoning represents a conceptual transformation in how religion (and Islam) is imagined in Muslim public life. Although Muslim intellectuals from as early as Abbasid times paired *dīn* with *dawla,* or government, they emphasized the complementarity of these two domains, which contrasts with how many reformists in the twentieth century drew a sharper line dividing religion from government within the political context of the nation-state.[49] Even the conservative Azhari jurist and opponent of reformist thought Muhammad Bakhīt al-Muṭīʿī (d. 1935) shifted the zone of "religious matters" (*umūr al-dīniyya*) from the public realm of the court to the private realm of the individual in order to authorize the sighting of the Ramadan moon by a single upright witness.[50] Bakhīt's understanding of "religion," observes Quadri, "is indebted to the modern transformations associated with new conceptions of the secular."[51] These modern conceptions of religion are also different from how classical Islamic manuals of positive law across the major schools distinguished between ritual (*ʿibādāt*) and social practices (*muʿāmalāt*) but nonetheless included both domains within the normative universe of the shariʿa.

But this did not mean that ʿAbduh himself aspired to shrink the role of religion in public life. For him, Islam was not an obstacle but the key to Muslim civilizational progress. In a widely publicized debate with the Syrian Christian émigré Faraḥ Antūn, ʿAbduh expressed his disagreement with the view that religion should be separated from politics.[52] That he sought to effect Islamic reform through the administrative levers of the Egyptian government suggests that he was willing to mix religion and politics, despite his aversion to direct involvement in political affairs. He also disagreed with Antūn's claim that religion is inherently hostile to reason and science. ʿAbduh argued that religion, and Islam in particular, is not against science but in harmony with it. In his view, both share the same epistemological objective of uncovering the natural laws of the universe. In this way, Islam and science enrich one another. ʿAbduh's desire to have the natural sciences taught at Azhar should not be interpreted as an attempt to diminish the status of "religion" or to secularize the institution, as some thought, but rather to update and expand its vision of Islam to meet the challenges of modernity.

ʿAbduh passed away from cancer in 1905. But the controversy over wearing foreign headgear was rekindled a few decades later, after the fall of the caliphate in 1924. The stakes of the ensuing debate escalated: in 1924, Turkish Ḥanafī religious scholar Iskilipli Mehmet Âṭıf Hoca (d. 1926) published a treatise against imitating unbelievers that forbade Muslims to wear European-style hats; but he was subsequently put on trial and executed by Mustafa Ataturk for undermining a state law banning the tarbush in the newly formed Turkish republic that was enacted in 1925, one year *after* Âṭıf Hoca's treatise was published (figure 17).[53] "A civilized international dress is worthy and appropriate for our nation, and we will wear it," proclaimed Ataturk in 1925. "Boots or shoes on our feet, trousers on our legs, shirt and tie, jacket and waistcoat—and of course, to complete these, a cap with a brim on our heads. I want to make this clear. This head-covering is called a 'hat' [*şapka*]."[54] Not wearing a European hat was thus viewed as a rejection of civilization, secularism, and progress.

Figure 17. Cover page of *İskilipli Atıf Hoca: nasıl idam edildi?* Istanbul: Sinan Matbaası ve Neşriyat Evi, 195–? (Courtesy of the Princeton University Library.)

But subjects of the Ottoman Empire had already begun to emulate European sartorial styles in the nineteenth century. In 1826, Sultan Mahmud II (d. 1839) replaced his turban with the fez, which was, visually and symbolically, a more dramatic transformation than Ataturk's replacement of the fez with the brimmed hat.[55] The military followed, as did elite Ottoman men, who adopted jackets and fitted trousers as well.[56] It was not long before other European fashion trends caught on, including European-style brimmed hats, which Sultan Abdul-Hamid II banned in 1877 to safeguard the fez's symbolic supremacy.[57] Ataturk's 1925 hat law inverted this decree, recoding the fez from a symbol of progress to a symbol of backwardness, and paradoxically continuing the old Ottoman tradition of linking national identity to headgear. Some citizens of the new Turkish republic resisted this transition. As the spattering of public protests of the law were ruthlessly put down, others resisted through more subtle means, either avoiding the public altogether by staying at home or wearing the hats crookedly, with the brims defiantly pushed to the side.[58]

In Egypt, the tarbush "had become recoded during the First World War as a specific Egyptian nationalist symbol through its public expression of opposition to the British."[59] As with elite Ottoman men, a tarbush, coupled with a European-style suit, had come to signal effendis, educated Egyptian men—although some women did wear it too. To ally themselves with this new class of educated elites and signal their desire for progress, in February 1926, students at an Islamic seminary, the Dār al-ʿUlūm, replaced their traditional uniform of a turban and caftan with the tarbush—without authorization from the school.[60] In response, the education minister issued a decree banning six hundred students from entering the seminary. As tensions escalated, the students obtained a fatwa from Aḥmad Muḥammad Shākir (d. 1958), the well-respected deputy director of the Azhar seminary, who sided with them, saying that "religion doesn't tell people in which style to dress, so long as they are appropriately modest. . . . Wear whatever makes you proud," he proclaimed, "even indeed a cross."[61]

Meanwhile, some Egyptian students at nonreligiously affiliated schools took the more radical step of demanding a replacement of the tarbush with European-style hats! Egyptian men wore European-style jackets and pants without a fuss, so why not complete the ensemble with brimmed hats as well? The tarbush was no longer progressive enough. But in the face of such brazen aping of the West, other students drew the line. The Wafd student party issued the following statement: "The call for dismissing the tarboush in favour of hats is unjustified and unacceptable. Stop telling us that the Turks have done just that. They have their ways and we have ours."[62] The Wafdists thus called on these Egyptian students to stop imitating the Turks in how they were imitating Europeans.

This patriotic spirit materialized into a new grassroots movement in the following decade to nationalize several industries, including the manufacture of tarbush caps which, despite their native symbolism, were imported from other North African countries and Austria. Devised by university students in the early 1930s, the Piastre Plan (*mashrūʿ al-qirsh*) harnessed nationalist fervor to motivate Egyptians to buy tarbush caps produced in local factories, not abroad, which diffused the cap's national symbology beyond effendi elites who

Figure 18. (*left*) Piastre Plan advertisement for the "Muhammad Ali" model of the tarbush, likely from the mid- to late 1930s. Figure 19. (*right*) The Piastre Plan continued until at least October 1951, when the tarbush was portrayed as a "symbol of national pride" (*shiʿār al-ʿizza al-qawmiyya*). *al-Ahram*, October 28, 1951.

consumed the product to encompass the ordinary Egyptians who now produced it. Advertisements linked specific models of tarbush caps to particular factories and memorable historical events connected to their production (figures 18 and 19). As Nancy Reynolds observes, "Tarabish and tea glasses formed important consumption items that began to unite Egyptian consumers into self-conscious communities and to mark out commerce and consumption as areas of politics."[63] The symbolic meaning and value of the tarbush continued to transform.

How did religious scholars respond to these socio-political developments? A few months after the tarbush incident at the Islamic seminary, a group of scholars from Alexandria, Egypt, published a fatwa against wearing the European hat in the April 13, 1926, issue of *The Lighthouse*.[64] Based on their reading of scriptural evidence, including the hadith "Whoever imitates a people becomes one of them," they concluded that imitating non-Muslims is prohibited. What is more remarkable, however, is that Riḍā's views on wearing foreign clothing—including European hats—evolved. As Leor Halevi has persuasively argued, a confluence of ideological currents, including the rise of Egyptian nationalism, Ataturk's hat reforms, and Mahatma Gandhi's nonviolent protest movement in British India, factored into Riḍā's new outlook on the value of Muslim indigenous dress.[65]

In yet another fatwa on European-style hats, published in *The Lighthouse* across two issues from October 1925 to January 1926, Riḍā places a new focus on cultural authenticity.[66] While he upholds his original position on the permissibility of wearing trousers and hats, he now suggests that Muslims who adopt European sartorial styles also inhabit an alternate moral imaginary. They "usually abandon prayer . . . tend to sit in bars, drink alcohol in public and openly frequent places of dancing, licentiousness, and adultery." Far from being exemplars of virtue, these people are inauthentic believers predisposed to vice who "deny their own tradition" and pretend "they are like the peoples of those [European] countries." Riḍā's portrayal of the Prophet's sartorial *sunna* also evolves. Yes, the Prophet wore foreign clothing, but he also exhorted believers to be different in religious as well as cultural matters (*ʿādāt*), including dress. Riḍā's new reading of the Islamic tradition is a stunning reversal from past fatwas in which he limited the prohibition of imitation to "religious matters" (*dīn*) alone. He also digs up a new anecdote from the generation of the *salaf* in which the second caliph, ʿUmar b. al-Khaṭṭāb, shuns cultural assimilation. When traveling to the recently conquered territory of Syria for the first time, ʿUmar is urged to adopt an extravagant ceremonial display reminiscent of its former Byzantine rulers. ʿUmar, however, has no interest in emulating them: "We have come to teach them how we rule, not to learn from them how to rule." Riḍā's citation of this anecdote in the fatwa signals his blossoming nationalism. He argues that Muslims, in fact, originated the idea of maintaining a "strong national culture" by refusing to imitate others, which European empires then copied, leading to their success. "When one people imitates another that it regards as more advanced, its own traditional values are weakened and become contemptible in the eyes of its own people. Correspondingly, the people who are imitated take on a higher status." Based on this Khaldunian rationale, he rejects Ataturk's reforms as debasing the Turks and destroying Islam under the pretext of Westernization, which Riḍā sarcastically dubs "Frankification." So although adopting European attire is permissible in principle, Riḍā concludes, "it is forbidden in that it weakens the national-confessional bond and shows a preference for the ways of our grasping adversaries as opposed to the ways of the Islamic community." Put differently, modern Muslims must shift the emphasis of their Europeanization from its external cultural forms to its manner of *resisting acculturation*, a pathway to flourishing that in fact originated with Muslims.

Five years later, Riḍā reiterated his disdain for imitating foreigners (Europeans) in a lecture he gave on the subject of Islamic renewal (*tajdīd*).[67] Recycling arguments and scriptural evidence first advanced in his 1925–26 fatwa, he blames a host of modern geopolitical failures—the collapse of the Ottoman caliphate, the weakness of the modern Egyptian state, the abdication of Afghanistan's king, Amanullah Khan (r. 1919–29), and the Turkish republic's abandonment of Islam—on attempts at national renewal that reeked of mimicry. Instead, he calls for an "independent renewal" among Muslims modeled on that of the Meiji restoration in Japan. "Rational and independent people do not shun the old and turn to the new unless there is a reason." An authentic renewal of Islamic civilization must thus start from within.

Other reformist scholars, however, maintained their liberal views. In a scenario reminiscent of the original Transvaal fatwa, on November 26, 1928, the current grand mufti of Egypt, ʿAbd al-Majīd Salīm (d. 1954), issued a fatwa in response to a petition from the mufti of Greece regarding the permissibility of wearing the European hat.[68] Like the Muslims of Transvaal, Greek Muslims were a minority living among a non-Muslim majority; they were feeling pressure to wear the hat as a result of the ongoing reforms in the Turkish republic. Salīm was, in fact, a student of ʿAbduh, and his fatwa was modeled along the lines of his teacher's. But whereas ʿAbduh delivered his ruling with minimal explanation, Salīm explained in detail how the Islamic tradition authorizes his opinion.

Simply wearing a European hat is not unbelief, Salīm states, because the act does not provide clear evidence that the Muslim has renounced Islam—either by rejecting belief in the religion's divine origins or by seeking to publicly insult or disparage it. Additional evidence that clarifies the motive behind the act is needed to anathematize the believer: "A person's belief in Islam is assumed to be firmly established [*thābit*] and is therefore not superseded by doubt." Salīm paraphrases the well-known Islamic legal maxim "Certainty is not superseded by doubt" (*al-yaqīn lā yazūlu bi'l-shakk*), which means that the default legal status of something remains in force unless there is sufficient evidence to the contrary. In a criminal context, this statement resembles the Anglo-American legal maxim that a person remains innocent until proven guilty.[69]

To bolster the authority of his opinion, Salīm draws on key classical Islamic religious texts, including Ibn Taymiyya's commentary on the imitation hadith in *The Obligation of Following the Straight Path.* He contends that adopting the distinctive practices of unbelievers does not lead to unbelief, only to sin, if the act copied is sinful and the motive behind the act is not to renounce or smear Islam. To legitimize this opinion within the Ḥanafī school in particular, Salīm cites a number of classical Ḥanafī legal texts as well.

Like some of his reformist predecessors, Salīm carves out a distinct zone for *dīn.* He claims that the Mughal *qalansuwa,* a style of headgear worn originally by Zoroastrian Persians and adopted by Muslim elites during the formative period of Islam, is a symbol of kingship (*mulkiyya*), not *dīn.* Here, Salīm makes an explicit distinction between the domains of *dīn* and politics that parallels modern conceptualizations of the term *religion*—in this discursive context, the two terms are nearly interchangeable. Following Salīm's line of reasoning, a *qalansuwa* is not a foreign religious symbol and is thus not sinful for a Muslim to appropriate. By weaving this semantic distinction into his legal argument, Salīm sharply defines—and thus restricts—the domain of religion (and Islam) in Muslim public life.

In 1942, more than a decade after he issued the fatwa, Salīm reflects back on his rhetorical approach in an interview with *The Message* (*al-Risāla*):

> In his fatwas, he [ʿAbduh] depended upon comprehending the spirit of the law [*rūḥ al-sharīʿa*] and explaining its general objectives, not upon internal debates between the legal schools or determining which of the jurists' existing opinions were strongest [*tarjīḥ*]. For that reason, he usually issued brief fatwas, which provoked debate and disagreement among the religious scholars. One example is his famous fatwa permitting the [Muslims in Transvaal] to wear the European hat; as a result, a terrible outcry between scholars and the Azhari scholars at that time arose. So when I wanted to offer an opinion on this matter, I benefited from the lesson learned from this event, so that when I published my fatwa that permitted Muslims to wear the hat, I supported it with the opinions of the classical scholars, following their way of establishing textual proof and their process of determining the strongest opinion.[70]

According to Salīm, it was not only the controversial content of ʿAbduh's fatwa but also its manner of delivery that stoked controversy. Although he applauds ʿAbduh's ability to comprehend the spirit of the law [*rūḥ al-sharīʿa*], he obliquely criticizes the fatwa's brevity, which failed to instill confidence among both religious scholars and laypeople that it was sufficiently grounded in the Islamic tradition and not born of a desire to pander to European civilization. In his fatwa, Salīm thus followed the long-standing conventions of Islamic legal reasoning to placate skeptics.

Nevertheless, this transparency did not shield Salīm from criticism. The conservative Ḥanafī scholar, and the most learned Islamic manuscript expert of his generation, Muḥammad Zāhid al-Kawtharī (d. 1952), composed a stinging rebuke of Salīm's fatwa.[71] Kawtharī fled from Istanbul to Egypt in 1922, but continued to employ his official title, assistant to the shaykh al-Islam of the Ottoman Empire, even after the empire's decline and fall.[72] Echoing conservative thinkers like ʿIlīsh, in his published writings he blasts reformists who dismiss *taqlīd* and let "anyone who wears a turban" define Islam through *ijtihād.* His refutation of Salīm's fatwa reflects nostalgia for an old order in which *ʿulamāʾ* adhered to their respective schools of law and exercised control over Islamic orthodoxy.

Kawtharī ruthlessly attacks Salīm's fatwa at every level. First, Kawtharī claims that in his 1942 interview with *The Message,* Salīm misrepresents the diversity of viewpoints on the matter among Azhari scholars; he mentions ʿAbduh's fatwa in favor of wearing the hat but not the prominent Azhari scholars who issued fatwas against it, such as Muḥammad al-Bakhīt. Second, he criticizes Salīm's superficial style of legal reasoning (*ijtihād*). If he arrogantly claims the authority of an independent scholar (*mujtahid muṭlaq*), bypassing *taqlīd,* then he must derive an original ruling directly from the primary sources of Islamic jurisprudence—the Quran, *sunna,* analogical reasoning (*qiyās*), and consensus (*ijmaʿ*)—but he does not follow this protocol; instead, he draws from secondary sources, as would a lower-rank scholar (*muqallid*), a status that requires him to remain within the bounds of scholarly consensus. As a case in point, Kawtharī pedantically draws attention to the mufti's misspelling of "Abū *Munīb* al-Jurashī" as "Abū *Junīb* al-Jurashī," caustically remarking: "This [error] should not be surprising from someone who does not directly access the hadith through the door of *ijtihād.*"

But Kawtharī's most substantive critiques focus on Salīm's (mis)interpretations of the classical tradition of Islamic scholarship. Kawtharī accuses Salīm of disregarding the standards of evidence upheld by the Islamic legal tradition concerning matters of faith (that is, determining whether someone is a believer or unbeliever), which rely upon external signs like dress. Since only God truly knows what is in a person's heart, such methods, which rely upon an anthropology of everyday experience, only lead to probabilistic legal outcomes; but this is nonetheless how jurists conventionally determined the law throughout Islamic history. To now claim that absolute certainty is required to arrive at conclusions about matters of faith is a clean break from precedent. "How can he permit Muslims to adopt the distinctive markers of non-Muslims [*ghayr-muslimīn*] when the received tradition condemns such behavior?" Kawtharī concludes that Salīm incorrectly applies the legal maxim "Certainty is not superseded by doubt" to this situation.

Kawtharī also argues that Salīm misrepresents the position of the Ḥanafī legal canon on this subject. For example, Salīm cites from *Jāmiʿ al-Fuṣūlayn,* an important legal manual taught in the Ottoman madrasa system composed by the Transoxianian Sufi jurist Badr al-Dīn b. Qāḍī Samāwna (d. 1416), who wrote, "Wearing the *zunnār* around the waist and entering non-Muslim territory in order to conduct business is infidelity," but public acts such as dressing in the color black or wearing a Moghul cap is not; the latter is a "symbol of kingship [*mulkiyya*], not religion [*dīn*]." Salīm concludes that Ibn Qāḍī Samāwna's views on symbolic markers like the Moghul cap, not the *zunnār,* apply to the case of European hats. Kawtharī disagrees, contending that unlike brimmed hats, dressing in black and wearing the Moghul cap were historically associated with Muslim polities. The *zunnār,* on the other hand, has always been a distinctive marker of Christian identity. "So the evidence upon which the respected mufti bases his opinion," concludes Kawtharī, "does not [in fact] have any foundations."

Salīm's mischaracterization of the Islamic scholarly tradition, Kawtharī claims, is not limited to the Ḥanafī school. He mischaracterizes the views of Ibn Taymiyya, portraying him as lenient on the issue, when in fact he firmly opposed Muslim adoption of foreign practices. Although Salīm argues, as did ʿAbduh before him, that intent is a key factor in determining the legal status of wearing European headgear, according to Kawtharī's reading of Ibn Taymiyya, emulating unbelievers, even in the minimal case of refusing to dye the beard, is reprehensible, regardless of intent.

Kawtharī concludes that Salīm's fatwa goes farther askew than even ʿAbduh's because it is far more liberal. Despite departing from scholarly consensus, at least ʿAbduh imposed preconditions for wearing foreign headgear. Salīm, however, fails to impose any, ostensibly permitting Muslims to wear brimmed hats without any restrictions.[73]

MADE IN EUROPE'S IMAGE

In his eulogy of Kawtharī, the Egyptian biographer Muḥammad Abū Zahra (d. 1974) lauded his resistance to those who wished to confine religion to a distinct domain: "He reached the point when he was confronted by those who wanted to separate the world from religion (*dīn*) in order to rule the world by other than what God has revealed, but he stood in ambush for them."[74] The decades-long debate over wearing the European hat during the British occupation and control of Egypt reflects competing visions among Muslim thinkers over the place of religion—and thus Islam—in public life. For some, the way for Islamic civilization to reclaim its lost glory lay in removing the barriers inhibiting Muslims from adapting to modernity—even if that meant adopting foreign cultural norms—while for others, the way forward was to resist these temptations and retain fidelity to the Islamic past and preserve Muslim difference. These competing imaginations of modern religion lay bare how the dynamic process of meaning-making within Islam is, as Shahab Ahmed argued, defined by its differences, contrasts, and contradictions.[75]

Of course, the spectrum of Muslim attitudes toward emulating Europe cannot be reduced to a rigid dichotomy of liberal versus conservative (or modernist versus traditionalist), as Riḍā's dramatic reversal on adopting foreign dress illustrates. Although there are substantive differences between Riḍā's early and later writings on this issue, the collective interest of the Muslim community remained the cornerstone of his legal rulings. After the dramatic sociopolitical and economic transformations of the first quarter of the twentieth century, Riḍā came to see the adoption of Europe's cultural forms as an obstacle to Muslim progress toward their own modernity, and his legal argumentation merely traced the arc of this new point of view. Although some may describe his shift as a turn toward conservativism, he continued to believe that "both the old and the new" have their place.[76]

Aided by the rise of print media, modern Muslim thinkers from all ideological orientations—reformist, conservative, and those in between—intensified their focus on the image of Muslims and Islam. For the Muslim minorities living abroad who wore brimmed hats to look European, or the conservatives who shunned them to look distinctively Muslim, the external form of Muslim difference remained paramount. What they could not agree upon, however, were the meanings of these images. Did adopting the European hat signal Muslim humiliation, as many conservatives feared, civilizational progress, as some reformists claimed, or was it simply inconsequential?

Ultimately, Egypt's reformists prevailed. King Farouk was overthrown on July 23, 1952, and his successor appeared in public without a tarbush, which no Egyptian leader had done in more than 150 years. The independence of Egypt led to the resignification of headgear (and the body). Once a marker of Egyptian nationalism, the tarbush came to symbolize the vanished monarchy, thus opening the door for Egyptian Muslims to wear any style of hat, including brimmed hats. As representatives of the government's new visual language, police officers began donning berets, a material symbol of Egypt's transformation into a modern state made in Europe's image.

Epilogue

SEEING THE OTHER IN THE LIGHT OF GOD

The physical appearances of people become alike only when their hearts are aligned.

—ʿABD ALLĀH B. MASʿŪD (d. 653)

THE ELEMENTS OF MUSLIM STYLE

The heated debates within and beyond Egypt over wearing European brimmed hats cap the long history narrated in this book of how Muslims cultivated distinctive styles of difference from the origins of Islam to global modernity. I thus conclude with an argument for thinking of Muslim difference as a distinct style of being in the world. I construe style as a frame concept that weaves together the threads of Muslim difference, summarizing, in the process, this study's key findings. It also furnishes a point of entry into the critical task of reimagining Muslim difference in late modernity.

In the epigraph, the prominent Companion ʿAbd Allāh b. Masʿūd reminds us that mimesis is a connective practice that binds the bodies and emotions of people together.[1] Mimesis draws out people's hidden emotional and spiritual affinities onto the surfaces of their physical bodies for all to see. Rendered above as "physical appearance," the Arabic term *ziyy* inhabits a robust semantic field that encompasses the external forms of life from sartorial codes to distinctive gestures and bodily comportment—what we may alternatively refer to as a person's (or people's) distinctive style. *Style* is derived from the Latin root *stilus,* which originally signified the instrument as well as the act of composition.[2] However, with the Latin term's adaptation into Middle English (by means of Old French), *stilus* became "style," a reference not only to the craft of writing but to the aesthetic sensibilities associated with nearly all forms of cultural production, from architecture and furniture to art, fashion, and music. Today, this repertoire also includes people's distinctive physical bearings, their gestures, postures, and mode of speaking. In this way, the semantic field of style converges with that of *ziyy*, which retains its primary association with sartorial codes but may refer to other cultural forms as well. The semantic fields of *style* and *ziyy* thus focus our attention on the material forms of Muslim life, which aligns with how Muslim religious thinkers defined the lines between believers and unbelievers in public life through quotidian practices, not esoteric theological disputes on the Trinity or salvation.

Some styles are iconic—in the sense of being representative symbols of a society or culture. Overflowing with meaning and value, iconic styles across the fields of architecture, fashion, and art draw our attention to the semiotic. As we have seen, Muslim thinkers across time and place espoused a semiotic imaginary of difference in which symbols (*shiʿār*) are consequential to safeguarding religious and other social boundaries. The danger of imitating styles, then, lies in trafficking symbols across these boundaries.

The concept of style is thus not confined to external form alone. Reaching beneath the surface of the skin into the human inner sanctum, style also characterizes a person's subjective attitudes and everyday conduct. Some common phrases in the Egyptian colloquial dialect of Arabic, for example, illustrate how *ziyy* evolved into a general expression of how someone feels and thinks—as in the greetings "Iz-zayyak" (How are you)? and "Iz-zayyak fi kada" (What is your opinion on this)? In its most capacious sense, then, *ziyy* reflects one's "personal style."

This capacious sense of style is also implied in yet another version of the imitation hadith transmitted on the authority of the Companion Ḥudhayfa b. al-Yamān that bears a striking resemblance to the tradition transmitted on the authority of Ibn Masʿūd above: "People's physical appearances do not become alike until their morals [*khuluq*] do. Whoever imitates a people becomes one of them."[3] This obscure version, likely a composite of two traditions that were transmitted independently (with slight variations), was collected by Abū Shujāʿ al-Daylamī (d. 1115) in a relatively late compilation of traditions that was rearranged by his son Abū Manṣūr al-Daylamī (d. 1163). Daylamī's narration uses the term *khuluq* (morals) in place of the term *qulūb* (hearts), adding another shade of meaning. In this textual context, "Whoever imitates a people becomes one of them" becomes a commentary on the preceding statement that elaborates the meaning of style (*ziyy*)—that the alignment of a people's aesthetic and moral sensibilities reflects a shared sense of belonging.

The concept of style thus invites us to jettison letter-spirit dichotomies that sever the aesthetic from the moral. Although style draws attention to the external forms of life, it nonetheless elides the visible and invisible. Muslim imaginations of difference assume that visible and invisible forms of life are entwined. Both Ibn Taymiyya and Ghazzī admonished their readers to beware of the affective and spiritual power of outward imitation. In binding the aesthetic to the moral, the concept of style reframes ordinary practices as technologies of the self.

Through this conceptual lens, we are more apt to see Muslims as active agents whose alterity grew organically out of their historical conditions. Style, like difference, is a historically dynamic concept. Styles of Muslim difference are contingent upon the surrounding environment and indebted to a history of accidental encounters with a variety of foreigners. The specific embodied and material forms of Muslim difference, in other words, were not inevitable; if Medinan Jews and Meccan Arabs observed different styles of dress and ritual worship, then Muhammad's followers would have done so too.

Nor did these styles remain frozen in time. Defined by the present as much as the past, the forms of Muslim difference continued to *transform* across time and place. Islam has always been a dynamic tradition of progress—a discursive tradition that looks to the past but advances forward, balancing continuity and change as it adapts to new historical circumstances. Some markers of Muslim difference have been incredibly durable, like a fully grown beard, which, as discussed, began as a style intended to set apart Arabs from Persians but transformed into a symbol of Muslim piety and religious difference over time. The public call to prayer (*adhān*) likewise remains the quintessential audible symbol of Muslim difference today. Other markers of difference, however, faded away. One notable example is wearing shoes during prayer. Although the Prophet commanded his followers to pray in mosques with shoes in opposition to the Jews, subsequent generations of Muslims reversed course and began to pray without their shoes to keep the mosques clean. Another is the tarbush, adopted as a national symbol of Egypt (and the Ottoman Empire) only to be cast aside with the country's independence in 1952. But why do some markers of Muslim difference endure while others do not, and why do some symbolic practices come into style as others go out of style?

I have argued that we must view these religious transformations alongside the social, political, and material transformations that took place both within and around the Realm of Islam (*dār al-Islām*).[4] Within *dār al-Islām,* I singled out the historical contingency of the political structures that constitute Muslim difference. Precolonial styles of Muslim difference carried the ideological freight of empire, which molded social relations into hierarchical strata. The diminished status of Jewish and Christian subjects in precolonial Muslim polities from the Umayyad dynasty to the Mamluk Sultanate and Ottoman Empire reflect this imperial imaginary.

When crises—social, political, economic, environmental—erupted that threatened to unravel this socio-symbolic order, so did Islamic discourses against imitation and sumptuary regulations modeled on the Pact of ʿUmar, which aimed to safeguard this order. The convergence of religious discourse and state policy indexes the shared interest among scholars and bureaucrats in safeguarding the Realm by enacting a hierarchy of religious differences among its subjects. Political crises involving violent encounters with unbelievers that bloodied the borders of *dār al-Islām* precipitated the exchange of social practices and material objects across communal lines that became charged with new symbolic value. The looming Mongol presence along the borders of the Mamluk Sultanate fed Ibn Taymiyya's anxieties over Muslims and Christians celebrating Maundy Thursday together in the heart of Damascus. Ottoman rivalries with the Austrian-Habsburg and Safavid Empires informed Ghazzī's portrayal of the coffeehouse as the devil's lair that lured unsuspecting believers into a web of vices. Few Egyptians would have cared if Muḥammad ʿAbduh permitted Muslims on the opposite side of the African continent to wear brimmed hats if Europe had not aggressively colonized lands that once belonged to *dār al-Islām.*

The contours of Muslim difference transformed once the imperial political structures that constituted it fell apart. Reformists who categorized the brimmed hat as a cultural practice indigenous to Europe and not a "Christian" religious practice reflect a modern social imaginary that redefined the place of religion in public life. The marginal view that limited reprehensible imitation exclusively to "religious" markers of difference, such as the ritual practices (*ʿibādāt*) of taking Communion or wearing a crucifix, became normative. In contrast to Ibn Taymiyya, who forbade imitating the practices of unbelievers due to their foreign origins, this reformist logic privileges the taxonomy of a practice ("religious" versus "cultural") over its etiology. And yet, there remained (and still remain) conservative thinkers like ʿIlīsh and Kawtharī who grasped tightly onto traditional views enshrined in the schools of jurisprudence that resisted these new taxonomies. Adapting this discourse to today's culture wars, many conservative Muslims in America point to the "un-Islamic" origins of "secular" holidays such as Halloween, Thanksgiving, New Year's Day, and Valentine's Day.[5]

These contrasting styles of Islamic legal reasoning indicate that the concept of style is itself constituted by difference; to identify a style is to acknowledge the presence of alternative styles, whether between individuals or groups. At the collective level, style equips scholars in the humanities and social sciences with a powerful language of comparison to analyze cultural forms such as architecture, fashion, and worship. At the individual level, it exposes the tension between the one and the many, how the individual at once stands out from and conforms to the group.

Style offers scholars of religion a way to talk about diversity both within and beyond Islam. Although it is possible to compare Muslim styles of worship with Christian, Jewish, or Buddhist styles of worship, it is also possible to compare styles of worship within the Muslim community (*umma*). The *umma* does not constitute a single uniform entity and is itself highly differentiated. The preceding chapters have showcased diverse styles of being Muslim that cut across categories of gender, sect, ethnicity, and class. The vocabulary of style thus helps scholars to avoid the cardinal sin of essentializing Muslims, the reductive habit of typecasting the entire community by falsely claiming that all members share certain essential qualities.

As we shift our gaze to the present and future of Muslim difference, we can expect to see it follow multiple trajectories along a wide spectrum of sociocultural orientations that range from opposition to assimilation.

DISGRACED

A powerful but dark meditation on modern Muslim identity and difference is found in Ayad Akhtar's Pulitzer Prize–winning play, *Disgraced.* Akhtar tells the tragic story of Amir Kapoor, a self-described Pakistani Muslim apostate whose life quickly unravels in post-9/11 America. In the opening scene, the audience encounters Amir as a successful New York lawyer on the verge of becoming partner at his firm who is happily married to an artist, Emily. But by the final scene, Amir has lost both his job and his wife—a collapse that takes place at one fateful dinner party fueled by a combustible mix of alcohol, infidelity, and a heated interfaith debate on the Quran.

Amir also loses the respect of his teenage nephew Abe. Throughout the play, Abe expresses admiration for his uncle. But by the end, Abe is shattered by Amir's fall. He accuses him of turning on his Pakistani Muslim heritage so he can assimilate into mainstream American culture: "You want something from these people that you will never get."[6] In Amir's failure, Abe sees his own bleak future. Abe's resentment and despair at his own crumbling sense of self boils over into a denunciation of Western civilization:

> ABE. The Prophet wouldn't be trying to be like one of them. He didn't conquer the world by copying other people. He made the world copy him.
> AMIR. Conquer the world?
> ABE. That's what they've done. They've conquered the world. We're gonna get it back. For three hundred years they've been taking our land, drawing new borders, replacing our laws, making us want to be like them. Marry their women. They disgraced us. They disgraced us. And then they pretend they don't understand the rage we've got![7]

Abe expresses the anger and frustration of many young diasporic Muslims today who feel pressured to forfeit their faith in order to belong but are nonetheless spurned when they do so. Stuck between old and new, Abe feels neither authentically American nor authentically Muslim. He has little recourse but to fill this spiritual and social void with fantasies about a glorious Islamic past that vanished long ago. At the center of Abe's epic decline narrative is the magnetic force of imitation, which serves as a metacommentary on the Prophetic hadith "Whoever imitates a people becomes one of them." After the utopian era of the Prophet, in which Muhammad "made the world copy him," the historical fortunes of the Muslim *umma* go south: Muslims are now the ones copying everyone else, that is, Western civilization. Abe laments that the West has succeeded utterly in "making us want to be like them." Abe's discourse of power ignites his indignation at the *umma*'s precipitous fall from grace. But he is convinced that the *umma* will reclaim the dignity that properly belongs to it, confidently proclaiming, "We're gonna get it back."

Over the course of the play, we see a dramatic transformation in Abe's character. When we are introduced to Abe, he dresses like a "normal" American teenager, and has recently replaced his foreign, Muslim-sounding birth name, Hussein, with a conventional American-sounding name, "Abe Jensen," in order to blend into mainstream American culture. But by the final scene, his fortunes have changed; at a local Starbucks, fearing that Abe and his friend may belong to an Islamic extremist group, a barista calls the FBI, and they are taken in for interrogation. Abe fears that they will pressure him to spy on the Muslim community by threatening not to renew his visa and forcibly deport him back to Pakistan. Abe's world (and worldview) has begun to unravel—mirroring the downward spiral of his uncle Amir. This transformation is also displayed through Abe's physical appearance. Abe now wears a *kufi* and has disavowed the name "Abe Jensen" in favor of his real name, Hussein—both external markers of his Muslim identity. Abe's new self-consciously Islamic style does not reflect a spiritual revival but a new cultural orientation. Shattered by the failures of Amir, Abe has lost hope of fitting into mainstream American society and becoming "one of them." Speaking about the prospect of getting deported back to Pakistan, Abe wonders, "Maybe we never should've left. Maybe we never should have come to this one."[8] He is now stuck—confused about where he truly belongs. Amid this confusion, the pendulum of Abe's cultural orientation toward America abruptly swings from emulation to opposition.

POOR ASSES IN LION'S SKIN

The enigmatic figure of Muhammad Asad, on the other hand, saw the pendulum of his cultural orientation swing away from opposition. Fourteen years after his first critique of imitation in 1933, Asad refined his views in an article published in April 1947, "That Business of Imitation." Its content is devoted to answering the question "Why this seeming exaggerated anxiety when viewing our [Muslim] present position with regard to Western civilization?"[9] That is, why were Muslims so obsessed with copying the West? Geopolitically, much had changed between 1933 and 1947. From the ashes of World War II, the United States emerged as a global power. Muslims across the globe still found themselves looking toward Europe, and now the United States—as the construct called the "West" continued to evolve. It was strange that Muslims regularly compared Islam, a religion, to the West, an imagined geographic entity. Still, the comparison persisted.

Frustrated that his initial warnings against blind imitation were ignored, Asad complains that Muslim copycats are now everywhere, "confusing 'modernity' with an aping of Western customs."[10] These copycats refuse to accept the challenge to define their own modernity. Despite his firm opposition to the blind "aping" of Western cultural norms, Asad acknowledges that Islamic civilization once thrived due to the strategic appropriation of foreign cultural norms. But this is no longer the case. Asad wonders what is so different about the Western challenge. Proposing an answer to his own question, Asad claims that what has in fact changed is the character of Islamic civilization itself. In the past, Islamic civilization was strong, self-confident, and vigorous. Today, those attributes no longer belong to Muslims but to Western civilization. Islamic civilization is no longer equipped to imitate and assimilate foreign cultural norms in ways that are advantageous to the *umma.* Muslims can only imitate poorly—from a position of weakness and insecurity that leads to subservience and humiliation. *Tashabbuh,* in other words, is a pedagogy of the weak and dispossessed. Evoking René Girard's idea that a mimic becomes a double of his rival, Asad observes that "we [Muslims] have become as materialistic as our Western preceptors."[11] Muslims are imitating what is bad about the West, not what is good.

Asad's solution to this problem is similar to what he first proposed in 1933: Muslim cultural transformation should "come from *within.*"[12] Imitating the West "killed all pride and self-confidence," stripping Muslims of their "cultural autonomy" and making them into "poor asses" in a "lion's skin."[13] Above all, Asad wants Muslims collectively to reclaim their agency and determine their own destiny. Again, he states that the only way that Islamic civilization should imitate the West is by *not imitating* it.

Half a century later, in 1980, Asad once again counseled his fellow believers to be different from the West. Although the shape of geopolitics had transformed during the intervening period, the outlook for Islamic civilization as a whole remained poor. Now eighty years old, Asad had continued to refine his ideas on imitation—as signaled by his new gloss on "Whoever imitates a people becomes one of them." Whereas his initial commentary dwelled on the loss of Muslim difference that accompanies imitation, his new reading adds a positive moral spin to the Prophet's counsel. "This admonition cuts both ways," Asad writes. "It implies not only a condemnation of a Muslim imitating a non-Muslim people but also a recommendation of our imitating those whom we believe to be on the Right Way."[14] But who are the people on the "Right Way?" To clarify their identity, Asad turns to the final verses of *sūrat al-fātiḥa,* the opening chapter of the Quran: "Guide us on the straight path, those you have blessed" (Q 1:6–7). This supplication is first and foremost a moral imperative, he explains—an imperative to emulate those who are morally upright. In this more expansive reading of the hadith, imitating others, Muslim or non-Muslim, can be a force for good.

Elsewhere, he states, "[Muslims] have been low down for so many centuries that now they think they have to assert themselves by saying we are different. They are human beings. *They are not different* [emphasis added]."[15] Asad's unequivocal declaration that non-Muslims—Jews, Christians, Hindus, Buddhists, and other unbelievers—are "not different," expressed near the end of his life, is a categorical reversal from his original view, expressed first in *Islam at the Crossroads.* Asad no longer portrays the stubborn insistence on Muslim difference as a path to prosperity; he views it as an impulsive response to the rising tide of historical events that have overwhelmed and subdued the *umma.* This myopic view, he now states, obscures the shared humanity connecting Muslims to others, which transcends the religious divisions between them. That Asad chose to be buried in Granada, Andalusia, once part of al-Andalus, imagined as a place of multifaith *convivencia,* is a signpost of his evolution. But given his earlier views on the matter, Asad could not have been directing this critique toward contemporary Muslims alone, but toward himself as well. Asad's reversal is not only indicative of his personal spiritual and intellectual transformation; it also provides a hermeneutical key, I believe, for Muslims to unlock some of the mysteries of religious difference today.

REIMAGINING MUSLIM DIFFERENCE

This book provides copious evidence that cultivating a sense of belonging to the Muslim *umma* is a normative value within Islam. From the increased *baraka* (blessing) of praying together in the mosque to performing the Hajj pilgrimage to Mecca, Islamic ritual and law make it abundantly clear that connecting with fellow believers is a good thing. What is more ambiguous, however, is the value Islam attributes to cultivating a sense of belonging to a society that is predominantly non-Muslim.

Recall that, according to Muḥammad ʿAbduh and other reformists, cultivating a sense of belonging by assimilating into a majority non-Muslim society is in the collective interest (*maṣlaḥa*) of the Muslim community. This outlook was modeled on Ibn Taymiyya's pragmatic reasoning that the collective good is determined through a calculation that maximizes benefit and minimizes harm. But while Ibn Taymiyya defined the zone of reprehensible imitation holistically to encompass ritual and cultural practices such as wearing foreign attire and attending festivals, reformists reduced that zone to exclude cultural practices like dress, granting Muslims more individual autonomy and redefining religion in the process. Muslims today living in sovereign nation-states may adhere to this pragmatic logic, adding that empirical studies demonstrate it is harmful for Muslim mental and spiritual health to be disconnected from mainstream society and that Islamophobia will intensify in the absence of deep and meaningful social connections with non-Muslims.

The problem with this self-interested utilitarianism, however, is that it is ethically thin. It is important to take a step back and recall that the shariʿa is not merely "law," and thus concerned with rule-making alone; rather, it is a normative universe that sets forth a virtuous path of how to live a good life. At its core, shariʿa-based reasoning is an aspirational ethical endeavor. At the turn of the twentieth century, the utilitarian spirit behind ʿAbduh's fatwa and its subsequent elaborations trailblazed a new Muslim cultural orientation toward Europe. But in today's religiously plural societies, the fatwa's cold utilitarian logic falls short of establishing a deep connection with the Religious Other. It instrumentalizes the social technology of imitation to achieve the political, scientific, and military interests of the Muslim community, but ignores the underlying ethical problem: that contempt for and subjugation of the religious Other remains a normative ideal. The form of social belonging this attitude enables is surface level at best. It bars Muslims from truly belonging in a cosmopolitan society and, in a sense, fails to attain the *maṣlaḥa* it sets out to achieve.

Imitation, as we have seen, is a social relationship of power and prestige in which the imitator looks up to the model as "the original." In the eyes of religious authorities, Muslims who imitated non-Muslims inverted the ideal religious hierarchy in which "Islam is above, not below." To preserve this hierarchy, they drew on the Prophet's authority to stigmatize imitation that crosses confessional lines due to its implicit flattery of the religious Other. Over time, the dictum "Whoever imitates a people becomes one of them" came to encode a logic of difference in which the religious Other was assumed to be morally inferior.

This categorically negative outlook toward the religious Other does not cohere with contemporary moral sensibilities in which we evaluate the behavior of individuals, not groups. We assume that anyone, Muslims or non-Muslim, has the capacity to be a moral exemplar (or moral failure). For Muslims to belong in a religiously plural society and not be mere spectators on its margins, closing the gap between these outlooks is essential.

As this descriptive history blurs into constructive engagement with the Islamic discursive tradition, my identity as a Muslim of South Asian descent becomes more salient. As a person of color who immigrated to America, fleeing racial discrimination, I have experienced how elusive a sense of true belonging can be. In what follows, I argue that cultivating a more inclusive style of Muslim difference that displays genuine respect and sincere affection for the religious Other is a moral imperative in our intertwined world.[16]

Quran scholar Mun'im Sirry complains that although some Muslim reformists have boldly reinterpreted the Quran to advance interreligious harmony, they have not been courageous enough to "revisit the applicability of *dhimmī* status" in modern nation-states.[17] His observation begs the question: is the hierarchical ideal behind the *dhimmī* system that assigns to non-Muslims a diminished socio-political status relative to Muslims a transhistorical "Islamic" ideal or a historically contingent one? I have argued that the Partisans of Hadith's hierarchical vision of an ideal Islamic society, as conveyed through the hadith traditions against imitation, reflects an imperial imaginary extrinsic to the texts. However, the political reality that conditioned how these difference-makers drew the line between self and other has transformed in modernity. Empire has given way to the sovereign nation-state as the dominant political form. Philosopher Charles Taylor has persuasively argued that a modern social imaginary is defined not by the ideal of hierarchy but by the ideal of equality between citizens.[18] "Modern universal citizenship," adds Andrew March, "presents expectations of moral recognition and social solidarity across communal and confessional lines."[19] How can the categorical inferiority of unbelievers instituted within premodern Islamic prescriptive discourses cohere with this distinctively modern worldview?

Recent scholarship has shown how the political transformations of modernity have spawned new Muslim social imaginaries. Mohammad Fadel demonstrates how the prospect of liberal democracy in Egypt prompted Muslim reformists to adopt more tolerant attitudes toward unbelievers, such as optimism for their salvation and aversion to the *dhimmī* system.[20] These transformations have reshaped not only hierarchical ideals of religious difference but also the ideals governing other differences such as gender, ethnicity, and status. Religious difference, I have shown in this book, intersects with other markers of difference. The illuminating studies of Kecia Ali, Jonathan Brown, and Zahra Ayubi on slavery and gender in classical Islam illustrate the sharp contrast between the hierarchical ideals implicit in those discourses and our modern egalitarian sensibilities.[21]

In light of these broader social transformations, it becomes apparent that the ideal of a religiously stratified society is historically contingent—that the Pact of ʿUmar can no longer be viewed as an ideal template for Muslim interreligious engagements and revived during moments of crisis, as it had been for a millennium. That some features of this system are in fact more "liberal" than the policies of modern nation-states, such as granting Jewish and Christian subjects a certain measure of legal autonomy, does not erase the categorical distinctions in religious status that this system was meant to impose. With the transformation from a pre-modern social imaginary to a modern social imaginary grounded in an egalitarian ethos that disavows hierarchy a fait accompli, what does the present and future of Muslim difference "look" like?

I believe that Muslims must adopt a logic of difference that disavows a hermeneutics of contempt for the religious Other. While all humans draw lines that distinguish self from other, it is not inevitable that outsiders be scorned; they may, instead, be viewed with indifference or reverence. Social psychologists have shown how demonizing language can push others outside of one's circle of moral concern, leading to their social death and, ultimately, their physical death.[22] It is incumbent upon Muslims to acknowledge the moral damage that exclusivist religious discourses may inflict upon others in order to apply the Prophet's universal ethical teaching: "Do not harm nor reciprocate harm."[23] This principle is particularly relevant today amid the alarming spread of Islamophobia across the globe, which has normalized anti-Muslim discrimination. Instead of reciprocating harm, Muslims must struggle to "respond in a better way [*aḥsan*]" by exhibiting self-restraint and refusing to categorically demonize the Other. The outcome of treating the religious Other with dignity, equality, and humanity, promises Q 41:34, is that "your bitter enemy will become like an old friend."

In this new paradigm, a social imaginary stratified along lines of group membership is superseded by one defined by individual achievement. This worldview is not alien to Islam. The oft-quoted Q 49:13 proclaims that sincere devotion to God (*taqwā*) is the cardinal virtue that sets apart one human being from another—not group membership.[24] Dramatic transformations in the logic and meaning of Muslim difference are also not new to Islam. Recall how the semiotic value of the headscarf evolved from a marker of class difference between slave and free women into a marker of religious difference that stressed modest relations between women and men. What would be new, then, is for this transformation to stop.

Skeptics may object that across all societies today, East and West, hierarchies persist. In the United States, there are stark inequalities that cut across race, gender, class, and religion. Skeptics may add that the spread of egalitarian beliefs among Americans is of recent vintage, roughly half a century. Why, they may wonder, is it essential to root the Islamic discursive tradition in the shifting sands of secular liberal democracies that are themselves unsure of who they are and what they believe? In modern societies defined by flux and fragmentation, what are Muslims attempting to assimilate into?

Such objections, though understandable, stem from anxieties over change—especially change perceived to originate from a nefarious European ("Western") colonial legacy intent on dominating Muslim civilization. Constructions of Muslim difference, as we have seen, are entangled in webs of power relations. From the eighteenth century, Muslim thinkers across the globe composed treatises against aping European civilization, wondering how they could limit the spread of this plague-like epidemic, which had become so pervasive that it inspired the Persian neologism *gharbzadegī* ("Westoxification" or "Occidentosis").[25] These treatises—some inspired by the Salafi ideology now dominant in Saudi Arabia—marginalize the positive valence of *tashabbuh,* as well as its Sufi-inspired meanings, condensing its interpretation into a uniform spectrum of gray that locks Muslims into a hostile confrontation between "us and them" (that is, Islam and the West). Seduced by the simplicity of Ibn Taymiyya's uncompromising scripturalism as well as the aura of authenticity and certainty that it promised, adherents of the modern-day Salafi movement have fiercely resisted the opposing currents of innovation and imitation.[26] These transformations, a response to the West's triumphalism, reflect broader discursive trends in modern Islam that include a contraction in the scope of Islamic orthodoxy as well as a reduced tolerance for epistemological ambiguity.[27] Today, scholars and intellectuals across a wide range of media stress the need to safeguard Muslim difference amid the flux of modern identity politics, the nation-state's ongoing efforts to domesticate religion, and new technologies that have enabled people to communicate and travel across land, sea, and air at a scale and speed unthinkable in the past. This increased mobility of people, ideas, and things across the globe has accelerated the pace of cultural change, leading to demographic shifts that have turned the trite binary of "Islam and the West," along with its implied essentialisms, into an anachronism.[28] With millions of Muslims now living in and actively shaping Europe and North America, Islam is now *in* the West. Contemporary religious discourses of Muslim difference ought to shed the outdated Islam/West dichotomy and reflect these new social entanglements.

Despite the persistent trope, shared by Islamophobes and puritans alike, that Islam is immune to change, this book has shown that change is built into the architecture of Islamic tradition. The *kaʿba* is an effective "Islamic" metaphor for tradition, argues Martin Nguyen, because while it is a symbol of deep spiritual meaning and value, it is nonetheless a physical structure constructed by human hands throughout history.[29] Change is also embedded into the matrix of this tradition—the origins of Islamic scripture itself. The Quran did not materialize into stone tablets made of sapphire like the Ten Commandments but through the medium of the Prophet's body—his heart and tongue—over a period of twenty-three years. This dynamic unfolding of divine revelation provides a master class in situational ethics, which adapts styles of life to changes in time and place. As already discussed, later jurists recognized that cultural norms (*ʿurf*/*ʿāda*) conditioned not only the Quran but also the *sunna,* and formally instituted this source as a dynamic legal mechanism to enable the shariʿa to adapt to local cultures. Accorded the weight of law, these norms include not only social practices but moral sensibilities as well.[30] The point, then, is not to anoint secular modernity as the pinnacle of human moral progress, but to do what Muslims across time and place have always done: connect Islam to the world in which they live. To reject change, wholesale, is to reject the Islamic tradition.

"Whatever Muslims deem good is good in the sight of God," stated Ibn Masʿūd, "and whatever they deem bad, it is bad in the sight of God."[31] There is a growing consensus among contemporary Muslim scholars across the ideological spectrum that hierarchical imaginations of the religious Other are no longer viable. Some progressive Muslim scholars, such as "Muslima" theologian Jerusha Tanner Rhodes (aka Jerusha Tanner Lamptey), have deconstructed stratified models of religious difference based on their original readings of the Quran.[32] A cluster of Egyptian reformists, from political analyst Fahmī Huwaydī to jurist-academic Khaled Abou El Fadl, disclaim the premises behind the *dhimmī* system.[33] But even arch-traditionalist T. J. Winter ("Abdal Hakim Murad"), who vigorously defends the Sunni theological doctrine that Islam supersedes all other religions, disavows the "medieval" sumptuary regulations inspired by the Pact of ʿUmar—despite the alleged consensus (*ijmāʿ*) on the obligation to impose them.[34] Publicly marking unbelievers, he suggests, is historically outmoded.

In line with this progressive spirit, Winter more recently expanded the Islamic theological zone of proximate others beyond the usual monotheist suspects to encompass atheists.[35] Instead of referring to them through existing Quranic labels of unbeliever (*kāfir*) or polytheist (*mushrik*), which are categorically negative, its members stigmatized, censured, and threatened with damnation, he gives them a brand-new name: *ahl al-kidhāb,* the people of denial. One might presume that those who lack faith altogether would be ranked lower in the Islamic hierarchy of religious Others than the *mushrik,* who at least possesses some faith, but Winter's clever play on the term *ahl al-kitāb* signals that *ahl al-kidhāb* ought to be treated as proximate others. Given the growing population of agnostics and atheists in Britain and other parts of Europe, he calls upon Muslims to disavow a hermeneutics of contempt and "develop an empathetic and compassionate theology of atheism and of the very new type of humanity it is creating."[36] Because the "entitlements of humans are innate" due to the radiance conferred upon them by God prior to ensoulment, he urges true believers to see the best in everyone, even those who openly reject faith, with sincere love and gratitude, in order to cultivate an "outlook of positivity towards others."[37] Loathing these deniers as hostile infidels (*kuffār*) is not an option. As a path toward interreligious cooperation, Winter opts not to fixate on what divides Muslims from deniers—belief—but on what they share—their humanity. Winter contrasts this "Sufi conception" of interreligious engagement with that of ISIS, which "sees the unbeliever only as the reassuring object of scorn."[38] Winter's conciliatory attempt to smooth over the rough edges of religious difference in contemporary British society is a striking reversal from his defiant proclamation two decades earlier that "it is religious truth claims which should generate tolerance—and not vice versa."[39] Now, it is precisely the "context of post-monotheistic society" and the need to construct a culture of religious tolerance that inspires his new anthropocentric theology in which the most remote religious Other becomes the near Other.[40]

Recent scholarship has thus shown that there are ample scriptural, ethical, and theological resources within Islam to reimagine the religious Other. But what would the proposed theological reframing of the religious Other mean for Islamic discourses against imitation? Recognizing the intrinsic worth of the unbeliever implies that the discourse no longer drips with contempt for the religious Other. There is no need to hold onto Ibn Taymiyya's "medieval" polemical reading of "Whoever imitates a people becomes one of them," in which the referent "them" is categorically negative, nor to the belief that non-Muslims, as a category, are unworthy of emulation and friendship. If God permits the believer to fall in love, marry, and have children with the unbeliever, wonders one German Muslim, why can't they be friends?[41]

Instead of hinging upon exterior markers of religious identity, contemporary Muslim thinkers may instead draw more heavily on Sufi discourses that stress interior ethical self-cultivation. In these discourses, the spiritual objective of subjugating the self to God prevails over the social objective of subjugating *others* to the self. In other words, it is not necessary to construct the non-Muslim as a foil to forge the ideal Muslim. The spiritually undisciplined self (*nafs*) obsessed with power seeks to be above others, but the spiritually disciplined self shuns self-aggrandizement, fearing abasement before God. By denying the impulse of the self to rise above the religious Other, the flattening of religious hierarchy onto a plane of social equality acts as a form of spiritual discipline (*taʾdīb*) that cultivates a virtuous self (*nafs*).

This sensibility is echoed in Muhammad Asad's rereading of the imitation hadith, which privileges the emulation of moral virtue over external markers of religious identity, a reading that aligns with the nonpolemical glosses of Suhrawardī and Ghazzī that fully embrace the positive transformative potential of imitation and define true belonging as the presence of mutual affection. Through the lens in which the religious Other has intrinsic value, these readings help us to envision a cosmopolitan society in which belonging is not confined by confessional boundaries.

One of my principle aims in this book has been to illuminate Ghazzī's contributions in the magisterial treatise *The Virtue of Awakening* to our understanding of the human subject. Against prevailing atomistic conceptions of the self, Ghazzī imagines a self holistically shaped by its environment. The human subject, according to him, is connected to a cosmic ecosystem through the spiritual and social technology of mimesis. The concept of mimesis, I have argued, helps us to see identity and difference in new ways. In a mimetic model of the self, identity is defined, dialogically, through encounter. Mimesis, in other words, is a relational practice that blurs the line between self and other. Instead of seeing self and other as a dichotomy in opposition, we come to the more nuanced view that the dyad is dynamically intertwined. The Other, according to Tanner Rhodes, is "never wholly other."[42] Mimesis, then, manifests the ongoing fluidity between self and other.

But in order to avoid falling into the narcissistic trap of seeing the Other only through the lens of the self, French Jewish philosopher Emmanuel Levinas urges us to first look into the face of the Other.[43] When the Other looks back at us it confers upon us an ethical responsibility to shun the impulse to dominate and assimilate the Other into ourselves. We instead surrender to its irreducible *difference.* For the true believer whose vision is illuminated by divine radiance, according to a famous hadith, to see the face of the Other is to see the face (*wajh*) of God.[44] Encounter is revelation. We may thus reimagine the religious Other as a conceptual *barzakh* or *dihlīz,* a threshold that is at once part of the self and irreducibly Other.[45]

If the religious Other is no longer to be scorned but embraced, does Muslim difference—the obligation for Muslims to set themselves apart from the religious Other—become obsolete? Winter proposes that, at the very least, Muslims in Britain tone down their difference:

> We need to reduce the superficial outward signs that suggest to secular *Lahabists* [*sic*] that we are exiles. For faith to prevail of its alternative, it must not be veiled by strangeness. . . . Our cultured despisers, who understandably judge by appearances, frequently object to spectacular outward tokens of foreignness and the ethnic exotica of where our grandmothers were born. Put crudely, a sharia-compliant headscarf of British inspiration is less likely to invite attack than headgear which proclaims adherence to the culture of a fair but distant land. A man walking the cold and rainy streets of Frankfurt in desert clothes is inviting all who see him to the *tanfīrī* [*sic*] conclusion that the ways of Islam do not belong. . . . *Tajwīd* and *adhān* modes ought to be local and not imported. *There exists no Sharia requirement to make a public statement that Islam is an alien religion* [emphasis mine].[46]

Adopting a nativist posture, Winter urges British Muslims, most of whom are ethnically South Asian, to leave behind their foreign cultural styles in their ancestral homes. He singles out ethnocultural markers of Muslim difference, visible and audible, that he believes build walls between Muslims and non-Muslims in British society. Although distinctive religious markers such as the call to prayer (*adhān*), recitation of the Quran (*tajwīd*), and adoption of the headscarf should publicly manifest, the particular *styles* of their performance that fail to conform to indigenous British aesthetic and cultural styles should be cast away.[47] Winter's admonitions assume that it is possible to characterize certain styles as "British," a view that is at odds with his portrayal of British society as a shifting sand too unstable for Muslims to assimilate into; if chicken tikka masala can become Britain's national dish, then these foreign styles, too, may one day be coded as British.[48] We also inadvertently hear in Winter's soft nativism faint echoes of the right-wing xenophobic discourses behind the heavy-handed measures undertaken by European states such as France and Switzerland to suppress public markers of Muslim difference from headscarves to minarets. Most American Muslims would likely scoff at the assertion that they should voluntarily suppress their individual freedom to express their difference—religious, racial, ethnic—to appease the white Anglo-Protestant religious majority. Although Winter is correct to point out that scholars never compelled Muslims to declare that "Islam is an alien religion," they did expect Muslims to set themselves apart in public life through small differences.

Within the United States, a religiously plural liberal democracy, it is critical that Muslims envision a form of religious difference that empowers ordinary believers to define their own personal style, or *ziyy.* Muslims should neither feel compelled to publicly display outward signs of their difference through an Islamic discourse that categorically demonizes the religious Other nor feel pressured to erase those signs to appease a white Anglo-Protestant religious majority. Neither can contemporary interpretations of the Islamic discursive tradition be indifferent to the local particularities of Muslims living in secular liberal democracies; nor can mainstream American society be indifferent, or hostile, to the particularities of being Muslim. If the loudest voices within the Islamic tradition and American society present Muslim citizens with the false choice that they must choose between being authentically Muslim or authentically American, they will find themselves stuck between alienation and assimilation. The inevitable outcome of such radically divergent discourses, as portrayed by the character Abe in *Disgraced,* is confusion, despair, and a fractured self.

According to Sherman Jackson, the persistent dichotomization of Muslim and American identities has been detrimental to Blackamerican Muslims. "Aided by the interpretive goadings and assurances of their immigrant brethren," laments Jackson, "Blackamerican Muslims commonly construe Islam as implying that any imitation of the infidel West is tantamount to Unbelief."[49] This outlook, he argues, has complicated their "quest for a constructive, dignified American identity" by convincing them they must look elsewhere: "'Islamic orthodoxy' now bans Blackamerican Muslim participation on pain of divine retribution. To bolster this position, a Prophetic hadith, ubiquitously cited in the 1970s and 1980s, is strategically pressed into service: 'Whoever imitates a people becomes one of them (*man tashabbaha bi qawmin fa huwa minhum*).' On this construction, not only is participation in the dominant order a violation of true blackness, it is additionally a violation of Islam—or more properly 'Islamic identity'—at least for Blackamerican Muslims."[50] The alleged religious imperative to be different has enhanced racialized sentiments that being authentically black means opposing mainstream American culture, even in areas that lead to prosperity, such as education. "This," bemoans Jackson, "is misguided protest at its worst."[51]

But history offers American Muslims guidance. By reading Islamic prescriptive discourses alongside historical and documentary sources over a grand sweep of time, I demonstrated how textual representations of religious difference overlay a complex social world in which the lines between believers and unbelievers often blurred. Muslims cultivated a style of being different that, although hierarchical, produced a culture of hospitality toward the religious Other. They consciously scaled down social distinctions to small differences that aligned with the Quranic ethos of moderation. Muslim efforts to stand out from the crowd were not spectacular and oppositional, but minimal and incremental, carefully calibrated to accommodate the presence of religious Others.

Although the scale of these differences was small relative to what Muslims had in common with unbelievers, they nonetheless possessed great symbolic value. Whether by means of distinctive styles of headgear, facial hair, or the cardinal direction of ritual prayer, Muslims drew from a shared ecosystem of symbols that were already in use among Jews, Christians, and others. Although Muslims adopted small differences that visibly set them apart in the public sphere, they drew from an ecosystem of symbols that cut across religious lines and paradoxically connected them to others.

One of the most important cultural strategies the Prophet employed to harmonize the dual aspirations of social distinction and connection was creatively synthesizing existing styles to produce new styles. Perhaps the best example of this cultural synthesis, discussed in chapter 4, is the institution of a distinctive style of Muslim headgear. By winding the turban around the *qalansuwa,* the Prophet blended two styles of headgear that Arabs wore, but not necessarily together, into a new style. On other occasions, the Prophet simply updated an existing style. Arab men customarily grew their beards, but the Prophet encouraged his followers to adopt a new style—not only to grow them but to dye them a different color. In both situations, the Prophet did not crudely import cultural norms entirely foreign and strange to the Arabs, but adopted norms that were indigenous and familiar to them, while infusing them with new symbolic meaning and value. In this way, he was able to connect Islam to the culture around him.

This connectivity is also reflected in how the Quran labels "People of the Book" as the proximate religious Other, which positions Muslims as mediators between—not opposite to—Jewish and Christian styles of monotheism. The label signals what they have in common, not what sets them apart; and what they have in common is not small but grand in scale: a shared belief that God is one and a shared ethos of doing good in the world (*āmanū wa-ʿamilū al-ṣāliḥāt*).[52] Indeed, it was the scale of this sharedness across creed and practice that paradoxically elevated the value of the small differences that set them apart. But today, a growing chorus of Muslim scholars suggests that this spiritual proximity extends to all humanity by virtue of the divine breath that inheres within everyone.

American Muslims, then, ought to feel empowered to shun misreadings of the Islamic tradition that claim the Prophetic *sunna* commands them to categorically oppose and reject social citizenship in the United States.[53] Muhammad's way suggests that public displays of Muslim difference need not be spectacular; small differences suffice. The ethical challenge for Muslims in America today, however, is to embrace a new social imaginary that recodes how the religious Other is perceived—to turn away from a hermeneutics of contempt and to affirm the intrinsic value of all people, regardless of religion.

To be clear, a semiotic reconfiguration of Muslim difference is not a call to erase the distinctive markers that define the *umma*. Across human societies, symbolic markers of difference have played a key role in drawing lines between self and other by infusing corporeal practices and material objects with meaning and value. Despite the privatization of faith, symbols continue to play an important role in defining religious difference in American public life. A call to reimagine the religious Other positively in nonbinary terms affirms the agency of Muslims to embody versatile styles of being and belonging that both set them apart and connect them to the world. Recall that Malcolm X's journey to Islam began with small differences. Even before Malcolm knew anything about Islam, his brother, Reginald, gave him the following instructions: "Malcolm, don't eat any more pork and don't smoke any more cigarettes."[54]

American Muslims will, of course, not conform to a single style—nor should they. As I have argued in this book, the orientation of Muslim difference throughout Islamic history is characterized by multiplicity. Muslim heterogeneity across markers of race, ethnicity, class, gender, ability, sect, generation, ideology, and geography ensures that the American *umma* today will likewise be characterized by multiplicity. While *some* South Asian immigrants will adopt white, upper-middle-class social norms and refrain from displaying any outward forms of their religious difference, *some* Blackamerican Salafis will outwardly manifest distinct forms of religious difference embedded in a racial logic of opposition to a long American history of systemic racism against blacks.[55] Although all Muslims are difference-makers, neither the motivations nor the styles that define the meaning and value of these differences are uniform.

The diverse expression of Muslim difference is itself quintessentially American. By permitting the free exercise of religion, the First Amendment of the U.S. Constitution laid the foundation for establishing religious pluralism as a normative ideal and a cornerstone of liberal democracy. Although this ideal has yet to be fully realized due to intermittent, often violent, persecution against different religious groups, it has enabled the United States to become one of the most religiously diverse nations in the world.[56] Muslim pluralists, excavating the Quran for a similar message, struck gold with Q 5:48, which not only endorses diversity but proclaims that it is divinely ordained: "We have assigned a law and a path to each of you. If God had so willed, He would have made you one community."[57] But God did not decree that everyone follow one religion and thus, they reason, humans should not have that expectation either. "There is no compulsion in religion" (Q 2:256).[58]

There is, of course, a darker side to difference: conflict. As I conclude this book, sharpening divisions between "red" and "blue" states and between rich and poor are fracturing the United States. Add mass shootings, gender violence, systematic racism against black and brown people, rising Islamophobia and anti-Semitism, and it appears that the country is falling into pieces—that America's experiment with difference is failing. But in this precarious moment, I believe that American Muslims have an opportunity to draw on the rich spiritual, ethical, and intellectual resources of Islam to heal and repair these divisions. By making Islam's core theological doctrine, *tawḥīd,* "to make one," the touchstone of this endeavor, Muslims can help reimagine and reunite a nation fractured by social atomism.[59]

It begins by expanding the circle of belonging. As we have seen, one of the most powerful statements of belonging in the Islamic tradition is the canonical hadith on imitation that thematically anchors this book. "Whoever imitates a people [*qawm*] becomes one of them" invites us to think about the nation as an imagined community. Although the hadith has historically signaled repudiation and disavowal from religious Others, it can be reframed to signal interreligious solidarity. There are two key steps in this hermeneutical process. The first step is to view "them," the religious Other, not with contempt but with respect, reverence, and love. "A person," taught the Prophet, "belongs with the one he loves." The second step is to conceptually expand the circle of *qawm,* people or nation, to be more inclusive. *Qawm* is an elastic term, applicable to wide range of collectivities, that authorizes Muslims to inhabit multiple circles of belonging. The term *qawmiyya* in Modern Standard Arabic means nationalism. In the context of the hadith, then, the semantic zone of *qawm* need not be religiously uniform, limited to Muslims alone, but can be reimagined as a religiously plural nation that encompasses all Americans—both Muslim and non-Muslim. Through this new frame of reference, suitable for a religiously plural liberal democracy, the hadith promotes an inclusive style of social citizenship that invites others to transcend confessional divisions, enter new circles of belonging, and come together as a single nation to pursue justice, virtue, and the collective good.

Before leaving Damascus in 2010, I gifted ten-year-old Saʿīd, the eldest of the three children in my host family, with a New York Yankees baseball cap. The navy blue cap put a big smile on Saʿīd's face. That he had never watched a Yankee game didn't matter. He recognized the iconic "NY" symbol on the front. Having grown up watching the Yankees, and having dreamed of playing for the team one day, I owned several caps. So I decided to offer Saʿīd some "insider" tips on how to wear it properly. I began to bend the brim of the cap into a crescent shape so that it would look "broken in." But Saʿīd abruptly stopped me. "No, Youshaa, that's not the right way," he said confidently. He took the cap, straightened the brim back to its original state, and put it on his head. "This is the right way."

Notes

INTRODUCTION

1. Asad, *Islam at the Crossroads,* 75. Asad composed this book—his first—at the age of thirty-three. Asad authored nearly forty works on Islam, including his autobiography, *Road to Mecca,* and a translation of the Quran, *The Message of the Quran.*
2. Ibid., 77.
3. Ibid., 78.
4. Ibid.
5. Ibid., 79–80.
6. *Man tashabbaha bi-qawm*^{in} *fa-huwa min-hum.* See *Sunan Abī Dāwūd, kitāb al-libās, bāb fī libs al-shuhra;* al-Ṭabarānī, *al-Muʿjam al-Awsaṭ,* 8:179; al-Quḍāʿī, *Musnad al-Shihāb,* 1:244; al-Bazzār, *Musnad al-Bazzār,* 7:368; al-Ṭabarānī, *Musnad al-Shāmiyyīn,* 3:94; al-Ṣanʿānī, *al-Muṣannaf,* 11:453–54. See chapter 2 for references to other narrations as well as rankings of its authenticity among hadith critics.
7. Asad, *Islam at the Crossroads,* 77.
8. Ibid., 79.
9. Misch et al., *A Road to Mecca.*
10. Asad, *Islam at the Crossroads,* 7.
11. On genealogical approaches to history, see Foucault, "Nietzsche, Genealogy, History," 76–100.
12. Freidenreich, *Foreigners and Their Food,* 5.
13. Appiah, *The Lies That Bind,* 202.
14. Twain, *Tom Sawyer Abroad,* 98.
15. I draw inspiration from Berkowitz, who writes, "I tell the story of how Jewishness was made." *Defining Jewish Difference,* 6.

16. Mahmood, *Religious Difference,* 11.
17. Although *The Muslim Difference* is the first book-length study on the Islamic doctrine of reprehensible imitation (*tashabbuh*), there are some studies of the subject in European languages, including Goldziher's brief but pioneering study in Goldziher, "Über jüdische," 302–15; Goldziher, "Usages juifs," 75–94; for an important follow-up to Goldziher, nearly a century later, see Kister, "'Do Not Assimilate Yourselves,'" 321–53; on usages of *tashabbuh* in modern South Asian legal discourses, see Masud, "Cosmopolitanism and Authenticity," 156–75; in medieval Sufi discourse, see Salamah-Qudsi, "The Idea of *Tashabbuh,*" 175–97. Also see my articles: Patel, "'Their Fires Shall Not Be Visible'"; Patel, "'Whoever Imitates a People Becomes One of Them'"; Patel, "The Islamic Treatises against Imitation."
18. *Ṣaḥīḥ Muslim, kitāb al-ḥayḍ, bāb jawāz ghusl al-ḥāʾiḍ raʾs zawjihā.*
19. Foucault, "Nietzsche, Genealogy, History," 76–100.
20. Emon, *Religious Pluralism and Islamic Law,* 34–76. Charles Taylor argues that premodern societies are "organized around a notion of hierarchy"—a way of viewing the cosmos that is distinctive from modern societies: Taylor, *Modern Social Imaginaries,* 9.
21. Marlow, *Hierarchy and Egalitarianism.*
22. Moving beyond structuralism, post-structuralist thinkers such as Gilles Deleuze reimagined binary oppositions (self/other, us/them, male/female) as multiplicities of difference—a philosophical framework that emphasizes conceptual threshold ("in-between") spaces: Deleuze, *Difference and Repetition.*
23. Bowen, *Why the French Don't Like Headscarves;* Miller, "Majorities and Minarets"; Weiner, *Religion Out Loud,* 158–94. For the U.S. Supreme Court decision on growing a beard in jail, see *Holt, aka Muhammad v. Hobbs, Director, Arkansas Department of Correction, et al.,* 574 U.S. 352 (2015).
24. By "unbeliever" I mean those who do not identify as Muslim, or non-Muslims. Occasionally, I use the word in a more specific sense, as a translation for the polemically charged Arabic-Quranic term *kāfir.*
25. al-Ghazzī, *Ḥusn al-tanabbuh;* al-Muḥibbī, *Khulāṣat al-athar,* 4:195.
26. Some Ottoman historians have made passing references to Ghazzī: Rafeq, "The Economic Organization of Cities," 107; see references to Ghazzī's treatise on imitation in Winter, "A Polemical Treatise." A few Muslim jurists who lived during the first half of the twentieth century allude to the value of Ghazzī's scholarship: the Moroccan jurist Muḥammad b. Jaʿfar al-Kattānī (d. 1927) summarizes the positions of Ghazzī on smoking in his legal compendium on the subject in al-Kattānī, *Iʿlān al-Ḥujja,* 134. Ḥanafī jurist Muhammad Zāhid al-Kawtharī (d. 1952) recommended that Ghazzī's treatise on imitation be published: al-Kawtharī, *Maqālāt al-Kawtharī,* 80.
27. Skovgaard-Petersen, *Defining Islam,* 128.
28. For an exceptional interdisciplinary historical study of premodern Muslim interreligious encounter, see Flood, *Objects of Translation.* For textual studies of how Muslims defined religious boundaries, see Goldziher, "Usages juifs"; Kister, "'Do Not Assimilate Yourselves'"; Friedmann, *Tolerance and Coercion;* Masud, "Cosmopolitanism and Authenticity"; for historical studies: Tritton, *The Caliphs and Their Non-Muslim Subjects;* Fattal, *Le statut légal;* Cohen, *Under Crescent and Cross;* Noth, "Problems of Dif-

ferentiation"; Levy-Rubin, *Non-Muslims in the Early Islamic Empire;* Constable, *To Live Like a Moor;* for legal studies: Freidenreich, *Foreigners and Their Food;* Emon, *Religious Pluralism and Islamic Law;* Safran, *Defining Boundaries in al-Andalus;* Fierro and Tolan, *The Legal Status of Dhimmīs.*

29. Berkowitz, *Defining Jewish Difference,* 5–6.
30. Lev. 18:3 states, "You shall not follow their laws (customs)." See Ydit, "Ḥukkat Ha-goi," *Encyclopaedia Judaica,* 9:580; and Berkowitz, *Defining Jewish Difference.*
31. Cor. 11:1 (Revised Standard Version); on Paul and imitation, see Castelli, *Imitating Paul.*
32. Castelli, *Imitating Paul,* 114.
33. Morony, "Religious Communities."
34. Simmel, *The Sociology of Georg Simmel,* 30; Jenkins, *Social Identity,* 16–27.
35. al-Ghazzī, *Itqān mā yaḥsun,* 449; al-Ṣāliḥī, *al-Shadhra fī al-aḥādīth al-mushtahara,* 2:161.
36. Durkheim, *The Elementary Forms of Religious Life,* 44.
37. Girard, *Things Hidden,* 7.
38. Ibid.
39. Kant, *Critique of Judgment,* 176.
40. See Adorno, *Minima Moralia;* Benjamin, "On the Mimetic Faculty," 720–22; Baudrillard, *Simulacra and Simulation;* Butler, "Imitation and Gender Insubordination"; Taussig, *Mimesis and Alterity.*
41. Mauss, "Techniques of the Body," 73–74, 85.
42. Mauss, *The Gift,* 103.
43. Aristotle, *Poetics* 1448b4–9.
44. Adorno, *Minima Moralia,* 154.
45. Rizzolatti and Craighero, "The Mirror Neuron System"; Iacoboni, "Imitation, Empathy, and Mirror Neurons."
46. Girard, *Things Hidden,* 7.
47. Bandura, Ross, and Ross, "Imitation of Film-Mediated Aggressive Models"; Anderson and Bushman, "Effects of Violent Video Games."
48. Girard, *Things Hidden,* 10. Plato's criticism of imitation supported the ideal of a complex social hierarchy. Citizens of the Republic should not imitate social inferiors or outcasts, including women, slaves, corrupt men, animals, or the insane. Instead, they should imitate men of elevated status, namely, the philosophers who strove to imitate God.
49. See Plato, *Republic,* 73–74.
50. See books 2 and 3 in ibid.
51. Aristotle, *Poetics* 1448b4–9.
52. E. W. Lane defines *tashabbaha* as the following: "He became assimilated to him or it. He assumed, or affected, a likeness, or resemblance to him, or it. He imitated him or it. He made himself to be like, or resemble him or it." See the entry for Sh-B-H in Lane and Lane-Poole, *An Arabic-English Lexicon.* Lane also quotes a saying attributed to the caliph ʿUmar b. al-Khaṭṭāb cited in the eighteenth-century lexicon *Tāj al-ʿArūs:* "Verily one becomes like [*yutashabbahu* or *yushbahu*] by feeding upon milk [*inna al-laban yutashabbahu/yushbahu ʿalayhi*]." Because the infant who is nursed takes on

the personal qualities of the wet nurse, ʿUmar admonishes parents to be careful when selecting a wet nurse.

53. al-Ghazzī, *Ḥusn al-tanabbuh,* 1:16; al-Luwayḥiq, *al-Tashabbuh al-manhī ʿanhu,* 31.

54. Walter Benjamin discusses how language enabled the "mimetic faculty" of human beings. Michael Taussig reworks Benjamin's definition of mimesis into his own. Benjamin, "On the Mimetic Faculty"; Taussig, *Mimesis and Alterity,* 19, xiii.

55. Donner, *Narratives of Islamic Origins,* 143–44, 60–73, 160–73.

56. al-Farāhīdī, *Kitāb al-ʿAyn.* Also see the entry for SH-B-H in al-Fīrūzʾābādī, *al-Qāmūs al-muḥīṭ,* 2:1638.

57. Philosopher Raymond Williams observes that *community* is a "warmly persuasive word to describe an existing set of relationships," where "signs of distinction" are especially significant. Williams, *Keywords,* 76. See the entry for Q-W-M in Lane and Lane-Poole, *An Arabic-English Lexicon.*

58. Muslims were attentive to the social dimension of religious life from the beginnings of Islam. Inspired by the Quran, Muslims conceptualized community through a variety of terms: *umma,* a people, nation, or community, originally included Muslims as well as non-Muslims, but eventually signified the exclusive international (and now global) community of Muslims; *dīn* emphasizes the collective way of life shared among the members of a group, and in some contexts, may be translated as "religion"; *milla* fuses the meanings of *umma* and *dīn,* signifying "religious community," as in "the *milla* of Abraham"; *qawm* often has ethno-national undertones, and is perhaps best translated as "people," as in "the *qawm* of Abraham." Other Quranic terms such as *shaʿb,* people, and *qabīla,* tribe, mark subgroups within the super-community of Muslims. The Tunisian historian Ibn Khaldūn highlighted the importance of group solidarity (*ʿaṣabiyya*) to the unfolding of human civilization. All these terms can be applied to other forms of community as well. See Ibn Khaldūn, *The Muqaddimah.*

59. Q 11:89, 9:24, 10:87.

60. al-Iṣfahānī, *Mufradāt alfāẓ al-Qurʾān,* 693.

61. Moosa and Tareen, "Revival and Reform," 463.

62. The concept and practice of following the *sunna* (*ittibāʿ al-sunna*) signaled both a believer's personal piety and membership in the Muslim community. The normative authority of the *sunna* is second only to that of the Quran in the derivation of Islamic law (*fiqh*), and is found in both in both Sunni and Shiʿi collections of hadith. The Quran (33:21) describes Muhammad as a worthy exemplar (*uswa ḥasana*). Speaking on behalf of Muhammad, Q 3:31 exhorts, "If you love God, then follow me, and God will love you" (*In kuntum tuḥibbūnī fa-ittabiʿūnī, yuḥbibkum Allāh*).

63. Many scholars of Islam render *taqlīd* as "imitation." See, for example, Berkey, *The Formation of Islam,* 219. Among Muslims who advocate adhering to a single school of jurisprudence, *taqlīd* is necessary. However, since the nineteenth century, reformist thinkers have criticized *taqlīd,* favoring *ijtihād,* the exercise of independent reason, to determine Islamic law (see chapter 8). But even among premodern scholars, it was considered blameworthy for jurists with the requisite training and ability to blindly imitate past precedent when they could exercise their independent judgment. See Hallaq, *Authority, Continuity and Change in Islamic Law,* 86–120; al-Jurjānī, *Kitāb*

al-Taʿrīfāt, 129; Kurzman, *Modernist Islam,* 9–11; Hodgson, *The Gunpowder Empires,* 274–75.

64. But, as Ghazzī's definition suggests, *tashabbuh* may carry a positive connotation in Sufi discourses, discussed in chapters 6 and 7.
65. Dissimulation, *taqiyya,* is accepted by Sunnis in limited circumstances, but not to the degree most Shiʿis accept it. On the significance of *taqiyya* as a pivotal doctrine of Shiʿism, see Kohlberg, "Taqiyya in Shīʿī Theology"; Kohlberg, "Some Imāmī-Shīʿī Views on Taqiyya"; on *taqiyya* as a historical performance, see Stewart, "Taqiyya as Performance."
66. This conclusion is based on an exhaustive study of canonical Sunni and Imāmī Shiʿi collections of hadith. See chapter 3.
67. Ahmed, *Before Orthodoxy,* 3.
68. Asad, "The Idea of an Anthropology of Islam," 15.
69. Against the notion that power is (mainly) the capacity to set limits upon human activity, Michel Foucault conceived power as the capacity to *produce* new subjects. *Discipline and Punish.*
70. Ibn Khaldūn, *The Muqaddimah,* 116.
71. Ibid.
72. The famous saying "Imitation is the sincerest form of flattery" is a mutation of the original saying, "Imitation is the sincerest of flattery," coined by the eccentric Victorian English cleric Charles Caleb Colton in 1820: *Lacon,* 113.
73. Mauss, "Techniques of the Body," 73.
74. Asad, *Islam at the Crossroads,* 14.
75. Asad, "The Idea of an Anthropology of Islam," 15.
76. To fill this scholarly lacuna, I have created a bibliographical archive of available treatises against imitation, premodern and modern: Patel, "The Treatises against Imitation." By contrast, scholars have documented the treatises against innovation (*bidʿa*). See Fierro, "The Treatises against Innovations."
77. By employing the term *discourse,* I conceptualize the making of knowledge as a social practice. Discourse, then, is not a collection of abstract ideas but an array of concepts, forms of reasoning, and literary genres that are mediated through both history (Islamic scripture and tradition) and the present (the social and political life of the actor) to construct a normative way of knowing and being in the world.
78. Freud, *Sexuality and the Psychology of Love,* 66.
79. Ibid., 67.
80. Ibid.
81. Freud, *Civilization and Its Discontents,* 72.
82. Ibid.
83. Ibid., 72–73.
84. Freud, *Sexuality and the Psychology of Love,* 66–67; Freud, *Civilization and Its Discontents,* 72.
85. Morony, "Religious Communities."
86. After the Christian conquest of Granada, converted Christians, Moriscos, "had to both be and appear to be Christians," lest they retain their old "Muslim" habits like eating

couscous and putting henna on their hands and feet. Constable, *To Live Like a Moor,* 1–62.

87. Girard laments that moderns have excluded imitation "from just about everything, including our aesthetics." Girard, *Things Hidden,* 17. See Meyer and Verrips, "Aesthetics"; Elias, *Alef Is for Allah,* 10–14.
88. *Sunan Abī Dāwūd, kitāb al-jihād, bāb al-nahy ʿan qatl man iʿtaṣama biʾl-sujūd.*
89. al-ʿAẓīm Ābādī, *ʿAwn al-Maʿbūd,* 7:305.
90. Mauss, "Techniques of the Body," 73.
91. Douglas, *Purity and Danger.*
92. Merleau-Ponty, *Phenomenology of Perception,* 94–95.
93. The hadiths, in fact, became a synecdoche of Muhammad's exemplary conduct (*sunna*). Brown, *The Canonization of al-Bukhārī and Muslim,* 339.
94. The earliest collections of traditions, such as the *Muṣannaf* of ʿAbd al-Razzāq, which preceded the movement to authenticate Prophetic traditions, did not apply this classification system. Hadith collectors, beginning in the second half of the ninth century, began to subject the transmitters of hadiths to greater scrutiny, seeking to include only those hadiths that were considered authentic (*ṣaḥīḥ*). For an overview of the types of hadith collections and their development, see Brown, *Hadith,* 15–65.
95. Most hadith scholars settled for transmitting the general meaning of the hadith (*riwāya biʾl-maʿna*) instead of the exact word-for-word transmission (*riwāya biʾl-lafẓ*). Had they required the latter, very few hadiths would have been accepted into the canon. Brown, *Hadith,* 23.
96. Euro-American scholars of early Islam are divided into two camps over the historicity of hadith. While "skeptics" deny that there is a reliable empirical method of extracting the historical kernels of truth contained in the hadiths, "sanguine" scholars disagree, claiming that, with the proper methods, historical kernels of truth can in fact be found. See Berg, "Competing Paradigms"; Brown, *Hadith,* 197–239.
97. Keane, "Semiotics."
98. Ibid., 410.
99. This historical approach focuses on the *circulation* of ideas, practices, and meanings connected with the hadiths instead of their origins. For an exemplary demonstration of this approach, see Halevi, *Muhammad's Grave.*

1. TURNING AWAY FROM CHRISTIANS AND JEWS?

1. *Ṣaḥīḥ al-Bukhārī, kitāb al-libās, bāb al-farq; Ṣaḥīḥ Muslim, kitāb al-faḍāʾil, bāb fī sadl al-nabī shaʿrihi wa farqihi.* Citations are from Muslim's version.
2. *Ṣaḥīḥ al-Bukhārī, kitāb al-ṣawm, bāb ṣiyām yawm ʿĀshūrāʾ; Ṣaḥīḥ Muslim, kitāb al-ṣiyām, bāb ṣawm yawm ʿĀshūrāʾ.*
3. I examine these funerary traditions below.
4. Shāh Walī Allāh al-Dihlawī, *The Conclusive Argument,* 361–75.
5. Ibid., 368–69.
6. Donner, *Muhammad and the Believers,* 69.
7. Crone, "Among the Believers." More recently, Jack Tannous offered a rebuttal of

Donner's thesis based, in part, on a cluster of polemical Quranic verses against Jews and Christians: Tannous, *The Making of the Medieval Middle East,* 394–97, especially 394–95, n. 158. Robert Hoyland expressed his disagreement with the original formulation of Donner's thesis in *Seeing Islam as Others Saw It,* 550, n. 22.

8. Girard downplays this feature, preferring the Greek term *mimesis* to the "exhausted word" *imitation* because the latter highlights representational practices such as gestures, speech, and appearance, while the former emphasizes the possibilities of conflict. In this book, I use the terms interchangeably. Girard, *Things Hidden,* 18.
9. Ibid., 295.
10. Ibid., 26.
11. Ibid., 12.
12. Girard's theory of mimetic rivalry also helps to explain conflict *between* Muslims, such as sectarianism between Sunnis and Shiʿis, who each make exclusive claims on Islamic orthodoxy.
13. As discussed below, Jerusalem is explicitly mentioned not in the verse but in commentaries on the Quran.
14. *Ṣaḥīḥ al-Bukhārī, kitāb al-tafsīr,* Q 2:145.
15. See Q 2:115: "To God belong the East and the West; wherever you turn, there is the Face [*wajh*] of God." God, in other words, is everywhere. To unlock the mysteries hidden behind faces, Muslim thinkers cultivated the art and science of physiognomy, the study of facial structures and expressions to elicit a person's character. For a masterful study of how Muslims translated and preserved Polemon of Laodicea's classic work on physiognomy, see Swain and Boys-Stones, *Seeing the Face, Seeing the Soul.*
16. Q 2:148 may also be rendered as "Everyone has a direction to which he turns" (*Wa li-kull^{in} wijhat^{un} huwa muwallīha*). But the context of the verse, which addresses interreligious relations, indicates that the intended subject is a community, not an individual. The Quran translations of Muhammad Asad and M. S. Abdel Haleem agree with this reading.
17. Rubin, "Ḥanafiyya and Kaʿba."
18. On Daniel praying toward Jerusalem: "Now when Daniel knew that the writing was signed, he went into his house; and his windows being open in his chamber toward Jerusalem, he kneeled upon his knees three times a day, and prayed, and gave thanks before his God, as he did aforetime." Dan. 6:10 (King James Version).
19. Bashear, "Qibla Musharriqa and Early Muslim Prayer in Churches"; Donner, *Muhammad and the Believers,* 115.
20. al-Ṭabarī, *Tafsīr al-Ṭabarī,* 2:640–41.
21. Q 9:56–57 (Abdel Haleem) describes the hypocrites: "They swear by God that they belong with you, but they do not. They are cowardly; if they could find a place of refuge, or a cave, or somewhere to crawl into, they would run there with great haste." Some Quran commentators likened them to sheep that joined one flock, then another. See *Encyclopaedia of the Qurʾān,* s.v. "Hypocrites and Hypocrisy" (C. Adang).
22. Muqātil b. Sulaymān, *Tafsīr Muqātil b. Sulaymān,* 1:146. Also cited in Shtober, "Lā Yajūz," 91–92. The *Tafsīr* of Muqātil b. Sulaymān (d. 767) is the earliest major Quran commentary that has survived, although later exegetes marginalized it. Muqātil's com-

mentary privileges narrative over linguistic interpretations. *Encyclopaedia of Islam,* 2nd ed., s.v. "Muḳātil b. Sulaymān" (M. Plessner and A. Rippin).

23. al-Ṭabarī, *Tafsīr al-Ṭabarī,* 2:658.
24. Margoliouth, *Mohammed and the Rise of Islam,* 247–50. Bell, *Introduction to the Quran,* 137, 166; Watt, *Muhammad at Medina,* 198–204.
25. Margoliouth, *Mohammed and the Rise of Islam,* 249.
26. al-Ṭabarī, *Tafsīr al-Ṭabarī,* 2:657.
27. Ibn Taymiyya, *Iqtiḍāʾ al-ṣirāṭ al-mustaqīm,* 1:88; Memon, *Ibn Taimiya's Struggle,* 100–101, 188. Memon just summarizes Ibn Taymiyya's exegesis.
28. For example, the Prophet is reported to have said: "A prayer in Mecca is worth one hundred thousand times, a prayer in my mosque [in Medina] is worth one thousand times, and a prayer in the al-Aqṣā Sanctuary [in Jerusalem] is worth five hundred times more than anywhere else." al-Suyūṭī, *Jamʿ al-jawāmiʿ,* 5:475. Other traditions measure the relative worth of prayer at one hundred thousand in Mecca, fifty thousand in Medina, and five thousand in Jerusalem. See *Sunan Ibn Mājah, kitāb iqāmat al-ṣalāt wa'l-sunna, bāb lā jāʾa fī al-ṣalāt fī al-masjid al-jāmiʿ.* Although the hierarchy is the same, the variation in relative values suggests that Muslim perceptions of the relative holiness of these sacred spaces varied.
29. Q 2:158 declares that Ṣafā and Marwa, two geographic landmarks of the Hajj pilgrimage, are the *shiʿār* of God. Abraham's servant-wife Hagar is said to have run back and forth between these two poles as she frantically searched for water in order to slake the thirst of her son Ishmael.
30. Q 2:140: "Or are you saying that Abraham, Ishmael, Isaac, Jacob, and the Tribes were Jews or Christians? Ask them, 'Who knows better: you or God?'" Q 3:67 is even more explicit: "Abraham was neither a Jew nor a Christian. He was a pure monotheist [*ḥanīf*]—a Muslim, not an idolater."
31. See Q 2:111: "They also say, 'No one will enter Paradise unless he is a Jew or a Christian.' This is their own wishful thinking. [O Prophet], say, 'Produce your evidence, if you are telling the truth'"; and Q 2:120: "The Jews and the Christians will never be pleased with you unless you follow their ways."
32. The mosque in which Muslims were praying as the Quranic verses commanding Muslims to turn around were revealed was named, appropriately, *masjid al-qiblatayn*—the mosque of two directions; it is unique among mosques for having prayer niches facing both Jerusalem and Mecca.
33. al-Zarnūjī, *Instruction of the Student,* 44–45. In one anecdote, two students traveled abroad seeking religious knowledge, but only one returned a jurist. The reason for the distinct outcomes, according to the author, is that the jurist obtained blessings from the habit of facing Mecca while studying, while the other did not. al-Qurṭubī, *al-Jāmiʿ li-aḥkām al-Qurʾān,* 1:27. Cited in al-Miṣrī, *Reliance of the Traveller,* 875.
34. Ghazālī categorizes four different ways of orienting the body when sleeping: "Sleep is of four types: 1) sleeping on one's back: that is the way of the prophets who contemplate the creation of the heavens and the earth; 2) sleeping on one's right side: that is the way of the religious scholars and devotees; 3) sleeping on one's left side: that is the way of the kings in order to digest their food; and 4) sleeping face down: that is the way

of Satan." al-Ghazālī, *Iḥyāʾ ʿulūm al-dīn,* 2:30. Drawing attention to the social significance of burial orientation, Halevi observes, "By burying the dead in low graves facing Mecca, Muslims promoted a sense of belonging to a single community, a community whose members, no matter where in the world they died, would all seem equal to one another—yet manifestly different from outsiders." Halevi, *Muhammad's Grave,* 187–91 (quote on 189), 320–21, n. 93.

35. Wensinck, "The Origin of the Muslim Laws of Ritual Purity," 91; Wensinck, "Die Entstehung." Wensinck mentions Islamic parallels to Jewish law, which also forbids urinating in the direction of Jerusalem.

36. Even the Khārijī rebels called the Muslims against whom they fought jihad the *ahl al-qibla.* See al-Ṭabarī, *The History of al-Ṭabarī: Between Civil Wars,* 24.

37. Donner, *Early Islamic Conquests;* Hoyland, *In God's Path;* Kaegi, *Byzantium and the Early Islamic Conquests.*

38. It is unclear to what extent Muslim state authorities in fact regulated the hairstyles of their Christian subjects. Late antique Byzantine coinage depicts figures such as Jesus or an emperor with a range of hairstyles, indicating that Christian sartorial norms shifted. See Neuwirth, Sinai, and Marx, *The Qurʾān in Context,* 176.

39. Ironically, this new Muslim style was also a Persian style; Persian elites grew out and parted their hair. Efforts among Arab Muslims to appropriate this style suggest that parting the hair carried cultural prestige in the late antique Near East. Levy-Rubin, *Non-Muslims in the Early Islamic Empire,* 153.

40. The clipped forelock, the anecdote suggests, distinguished Arab Muslims from Arab Christians. Without this distinguishing marker, Christians who spoke Arabic and dressed like Muslims could pass as Muslim. By using dress codes to visibly distinguish Muslims from non-Muslims, ʿUmar II achieved two political objectives: (1) the enforcement of state security by preventing "foreign" spies from interfering in state affairs and non-Muslims from posing as Muslim soldiers in the military; and (2) tax revenue from *dhimmīs,* who paid a poll tax in exchange for protection. Sumptuary laws not only set apart Muslims from unbelievers but also advanced the caliphate's political and economic interests. Levy-Rubin, *Non-Muslims in the Early Islamic Empire,* 88–96; Fattal, *Le statut légal,* 98–99.

41. Levy-Rubin, *Non-Muslims in the Early Islamic Empire,* 88–96.

42. Margoliouth, *Mohammed and the Rise of Islam,* 226; Watt, *Muhammad at Medina,* 199; Mazuz, *The Religious and Spiritual Life,* 28–33.

43. When Muhammad first immigrated to Medina from Mecca, he observed local Jews fasting on the day of ʿĀshūrāʾ, the tenth day of Muḥarram, the first month in the Muslim lunar calendar, to honor the triumph of Moses over Pharaoh. He responded by ordering his followers to fast as well, explaining to the Jews, "We are closer to Moses than you." But other traditions tell a different story. Some traditions claim that ʿĀshūrāʾ was originally a pre-Islamic Arab practice that Muslims assimilated, not a Judeo-Christian custom. Other traditions say the Prophet fasted on the ninth, not the tenth day of Muḥarram. How to properly observe ʿĀshūrāʾ thus confused early Muslims. Some early Muslims fasted on the tenth day of Muḥarram, others on the ninth, others on the ninth, tenth, and eleventh, and others on the ninth and tenth. Muslims

also disagreed on the holiday's legal status: some believed it was required until the Ramadan fast was legislated, and then became voluntary; others believed that fasting on the day became detested after Ramadan; and yet others believed that it had always been voluntary, before and after Ramadan. So Muslims disagreed not only on whether ʿĀshūrāʾ was a Jewish custom but, if it was, whether they should copy the Jews (fast on the tenth), be slightly different from them (fast on the ninth and tenth), or be very different from them (not fast at all). Shiʿis adopted a completely different practice from the Sunnis. Instead of fasting and celebrating the tenth day of Muḥarram with the Sunnis, they did the opposite, mourning the day to honor the martyrdom of the Prophet's grandson Ḥusayn. Bashear, "ʿĀshūrā, an Early Muslim Fast."

44. *Ṣaḥīḥ Muslim, kitāb al-ṣiyām, bāb ay yawm yuṣām fī ʿĀshūrāʾ*.
45. *Ṣaḥīḥ al-Bukhārī, kitāb al-janāʾiz, bāb man qāma li-janāzat yahūdī.*
46. Ibid.
47. Ibn Ḥanbal, *Musnad,* 2:381–83. The *Musnad*'s editor, Shuʿayb Arnāʾūṭ, grades this hadith authentic (*ṣaḥīḥ*).
48. On *naskh,* see Hallaq, *A History of Islamic Legal Theories,* 68–74; Kamali, *Principles of Islamic Jurisprudence,* 202–27. Also see *Encyclopaedia of Islam,* 3rd ed., s.v. "Abrogation" (A. Rippin).
49. Goldziher, "Usages juifs," 77.
50. *Sunan Ibn Mājah, kitāb al-janāʾiz, bāb jāʾa fī al-qiyām liʾl-janāza.*
51. According to a hadith collected by Ibn Mājah, "We used to pray with the Messenger of God towards Jerusalem eighteen months and then the direction of prayer was changed to the *kaʿba* two months after his entry into Medina." This tradition suggests that the Prophet prayed toward Jerusalem for sixteen months while still in Mecca. See *Sunan Ibn Mājah, kitāb iqāmat al-ṣalāt waʾl-sunna, bāb al-qibla.* Most traditions, however, such as those in Ṭabarī's Quran commentary, indicate that the Prophet began to face Mecca about eighteen months after immigrating to Medina.
52. On the historical challenges of studying Arabian Jews, see Mazuz, *The Religious and Spiritual Life,* 1–8.
53. Neuwirth, "From the Sacred Mosque to the Remote Temple"; Rubin, "The Kaʿba," 103–4, n. 29.
54. Ibn Hishām, *al-Sīra al-nabawiyya,* 160–61; Rubin, "Between Arabia and the Holy Land," 350–51. According to this narrative, before immigrating to Medina, the Prophet would pray behind the *kaʿba* while facing north toward Syria, suggesting that Muslims faced Jerusalem *before* the emigration. In Medina, Muslims may have faced Jerusalem exclusively with the intent of emulating Jewish ritual practice before being commanded to face Mecca.
55. al-Ṭabarī, *The History of al-Ṭabarī: The Victory of Islam,* 38. One Companion of Muhammad (Salmā bint Qays) is described as having prayed toward two different directions (*qiblatayn*).
56. Imbert, "La nécropole islamique," 20; Toombs, *Tell El Hesi,* 77–80. Cited in Halevi, *Muhammad's Grave,* 321, n. 99. Toombs suggests that some (wayward?) Muslims were intentionally buried facing Jerusalem instead of Mecca. According to Hoyland, the lack of consensus over how to calculate the direction of the *qibla* explains why the

Umayyad caliphs ʿAbd al-Mālik (r. 685–705) and Walīd (r. 705–15) realigned *qibla*s in mosques across the caliphate. Hoyland, *Seeing Islam as Others Saw It,* 560–73, especially 567–68.

57. Compilations of oral traditions on the religious merits of Jerusalem developed into a distinct genre of treatises. See Mourad, "A Note on the Origin of *Faḍāʾil Bayt al-Maqdis* Compilations." According to Islamic tradition, one inspiration for these compilations was the Prophet's ascension to heaven from Jerusalem during the night journey. See Q 17:1, although the toponym of Jerusalem is absent.
58. Bashear, "Qurʾān 2:114 and Jerusalem," 237; Shtober, "Lā Yajūz," 97.
59. On the virtues of ʿAlī, see, for example, al-Quḍāʿī, *A Treasury of Virtues.* For a summary of sources on the saying that the Prophet is the city of knowledge and ʿAlī is its door, see Rosenthal, *Knowledge Triumphant,* 144, n. 245.
60. Al-Azmeh, *The Emergence of Islam,* 419–20.
61. Rahman, *Major Themes of the Qurʾān,* 131–49, especially 146–49.
62. Neuwirth, *The Qurʾan and Late Antiquity,* 333–34.
63. Goldziher, *Muslim Studies,* 2:44–46. For H.A.R. Gibb's rejection of Goldziher's theory, see *Encyclopaedia of Islam,* 1st ed., s.v. "al-Ḳuds" (H.A.R. Gibb).
64. See n. 28 above.
65. According to one well-known tradition, with narrations in all Sound Six Sunni hadith collections: "You shall set out only for three mosques: the Holy Sanctuary [in Mecca], the Farthest [al-Aqṣā] Mosque, and my mosque." *Ṣaḥīḥ al-Bukhārī, kitāb faḍl al-ṣalāt, bāb faḍl al-ṣalāt fī masjid makka waʾl-madīna; Ṣaḥīḥ Muslim, kitāb al-ḥajj, bāb lā tushadd al-riḥāl illā ilā thalātha masājid; Sunan Abī Dāwūd, kitāb al-manāsik, bāb fī ityān al-madīna; Sunan al-Tirmidhī, kitāb abwāb al-ṣalāt, bāb ay al-masjid afḍal; Sunan Ibn Mājah, kitāb iqāmat al-ṣalāt, bāb mā jāʾa fī al-ṣalāt fī masjid bayt al-maqdis; Sunan al-Nasāʾī, kitāb al-jumʿa, bāb dhikr al-sāʿa allatī yustajāb fīhā al-duʿāʾ yawm al-jumʿa.* Also see Kister, "You Shall Only Set out for Three Mosques."
66. El-Hawary, "The Most Ancient Islamic Monument Known"; Halevi, *Muhammad's Grave,* 14–17; Al-Ghabbān, "The Evolution of the Arabic Script," 97–98.
67. Halevi, *Muhammad's Grave,* 20.
68. The parchment of the Birmingham Quran manuscript has been radiocarbon dated to 568–645, with a 95.4 percent probability, although some scholars propose a date near the end of the seventh century or later based on its orthography, which is shared with sixteen leaves from BnF Arabe 328(c) in the Bibliothèque Nationale de France. The arrangement of the *sūra*s and verses contained in the fragment conforms to that of the standardized Quran used by Muslims today—with minor variations. The manuscript contains a cluster of polemical verses from the conclusion of *sūra* Maryam defining religious boundaries along doctrinal lines, including Q 19:91–92: "That they attribute to the Most Merciful a son when it does not befit the Most Merciful to have a son." See https://www.birmingham.ac.uk/facilities/cadbury/birmingham-quran-mingana-collection/birmingham-quran/what-is.aspx. On the orthography of BnF Arabe 328(c), see Déroche, *Qur'ans of the Umayyads,* 67–69; on the Sanaa palimpsest, a Quran manuscript whose lower text has been dated to the seventh century, see Hilali, *The Sanaa Palimpsest;* and on the Corpus Coranicum project to establish a critical edition of the

Quran based on the earliest existing manuscripts, including BnF Arabe 328(c), see https://corpuscoranicum.de.

69. Neuwirth, *The Qur'an and Late Antiquity,* 271
70. Grohmann, "Aperçu de papyrologie arabe," 40–43. On this and other early papyri, see Anthony, *Muhammad and the Empires of Faith,* 27. Although the *basmala* prefaces all but one *sūra* in the Quran, early jurists nonetheless debated whether those invocations were part of the Quran or not, resulting in different practices of reciting the formula, silently or out loud, during ritual prayer. Pre-Islamic precedents for and parallels with the *basmala* are also to be found, although I have yet to see evidence for the specific formula *bi-smillāh al-raḥmān al-raḥīm* outside of distinctively Arabo-Islamic literary and material contexts. *Encyclopaedia of Islam,* 3rd ed., s.v. "*Basmala*" (W. H. Graham).
71. The Quran pairs the emigrants, *muhājirūn,* with their counterparts, the helpers, or *anṣār* (Q 9:100, 117). Other verses associate the act of emigration with persecution and war (Q 3:195, 4:97, 8:72, and 22:58). In Q 29:26, Abraham proclaims, "I will flee to my Lord" (*innī muhājir ilā rabbī*), which reframes emigration as a spiritual practice.
72. Syriac and Greek references to the community of Muhammad as emigrants, not Muslims, have provoked debates among scholars for decades over their implications for the historiography of early Islam. The Greek *magaritai* is attested in PERF 564, dated 21/642, and PERF 558, dated 22/643, and Syriac *mhaggrē* is attested in the writings of Isho'yahb III (d. 659). See Cook and Crone, *Hagarism,* 8–9, 159, n. 51; Crone, "The First-Century Concept of *Hiǧra,*" 359; Hoyland, *Seeing Islam as Others Saw It,* 76, 179–80; Trombley, "Fiscal Documents," 27–28, 31–33; Donner, *Muḥammad and the Believers,* 86; Lindstedt, "Muhājirūn"; Webb, *Imagining the Arabs,* 170.
73. The earliest documentary and material evidence does not label the year *hijrī,* suggesting that the audience knows which epoch is being referred to. Despite the absence of the term, Sean Anthony considers the claim "virtually irrefutable" that the dates refer to the *hijrī* calendar, not to another calendar: Anthony, *Muhammad and the Empires of Faith,* 27.
74. Anthony, *Muhammad and the Empires of Faith,* 26; Stowasser, *The Day Begins at Sunset,* 16; Blake, *Time in Early Modern Islam,* 10.
75. Grohmann, "Aperçu de papyrologie arabe," 40–43; Anthony, *Muhammad and the Empires of Faith,* 27; Trombley, "Fiscal Documents," 32.
76. *Ṣaḥīḥ al-Bukhārī, kitāb bad' al-khalq, bāb mā jā'a fī sab' arḍīn; Ṣaḥīḥ Muslim, kitāb al-qasāma wa'l-muḥāribīn wa'l-qiṣāṣ wa'l-diyāt, bāb taḥrīm taghlīẓ al-dimā' wa'l-a'rāḍ wa'l-amwāl.* Also see Al-Azmeh, *The Emergence of Islam,* 194.
77. Blake, *Time in Early Modern Islam,* 179.
78. Carlebach, *Palaces of Time,* 5.
79. Anthony, *Muhammad and the Empires of Faith,* 26.
80. Q 9:36 (Arberry).
81. Neuwirth, *The Qur'an and Late Antiquity,* 278, 316.
82. Donner, *Muhammad and the Believers,* 87.
83. Ibid., 112.
84. Donner nonetheless acknowledges, "Even more than theological differences, it is dif-

ferences in cultic practice that set one religious community apart from others." Ibid., 214.

85. See, for example, the importance of mobility and everyday practice in Thomas Tweed's theory of religion: Tweed, *Crossing and Dwelling.*
86. Reza Aslan describes the new Meccan *qibla* as an index of "the maturing of Islam into its own independent religion." Aslan, *No god but God,* 102.
87. Hoyland, *Seeing Islam as Others Saw It,* 549–50.
88. Tannous, *The Making of the Medieval Middle East,* 46–81, 225–309.
89. Gibb, "Arab-Byzantine Relations," 77.
90. Ibn Ḥajar al-ʿAsqalānī, *Fatḥ al-Bārī,* 1:402.

2. *FROM NARRATIVE TO NORMATIVE*

1. Koselleck, "Linguistic Change," 653.
2. Goldziher, "Über jüdische"; Goldziher, "Usages juifs"; Kister, "'Do Not Assimilate Yourselves'"; Vajda, "Juifs et musulmans." Goldziher acknowledges that the semantic usage of *bidʿa* (innovation) evolves, but not *tashabbuh.* Kister's title implies that imitating unbelievers is reprehensible.
3. Form V of SH-B-H, *tashabbuh,* is not found in the Quran (although other forms are). I did not find this form in pre-Islamic collections of poetry (*al-Asmāʿiyyāt, al-Mufaḍḍaliyyāt, al-Muʿallaqāt,* and the *Diwān al-Ḥamāsa*) or in Abbasid collections of proverbs and sayings such as Jāḥiẓ's *al-Bayān.* Although some scholars dispute the attribution of *Kitāb al-ʿAyn* to Khalīl b. Aḥmad, its phonetic arrangement of words suggests an early historical provenance. His students include Sibawayh (d. 796) and al-Asmaʿī (d. 831). Talmon, *Arabic Grammar in Its Formative Age.*
4. Like *tashabbuh,* all the aforementioned entries are form V. al-Farāhīdī, *Kitāb al-ʿAyn,* 7:297, 8:137, 8:265.
5. Ibid., 3:386–87. *Hājarū wa lā tahajjarū! Ay: Akhliṣū al-hijra li'llah wa lā tashabbahū bi'l-muhājirīn.* Although not found in canonical hadith collections, a variant of this tradition is found in Ibn Saʿd, *al-Ṭabaqāt,* 3:301.
6. "Kamā taqūl yataḥallam wa laysa bi-ḥalīm." al-Farāhīdī, *Kitāb al-ʿAyn,* 3:386–87.
7. I am grateful to Mustafa Macit Karagözoğlu for correctly identifying the Shāfiʿī jurist being paraphrased here, Shams al-Dīn al-ʿAlqamī (d. 1561–62), not ʿAlqama b. Qays, as I originally believed. See al-ʿAẓīm Ābādī, *ʿAwn al-Maʿbūd,* 11:74–76.
8. I distinguish between a hadith, or tradition, and its "varying transmissions," or narrations. Brown, *Hadith,* 7.
9. In my usage, each version of the imitation hadith—the concise version and the apocalyptic version—consists of different narrations. I compare and analyze these narrations in Patel, "'Whoever Imitates a People Becomes One of Them,'" 404–26. There is also a third version, which I discuss in the epilogue.
10. *Buʿithtu bayna yaday al-sāʿa bi'l-sayf ḥattā yuʿbad Allāh waḥdahu lā sharīka lahu wa juʿila rizqī taḥta ẓill rumḥī wa juʿila al-dhillatu wa'l-ṣaghāru ʿalā man khālafa amrī wa man tashabbaha bi-qawm[in] fa huwa min-hum.* Ibn Ḥanbal, *Musnad,* 9:123–126, 9:478;

Ibn Abī Shayba, *al-Muṣannaf,* 7:29, 7:38; al-Būṣīrī, *Itḥāf al-khiyara,* 4:484; 5:203. Būṣīrī includes two different narrations of the imitation hadith from *Musnad Abī Yaʿlā,* although I did not find either narration in the printed edition of the *Musnad.* It is possible, however, that some manuscripts contain it, as indicated by Būṣīrī. Ibn Ḥumayd, *al-Muntakhab min musnad ʿAbd b. Ḥumayd,* 2:57; Ibn Manṣūr, *Sunan,* 2:143–44; al-Ṭabarānī, *Musnad al-Shāmiyyīn,* 1:135–6; al-Harawī, *Dhamm al-kalām,* 124; al-Ṭaḥāwī, *Sharḥ Mushkil al-āthār,* 1:212–13; al-Aṣbahānī, *Akhbār Aṣbahān (Iṣfahān),* 1:165.

11. *Ṣaḥīḥ al-Bukhārī, kitāb al-jihād wa'l-siyar, bāb al-janna taḥta ẓill al-suyūf; Ṣaḥīḥ Muslim, kitāb al-imāra, bāb thubūt al-janna li'l-shahīd.* The Prophet paradoxically stated, "Paradise lies beneath the shade of swords," after advising his audience *not* to hope to meet the enemy. *Ṣaḥīḥ al-Bukhārī, kitāb al-jihād wa'l-siyar, bāb lā tamannaw liqāʾ al-ʿaduww.*
12. "Fight those who have been given scripture yet do not believe in God nor the Last Day, and who do not prohibit what God and His messenger have prohibited nor follow the religion of truth until they pay the tribute with their hands, humbled and subdued [*ṣāghirūn*]." On interpretations of Q 9:29 past and present, see Sirry, *Scriptural Polemics,* 168–82, 261, n. 9.
13. See n. 10 for reference to Ibn Ḥanbal's narration. For other variants of the apocalyptic version, see al-Harawī, *Dhamm al-kalām,* 124. In his collection, Bukhārī omits the parts of the hadith unrelated to spears (see below). Bukhārī is not included in my list of collectors of this version.
14. See my list of compilations that collect the hadith in both versions in Patel, "'Whoever Imitates a People Becomes One of Them,'" 404–7.
15. Ibn ʿUmar was a prolific Companion transmitter of Sunni hadiths (around twenty-six hundred), second only to Abū Hurayra. Brown, *Hadith,* 19. On Ibn ʿUmar's jurisprudence, see Qalʿarjī, *Mawsuʿat Fiqh ʿAbd Allāh b. ʿUmar.* Also see *Encyclopaedia of Islam,* 3rd ed., s.v. "ʿAbd Allāh b. ʿUmar b. al-Khaṭṭāb" (A. Görke). Other prominent Companions allegedly transmitted different versions of the imitation hadith from the Prophet; Anas b. Mālik (d. 709) and Abū Hurayra (d. 678) transmitted the apocalyptic version, while Ḥudhayfa b. al-Yamān (d. 656) transmitted the concise version.
16. al-Ṣanʿānī, *al-Muṣannaf,* 11:453–54.
17. See my analysis of the *isnād*s in the appendix of Patel, "'Whoever Imitates a People Becomes One of Them,'" 404–26. Also see the summary evaluations in al-ʿAẓīm Ābādī, *ʿAwn al-Maʿbūd,* 11:74–76; Luwayḥiq, *al-Tashabbuh al-manhī ʿanhu,* 37–43.
18. Ibn Ḥanbal based his evaluation on the *isnād*s associated with the Companion ʿAbd Allāh b. ʿUmar (Ibn Thawbān-> Ḥassān b. ʿAṭiyya-> Abū al-Munīb al-Jurashī-> Ibn ʿUmar-> Prophet). The editor of the *Musnad,* Shuʿayb al-Arnāʾūṭ (d. 2016), concurred with Ibn Ḥanbal's evaluation. It is also possible that Ibn Ḥanbal viewed the chain as fair, despite perceiving weakness in it. Ibn Ḥanbal, *Musnad,* 9:123–26, 9:478; al-Sakhāwī, *al-Maqāṣid al-ḥasana,* 639; al-Kawtharī, *Maqālāt,* 78–80.
19. Ibn Taymiyya, *Iqtiḍāʾ al-ṣirāṭ al-mustaqīm,* 1:240–41; al-Ghazzī, *Ḥusn al-tanabbuh,* 1:17; Ibn Ḥajar al-ʿAsqalānī, *Fatḥ al-Bārī,* 6:120–21; al-ʿAql, *Man tashabbaha biqawm fa-huwa min-hum,* 3; al-Kawtharī, *Maqālāt,* 79.
20. al-Albānī, *Irwāʾ al-ghalīl,* 5:109–10; al-Kawtharī, *Maqālāt,* 78–80. During a discussion

at his residence in Damascus in February 2010, Nūr al-Dīn ʿItr explained his view that the hadith is authentic due to the corroborating evidence of other *isnāds*. Also see the evaluations of the following Saudi scholars: al-Luwayḥiq, *al-Tashabbuh al-manhī ʿanhu,* 43; ʿAbd al-Ghaffār, *al-Sunan waʾl-āthār,* 102.

21. Robinson, *Islamic Civilization in Thirty Lives,* 42.
22. Both Euro-American academic scholars and Muslim hadith critics rightly question the historicity of these *isnāds*. Hadith critics found fault in the *isnāds*—even the most authoritative ones. But Behnam Sadeghi has demonstrated that a hadith's *isnād* network often yields distinctive regional variations in the wording, offering us historical information. Sadeghi, "The Traveling Tradition Test," 204–5.
23. The proposition, though tantalizing, is speculative; *qawm* can also mean tribe.
24. Additionally, the Syrian *Musnad* of al-Ṭabarānī (*Musnad al-Shāmiyyīn*) includes several *isnāds* with Syrian transmitters of the imitation hadith. See figure 8. Determining when and where a hadith circulated is a less nebulous and more historically reliable alternative to determining when and where it originated. As mentioned above, *isnāds* may offer us historical evidence. Here, the transmission network tells us not only the figures responsible for circulating the imitation hadith, but also when and where it circulated. I employ the term "primary circulator" to identify the earliest figure(s) after the Prophet Muhammad to transmit a tradition to multiple sources. This figure is analogous to Joseph Schacht's "common link" except that, unlike Schacht, I do not assume that this figure originated the tradition and falsely ascribed it to the Prophet (or another past authority). Such an assumption, in my view, is far too speculative and subjective. By naming the common link a "collector" in "Dating Muslim Traditions," Harald Motzki seems to agree with this view. Andreas Görke identifies no fewer than three different ways of conceptualizing "common link." By stipulating new terms, I avoid misleading the reader. Epistemologically, examining the primary circulator(s) in a network of *isnāds* tells us when and where the imitation hadith *circulated*—not when and where it originated; the statement may have been coined by any number of authorities across the *isnād*—Ibn Thawbān, al-Awzāʿī, Ḥassān b. ʿAṭiyya, the Prophet Muhammad, Qatāda b. Diʿāma, or someone else. The hadith critics' evaluations of the individual *isnāds* assumed sufficient doubt in their authenticity to permit a range of possible scenarios. To speculate that the hadith originated with Ibn Thawbān—even if likely—excludes these alternative possibilities. Put differently, to assert that the imitation hadith "originated" in Damascus reflects a confirmation bias of the hadith's inauthenticity and exceeds what the *isnād* evidence actually tells us. I define the related term "secondary circulator" as a figure who chronologically postdates the primary circulator and transmits the same tradition to multiple sources—analogous to G.H.A. Juynboll's "Partial Common Link." Readers may speculate upon the provenance of the hadith based upon the objective evidence and analysis presented here and upon their own subjective assumptions about the historicity of hadith transmission. Schacht, *The Origins of Muhammadan Jurisprudence,* 163–75; Juynboll, "(Re)Appraisal," 306; see Brown's criticisms of Schacht's and others' skeptical approaches to the canon of hadiths in *Hadith,* 197–239. Also see Motzki, "Dating Muslim Traditions," 228; Görke, "Eschatology, History, and the Common Link," 188.

25. Awzāʿī was better known as a traditionist than Ibn Thawbān, but the latter transmitted this hadith to more individuals (six versus four). See figure 8. Awzāʿī criticized Ibn Thawbān's indecisiveness on the subject of leaving the Friday prayer, first saying it is unlawful, then saying it is permissible. al-Dhahabī, *Siyar aʿlām al-nubalā'*, 7:314.
26. Ibn Ḥajar al-ʿAsqalānī alleges that the transmitter al-Jurashī is unknown. Of The Sound Six, the *Sunan* of Abū Dāwūd is the only one that includes al-Jurashī as a transmitter—just one hadith, the imitation hadith. Still, Ibn Taymiyya asserts that both al-Jurashī and Ibn Thawbān are upright. al-Mizzī, *Tahdhīb al-kamāl,* 34:324–25; Ibn Taymiyya, *Iqtiḍā' al-ṣirāṭ al-mustaqīm,* 1:241; Ibn Ḥajar al-ʿAsqalānī, *Fatḥ al-Bārī,* 6:120–21.
27. The transmitters preceding Ibn Thawbān—Ḥassān b. ʿAṭiyya and Abū al-Munīb al-Jurashī—are Damascene, except for the Companion transmitter ʿAbd Allāh b. ʿUmar, who resided in Medina. Juynboll links hadiths that contain the phrase *lā tashabbahū* to Medina and those that have *khālifūhum* to Syria. He bases this conclusion exclusively upon the traditions transmitted by Ibn Saʿd on dyeing hair in his *al-Ṭabaqāt:* Juynboll, "Dyeing the Hair and Beard in Early Islam," 60; Ibn Saʿd, *al-Ṭabaqāt,* 1:378. Pace Juynboll, my survey of the *isnād*s of *lā tashabbahū* traditions indicates that the phrase was expressed outside Medina as well.
28. In Baghdad, Ibn Thawbān reportedly spoke harshly to the third Abbasid caliph al-Mahdī (r. 775–85), who became enraged at his insolence. al-Dhahabī, Siyar aʿlām al-nubalā', 7:314. See n. 24 for an explanation of my terminology, e.g., "secondary circulator."
29. See Figures 8 and 9.
30. Ibn Thawbān transmitted the imitation hadith to six figures: four Iraqis—Abū al-Naḍr of Baghdad, Sulaymān b. Dāwūd al-Ṭayālisī of Basra, Muḥammad Yazīd of Wasit, and Ghassān b. al-Rabīʿ of Kufa—and two Syrians—ʿAlī b. ʿAyyāsh al-Ḥimṣī from Homs and Muḥammad b. Yūsuf al-Firyābī of Qaysāriyya, a coastal city in southwest al-Shām. See figures 8 and 9, as well as my analysis in Patel, "'Whoever Imitates a People Becomes One of Them,'" 422–23.
31. The compilers who collected narrations of the imitation hadith from Ibn Thawbān include Abū Yaʿlā al-Mawṣilī (d. 919), Aḥmad b. Ḥanbal, Ibn Abī Shayba (d. 849), ʿAbd b. Ḥumayd (d. 863), and Abū Dāwūd. See n. 10 above for the references. *Isnād*s of the imitation hadith that include either of the Syrian authorities, ʿAlī b. ʿAyyāsh al-Ḥimṣī or Muḥammad b. Yūsuf al-Firyābī, are found in later collections of hadiths: *Musnad al-Shāmiyyīn* of al-Ṭabarānī, the second half of the tenth century; and *Dhamm al-kalām* of al-Harawī and *Shuʿab al-īmān* of Abū Bakr al-Bayhaqī, both eleventh-century compilations.
32. Critics had mixed opinions of Ibn Thawbān. Nasā'ī and Sakhāwī impugned Ibn Thawbān's reliability and credibility, while Yaḥyā b. Maʿīn did not criticize him. Abū Dāwūd, Tirmidhī, and Ibn Mājah transmitted hadiths from him, but Ibn Ḥanbal opined, "Some of his hadith are disclaimed," and Nasā'ī concluded, "He is not trustworthy [*thiqa*]." On Ibn Thawbān's credibility as a hadith transmitter, see al-Dhahabī, *Siyar aʿlām al-nubalā'*, 7:313–14; al-Mizzī, *Tahdhīb al-kamāl,* 17:12–26; Ibn Ḥanbal, *Musnad,* 9:123–26, 9:478.
33. On Awzāʿī, see Ibn ʿAsākir, *Ta'rīkh Madīnat Dimashq,* 35:147–229; al-Dhahabī, *Siyar*

aʿlām al-nubalāʾ; for an evaluation of his ability to transmit hadiths, see al-Dhahabī, *Mīzān al-iʿitidāl,* 4:305; for secondary sources, see Judd, "Competitive Hagiography." Also see *Encyclopaedia of Islam,* 2nd ed., s.v. "Awzāʿī" (J. Schacht).

34. Abū Dāwūd and Ibn Ḥanbal each transmit different versions of the imitation hadith, discussed below. Ibn Abī Shayba is the only authority to collect narrations of the imitation hadith from both Ibn Thawbān and Awzāʿī. Ibn Abī Shayba, *al-Muṣannaf,* 7:29, 7:38.
35. Based on my analysis of both the textual content (*matn*) and the *isnād* of the imitation hadith's apocalyptic version, I conclude that there are no significant regional variations (Syria versus Iraq) among the different narrations. This conclusion supports my claim that the apocalyptic version was circulating in Damascus during the first half of the eighth century. Patel, "'Whoever Imitates a People Becomes One of Them,'" 407–12.
36. Ḥassān b. ʿAṭiyya allegedly transmitted hadiths to a total of eight students, so it is plausible that he transmitted the imitation hadith only to two of them. Had he transmitted hadiths to a large number of students, one would then wonder why he transmitted the imitation hadith only to two of them. al-Mizzī, *Tahdhīb al-kamāl,* 6:34–40.
37. Most narrations place the Pact of ʿUmar in Damascus, while others place it in the Hijaz.
38. On the Pact of ʿUmar, see Noth, "Problems of Differentiation"; Tritton, *The Caliphs and Their Non-Muslim Subjects;* Fattal, *Le statut légal;* Levy-Rubin, *Non-Muslims in the Early Islamic Empire;* Cohen, "What Was the Pact of ʿUmar?"; Emon, *Religious Pluralism and Islamic Law.*
39. My translation is based on a version of the pact found in Mark Cohen's Arabic edition of Ibn Zabr's manuscript, dated to the first half of the tenth century. Cohen, "What Was the Pact of ʿUmar?" 137.
40. Abū al-Munīb al-Jurashī of Damascus is listed among the transmitters of the imitation hadith in *Sunan Abī Dāwūd, kitāb al-libās, bāb fī libs al-shuhra.*
41. al-Ṣanʿānī, *al-Muṣannaf,* 11:453–54.
42. I did not find significant correspondences between the transmitters of the imitation hadith and the Pact of ʿUmar. Curiously, the one common transmitter of both texts, Ismāʿīl b. ʿAyyāsh (d. 797–98) from Homs, Syria, transmits the version of the Pact of ʿUmar said to have taken place in al-Jazīra, not Syria! One would have expected him to transmit the Syrian version of the pact. See Ibn al-Qayyim al-Jawziyya, *Aḥkām ahl al-dhimma,* 2:658.
43. Concerning the subjectivity of hadith collection and interpretation, see Fadel, "Ibn Hajar's *Hady al-Sārī*"; Fadel, "Is Historicism a Viable Strategy for Islamic Law Reform?"
44. "The classification of things reproduces this classification of men." Durkheim and Mauss, *Primitive Classification,* 7.
45. Some recent studies, however, seek to fill this lacuna: Burge, "Reading between the Lines"; and Blecher, *Said the Prophet of God,* 111–28.
46. The related term *tarjumān,* also derived from the trilateral root T-R-J-M, refers to the practice of translation, widely understood as a form of interpretation. Ibn ʿAbbās was dubbed *Tarjumān al-Qurʾān,* the interpreter of the Quran.
47. Blecher, *Said the Prophet of God,* 111–28.

48. For a focused study on the chapter headings in *Ṣaḥīḥ al-Bukhārī,* see al-Kandhlawī, *al-Abwāb wa'l-tarājim li'l-Bukhārī.* Explanations of chapter headings are also included in general hadith commentaries like Ibn Ḥajar's *Fatḥ al-Bārī.* For other commentaries, see Blecher, *Said the Prophet of God,* 111–28; Fadel, "Ibn Hajar's *Hady al-Sārī*"; Fadel, "Is Historicism a Viable Strategy for Islamic Law Reform?" I am unaware of any studies of the chapter headings in Abū Dāwūd's *Sunan.*
49. Goldziher, *Muslim Studies,* 2:218, cited in Burge, "Reading between the Lines," 170, n. 11.
50. Goldziher, *Muslim Studies,* 2:217, cited in Fadel, "Ibn Hajar's *Hady al-Sārī,*" 173–74; Tokatly, "The *A'lām al-ḥadīth* of al-Khaṭṭābī," 55, n. 12; Blecher, *Said the Prophet of God,* 112.
51. Tokatly, "The *A'lām al-ḥadīth* of al-Khaṭṭābī," 55.
52. Burge, "Reading between the Lines"; Blecher, *Said the Prophet of God,* 111–28.
53. See Melchert, "The Life and Works of Abū Dāwūd al-Sijistānī"; *Encyclopaedia Islamica,* s.v. "Abū Dāwūd al-Sijistānī" (A. Pakatchi).
54. Were the chapter and section headings original to Abū Dāwūd's *Sunan* (as with al-Bukhārī's *Ṣaḥīḥ*) or inserted later by a copyist or commentator (as with Muslim's *Ṣaḥīḥ*)? Without having compared all nine recensions of the *Sunan,* I assume that Abū Dāwūd inserted them himself, based on the *Sunan*'s emphasis on adducing legal rulings (*aḥkām*) whose meanings are clarified by the presence of subject headings. The earliest commentary on the *Sunan, Ma'ālim al-sunan,* by the Central Asian scholar Abū Sulaymān al-Khaṭṭābī (d. 998), retains both the chapter and section headings (although the chapter headings are ordered differently), which suggests an early provenance to the arrangement of the *Sunan,* as noted by Christopher Melchert in personal correspondence. See al-Khaṭṭābī, *Ma'ālim al-sunan.*
55. *Sunan Abī Dāwūd, kitāb al-libās, bāb fī libs al-shuhra.*
56. Ibid.
57. Burge advocates examining both the categorization and arrangement of hadiths to understand how a collector interpreted its meanings. Burge, "Reading between the Lines," 166–77.
58. For the argument that the *Muṣannaf* of 'Abd al-Razzāq contains hadiths dating to the first Islamic century, see Motzki, "The *Muṣannaf* of 'Abd al-Razzāq al-Ṣan'ānī"; also see Motzki, *The Origins of Islamic Jurisprudence,* 51–74.
59. 'Abd al-Razzāq, though influential, was not as discriminating as Abū Dāwūd. Since 'Abd al-Razzāq compiled his *Muṣannaf* prior to the *sunan* movement, which restricted hadiths exclusively to Prophetic origin, he collected traditions from a wide range of early Muslim authorities, including the Prophet, his Companions, and Successors. Whereas nearly 90 percent of the traditions in Abū Dāwūd's *Sunan* originate with the Prophet, fewer than 25 percent of the traditions in 'Abd al-Razzāq's *Muṣannaf* do. Although Abū Dāwūd may have appended over five hundred broken-chained reports (*marāsīl*) to his *Sunan,* he and other members of the *Sunan/Ṣaḥīḥ* movement, such as Bukhārī and Muslim, focused on collecting hadiths that they could trace back to Muhammad (*marfū' isnāds*) and, more importantly, focused on hadiths that had con-

tinuous chains of transmission (*muttaṣil isnāds*). On the other hand, ʿAbd al-Razzāq, who compiled his *Muṣannaf* prior to the *sunan* movement, did not. And so, the ratio of weak hadiths relative to good and sound hadiths in Abū Dāwūd's *Sunan* is far less than the same ratio in ʿAbd al-Razzāq's *Muṣannaf.* Brown, *Hadith,* 25–34; Sayeed, *Women and the Transmission of Religious Knowledge in Islam,* 13, n. 24. On whether *marāsīl* should be considered part of Abū Dāwūd's *Sunan,* see Abū Dāwūd al-Sijistānī, "Risāla li'l-Imām Abī Dāwūd," 51; Melchert, "The Life and Works of Abū Dāwūd al-Sijistānī," 18, n. 52.

60. al-Ṣanʿānī, *al-Muṣannaf,* 11:453–54.
61. See, for example, the brief discussion on silk in Ibn Taymiyya, *Iqtiḍāʾ al-ṣirāṭ al-mustaqīm,* 1:306–8.
62. Ibid., 1:182–85.
63. Mattson, "A Believing Slave," 20–79.
64. Ibid.
65. Melchert, "Aḥmad Ibn Ḥanbal's Book of Renunciation"; Melchert, *Ahmad Ibn Hanbal.*
66. al-Marwadhī, *Kitāb al-Waraʿ,* 176–77.
67. Ibn al-Mubārak, *Kitāb al-Jihād,* 116–17; Melchert, "Ibn al-Mubārak's *Kitāb al-Jihād*"; Salem, *The Emergence of Early Sufi Piety and Sunnī Scholasticism,* 42–3, 92–100. See my analysis of the narrations collected by Ibn al-Mubārak in Patel, "'Whoever Imitates a People Becomes One of Them,'" 417–24.
68. See *Bāb man qāla al-jihād māḍ*[in] in Ibn Manṣūr, *Sunan,* 2:143–44.
69. Ibn Abī Shayba, *al-Muṣannaf,* 7:29, 7:38.
70. al-Ṭaḥāwī, *Sharḥ Mushkil al-āthār,* 1:212–13. Also see Abū Yūsuf, *Kitāb al-Kharāj,* 127.
71. Brown, *The Canonization of al-Bukhārī and Muslim,* 278–80.
72. *Ṣaḥīḥ al-Bukhārī, kitāb al-jihād, bāb mā qīla fī al-rimāḥ.*
73. Ibn Ḥajar al-ʿAsqalānī, *Fatḥ al-Bārī,* 6:120–21.
74. For a different narration of the apocalyptic version of the imitation hadith, see the *kitāb al-jihād* in Ibn Abī Shayba, *al-Muṣannaf,* 7:29. See my comparison and analysis of the apocalyptic version's different narrations in Patel, "'Whoever Imitates a People Becomes One of Them,'" 407–12.
75. *Sunan Abī Dāwūd, kitāb al-libās, bāb fī libs al-shuhra;* Ibn Ḥanbal, *Musnad,* 9:123–26, 9:478.
76. Muhammad Khalid Masud comes to the same conclusion independently, but does not explain why. Masud, "Cosmopolitanism and Authenticity," 160.
77. According to Juynboll, a composite text assembles parts of multiple traditions—prophetic and nonprophetic—into a single narration. The more component traditions a composite includes, Juynboll asserts, the later its date of origin because the process of synthesizing traditions requires time. Based on this rationale, Juynboll would likely date the apocalyptic version of the imitation hadith later than the concise version, although my analysis of the *isnād* evidence does not support this conclusion. See Juynboll, *Encyclopedia of Canonical Ḥadīth,* xxviii.
78. Abū Dāwūd al-Sijistānī, "Risāla li'l-Imām Abī Dāwūd," 31–32.

79. We need not assume that Abū Dāwūd was disingenuous. During his extensive travels, he likely heard *man tashabbaha bi-qawm*[in] *fa-huwa min-hum* spoken as an independent statement.

80. We lack conclusive evidence that demonstrates whether the concise version or the apocalyptic version of the imitation hadith came first. Based on my analysis of the hadith's most authoritative and widely transmitted narration going back to the Prophet, I confidently demonstrate that Abū Dāwūd extracted the phrase "Whoever imitates a people becomes one of them" from a longer statement, which casts doubt on whether the Prophet himself proclaimed "Whoever imitates a people becomes one of them" as an independent statement. If the apocalyptic version is a composite of multiple traditions, we lack evidence that clearly identifies who assembled it, or when this event took place. I thus refrain from asserting whether the concise version or the apocalyptic version of the hadith is the "original," a dilemma that resembles the age-old debate over the chicken and the egg.

3. EMPIRE OF SMALL DIFFERENCES

1. Douglas, *Purity and Danger,* 54.
2. *al-nabī nahā an yujlas bayna al-ḍaḥ wa'l-ẓill wa qāla majlis al-shayṭān.* Ibn Ḥanbal, *Musnad,* 24:147. In his edition of the *Musnad,* Shuʿayb al-Arnāʾūṭ notes that the hadith is authentic (*ṣaḥīḥ*), but this specific narration is fair (*ḥasan*). Other narrations are categorized under the subheading "Sitting in between Sunlight and Shade" in the following collections: *Sunan Abī Dāwūd, kitāb al-adab, bāb fī al-julūs bayna al-shams wa'l-ẓill; Sunan Ibn Mājah, kitāb al-adab, bāb al-julūs bayna al-shams wa'l-ẓill.*
3. Melchert, "The Piety of the Hadith Folk," 429, 431. Melchert bases his conclusions on evidence drawn mainly from ninth-century Baghdad.
4. Marlow, *Hierarchy and Egalitarianism,* 76.
5. Ibid., 88. The medieval Iranian polymath al-Bīrūnī (d. 1048) perceived Islamic civilization as egalitarian, writing, "All men are equal except in piety," in comparison to Indian civilization, which he considered sharply hierarchical.
6. Burbank and Cooper, *Empires in World History,* 8.
7. Fowden, *Empire to Commonwealth,* 137.
8. By "imperial imaginary," I allude to Burbank and Cooper's (*Empires in World History*) emphasis upon maintaining "distinction and hierarchy."
9. Zaman, *Religion and Politics.*
10. *al-Islām yaʿlū wa lā yuʿlā.* In *Ṣaḥīḥ al-Bukhārī, kitāb al-janāʾiz, bāb idhā aslama al-ṣabiyy fa-māta hal yuṣallā ʿalayhi wa hal yuʿraḍu ʿalā al-ṣabiyy al-islām?* This tradition is a suspended tradition (*muʿallaq*), that is, Bukhārī may not have heard this tradition directly from his teacher, unlike the hadiths considered part of his authentic collection. Its chain of transmission (*isnād*) is thus defective. Since the tradition is attributed to a Companion, not the Prophet, its primary purpose is to serve as a rhetorical entry point into the main subject matter of the chapter, which concerns a boy whose parents are non-Muslim converts to Islam but then dies. Should the funeral prayer be offered on his behalf? In his commentary on this tradition, Ibn Ḥajar al-ʿAsqalānī mentions

that it is also transmitted as a Prophetic narration in the *Sunan* collection of Dāraquṭnī, although through a different line of transmitters that he deems to be fair (*ḥasan*). al-Dāraquṭnī, *Sunan,* 4:371; Ibn Ḥajar al-ʿAsqalānī, *Fatḥ al-Bārī,* 3:280.

11. Harari, *Lacan's Seminar on "Anxiety,"* 25.
12. Though comparatively few in number, Shiʿi usages of the term *tashabbuh* share three key features with Sunni usages: (1) *tashabbuh* carries a negative value; (2) it often applies to matters of ordinary life, such as dress and bodily comportment; and (3) it seeks to preserve social hierarchies. See the exhaustive compendium of Twelver Shiʿi hadiths, Barāzish, *al-Muʿjam al-Mufahras,* 1:410, 1:907, 1:951, 2:1907, 2:1968, 2:2265.
13. What I call a *semantic geography* maps the usage of a term contained in the hadiths across the major geographical centers of Islamic learning. When determining when and where a hadith circulated, I look for a hadith's primary and secondary circulators (see chapter 2). Most *tashabbuh*-related hadiths, however, are lone narrations, and thus lack a primary circulator who taught the tradition to multiple students who then circulated the tradition to their students. Therefore, we cannot confidently determine how frequently transmitters circulated these lone narrations in a given locale, nor the value attributed to this narration or the practice of which it speaks by the local community in which it circulated. I thus limit my semantic geography of *tashabbuh* only to those traditions with primary circulators. We can be reasonably confident about the information this approach provides. According to my findings, a majority of *tashabbuh* traditions traveled from Mecca or Medina in Arabia to almost every major center of the caliphate, especially Iraq. A typical chain of transmission looks like this: the Prophet Muhammad (Medina)-> Companion Ibn ʿAbbās (Mecca)-> ʿIkrima (Medina)-> Qatāda (Wasit, Iraq)-> Shuʿba (Basra, Iraq)-> numerous transmitters who eventually settled in Medina, Iraq, and elsewhere. The chains of transmissions of other oral traditions suggest that the geographic center of hadith transmission shifted from Medina to Iraq in the eighth century.
14. Based on close study of the *isnāds* of relevant hadiths, the phrase "Do not imitate" (*lā tashabbahū*) did not circulate widely in Ṣanʿāʾ, Yemen, a less important center of learning. I did not find primary circulators who transmitted traditions employing this phrase.
15. Ibn Saʿd, *al-Ṭabaqāt,* 1:378.
16. Barāzish, *al-Muʿjam al-mufahras.* Some Twelver Shiʿi legal positions concerning relations with Christians and Jews were stricter than those of Sunnis. Freidenreich, "The Implications of Unbelief."
17. Ibn Wahb, *al-Jāmiʿ fī al-ḥadīth,* 1:442. The editor of Ibn Wahb's collection, Muṣṭafā Ḥasan Ḥusayn Muḥammad, elevates his grade of the hadith's authenticity to fair (*ḥasan*) due to corroborating narrations that resemble its syntax.
18. Ibn Wahb helped compile the *Muwaṭṭaʾ* and spread the Mālikī school of jurisprudence. See ibid., 1:12–32.
19. *Ṣaḥīḥ al-Bukhārī, kitāb al-manāqib, bāb mā dhukira ʿan banī isrāʾīl,* and *kitāb al-iʿtiṣām bi'l-sunna, bāb qawl al-nabī la-tattabiʿanna sunan man kāna qablakum; Ṣaḥīḥ Muslim, kitāb al-ʿilm, bāb ittibāʿ al-yahūd wa'l-naṣārā.*
20. Ibn Ḥajar al-ʿAsqalānī, *Fatḥ al-Bārī,* 13:368. This interpretation illustrates how ethnic and religious differences intersected in the early Muslim social imagination.

21. *Ṣaḥīḥ al-Bukhārī, kitāb al-iʿtiṣām bi'l-kitāb wa'l-sunna, bāb la-tattabiʿanna sunan man kāna qablakum.*
22. Ibn Ḥajar al-ʿAsqalānī, *Fatḥ al-Bārī,* 13:366–69.
23. Ibn Taymiyya, *Iqtiḍāʾ al-ṣirāṭ al-mustaqīm,* 1:110; Memon, *Ibn Taimiya's Struggle,* 108.
24. Ibn Taymiyya, *Iqtiḍāʾ al-ṣirāṭ al-mustaqīm,* 1:110; Memon, *Ibn Taimiya's Struggle,* 109.
25. Pregill, *The Golden Calf.*
26. According to A. S. Tritton, "It is surprising how little Muslim authors have to say about the Jews; the law books rarely mention them, speaking only of *dhimmis* or Christians." Tritton's overgeneralization does not apply to the hadiths, which make copious references to the Jews, as observed by Goldziher and Kister. Tritton, *The Caliphs and Their Non-Muslim Subjects,* 92.
27. Goldziher arranged hadiths discouraging the imitation (*tashabbuh*) of Jews into three main categories: ritual, dogma, and ordinary life. Goldziher, "Über jüdische"; Goldziher, "Usages juifs." For the traditions on cleaning armpits, see *Sunan al-Tirmidhī, kitāb al-ṭahāra, bāb mā jāʾa fī al-naẓāfa;* dyeing hair, *Sunan al-Tirmidhī, kitāb al-libās, bāb mā jāʾa fī al-khiḍāb;* covering the faces of the dead, Ibn Abī Shayba, *al-Muṣannaf,* 5:435, in *kitāb al-ḥajj, bāb fī al-muḥrim yamūt yughaṭṭa raʾsuhu;* shunning the practice of hoarding goods, al-Mawṣilī, *Musnad Abī Yaʿlā,* 183; and shunning the practice of wrapping oneself up in a single garment, al-Ṣanʿānī, *al-Muṣannaf,* 1:352.
28. Luwayḥiq, *al-Tashabbuh al-manhī ʿanhu,* 185.
29. al-Bazzār, *al-Baḥr al-zakhkhār,* 5:21.
30. al-Suyūṭī, *Jamʿ al-jawāmiʿ,* 5:435. Suyūṭī mentions that Ṭabarānī includes this hadith in *al-Muʿjam al-kabīr.* For additional references, see Kister, "'Do Not Assimilate Yourselves,'" 338.
31. *Sunan Abī Dāwūd, kitāb al-libās, bāb al-ṣalāt fī al-naʿl;* Ibn Taymiyya, *Iqtiḍāʾ al-ṣirāṭ al-mustaqīm,* 1:185. For other sources, see Kister, "'Do Not Assimilate Yourselves,'" 338.
32. al-Ṣanʿānī, *al-Muṣannaf,* 1:352.
33. This tradition is attributed to ʿĀʾisha, but with a Kufan Iraqi *isnād.* Ibn Abī Shayba, *al-Muṣannaf,* 2:451.
34. *Sunan al-Tirmidhī, kitāb al-ṭahāra, bāb mā jāʾa fī al-naẓāfa.*
35. *Sunan al-Tirmidhī, kitāb al-istiʾdhān, bāb mā jāʾa fī karāhiyyat ishārat al-yad bi'l-salām.* The primary circulator of this hadith is the Meccan ʿAmr b. Shuʿayb (d. 736). Tirmidhī grades this chain of transmission as fair due to corroborating evidence, implying that the chain of transmission itself is weak.
36. Sijpesteijn, *Shaping a Muslim State,* 54.
37. Ibid., 77–78, 83–84.
38. *Laysa minnā man yatashabbahu bi-ghayrinā* versus *man tashabbaha bi-qawm^{in} fa-huwa minhum.*
39. Due to the weakness in the hadith's chain of transmission, the Andulusian Mālikī commentator Abū Bakr b. al-ʿArabī (d. 1148) saw no harm in greeting someone using a physical gesture. Ibn al-ʿArabī, *ʿĀriḍat al-aḥwadhī,* 10:171.
40. al-Bayhaqī, *al-Sunan al-kubrā,* 9:392; Ibn Taymiyya, *Iqtiḍāʾ al-ṣirāṭ al-mustaqīm,* 1:456–57.

41. Halevi, *Muhammad's Grave,* 143–64.
42. The Meccan Ibn Jurayj (d. 767) allegedly transmitted this tradition to several Iraqi personalities, Sufyān al-Thawrī, Ḥafs b. Ghiyāth, and ʿAlī b. ʿĀsim. Ibn Abī Shayba, *al-Muṣannaf,* 5:435.
43. This narration has a Kufan Iraqi *isnād.* Ibid., 4:445.
44. Ibn Taymiyya cites five "Be different" traditions—four of which focus on physical appearance.
45. Kister, "'Do Not Assimilate Yourselves,'" 335–68.
46. al-Marwadhī, *Kitāb al-Waraʿ,* 171–72.
47. *Farq mā baynanā wa bayn al-mushrikīn al-ʿamāʾim ʿalā al-qalānis.* Ibn Saʿd, *al-Ṭabaqāt,* 1:322.
48. *Ṣaḥīḥ al-Bukhārī, kitāb al-libās, bāb al-khiḍāb* and *kitāb al-anbiyāʾ, bāb mā dhukira ʿan banī isrāʾīl; Ṣaḥīḥ Muslim, kitāb al-libās waʾl-zīna, bāb fī mukhālafat al-yahūd fī al-ṣabgh; Sunan Abī Dāwūd, kitāb al-tarajjul, bāb fī al-khiḍāb; Sunan Ibn Mājah, kitāb al-libās, bāb al-khiḍāb biʾl-ḥinnāʾ.* A variant of this narration is contained in *Sunan al-Nasāʾī, kitāb al-zīna, bāb al-idhn biʾl-khiḍāb.*
49. The Medinese Hishām b. Urwa (d. 762) is said to have transmitted this tradition to various students from Iraq. *Sunan al-Nasāʾī, kitāb al-zīna, bāb al-idhn biʾl-khiḍāb.* Some narrations mention Jews only: *Sunan al-Tirmidhī, kitāb al-libās, bāb mā jāʾa fī al-khiḍāb;* Ibn Saʿd, *al-Ṭabaqāt,* 1:378; Juynboll, "Dyeing the Hair and Beard in Early Islam"; El Shamsy, "The Curious Case of Early Muslim Hair Dyeing."
50. *Ṣaḥīḥ al-Bukhārī, kitāb al-anbiyāʾ, bāb mā dhukira ʿan banī isrāʾīl; Ṣaḥīḥ Muslim, kitāb al-libās waʾl-zīna, bāb fī mukhālafat al-yahūd fī al-ṣabgh.*
51. Ibn Ḥanbal, *Musnad,* 36:613. The above phrase is an excerpt from a longer tradition, which suggests that Muslims wanted to be different from Jews and Christians in all sartorial matters: "'O Helpers, dye your beards red and yellow and be different from the People of the Book.' He said: So we said: 'O Messenger of God, the People of the Book do not wear trousers or sarongs [*izārs*].' So the Messenger of God said: 'Wear trousers and sarongs and be different from the People of the Book.' He said: we said: 'O Messenger of God, the People of the Book do not trim their moustaches and do not wear shoes [during prayer].' He said: the Prophet said: 'Trim your moustaches and wear shoes [during prayer] and be different from the People of the Book.' He said: we said: 'O Messenger of God, the People of the Book trim their beards [*ʿathānīnahum*] and grow out their moustaches [*sibālahum*].' The Prophet said: 'Trim your moustaches [*sibālakum*] and grow out your beards [*ʿathānīnakum*] and be different from the People of the Book.'"
52. While Twelver Shiʿis encouraged dissimulation, *taqiyya,* to manage tense relations with Sunnis, I did not find a single hadith explicitly condemning imitation (*tashabbuh*) of Sunnis.
53. al-Ṭabarānī, *al-Muʿjam al-kabīr,* 8:327–28. On this hadith, see the monograph composed by the great Yemenī reformer Muḥammad b. Ismāʿīl al-Ṣanʿānī, *Ḥadīth iftirāq al-umma,* especially 52, n. 1.
54. al-Ṣanʿānī, *Ḥadīth iftirāq al-umma,* 47–53.
55. Goldziher, "Le dénombrement des sectes mohamétanes."

56. al-Haythamī, *Bughyat al-rā'id fī majma' al-zawā'id,* 5:286.
57. Mālik b. Anas and al-Shaybānī, *Muwaṭṭa',* 146. To my knowledge, this is the lone *tashabbuh* tradition transmitted by the founding jurist, Mālik b. Anas, in his famous compilation of traditions, *The Well-Trodden Path* (*Muwaṭṭa'*). Although the chain of transmitters recorded by Mālik are Medinan ('Umar-> Ibn 'Umar-> Nāfi'-> Mālik), this tradition was transmitted to Iraq and Syria via the famous traditionist Ibn Shihāb al-Zuhrī (d. 742), who resided in both Medina and Damascus. Hadith compilers who transcribed this tradition usually did so through Syrian transmitters, who learned the tradition from Zuhrī during the first half of the eighth century. Also see *Ṣaḥīḥ al-Bukhārī, kitāb al-libās, bāb al-talbīd.*
58. Q 9:97 criticizes Bedouins for their harshness and hypocrisy. Despite criticizing Bedouin Arab norms, Ibn Taymiyya asserted that they could exceed urban Muslims in piety. Ibn Khaldūn preferred the Bedouin Arab to the urbanized Arab because of the latter's predilection for luxury and the spiritual diseases that spring from it. Ibn Taymiyya, *Iqtiḍā' al-ṣirāṭ al-mustaqīm,* 1:366–74; Memon, *Ibn Taimiya's Struggle,* 181–82; Ibn Khaldūn, *The Muqaddimah,* 297.
59. Luwayḥiq, *al-Tashabbuh al-manhī 'anhu,* 205–10; Memon, *Ibn Taimiya's Struggle,* 180–81.
60. *Ṣaḥīḥ al-Bukhārī, kitāb al-libās, bāb al-mutashabbihūn bi'l-nisā' wa'l-mutashabbihāt bi'l-rijāl; Sunan Abī Dāwūd, kitāb al-libās, bāb libās al-nisā'; Sunan al-Tirmidhī, kitāb al-adab, bāb mā jā'a fī al-mutashabbihāt bi'l-rijāl min al-nisā'; Sunan Ibn Mājah, kitāb al-nikāḥ, bāb fī al-mukhannathīn.* On the social role of effeminates during the first century of Islamic history, see Rowson, "The Effeminates of Early Medina."
61. Barāzish, *al-Mu'jam al-mufahras,* 1:951.
62. Alter, *The Five Books of Moses,* 986.
63. al-Quḍā'ī, *Musnad al-Shihāb,* 2:233.
64. al-Makkī, *Qut al-qulūb,* 2:243. See also Douglas, "The Beard," 106.
65. Brown, *Slavery & Islam,* 163, 294–98.
66. Ibn Abī Shayba, *al-Muṣannaf,* 3:127–28. For a variant narration, see al-Ṣan'ānī, *al-Muṣannaf,* 3:135–36. Both collectors categorize this tradition in chapters on prayer (*kitāb al-ṣalāt*).
67. Mikhail, *The Animal in Ottoman Egypt.*
68. "There is not an animal on earth, nor a bird that flies with its wings, but they form communities like yourselves" (Q 6:38). For exegesis of this verse as well as a list of animal species and categories in the Quran, see Tlili, *Animals in the Qur'an,* 138–220, 257–68.
69. al-Rāzī, *al-Tafsīr al-kabīr,* 4:526. I wish to thank Sarra Tlili for this reference.
70. "I am placing a steward [*khalīfa*] on earth" (Q 2:30). Tlili, however, refutes the claim that such verses imply that humans are meant to rule over nonhuman animals. Tlili, *Animals in the Qur'an,* 74–137.
71. *Sunan Abī Dāwūd, kitāb al-ṣalāt, bāb kayfa yaḍa' rukbatayhi qabla yadayhi; Sunan al-Nasā'ī; kitāb al-taṭbīq, bāb awwal mā yaṣilu ilā al-arḍ min al-insān fī sujūdihi;* Ibn Ḥanbal, *Musnad,* 14:515.
72. Abū Dāwūd al-Sijistānī, *al-Marāsīl,* 350.
73. *Lā ta'kulū bi'l-shimāl fa-inna al-shayṭān ya'kulu wa yashribu bi'l-shimāl.* In *Ṣaḥīḥ Mus-*

lim, kitāb al-ashriba, bāb ādāb al-ṭaʿām wa'l-sharāb wa aḥkāmihima. Also see *Ṣaḥīḥ al-Bukhārī, kitāb al-aṭʿima, bāb al-tasmiyya alā al-ṭaʿām wa'l-akl bi'l-yamīn.*

74. *Ṣaḥīḥ Muslim, kitāb al-ruʾyā, bāb qawl alladhī (ṣalla Allāhu ʿalayhi wa sallam) man raʾānī fi al-manām fa-qad raʾānī.*
75. al-Ṭabarānī, *al-Muʿjam al-kabīr,* 7:40–41.
76. Modified translation of these and other ordinances from Cohen, "What Was the Pact of ʿUmar?" 105–8.
77. Levy-Rubin, *Non-Muslims in the Early Islamic Empire,* 7.
78. Mark Cohen argues that the revival of these ordinances has the long-term effect of discriminating against non-Muslim populations. But Noth asserts that these stipulations are discriminatory in a "neutral," not a pejorative, sense, since Muslims were a minority seeking to protect themselves rather than to oppress their subjects. Noth, "Problems of Differentiation," 122; Cohen, "What Was the Pact of ʿUmar?" 129–30.
79. Noth, "Problems of Differentiation," 17–18.
80. Levy-Rubin, *Non-Muslims in the Early Islamic Empire,* 127.
81. Kister quotes Ibn al-Qayyim al-Jawziyya on this point: "'Do Not Assimilate Yourselves,'" 348–49.
82. *Ṣaḥīfat al-umma* translates literally as "document of the community." The most extensive study of the "The Constitution of Medina" to date is Lecker, *The "Constitution of Medina."* Also see Donner, *Muhammad and the Believers,* 227–32.
83. For a dissenting view, see Serjeant, "The 'Sunnah Jāmiʿah,' Pacts." For a review of existing secondary literature on this document, see Lecker, *The "Constitution of Medina,"* 1–4. Both "documents" are, of course, literary products that bear the possible alterations and emendations that accompany their passage over time into written form.
84. Lecker, *The "Constitution of Medina,"* 10. I have modified Lecker's translation.
85. Donner argues that Muhammad functioned as a political leader, not a "religious" leader, of the multiconfessional tribes that inhabited Medina. Donner, *Muhammad and the Believers,* 74–75.
86. Schaff and Wace, *Select Library,* 356–58.
87. Ibid., 370.
88. Ibid., 359–408.
89. A. S. Tritton first advanced the argument that the Pact of ʿUmar functioned as a normative template for Muslim interreligious relations, which supported his claim that the pact is misattributed to ʿUmar b. al-Khaṭṭāb; he deemed it unlikely that the first generation of Muslims were so future oriented. Tritton, *The Caliphs and Their Non-Muslim Subjects,* 10.
90. On Abū Yūsuf, see *Encyclopaedia of Islam,* 3rd ed., s.v. "Abū Yūsuf" (B. Wheeler). Historians have debated the authenticity of the *Treatise on Taxation* (*Kitāb al-Kharāj*). Calder claims that Abū Yūsuf's disciples composed it in the late ninth century, but Zaman argues Calder's claim is speculative. Melchert believes Zaman lacks sufficient evidence to claim Abū Yūsuf composed the treatise. Calder, *Studies in Early Muslim Jurisprudence,* 105–60; Zaman, *Religion and Politics,* 91–106; Melchert, "Review: Religion and Politics."

91. Abū Yūsuf, *Kitāb al-Kharāj*, 127.
92. Ibid.
93. Although Cohen claims *The Motherbook* (*Kitāb al-Umm*) of Shāfiʿī is the first text to reproduce a significant portion of the Pact of ʿUmar, Abū Yūsuf's *Treatise on Taxation*, which was likely composed earlier, also reproduces key features of the pact, albeit in summary form. Shāfiʿī omits the term *tashabbuh* in his version. The earliest surviving source to quote the Pact of ʿUmar verbatim, including the term *tashabbuh*, is an early tenth-century collection of responsa from Aḥmad b. Ḥanbal, collected by Ibn Khallāl. All the versions of the pact transmitted by Ibn Zabr include the term *tashabbuh*. Cohen, "What Was the Pact of ʿUmar?" 109.
94. Bosanquet, *Minding Their Place*, 69–98.
95. Ibn al-Qayyim al-Jawziyya, *Aḥkām ahl al-dhimma*, 2:657–872; Bosanquet, *Minding Their Place*, 262–322.
96. Ibn al-Qayyim al-Jawziyya, *Aḥkām ahl al-dhimma*, 2:736. This passage is also found in the unpublished treatise against employing Jews and Christians in government *al-Qawl al-mukhtār fī al-manʿ ʿan takhyīr al-kuffār* (*The Chosen View concerning the Prohibition on Preferring Infidels*), composed during the first half of the fourteenth century by an anonymous author who has yet to be identified, although he was a contemporary of Ibn al-Qayyim. The treatise references jurists from all major Sunni schools of jurisprudence and includes citations from some lost treatises concerning the Islamic rulings on *dhimmī*s. A lithograph of the manuscript, dated to 1856 or 1857, is held in Cairo (Maṭbaʿat Ḥajar). I accessed a manuscript copy held by the King Abd al-Aziz Public University library in Riyadh. Forthcoming references to *al-Qawl al-mukhtār* are from this copy. "al-Qawl al-mukhtār," F25r. See Yarbrough, "Al-Qawl al-mukhtār." On the literary genre of Islamic treatises against employing non-Muslims, see Yarbrough, "'A Rather Small Genre'"; Yarbrough, *Friends of the Emir.*
97. Ibn al-Qayyim al-Jawziyya, *Aḥkām ahl al-dhimma*, 2:736; "al-Qawl al-mukhtār," F36r–F36v.
98. al-Sunāmī, *Niṣāb al-iḥtisāb*, 111. There are two complete English translations of al-Sunāmī's treatise: ʿIzz ad-Dīn, *The Theory and the Practice of Market Law;* Partington, "The Niṣāb al-Iḥtisāb."
99. Buckley, "The Muḥtasib," 101–3. For primary and secondary sources on this office, see Stilt and Saraçoğlu, "Hisba and Muhtasib," 353–55.
100. Consider also Andalusian jurist Ibn Ḥazm's (d. 1064) exegesis of Q 9:29, which commands Muslims to fight *dhimmī*s until they pay the poll tax and are "humbled" (*ṣāghirūn*). In his compendium of Islamic jurisprudence, *The Brilliant Treatise* (*al-Muḥallā*), Ibn Ḥazm explains that the meaning of humbling non-Muslim subjects is "summed up by the ordinances of ʿUmar." Ibn Ḥazm, *al-Muḥallā*, 7:346, cited in Cohen, "What Was the Pact of ʿUmar?" 121.
101. Levy-Rubin argues that the Pact of ʿUmar and its subsequent manifestations were not intermittent but continuously applied throughout premodern Islamic history. Levy-Rubin, *Non-Muslims in the Early Islamic Empire*, 99–111.

4. THE SYMBOLIC POWER OF MUSLIM DIFFERENCE

1. Eliade, "Methodological Remarks," 95.
2. Geertz, *The Interpretation of Cultures,* 5.
3. Kugle, *Sufis & Saints' Bodies,* 123.
4. According to French theorist Roland Barthes, dress is a culturally and historically self-contained system, a vestimentary system that is built upon sartorial styles of the past. We may therefore view Muslim sartorial styles as a distinctive sartorial system. *The Fashion System.*
5. Describing the Israelites, Douglas observes, "The threatened boundaries of their body politic would be well mirrored in their care for the integrity, unity and purity of the physical body." *Purity and Danger,* 125.
6. Mauss, "Techniques of the Body," 73; Spencer, *The Principles of Sociology,* 207–8.
7. "Taqallub al-azyāʾ fī miʾat ʿāmm," 34.
8. There is a growing number of studies of hair in Islam, including a themed volume in *Al-Masāq,* "Hair in the Mediaeval Muslim World." Also see Pfluger-Schindlbeck, "On the Symbolism of Hair in Islamic Societies"; Bromberger, "Hair." On grooming hair in Islamic scripture and Sufism, see Ridgeon, "Shaggy or Shaved?" On the semiotics of the face in Islam, see Lange, "'On That Day When Faces Will Be White or Black.'"
9. Today, Muslim men with long dark beards are often vilified in the mainstream U.S. media. Culcasi and Gokmen, "The Face of Danger."
10. See, for example, Delaney, "Untangling the Meanings of Hair."
11. *Ṣaḥīḥ Muslim, kitāb al-ṭahāra, bāb khiṣāl al-fiṭra.*
12. *Ṣaḥīḥ al-Bukhārī, kitāb al-libās, bāb taqlīm al-aẓfār; Ṣaḥīḥ Muslim, kitāb al-ṭahāra, bāb khiṣāl al-fiṭra.*
13. al-Ṭabarī, *The History of al-Ṭabarī: The Victory of Islam,* 112–13. Also see Ibn Saʿd, *al-Ṭabaqāt,* 1:386.
14. al-Makkī, *Qut al-Qulūb,* 2:240. Selected translations in Douglas, "The Beard." Arabic translations are mine unless otherwise noted.
15. al-Makkī, *Qut al-Qulūb,* 2:240.
16. Ibid.
17. *Ṣaḥīḥ Muslim, kitāb al-ṭahāra, bāb khiṣāl al-fiṭra.*
18. Abū Yūsuf, *Kitāb al-Āthār,* 235. Many contemporary scholars, such as the well-known Egyptian jurist Yūsuf al-Qaraḍāwī, no longer believe that growing a beard is mandatory. Speculating that it was an Arab cultural norm, he writes, "Perhaps there was no need to shave, and perhaps growing the beard was a custom among them." al-Qaraḍāwī, *The Lawful and the Prohibited in Islam,* 91–93.
19. Ibn Qutayba al-Dīnawarī, *ʿUyūn al-akhbār;* al-Albānī, *Silsilat al-aḥādīth al-ḍaʿīfa wa'l-mawḍūʿa,* 13:52–53.
20. al-Ghazālī, *Iḥyāʾ ʿulūm al-dīn,* 1:203; al-Makkī, *Qut al-Qulūb,* 2:240.
21. Corradini, Diesenberger, and Reimitz, *The Construction of Communities,* 173; Constable, "Introduction: Beards in History," 60.
22. Sijpesteijn, "Shaving Hair and Beards," 16–17.
23. References in chapter 3.

24. Juynboll, "Dyeing the Hair and Beard," 55.
25. Several traditions enumerate the gray hairs in the Prophet's beard, which would have been impossible had he dyed it. There is a paucity of authentic hadiths that attest to the Prophet dying his beard. Anas b. Mālik believed that the Prophet "did not have enough gray hair to dye" or "only had a few gray hairs." *Ṣaḥīḥ al-Bukhārī, kitāb al-libās, bāb mā yudhkarū fī al-shayb.*
26. Dyes included saffron and colorful hues such as yellow, orange, and fiery red.
27. Ibn Saʿd, *al-Ṭabaqāt,* 1:379–80. Both Twelver Shiʿis and Sunnis encouraged the use of dye, except the color black. Some Sunni scholars permitted soldiers to use black dye to terrify the enemy.
28. al-Makkī, *Qut al-Qulūb,* 2:240.
29. Ibid.
30. See the anecdote of *ʿUmar b. ʿAbd al-ʿAzīz wa aḥad al-mukhannathīn* in Abū al-Faraj al-Iṣfahānī, *Kitāb al-Aghānī,* 6:352–53.
31. Shaving heads marked adherents of the Khārijī sect. Juynboll, "Dyeing the Hair and Beard," 68.
32. Ibn Saʿd, *al-Ṭabaqāt,* 3:23, 3:172, 3:303.
33. Levy-Rubin, *Non-Muslims in the Early Islamic Empire,* 147.
34. The third caliph, ʿUthmān, allegedly wore a *qalansuwa* to celebrate his wedding night with one of his wives. Ettinghausen, *From Byzantium to Sasanian Iran,* 30–31.
35. The Pact of ʿUmar mentions only the regular-sized *qalansuwa,* not the tall *qalansuwa.* It also denies non-Muslims the prestige of wearing the turban.
36. Ettinghausen, *From Byzantium to Sasanian Iran,* 30.
37. Dhalla, *Zoroastrian Civilization,* 3, 12; Curtis, Tallis, and André-Salvini, *Forgotten Empire,* 86, 90, 157.
38. Ibn Saʿd, *al-Ṭabaqāt,* 1:322.
39. See the erudite and impassioned historical study of the turban composed in 1923 by the Moroccan jurist Muḥammad b. Jaʿfar al-Kattānī: *al-Diʿāma li-maʿrifat aḥkām sunnat al-ʿimāma.*
40. Locke, *Two Tracts on Government,* 146; Matar, "John Locke."
41. Ibn Saʿd, *al-Ṭabaqāt,* 1:322.
42. al-Ṭabarī, *The History of al-Ṭabarī: Incipient Decline,* 89–90; Levy-Rubin, *Non-Muslims in the Early Islamic Empire,* 104, 106.
43. Tritton, *The Caliphs and Their Non-Muslim Subjects,* 120.
44. Ibid., 121.
45. *Encyclopaedia of Islam,* 1st ed., s.v. "Turban" (W. Björkman).
46. Ibn Ḥajar al-ʿAsqalānī, *al-Iṣāba fī tamyīz al-ṣaḥāba,* 6:24–25; ʿAthamina, "The Black Banners," 323.
47. Winter, *Egyptian Society under Ottoman Rule,* 206. Some hadiths criticize men for wearing yellow or red. Many religious authorities associated yellow with women and dishonorable professions such as singing. See "The Prohibition of a Man Wearing a Yellow Garment" in *Ṣaḥīḥ Muslim, kitāb al-libās wa'l-zīna, bāb al-nahy ʿan libs al-rajul al-thawb al-muʿaṣfar.*
48. Ibn Saʿd, *al-Ṭabaqāt,* 7:286.

49. Bauer, "Room for Interpretation," 143–49.
50. Ibn Taymiyya and al-Baʿlī, *Mukhtaṣar al-Fatāwa al-Miṣriyya,* 318–20; Chamberlain, *Knowledge and Social Practice,* 104.
51. Ibn Taymiyya and al-Baʿlī, *Mukhtaṣar al-Fatāwa al-Miṣriyya,* 318.
52. Ibn Qudāma, *al-Mughnī,* 1:383. Muwaffaq al-Dīn b. Qudāma compiled the most famous manual of law in the Ḥanbalī school, *al-Mughnī* (*The Enricher*), an extensive commentary on a cryptic tenth-century legal manual, *al-Mukhtaṣar* by al-Khiraqī (d. 945), that preserves disagreements between the Ḥanbalīs and other schools. *Encyclopaedia of Islam,* 2nd ed., s.v. "Ibn Kudāma" (G. Makdisi).
53. Ibn Taymiyya, *Iqtiḍāʾ al-ṣirāṭ al-mustaqīm,* 2:514; Memon, *Ibn Taimiya's Struggle,* 220. *Ṣaḥīḥ al-Bukhārī, kitāb al-nikāḥ, bāb mā yuttaqa min shuʾm al-marʾa; Ṣaḥīḥ Muslim, kitāb al-dhikr wa'l-duʿāʾ wa'l-tawba wa'l-istighfār, bāb akthar ahl al-janna al-fuqarāʾ wa akthar ahl al-nār al-nisāʾ.*
54. Ibn Taymiyya, *Iqtiḍāʾ al-ṣirāṭ al-mustaqīm,* 2:515; Memon, *Ibn Taimiya's Struggle,* 220.
55. Ahmed, *Women and Gender in Islam,* 55.
56. On ʿUmar's misogyny, see ibid., 60–61.
57. Ibn Abī Shayba, *al-Muṣannaf,* 3:127–28; al-Ṣanʿānī, *al-Muṣannaf,* 3:135–36. For variants of this tradition, see Anchassi, "Status Distinctions."
58. In other narrations, ʿUmar strikes the slave woman with a switch; in others, he does not strike her but verbally chastises either her or her owner. Anchassi, "Status Distinctions," 7–15.
59. Ibid.
60. The *ʿawra* for men usually includes the area between the belly button and the knees, whereas for (free adult) women, it includes the entire body except the hands, face, and feet. *al-Mawsūʿa al-fiqhiyya,* s.v. "*ʿawra.*"
61. Ahmed, *A Quiet Revolution.*
62. Alshech, "Out of Sight."
63. Ahmed, *Women and Gender in Islam,* 15.
64. For the Prophet's wives to remain behind a curtain is, according to the Quran, "purer for your hearts and for theirs" (33:53). Other women are excluded from this command because the Prophet's wives possess a unique status and "are not like other women" (Q 33:32). However, Q 24:31, which commands women to "draw a veil [*khimār*] over their chests," is not limited to the Prophet's wives exclusively.
65. In late antiquity, Jewish and Christian women also wore headscarves. Rabbinic law mandated that Jewish women who went out unveiled were liable to be divorced without return of their dower. The New Testament encourages women to attend church with their heads covered, although enforcement varied. Stillman and Stillman, *Arab Dress,* 144.
66. Ibid., 83.
67. Ibid., 67.
68. Graham, *Beyond the Written Word,* 79.
69. Kermani, *God Is Beautiful,* 303–11.
70. Weiner, *Religion Out Loud,* 158–94.

71. *al-adhān shiʿār al-īmān.* al-Ṣanʿānī, *al-Muṣannaf,* 1:483, 10:172.
72. Mālik b. Anas and al-Shaybānī, *Muwaṭṭaʾ*, 54.
73. *Ṣaḥīḥ al-Bukhārī, kitāb al-adhān, bāb badʾ al-adhān.* The horn may refer to the *shofar,* a ram's horn that has been associated with Rosh Hashanah since biblical times, or a trumpet, which is blown on significant days of the Jewish calendar. Another version credits the Companion ʿAbd Allāh b. Zayd, not ʿUmar, with having first shared the idea of the *adhān. Sunan Abī Dāwūd, kitāb al-ṣalāt, bāb badʾ al-adhān.*
74. *Ṣaḥīḥ al-Bukhārī, kitāb al-anbiyāʾ, bāb mā dhukira ʿan banī isrāʾīl.* It is unlikely that Jews had anything to do with fire, although substantial numbers of Jews resided within the Sasanian Empire, where Zoroastrians lit fires during their religious rituals.
75. Ibn Ḥajar al-ʿAsqalānī, *Fatḥ al-Bārī,* 2:105–6.
76. Howard, "The Development of the *Adhān,*" 219–28.
77. Ibid., 228; Becker, "Zur Geschichte," 387; Mittwoch, *Zur Entstehungsgeschichte,* 25.
78. Jurists considered ringing bells sinful if used to defend against the evil eye, but permissible if used for a genuine need. Ibn Ḥajar al-ʿAsqalānī, *Fatḥ al-Bārī,* 6:170–72.
79. *al-jaras mazāmīr al-shayṭān.* In *Ṣaḥīḥ Muslim, kitāb al-libās wa'l-zīna, bāb karāhat al-kalb wa'l-jaras fi al-safar.*
80. *Ṣaḥīḥ Muslim, kitāb al-libās wa'l-zīna, bāb karāhat al-kalb wa'l-jaras fi al-safar.*
81. Schaff, *History of the Christian Church,* 439–41. However, some early Syrian churches had apertures atop their towers through which religious sounds could be projected. Butler and Smith, *Early Churches in Syria,* 211.
82. Ibn Ḥajar al-ʿAsqalānī, *Fatḥ al-Bārī,* 6:170–72.
83. Hitti, *The Arabs,* 110.
84. Mālik b. Anas and al-Shaybānī, *Muwaṭṭaʾ*, 54. In his recension of Mālik's *Muwaṭṭaʾ*, Ḥanafī jurist Muḥammad al-Shaybānī rejects the authenticity of this tradition, despite its esteemed chain of transmission. It is absent from Yaḥyā b. Laythī's recension of the *Muwaṭṭaʾ*. Also see Howard, "The Development of the *Adhān*"; Lalani, *Early Shīʿī Thought,* 123–24.
85. al-Qāḍī al-Nuʿmān, *The Pillars of Islam,* 178–80.
86. Adopting a contrarian view, Shiʿi jurist Ibn Babawayh al-Qummī (d. 991–92) condemned the additions of "ʿAlī is the friend of God" and "Muhammad and ʿAlī are the best of mankind and their offspring are the best of offsprings" to the *adhān.* al-Qummī, *Man lā yaḥḍuruhu al-faqīh,* 1:289–90; Modarressi, *Crisis and Consolidation,* 43–44.
87. Hurgronje, *Mekka,* 63; De Sacy, *Chrestomathie Arabe,* 60, 169; Rabbat, "Al-Azhar Mosque," 53; Ibn Kathīr, *al-Bidāya wa'l-nihāya,* 15:328.
88. Ibn Kathīr, *al-Bidāya wa'l-nihāya,* 15:736, 16:71, 16:448.
89. al-Maqrīzī, *Mawāʿiẓ wa'l-iʿtibār,* 2:200.
90. Kendon, *Gesture,* 15. An involuntary nervous tick, by contrast, does not communicate an idea or emotion so would not be considered a "gesture" in this sense.
91. St. Félix, "What Will Taking the Knee Mean Now?"; Bilefsky, "Muslim Boys at a Swiss School Must Shake Teachers' Hands."
92. Mauss, "Techniques of the Body," 78.
93. Shiʿis argue that the verb *wipe* applies to both the head and feet, while Sunnis claim

it applies to the head only. On inter-Muslim debates on ritual ablution in the Quran, see Burton, "The Qurʾān and the Islamic Practice of Wuḍūʾ."

94. See the following traditions in Tirmidhī's *Sunan:* "The difference between faith and infidelity is [leaving] the prayer"; "The covenant that distinguishes us from them is the ritual prayer [*al-ṣalāt*]. So, whoever leaves it has left Islam [*kafara*]." *Sunan al-Tirmidhī, kitāb al-īmān, bāb mā jāʾa fī tark al-ṣalāt.*

95. Ibn Rushd, *The Distinguished Jurist's Primer,* 1:15–16. ʿAlī allegedly argued that if reasoning by analogy was the most authoritative legal tool, it would be incumbent to wipe under the boots, not above, since that is the dirtiest part of the boot.

96. An example of a sartorial practice that became a point of Islamic creed is wearing the *zunnār* belt; a Muslim who wears the belt in public signals unbelief.

97. Unlike their Sunni and Shiʿi co-religionists, Ḥanafī jurists permitted the drinking of *nabīdh,* a fermented drink usually made from barley, honey, raisins, dates, or grapes. Its inclusion in Ḥanafī books of creed indicates the degree of controversy this contrarian position provoked. *Encyclopaedia of Islam,* 2nd ed., s.v. "Nabīdh," (P. Heine) and *Encyclopaedia of Islam,* 2nd ed., s.v. "Khamr" (A. J. Wensinck and J. Sadan). On the development of Ḥanafī opinion, see Melchert, *The Formation of the Sunni Schools of Law,* 48–51.

98. *al-masḥ ʿalā al-khuffayn sunna.* Arabic edition with English translation of *al-Fiqh al-Akbar,* in Mangera, *Imām Abū Ḥanīfa's Al-Fiqh al-Akbar Explained,* 147, 155. Schacht, following Wensinck, argues that wiping over footgear was originally absent from the *al-Fiqh al-Akbar* and was a later interpolation originating from an inter-Sunni disagreement that evolved into a Sunni/Shiʿi creedal dispute. Western scholars have contested the provenance of Abū Ḥanīfa's *al-Fiqh al-Akbar.* But Mangera refutes this claim on two grounds. First, he rejects Wensinck's distinction between *al-Fiqh al-Akbar* I and II, arguing that *al-Fiqh al-Akbar* II is in fact the original *al-Fiqh al-Akbar,* and what Wensinck called *al-Fiqh al-Akbar* I is another treatise altogether, *al-Fiqh al-Absaṭ.* Second, he argues that later scholars, such as Ibn al-Nadīm in his *Fihrist,* point to Abū Ḥanīfa as the author of the treatise. Mangera's reassessment, in addition to the evidence presented below from the biographical dictionaries, strengthens the view that wiping over footgear is original to *al-Fiqh al-Akbar,* and that wiping over leather socks became a gesture that distinguished Sunnis from Shiʿis in the eighth century. Mangera, *Imām Abū Ḥanīfa's Al-Fiqh al-Akbar Explained,* 24–29; Schacht, *The Origins of Muhammad Jurisprudence,* 263–64; Wensinck, *The Muslim Creed,* 103.

99. al-Ṭaḥāwī, *The Creed,* 70–71; al-Taftāzānī, *Majmūʿat al-Ḥawāshī al-bahiyya,* 1:202–3.

100. al-Taftāzānī, *Majmūʿat al-Ḥawāshī al-bahiyya,* 1:202–3; al-Taftāzānī, *A Commentary on the Creed of Islam,* 155–56.

101. al-Taftāzānī, *Majmūʿat al-Ḥawāshī al-bahiyya,* 1:202; al-Taftāzānī, *A Commentary on the Creed of Islam,* 156.

102. al-Bahūtī, *Kashshāf al-qināʿ,* 1:255–56.

103. al-Nawawī, *al-Majmūʿ,* 1:478.

104. Dakake, *The Charismatic Community,* 197.

105. al-Qāḍī al-Nuʿmān, *The Pillars of Islam,* 136.

106. Ibid., 136, n. 48.

107. Haider, "Prayer, Mosque, and Pilgrimage," 161–62.
108. I was unable to locate the death date of Mūsā b. ʿUthmān in the biographical dictionaries I consulted, both Sunni and Shiʿi. However, the death dates of transmitters from whom he allegedly transmitted hadith, such as al-Aʿmash (d. 765), suggest that he lived during the eighth century.
109. al-Dhahabī, *Mīzān al-iʿtidāl,* 4:214; al-Tustarī, *Qāmūs al-rijāl,* 10:287.
110. According to Dhahabī, "He went to extremes in his Shiʿism [*gāla fi al-tashayyuʿ*]." al-Dhahabī, *Mīzān al-Iʿtidāl,* 4:214.
111. Haider, "Prayer, Mosque, and Pilgrimage," 161–62. Burton speculates that this debate originated in Iraq, based on a tradition set in Iraq in which the Companion ʿAbd Allāh b. ʿUmar witnesses another Companion (Saʿd b. Abī Waqqāṣ) wiping over leather socks. Ibn ʿUmar returns to Medina and questions his father, ʿUmar, who responds that the practice began with the Prophet himself. Burton's evidence is thin, but the corroborating evidence presented above strengthens his hypothesis. Burton, "The Qurʾān and the Islamic Practice of Wuḍūʾ," 48–49.
112. Ibn Ḥanbal, *Musnad,* 13:468.
113. Or pecking like a crow. Ibid., 24:292.
114. On the conflicting attitudes of Muslims toward dogs, see Berglund, "Princely Companion or Object of Offense?"; Mikhail, *The Animal in Ottoman Egypt,* 67–106. Also see Ibn Taymiyya, *Majmūʿat al-fatāwā,* 21:349–51.
115. *Sunan Abī Dāwūd, kitāb al-ṣalāt, bāb kayfa yaḍaʿ rukbatayhi qabla yadayhi; Sunan al-Nasāʾī; kitāb al-taṭbīq, bāb awwal mā yaṣilu ilā al-arḍ min al-insān fi sujūdihi;* Ibn Ḥanbal, *Musnad,* 14:515.
116. al-Ṣanʿānī, *Subul al-salām,* 2:306.
117. Translation from Sells, *Desert Tracings,* 24. On the poem's attribution to Shanfarā, see Stetkevych, "Archetype and Attribution."
118. Sells, *Desert Tracings,* 22–31.
119. Jāḥiẓ, *Kitāb al-Ḥayawān,* 1:213. Translation from Jāḥiẓ, *The Life and Works of Jāḥiẓ,* 137.
120. Jāḥiẓ, *Kitāb al-Ḥayawān,* 1:212.
121. See Ibn Taymiyya, *Iqtiḍāʾ al-ṣirāṭ al-mustaqīm,* 1:487; Memon, *Ibn Taimiya's Struggle,* 217; Ibn Taymiyya, *Majmūʿat al-fatāwā,* 32:160–62. See also volumes 11 and 12 in al-Ghazzī, *Ḥusn al-tanabbuh.*
122. Ibn Taymiyya, *Majmūʿat al-fatāwā,* 32:160–62.
123. Ibn Taymiyya acknowledges that some animals, like sheep, have positive influences—unlike non-Muslims. Ibn Taymiyya, *Iqtiḍāʾ al-ṣirāṭ al-mustaqīm,* 1:487; Memon, *Ibn Taimiya's Struggle,* 216–17.
124. Ibn Taymiyya, *Majmūʿat al-fatāwā,* 32:162. See references to the hadith in chapter 3.
125. *Ṣaḥīḥ Muslim, kitāb al-ashriba, bāb ādāb al-ṭaʿām wa'l-sharāb wa aḥkāmihima.* Also see *Ṣaḥīḥ al-Bukhārī, kitāb al-aṭʿima, bāb al-tasmiyya alā al-ṭaʿām wa'l-akl bi'l-yamīn.*
126. Freidenreich, *Foreigners and Their Food,* 4.
127. al-Ghazālī, *Iḥyāʾ ʿulūm al-dīn,* 2:3–86; al-Ghazālī, *Al-Ghazālī on the Manners Relating to Eating.*
128. "Imitating the devil and infidels is detested [*makrūh*] in matters outside ritual prayer."

al-Kāsānī, *Badā'i' al-ṣanā'i'*, 1:215. Shaybānī adds, "One should not eat or drink with the left hand unless there is good cause." Mālik b. Anas and al-Shaybānī, *Muwaṭṭa'*, 286–87.

129. *Ṣaḥīḥ Muslim, kitāb al-ashriba, bāb ādāb al-ṭa'ām wa'l-sharāb wa aḥkāmihima.*
130. *Ṣaḥīḥ al-Bukhārī, kitāb al-aṭ'ima, bāb al-tayammun fi al-akl wa ghayrihi.*
131. *Ṣaḥīḥ al-Bukhārī, kitāb al-ṭibb, bāb ruqyat al-nabī.*
132. *Ṣaḥīḥ al-Bukhārī, kitāb al-adhān, bāb maymanat al-masjid wa'l-imām.*
133. The following anecdote is narrated on the authority of Anas b. Mālik: "I saw the Messenger of God drinking milk. He came to my house and I milked a sheep. I then mixed the milk with water from the well for the Messenger of God. He took the bowl and drank. To his left was Abū Bakr, and to his right a Bedouin. So he gave what remained [of the milk] to the Bedouin and said, 'The right! The right [first]!'" *Ṣaḥīḥ al-Bukhārī, kitāb al-ashriba, shurb al-laban bi'l-mā'.*
134. *Ṣaḥīḥ al-Bukhārī, kitāb al-wuḍū', bāb lā yumsik dhakarahu bi-yamīnihi idhā bāl.* The left side is preferred in situations that have a negative value associated with them; when leaving the mosque or removing shoes, one should lead with the left foot: *Ṣaḥīḥ al-Bukhārī, kitāb al-libās, bāb yanzi' na'l al-yusrā.* One should spit toward the left side, not the right: *Ṣaḥīḥ al-Bukhārī, kitāb al-aṭ'ima, bāb al-tayammun fi al-akl wa ghayrihi.*
135. *Ṣaḥīḥ al-Bukhārī, abwāb al-qibla, bāb al-tayammun fi dukhūl al-masjid wa ghayrihi.*
136. Sabiq, *Fiqh Us-Sunnah,* 20.
137. "And he shall set the sheep on his right hand, but the goats on the left. Then shall the King say unto them on his right hand, Come, ye blessed of my Father, inherit the kingdom prepared for you from the foundation of the world. . . . Then shall he say also unto them on the left hand, Depart from me, ye cursed, into everlasting fire." Matt. 25: 33–34, 41 (King James Version).
138. Nahshon, *Jews and Shoes,* 3.
139. McManus, *Right Hand, Left Hand,* 32.

5. IBN TAYMIYYA AND THE INNOVATION OF IMITATION

1. Sivan, *Radical Islam,* 83–129; Meijer, *Global Salafism,* 305; Lawrence, *Messages to the World,* 9–11.
2. Little, "Did Ibn Taymiyya Have a Screw Loose?" 95–96. In addition to Little's article, other biographical sources for Ibn Taymiyya include Shams and al-'Imrān, *al-Jāmi' li-sīrat Shaykh al-Islām Ibn Taymiyya;* al-Jazarī, *Ta'rīkh ḥawādith al-zamān;* Ibn 'Abd al-Hādī, *al-'Uqūd al-durriyya;* al-Dhahabī, "al-Naṣīḥa al-dhahabiyya," 33–37; Laoust, *Essai sur les doctrines sociales;* Hoover, *Ibn Taymiyya;* Bori, "A New Source"; Bori, "The Collection and Edition of Ibn Taymiyya's Works." For an extensive bibliography of biographical sources, see Rapoport and Ahmed, *Ibn Taymiyya and His Times.*
3. al-Dhahabī, "al-Naṣīḥa al-dhahabiyya," 35, cited in Little, "Did Ibn Taymiyya Have a Screw Loose?" 101. Translation mine.
4. Little, "Did Ibn Taymiyya Have a Screw Loose?" 107.

5. Ibid., 110. His polemical treatises include the most elaborate polemic against Christianity in premodern Islam: Ibn Taymiyya, *A Muslim Theologian's Response to Christianity.*
6. Fierro, "The Treatises against Innovations"; Rispler, "Toward a New Understanding of the Term Bidʿa"; Berkey, "Tradition, Innovation and the Social Construction of Knowledge"; Masud, "The Definition of *Bidʿa*"; Ukeles, "Innovation or Deviation"; al-Ghazālī, *Within the Boundaries of Islam.*
7. Ibn Hishām, *al-Sīra al-nabawiyya,* 39–40; Ibn Taymiyya, *Iqtiḍāʾ al-ṣirāṭ al-mustaqīm,* 1:313–14; Memon, *Ibn Taimiya's Struggle,* 163.
8. Chamberlain, *Knowledge and Social Practice,* 27.
9. On Muslim emotional responses to the loss of the caliphate, see Hassan, *Longing for the Lost Caliphate.*
10. On Ibn Taymiyya's response to the Mongol occupation, see Amitai, "The Mongol Occupation of Damascus."
11. Meri, *The Cult of Saints,* 120–213.
12. Ibn Taymiyya, *Iqtiḍāʾ al-ṣirāṭ al-mustaqīm,* 2:617; Memon, *Ibn Taimiya's Struggle,* 11, 241–42.
13. *Ṣaḥīḥ al-Bukhārī, kitāb al-ʿīdayn, bāb sunnat al-ʿīdayn li-ahl al-Islām; Ṣaḥīḥ Muslim, kitāb ṣalāt al-ʿīdayn, bāb al-rukhṣa fī al-laʿib alladhī lā maʿṣiya fīhi fī ayyām al-ʿīd.*
14. Cohen, *Under Crescent and Cross,* 60.
15. Bakhtin, *Problems of Dostoevsky's Poetics,* 123.
16. Cohen, *Under Crescent and Cross,* 67.
17. Cohen also notes how the stability of "their legal status assured them a considerable degree of continuity." Ibid., 66, 74.
18. Mayer, *Mamluk Costume,* 65.
19. Subsequent decrees in 1354 limited the physical size of *dhimmī* turbans. Chamberlain, *Knowledge and Social Practice,* 100–106.
20. Mentioned in the ordinances of ʿUmar, the *zunnār* belt became a marker of Christian identity in Muslim societies. Mayer, *Mamluk Costume,* 65.
21. See Maqrīzī's description of the decree and the circumstances surrounding it in Lewis, *Islam,* 229–32; also see Stillman, *The Jews of Arab Lands,* 69.
22. Cohen, *Under Crescent and Cross,* 68.
23. Ward, "Taqī al-Dīn al-Subkī on Construction." After the decree, some churches were allegedly razed and the upper stories of some Christian dwellings that stood above those of Muslim neighbors were torn down. Petitions to relax the application of the laws for *dhimmī* elites suggest that they were enforced in urban areas.
24. Lewis, *Islam,* 232–33.
25. Hoover, "Kitāb Iqtiḍāʾ al-ṣirāṭ al-mustaqīm," 866.
26. For citations from the now lost works of Abū Yaʿlā b. al-Farrāʾ and Abū al-Shaykh al-Iṣbahānī, see Ibn Taymiyya, *Iqtiḍāʾ al-ṣirāṭ al-mustaqīm,* 1:243, 1:328–29, 1:428, 1:455, 1:459.
27. Ibn Taymiyya, *Iqtiḍāʾ al-ṣirāṭ al-mustaqīm,* 1:176–82; Memon, *Ibn Taimiya's Struggle,* 125.
28. Ibn Taymiyya, *Iqtiḍāʾ al-ṣirāṭ al-mustaqīm,* 1:241; Memon, *Ibn Taimiya's Struggle,* 148–50.

29. Q 5:51: *Man yatawallahum min-kum fa-innahum min-hum.* Ibn Taymiyya, *Iqtiḍāʾ al-ṣirāṭ al-mustaqīm,* 1:240. Although Ibn Taymiyya interprets the imitation hadith though the lens of the Quran, this hermeneutical strategy reversed the established practice of interpreting the Quran through the lens of hadith (i.e., the Sunna). Exegetes would commonly refer to the Prophet's normative practice to define the meaning of ambiguous Quranic verses, but rarely referred to the Quran to define the meaning of the Sunna. Early Sunnis therefore held that the Sunna may restrict the meaning of the Quran, but the Quran may not restrict the meaning of the Sunna, as expressed by the maxim "The Sunna rules over the Book of God, the Book of God does not rule over the Sunna." Brown, *Misquoting Muhammad,* 37.
30. Both the imitation hadith and the excerpt cited from Q 5:51 are quasi-conditional statements that fulfill the minimum criteria for an Arabic conditional statement. They possess the protasis, or *sharṭ* (lit., condition); a particle *fā* (not translated), which introduces the prostasis, or *jawāb* (lit., response); and the *jawāb.* As a quasi-conditional statement, neither text is normally translated according to the "if . . . then" template of standard conditional statements.
31. Ibn Taymiyya, *Iqtiḍāʾ al-ṣirāṭ al-mustaqīm,* 1:241–42. Ibn Taymiyya considers this hadith, collected by al-Bayhaqī, to be authentic. al-Bayhaqī, *al-Sunan al-kubrā,* 9:392.
32. Ibn Taymiyya, *Iqtiḍāʾ al-ṣirāṭ al-mustaqīm,* 1:240.
33. For other derivatives of SH-B-H in the Quran, see Q 2:70 and Q 3:7.
34. Like *tashabbuh, tawall*^{in} is a form V verbal noun.
35. See the entry for W-L-Y in al-Iṣfahānī, *Mufradāt alfāẓ al-Qurʾān,* 885–87.
36. Schmitt, *The Concept of the Political,* 26–27. The significance of Schmitt's theory is not that he recognized the distinction between friend and enemy—an observation that is obvious to the most casual observer of human behavior—but his claim that the formation of hostile groups into friend and enemy defines the concept of the "political" itself.
37. Ibn Taymiyya, *Iqtiḍāʾ al-ṣirāṭ al-mustaqīm,* 1:488; Memon, *Ibn Taimiya's Struggle,* 218.
38. *Man wādda al-kuffār fa-laysa bi-muʾmin.* Ibn Taymiyya, *Iqtiḍāʾ al-ṣirāṭ al-mustaqīm,* 1:490.
39. Ibn Taymiyya, *Iqtiḍāʾ al-ṣirāṭ al-mustaqīm,* 1:354.
40. Ashʿarī theologian, exegete, and Shāfiʿī jurist Fakhr al-Dīn al-Rāzī (d. 1209) proclaims that a Muslim who intentionally wears the *zunnār* belt has committed an act of unbelief (*kufr*). al-Rāzī, *al-Maḥṣūl,* 4:38.
41. On modern interpretations of Q 5:51, see Pink, "Tradition and Ideology."
42. Ibn Taymiyya, *Iqtiḍāʾ al-ṣirāṭ al-mustaqīm,* 1:243; Ibn al-Qayyim al-Jawziyya, *Aḥkām ahl al-dhimma,* 2:736; "al-Qawl al-mukhtār," F25r.
43. al-Munāwī, *Fayḍ al-qadīr,* 6:104; al-Dhahabī, *Tashabbuh al-khasīs,* 34. See Ibn al-Qayyim's commentary in al-ʿAẓīm Ābādī, *ʿAwn al-Maʿbūd,* 11:74–76.
44. Ibn Taymiyya, *Iqtiḍāʾ al-ṣirāṭ al-mustaqīm,* 1:314; Memon, *Ibn Taimiya's Struggle,* 164.
45. This *jāhiliyya* includes reprehensible innovations and abrogated doctrines that preceded Islam regardless of origin. Ibn Taymiyya, *Iqtiḍāʾ al-ṣirāṭ al-mustaqīm,* 1:231; Memon, *Ibn Taimiya's Struggle,* 146.
46. Ibn Taymiyya, *Iqtiḍāʾ al-ṣirāṭ al-mustaqīm,* 1:177; Memon, *Ibn Taimiya's Struggle,* 130.

47. Ibn Taymiyya, *Iqtiḍāʾ al-ṣirāṭ al-mustaqīm,* 1:65–79; Memon, *Ibn Taimiya's Struggle,* 92–96.
48. Ibn Taymiyya, *Iqtiḍāʾ al-ṣirāṭ al-mustaqīm,* 1:190–92; Memon, *Ibn Taimiya's Struggle,* 134.
49. Ibn Taymiyya, *Iqtiḍāʾ al-ṣirāṭ al-mustaqīm,* 1:191; Memon, *Ibn Taimiya's Struggle,* 134. Translation mine.
50. "But this does not mean that he is to be considered an unbeliever or impious." Ibn Taymiyya, *Iqtiḍāʾ al-ṣirāṭ al-mustaqīm,* 1:224; Memon, *Ibn Taimiya's Struggle,* 143.
51. In his compendium on religious sects (*al-Milal waʾl-nihal*), the Persian heresiographer Shahrastānī (d. 1153) divides sects into those that possess a scripture and those that don't. The latter he labels *ahl al-ahwāʾ*, which, according to Goldziher, is "a term applied by the orthodox theologians to those followers of Islām, whose religious tenets in certain details deviate from the general ordinances of the Sunnite confession." *Encyclopaedia of Islam,* 1st ed., s.v. "*ahl al-ahwāʾ*" (I. Goldziher).
52. Slovenian philosopher Slavoj Žižek draws our attention to the disruptive capacity of desire: "Desire's *raison d'être* is not to realize its goal, to find full satisfaction, but to reproduce itself as desire." Desire's unboundedness, in other words, endangers the bounded order of orthodoxy. Žižek, *The Plague of Fantasies,* 39.
53. Ibn Taymiyya, *Iqtiḍāʾ al-ṣirāṭ al-mustaqīm,* 1:359; Memon, *Ibn Taimiya's Struggle,* 178. Ibn Taymiyya derogatively refers to Shiʿis as *rāfiḍa/rawāfiḍ* (2:759–60). A tradition contained in an important Twelver Shiʿi collection expresses the positive value and unique association of wearing a ring on one's right hand: "'Inform me of the ring worn by the Commander of the Faithful. Was it on his right hand or what?' He replied: 'He used to wear it on his right hand because the imam is the companion of the right hand after the Messenger of God. God also praised the companions of the right hand, but condemned the companions of the left hand. The Messenger of God used to wear a ring on his right hand and it is a well-known sign of the Shiʿa.'" There are other traditions, however, that do not indicate a preference for one hand or the other. al-Āmilī, *Wasāʾil al-Shiʿa,* 5:82.
54. al-Jamil, "Ibn Taymiyya and Al-Muṭahhar Al-Ḥillī."
55. Makdisi, "Ibn Taimiya: A Sufi of the Qadiriya Order." For an opposing view, see Meier, "The Cleanest about Predestination."
56. Ibn Taymiyya, *Iqtiḍāʾ al-ṣirāṭ al-mustaqīm,* 1:69; Memon, *Ibn Taimiya's Struggle,* 93.
57. Ibn Taymiyya, *Iqtiḍāʾ al-ṣirāṭ al-mustaqīm,* 1:319; Memon, *Ibn Taimiya's Struggle,* 165–66. I have slightly modified Memon's translation.
58. Ibn Taymiyya, *Iqtiḍāʾ al-ṣirāṭ al-mustaqīm,* 1:366–74, 1:400; Memon, *Ibn Taimiya's Struggle,* 181–82, 184.
59. Ibn Taymiyya, *Iqtiḍāʾ al-ṣirāṭ al-mustaqīm,* 1:455; Memon, *Ibn Taimiya's Struggle,* 203.
60. Ibn Taymiyya, *Iqtiḍāʾ al-ṣirāṭ al-mustaqīm,* 1:401; Memon, *Ibn Taimiya's Struggle,* 184–85.
61. Ibn Taymiyya, *Iqtiḍāʾ al-ṣirāṭ al-mustaqīm,* 1:405; Memon, *Ibn Taimiya's Struggle,* 185.
62. Goldziher, "Usages juifs," 78. See, for example, the following medieval compendia of law: in the Ḥanafī school, al-Shaybānī and al-Sarakhsī, *Sharḥ Kitāb al-Siyar al-kabīr,* 1:12–14; Mālikī school, Ibn ʿAbd al-Barr, *al-Tamhīd,* 5:51; Ḥanbalī school, Ibn Qudāma, *al-Mughnī,* 2:373–4; Shāfiʿī school, al-Māwardī, *al-Ḥāwī al-kabīr,* 15:223–24. We may

call *tashabbuh* a doctrine—a precept, principle, or teaching—in light of these sources. A scholarly consensus emerged that *tashabbuh,* in some situations, is blameworthy.

63. "al-Qawl al-mukhtār," F25r.

64. Ibn Taymiyya, *Iqtiḍāʾ al-ṣirāṭ al-mustaqīm,* 1:492. Memon, *Ibn Taimiya's Struggle,* 219. I have modified Memon's translation.

65. Ḥanafī jurists added two more categories, distinguishing between mildly detested (*makrūh tanzīhī*) and strongly detested (*makrūh taḥrīmī*), and between necessary (*wājib*) and obligatory (*farḍ*). Kamali, *Principles of Islamic Jurisprudence,* 410–54; Reinhart, "'Like the Difference between Heaven and Earth.'"

66. al-Sarakhsī, *al-Mabsūṭ,* 1:201. I was unable to locate this citation in Shāfiʿī's published writings. Sarakhsī makes this attribution in a summary of debates between Ḥanafī and Shāfiʿī jurists over the permissibility of reading from a printed copy of the Quran while performing the ritual prayer. Shāfiʿīs permit the practice while Ḥanafīs prohibit it due to its resemblance to Jewish and Christian ritual.

67. See chapter 3.

68. al-Kāsānī, *Badāʾiʿ al-ṣanāʾiʿ,* 1:215.

69. *Ṣaḥīḥ al-Bukhārī, kitāb badʾ al-khalqi, bāb ṣifat Iblīs wa junūdihi; Ṣaḥīḥ Muslim, kitāb al-masājid wa'l-mawāḍiʿ al-ṣalāt, bāb awqāt ṣalawāt al-khams.*

70. Rizzo and Whitman, "The Camel's Nose Is in the Tent"; Volokh, "The Mechanisms of the Slippery Slope."

71. Posner, "Rick Hills on Slippery Slopes."

72. Kamali, *Principles of Islamic Jurisprudence,* 397–409; Ibn al-Qayyim al-Jawziyya, *Iʿlām al-muwaqqiʿīn;* al-Shāṭibī, *al-Muwāfaqāt,* 2:434–37.

73. Ibn al-Qayyim al-Jawziyya, *Iʿlām al-muwaqqiʿīn,* 3:108–26.

74. See chapters 3 and 4.

75. However, what a jurist claims is the "cause" that led to a particular ruling may in fact be a retroactive "rationalization" that justified an already established ruling. The earliest treatises of Islamic jurisprudence often provided little or no explanation for specific rulings.

76. Ibn Taymiyya, *Iqtiḍāʾ al-ṣirāṭ al-mustaqīm,* 2:621–22; Memon, *Ibn Taimiya's Struggle,* 245; Ukeles, "The Sensitive Puritan?"

77. This widely circulated hadith is in every collection of the Sunnī Sound Six: *Ṣaḥīḥ al-Bukhārī, kitāb al-badʾ al-waḥī, bāb kayfa kāna badʾ al-waḥī ilā rasūl Allāh; Ṣaḥīḥ Muslim, kitāb al-imāra, bāb qawlihi (ṣ) innamā al-aʿmāl bi'l-niyya; Sunan Abī Dāwūd, kitāb al-ṭalāq, bāb fīmā ʿuniya bihi al-ṭalāq wa'l-niyyāt; Sunan al-Tirmidhī, kitāb faḍāʾil al-jihād, bāb mā jāʾa fī-man yuqātil riyāʾan wa li'l-dunyā; Sunan al-Nasāʾī, kitāb al-ṭahāra, bāb al-niyya fī al-wuḍūʾ; Sunan Ibn Mājah, kitāb al-zuhd, bāb al-niyya.*

78. Ibn Taymiyya, *Iqtiḍāʾ al-ṣirāṭ al-mustaqīm,* 2:622; Memon, *Ibn Taimiya's Struggle,* 245.

79. Ibn Taymiyya, *Iqtiḍāʾ al-ṣirāṭ al-mustaqīm,* 1:420–21; Memon, *Ibn Taimiya's Struggle,* 190. Translation mine.

80. Rahman, *Revival and Reform in Islam,* 132–44; in comparison to Ghazālī's emphasis on "personal purity and piety," see Rahman, *Islam,* 110.

81. Michael Cook observes, "'Utilitarianism' is a well-attested feature of Ibn Taymiyya's thought." *Commanding Right and Forbidding Wrong,* 154.

82. Ibn Taymiyya, *Majmūʿat al-fatāwā,* 20:30. English translation, with modifications, based on al-Gamāʿah al-Islāmīyah and Jackson, *Initiative to Stop the Violence,* 63.
83. Ibn Taymiyya, *Majmūʿat al-fatāwā,* 20:33; al-Gamāʿah al-Islāmīyah and Jackson, *Initiative to Stop the Violence,* 63.
84. Describing Ibn Taymiyya's approach to *maṣlaḥa* as "more inclusive" than Ghazālī's should not be misconstrued as suggesting it will necessarily lead to a "more liberal" legal ruling. Rather, Opwis is claiming that Ibn Taymiyya has more flexibility than Ghazālī to deploy *maṣlaḥa* in his legal reasoning. Opwis, *Maṣlaḥa,* 198.
85. Ibn Taymiyya, *Iqtiḍāʾ al-ṣirāṭ al-mustaqīm,* 2:553; Memon, *Ibn Taimiya's Struggle,* 226–27. I have modified Memon's translation.
86. Ibn Taymiyya, *Iqtiḍāʾ al-ṣirāṭ al-mustaqīm,* 2:527. Memon, *Ibn Taimiya's Struggle,* 225.
87. Ibn Taymiyya, *Iqtiḍāʾ al-ṣirāṭ al-mustaqīm,* 1:491; Memon, *Ibn Taimiya's Struggle,* 219.
88. Ibn al-Qayyim al-Jawziyya, *Aḥkām ahl al-dhimma,* 2:763–64.
89. Ibn Taymiyya, *Iqtiḍāʾ al-ṣirāṭ al-mustaqīm,* 2:553–54; Memon, *Ibn Taimiya's Struggle,* 227.
90. Ibn Taymiyya, *Iqtiḍāʾ al-ṣirāṭ al-mustaqīm,* 2:553–54; Memon, *Ibn Taimiya's Struggle,* 227.
91. James, *Writings, 1878–1899,* 742. James explored the role of imitation in education.
92. Ibn Taymiyya, *Iqtiḍāʾ al-ṣirāṭ al-mustaqīm,* 1:425; Memon, *Ibn Taimiya's Struggle,* 193. Translation and emphasis mine.
93. Fierro astutely recognizes that certain rulings are innovations (*bidʿa*) because they are reprehensible imitations (*tashabbuh*). Fierro, "The Treatises against Innovations," 237.
94. Ibn Taymiyya, *Iqtiḍāʾ al-ṣirāṭ al-mustaqīm,* 1:425; Memon, *Ibn Taimiya's Struggle,* 193.
95. Fierro, "The Treatises against Innovations," 212.
96. For a bibliography of premodern treatises against innovation that includes Ibn Taymiyya's *The Obligation of Following the Straight Path,* see Fierro, "The Treatises against Innovations."
97. Meri, *The Cult of Saints,* 123; Ibn al-Ḥājj, *al-Madkhal,* 2:54–55.
98. Ibn al-Ḥājj, *al-Madkhal,* 2:54.
99. Clerics like Ibn Taymiyya and his student Dhahabī associate Maundy Thursday with the end of Lent festivities on Good Friday or Easter Sunday. Ibn al-Ḥājj, by contrast, concentrates on the potential for sexual arousal arising from the public presence of women during these festivals. Memon, *Ibn Taimiya's Struggle,* 210–14; Ibn Taymiyya, *Iqtiḍāʾ al-ṣirāṭ al-mustaqīm,* 1:476–81; Ibn Taymiyya, *Majmūʿat al-fatāwā,* 25:170–177; Ibn al-Ḥājj, *al-Madkhal,* 2:54–55.
100. Memon, *Ibn Taimiya's Struggle,* 225; al-Ghazzī, *Ḥusn al-tanabbuh,* 8:273. I have modified Memon's translation.
101. Shoshan, *Popular Culture,* 40–51.
102. Ibn Taymiyya, *Iqtiḍāʾ al-ṣirāṭ al-mustaqīm,* 2:581; Memon, *Ibn Taimiya's Struggle,* 229.
103. *Sunan al-Nasāʾī, kitāb ṣalāt al-ʿīdayn, bāb kayfa al-khuṭba.* Ibn Taymiyya cites an abbreviated narration of this hadith: "The worst things are inventions. Every innovation leads astray. And every stray deed leads to the hellfire." Ibn Taymiyya, *Iqtiḍāʾ al-ṣirāṭ al-mustaqīm,* 2:581; Memon, *Ibn Taimiya's Struggle,* 229.

104. Ibn Taymiyya, *Iqtiḍā᾿ al-ṣirāṭ al-mustaqīm,* 2:586; Memon, *Ibn Taimiya's Struggle,* 231–37.
105. Ibn Taymiyya, *Iqtiḍā᾿ al-ṣirāṭ al-mustaqīm,* 2:581; Memon, *Ibn Taimiya's Struggle,* 229.
106. al-Dhahabī, *Tashabbuh al-khasīs,* 39; al-Dhahabī, *Imitating the Disbelievers,* 26. I have modified Abū Rumaysah's translation in *Imitating the Disbelievers.*
107. Ibn al-Qayyim al-Jawziyya, *Aḥkām ahl al-dhimma.*
108. For references to Ibn Taymiyya, see "al-Qawl al-mukhtār," F32v, F35r, F39r.
109. On Dhahabī, see *Encyclopaedia of Islam,* 3rd ed., s.v. "al-Dhahabī" (C. Bori), which includes his biography, bibliography, and biographical notices, including Ibn Ḥajar al-ʿAsqalānī, *al-Durar al-kāmina,* 3:204–5; al-Ṣafadī, *Kitāb al-wāfī bi'l-wafayāt,* 2:163–68; al-Subkī, *Ṭabaqāt al-Shāfiʿiyya al-kubrā,* 9:100–122. To my knowledge, there are three published editions of Dhahabī's treatise against imitation (*Tashabbuh al-khasīs*): the 1988 Amman edition, edited by ʿAlī ʿAbd al-Ḥamīd; the 2002 Beirut edition, edited by Muḥammad Ismāʿīl; and a 2005 edition edited by Mashhūr Āli Salmān. ʿAbd al-Ḥamīd and Ismāʿīl rely on MS 4908 from the *Dār al-kutub al-Miṣriyya* in Egypt dated to the sixteenth century, while Salmān relies upon two manuscripts: MS 4908 from the *Dār al-kutub al-Miṣriyya* and MS 4669 from the Asad National Library in Syria, dated 1473–74. Salmān claims that, because it has fewer omissions, the Asad manuscript is superior to the Egyptian copy. (He claims to have discovered a third manuscript copy, also from the Asad National Library, which differs slightly from MS 4669, and plans to incorporate that copy into an updated edition.) The title of Salmān's edition, *Tashbīh al-khasīs,* also differs from the other editions, using the form II (*tashbīh*) in place of form V (*tashabbuh*), which is conventionally used in this context. Dhahabī, for example, never employs form II in his treatise. Salmān prefers *tashbīh* because that is the title preserved in the Asad manuscript, which he deems more authoritative. But ʿAbd al-Ḥamīd argues that *tashabbuh* makes more linguistic sense in this context. I agree with ʿAbd al-Ḥamīd's view. My references are to the 1988 Amman edition.
110. al-Dhahabī, *Tashabbuh al-khasīs,* 35; al-Dhahabī, *Imitating the Disbelievers,* 23.
111. *Encyclopaedia of Islam,* 3rd ed., s.v. "al-Dhahabī" (C. Bori); Jones, *The Power of Oratory,* 38–100.
112. Ukeles, "The Sensitive Puritan?" 324–25.
113. Douglas, *Purity and Danger,* 97.

6. "A PERSON BELONGS WITH THE ONE HE LOVES"

1. Abū Naṣr al-Sarrāj, *The Kitāb al-Lumaʿ,* 362; Salamah-Qudsi, "The Idea of *Tashabbuh,*" 177.
2. al-Ghazālī, *Iḥyāʾ ʿulūm al-dīn,* 1:377.
3. Ibid., 3:225.
4. Ibid., 2:234.
5. al-Hujwīrī, *The Kashf al-Maḥjūb,* 389; Salamah-Qudsi, "The Idea of *Tashabbuh,*" 177.
6. al-Sulamī, *al-Muqaddima fī al-taṣawwuf,* 72; also see Salamah-Qudsi, "The Idea of *Tashabbuh,*" 177; Ohlander, *Sufism in an Age of Transition,* 192.

7. The Syrian geographer Yāqūt al-Ḥamawī (d. 1226) quotes Shihāb al-Dīn al-Suhrawardī's most famous poem, "al-Qasīda al-ha'iyya," which includes the following verse still popular among Sufis today: "Imitate [*tashabbahū*], if you cannot be like them / For Imitating [*al-tashabbuh*] the virtuous leads to success" (*Fa-tashabbahū in lam takūnū mithlahum / inna al-tashabbaha bi'l-kirāmi falāḥ*). al-Ḥamawī, *Mu'jam al-udabā'*, 6:2808. On Suhrawardī, see Corbin, *Suhrawardî d'Alep;* Ziai, *Knowledge and Illumination.*
8. al-Suhrawardī, *Ādāb al-murīdīn;* see Milson's abridged translation, along with a biographical sketch of the author in al-Suhrawardī, *A Sufi Rule for Novices.*
9. al-Suhrawardī, *Ādāb al-murīdīn,* 81–82; al-Suhrawardī, *A Sufi Rule for Novices,* 73.
10. al-Suhrawardī, *Ādāb al-murīdīn,* 98; al-Suhrawardī, *A Sufi Rule for Novices,* 82.
11. al-Suhrawardī, *A Sufi Rule for Novices,* 8–9; Salamah-Qudsi, "The Idea of *Tashabbuh,*" 179.
12. al-Suhrawardī, *Ādāb al-murīdīn,* 98; al-Suhrawardī, *A Sufi Rule for Novices,* 82.
13. Ohlander, *Sufism in an Age of Transition,* 245.
14. On Abū Ḥafṣ al-Suhrawardī's life, works, and pivotal role in establishing Sufi orders across the Muslim world, see Ohlander, *Sufism in an Age of Transition;* Huda, *Striving for Divine Union.*
15. al-Suhrawardī, *'Awārif al-ma'ārif,* 84–85.
16. *Hum al-julasā' wa lā yashqā bi-him jalīsuhum.* See *Ṣaḥīḥ al-Bukhārī, kitāb al-da'wāt, bāb faḍl dhikr Allāh; Ṣaḥīḥ Muslim, kitāb al-dhikr wa'l-du'ā' wa'l-tawba.*
17. Salamah-Qudsi, *Sufism and Early Islamic Piety,* 228–37; Ernst, *Eternal Garden,* 13–15; al-Sulamī, *Kitāb Ādāb al-ṣuḥba.*
18. Salamah-Qudsi, "The Idea of *Tashabbuh,*" 196.
19. Elias, "The Sufi Robe," 286–87.
20. On the Sufi robe, or *khirqa,* see al-Suhrawardī, *'Awārif al-ma'ārif,* 108–15; Elias, "The Sufi Robe."
21. al-Suhrawardī, *'Awārif al-ma'ārif,* 83–84; also translated in Salamah-Qudsi, "The Idea of *Tashabbuh,*" 185–86.
22. al-Suhrawardī, *'Awārif al-ma'ārif,* 112; Salamah-Qudsi, "The Idea of *Tashabbuh,*" 184–85.
23. Salamah-Qudsi, "The Idea of *Tashabbuh,*" 185.
24. Ibid.
25. *al-mar'u ma'a man aḥabb.* See al-Suhrawardī, *'Awārif al-ma'ārif,* 80. *Ṣaḥīḥ al-Bukhārī, kitāb al-adab, bāb 'alāmat ḥubb Allāh 'azza wa jall; Ṣaḥīḥ Muslim, kitāb al-birr wa'l-ṣila wa'l-ādāb, bāb al-mar'u ma'a man aḥabb; Sunan al-Tirmidhī, kitāb al-zuhd 'an rasūl Allāh, bāb mā jā'a anna al-mar'a ma'a man aḥabb; Sunan Abī Dāwūd, kitāb al-adab, bāb ikhbār al-rajul bi-maḥabbatihi iyyāh.*
26. Ibid.
27. Ibid., 81.

7. ESCAPING THE DEVIL'S LAIR

1. al-Muḥibbī, *Khulāṣat al-athar,* 4:195.
2. *Encyclopaedia of Islam,* 3rd ed., s.v. "Encyclopaedias, Arabic" (E. Muhanna).
3. El-Rouayheb, "Opening the Gate of Verification." El-Rouayheb illustrates how trea-

tises, commentaries, and supercommentaries on logic and other "rational" sciences traveled from Persian- to Arab-speaking lands during the seventeenth century.

4. See chapter 6 for references to this hadith.
5. There are important intellectual distinctions between the two scholars, however. Ghazzī excelled in hadith, while Ghazālī excelled in "rational" disciplines such as philosophy and speculative theology (*kalām*). Nevertheless, the editors of the critical edition of *The Virtue of Awakening* complain that Ghazzī draws many hadiths from secondary rather than primary sources, resulting in occasional errors in transcription and the inclusion of weak and forged traditions. al-Ghazzī, *Ḥusn al-tanabbuh,* 1:54. On Ghazālī, see Moosa, *Ghazālī and the Poetics of Imagination;* on Ghazālī's double identity as Sufi and jurist, see al-Ghazālī, *Al-Ghazālī on Disciplining the Soul,* xv.
6. See introduction, n. 26, for references to Ghazzī in modern scholarship.
7. See volumes 11 and 12 in al-Ghazzī, *Ḥusn al-tanabbuh.*
8. Muhanna, *The World in a Book,* 72.
9. Ibid., 29–55.
10. al-Ghazzī, *Ḥusn al-tanabbuh,* 10:434.
11. Ibid., 1:71–72.
12. Ibid., 1:447–50, 8:198. The editors of the critical edition, who are sympathetic to the Ḥanbalī school, take issue with Ghazzī's treatment of Ibn Taymiyya, suggesting his criticisms were "unfair."
13. Nearly a century ago the Ḥanafī jurist and manuscript expert Muḥammad Zāhid al-Kawtharī recommended that Ghazzī's treatise on imitation, which he referred to as *Ḥusn al-tanabbuh li-aḥkām al-tashabbuh,* be published. al-Kawtharī, *Maqālat al-Kawtharī,* 80. The first three of five volumes of the manuscript in the original handwriting of the author survive: volumes 1 and 2, completed in 1615 and 1617, respectively, are held in Damascus at the Asad National Library (nos. 8585 and 8586). The third volume, completed in 1626, is held in Dublin at the Chester Beatty Library (Arabic 3216). A complete copy of the manuscript in seven volumes, handwritten by a contemporary of Ghazzī's and completed in 1632, is held at the Asad National Library (nos. 4054, 3890, 3277–3281). Another complete copy of the manuscript is held in Istanbul at the Süleymaniye Library—although the copyist and copy date are unknown (*Tekkeler Murad,* no. 69). The published edition is a critical edition based on these three manuscripts. al-Ghazzī, *Ḥusn al-tanabbuh,* 1:73–80.
14. The most important biographical source for Ghazzī, which relies on two of his autobiographical accounts, one of which is now lost (*Bulghat al-wājid fī tarjama shaykh al-islām al-wālid*), was written by his contemporary Muḥammad al-Muḥibbī: al-Muḥibbī, *Khulāṣat al-athar,* 4:189–200; also see al-Muḥibbī, *Nafḥat al-rayḥāna,* 1:540–46. Other biographical accounts include al-Ḥanbalī, *Mashyakha,* 63–71; Ibn Shāshū (d. 1716), *Tarājim ba ʿḍ al-a ʿyān dimashq,* 101–4; also see the excerpt in Samer Akkach's critical edition of *al-Wird al-unsī waʾl-wārid al-qudsī fī tarjamat al ʿĀrif ʿAbd al-Ghanī al-Nābulusī* in al-Ghazzī, *Intimate Invocations,* 126–131. The most comprehensive contemporary biography of Ghazzī to date was composed by Maḥmūd al-Shaykh in al-Ghazzī, *Luṭf al-samar,* 1:5–216. Also see al-Ghazzī, *Ḥusn al-tanabbuh,* 1:11–37; Ḥāfiẓ and Abāzah, *ʿUlamāʾ Dimashq wa aʿyānuhā,* 2:67–81.

15. al-Muḥibbī, *Khulāṣat al-athar,* 4:192.
16. The first occurred when he was just eighteen years old and had begun to teach publicly; a trio of senior *ʿulamāʾ* rekindled a controversy over his father's versified exegesis of the Quran, which Ghazzī was teaching. The controversy, which had originated decades earlier when his father, Badr al-Dīn al-Ghazzī, was still alive, revolved around the Quran's inimitability—whether the versified exegesis erased the fine line between the Quran and poetry. To transform the sacred language of God into the profane language of humans bordered on heresy. It resulted in several treatises being composed on the subject by Ghazzī's teachers and allies in response to his detractors. Pfeifer, "Encounter After the Conquest." The second controversy involved Ghazzī and another rival scholar wrangling over a teaching position at the al-Shāmiyya al-Barāniyya madrasa. Ghazzī had been teaching there, but a decree was issued from the Ottoman administration requesting that he step down to make room for someone else. Because Ghazzī would lose part of his annual salary by this removal, he traveled to Istanbul to lodge a complaint. He was partially successful in achieving his objective, agreeing to a compromise whereby he would split teaching duties with his rival at the madrasa. al-Muḥibbī, *Khulāṣat al-athar,* 4:197–200.
17. For a list of his authored works, see al-Ghazzī, *Ḥusn al-tanabbuh,* 20–37; al-Ghazzī, *Lutf al-samar,* 1:105–21.
18. Ghazzī's biographical compendia of notables include al-Ghazzī, *al-Kawākib al-sāʾira;* al-Ghazzī, *Lutf al-samar.*
19. Atçıl, *Scholars and Sultans,* 214
20. Ibid., 119.
21. al-Ghazzī, *Lutf al-samar,* 1:61.
22. Ibid.
23. Ibid., 1:62–63.
24. White, *The Climate of Rebellion.* A state of crisis was not limited to the Ottoman Empire, however. Historians have characterized this seventeenth-century calamity as a "global crisis" that encompassed Europe, North America, South Asia, Southeast Asia, and East Asia as well. See Goldstone, *Revolution and Rebellion;* Parker, "Crisis and Catastrophe"; Parker and Smith, *The General Crisis of the Seventeenth Century.*
25. White, *The Climate of Rebellion;* Faroqhi, "Crisis and Change"; Griswold, *The Great Anatolian Rebellion,* 13–14; Fleisher, "Mahdi and Millennium"; Tezcan, "The Ottoman Monetary Crisis."
26. Ferguson, *The Proper Order of Things,* 238.
27. al-Ghazzī, *Ḥusn al-tanabbuh,* 11:490.
28. Masters, *The Arabs of the Ottoman Empire,* 13.
29. Winter, "A Polemical Treatise," 95.
30. Ibid.
31. al-Muḥibbī, *Khulāṣat al-athar,* 4:190.
32. Winter, *The Shiites of Lebanon,* 15–20; Terzioğlu, "How to Conceptualize Ottoman Sunnitization," 312–13.
33. Terzioğlu, "How to Conceptualize Ottoman Sunnitization"; Krstić, *Contested Con-*

versions. Terzioğlu argues that as hostility between the Ottoman and Safavid Empires waned in the 1630s, so did its role in shaping the Ottoman Empire's Sunni identity.

34. Battle of *Keresztes* (*Haçova*), *Dīvān* of Nadiri, Istanbul, ca. 1603–17. Topkapı Palace Museum, H. 889, fols. 6b-7a.
35. Brummett, *Mapping the Ottomans,* 136–38.
36. In 1569, Ottoman tax collectors counted 7,054 Muslim, 1,021 Christian, and 546 Jewish households in Damascus. However, in 1597, they counted just 20 Damascene Jewish families and 6 Jewish bachelors. These dramatic swings in the population data elicit skepticism regarding their accuracy. See Bakhit, "The Christian Population."
37. Spanish and Portuguese Jewish exiles accounted for the majority of Ottoman Jewry. Ben-Naeh, *Jews in the Realm of the Sultans,* 422.
38. The Chicken Market, MCC, Cod. Cicogna 1971, fol. 27r. On this Ottoman miniature album, see Rothman, "Visualizing a Space of Encounter."
39. Ibid., 49–50.
40. Mansel, *Dressed to Rule,* 43.
41. Kohen, *History of the Turkish Jews,* 103.
42. Ibid.
43. Ibid., 104.
44. Kurz, *European Clocks,* 47.
45. al-Ghazzī, *Ḥusn al-tanabbuh,* 7:499. The first book authored by a Muslim on clock making, by fellow Damascene Taqī al-Dīn b. Maʿrūf (d. 1585), was published in 1559, shortly before Ghazzī's birth.
46. Sajdi, "Decline," 32.
47. Elias Muhanna argues that knowledge produced in the service of governance is contemporary in character in comparison to scholastic knowledge disseminated in a madrasa setting. In composing *The Virtue of Awakening,* Ghazzī intended to reach an elite audience of scholars within and beyond government bureaucracy. Muhanna, *The World in a Book,* 86.
48. al-Ghazzī, *Ḥusn al-tanabbuh,* 1:18.
49. *al-maḥabba hiya al-muwāfaqa.* See Ibid.
50. Ibid.
51. *al-marʾu maʿa man aḥabb.* Ibid., 1:23–24.
52. Ibid., 1:19. I was unable to find a corroborating reference to this quotation in Euclid's published writings.
53. al-Ghazzī, *Ḥusn al-tanabbuh,* 1:41; al-Suhrawardī, *ʿAwārif al-maʿārif,* 81.
54. al-Ghazzī, *Ḥusn al-tanabbuh,* 1:41; al-Suhrawardī, *ʿAwārif al-maʿārif,* 81.
55. al-Ghazzī, *Ḥusn al-tanabbuh,* 1:42.
56. Ibid.
57. *Man aḥabba qawm*^{an} *ḥasharahu Allāh fī zumratihim.* Ibid., 1:21.
58. *Man wāfaqa qawm*^{an} *wa aḥabbahum kāna min-hum wa maʿa hum fī al-dunyā wa'l-ākhira.* Ibid.
59. Ibid., 1:20–21.
60. Ibid., 1:17–18. Ghazzī cites a number of prophetic traditions that evoke both the syn-

tax and rhetorical force of the imitation hadith: "When a person is content with the guidance and activities of another he is like him [*mithlihi*]"; "Whoever admires the conduct of a person he is like him"; "None of you has true faith until his desires conform to what I [Muhammad] have brought." These prophetic traditions describe belonging in affective terms.

61. Ibid., 1:20.
62. Ibid., 1:25–27.
63. Ibid., 1:25–26.
64. Ibid., 1:26.
65. Ibid., 1:26–27.
66. According to Ghazzī, religious hostility includes inter-Muslim religious difference between orthodox Sunni and non-Sunni heretics. Muslim heretics who embody unbelief through religious innovations are more dangerous than non-Muslims because their wrongdoing is covert. Ibid., 1:77.
67. Ibid., 1:27.
68. Ibid.
69. Ibid., 1:76.
70. Ibid., 1:54.
71. Ibid., 1:57. Explaining the consequences of blind social conformity in *The Revival,* Ghazālī narrates the following anecdote regarding the Children of Israel: "God revealed to Joshua (Yūshaʿ b. Nūn), 'I killed forty thousand good people from your community and sixty thousand bad people.' Yūshaʿ replied, 'What was the matter with the good people?' God responded, 'They did not become angry for my sake [at the wrongdoing of the bad people] so they ate and drank with the bad people.'" al-Ghazālī, *Iḥyāʾ ʿulūm al-dīn,* 2:151.
72. al-Ghazzī, *Ḥusn al-tanabbuh,* 1:79–80.
73. Ibid., 1:77.
74. Ibid., 1:27–28.
75. *Man raghaba ʿan sunnatī fa-laysa minnī.* Ibid., 1:27.
76. *Dalīl ʿalā anna al-maḥabbatahu tilka lā ḥaqiqata laha.* Ibid.
77. Ibid., 1:31.
78. Ibid., 1:38.
79. On coffee drinking in Islamic civilization, see Hattox, *Coffee and Coffeehouses;* Grehan, "Smoking."
80. Grehan, "Smoking."
81. al-Ghazzī, *al-Kawākib al-sāʾira.*
82. Grehan, "Smoking," 1358.
83. al-Ghazzī, *al-Kawākib al-sāʾira,* 1:115.
84. Hattox, *Coffee and Coffeehouses,* 46–60.
85. Pamuk, *My Name Is Red,* 20.
86. al-Ghazzī, *al-Kawākib al-sāʾira,* 4:32–3.
87. Imber, *Ebuʾs-suʿud,* 93.
88. Ibid., 93–4.
89. al-Ghazzī, *al-Kawākib al-sāʾira,* 3:32–33; al-Ghazzī, *Ḥusn al-tanabbuh,* 6:98–99. Ghazzī

was not the first jurist to deliver a versified fatwa on consuming coffee. Bostanzade Mehmed Efendi (d. 1598), who served as Ottoman *şeyhülislam* during the last decade of the sixteenth century (1589–92, 1593–98), issued a versified fatwa that helped resolve the dispute among Ottoman *ʿulamāʾ* over the permissibility of drinking coffee. Çelebi, *The Balance of Truth,* 60; Lewis, *Istanbul,* 135.

90. Prior to the emergence of the coffeehouse, coffee was consumed in wine taverns. Mikhail, "The Heart's Desire," 163.
91. al-Ghazzī, *Ḥusn al-tanabbuh,* 6:98.
92. Mikhail, "The Heart's Desire," 137. The idea of the coffeehouse as a heterotopic space eschews the sharp Habermasian distinction between public and private. On the inversion of private and public in the coffeehouse, see Clery, "Women, Publicity and the Coffee-House Myth," 175.
93. Foucault, "Of Other Spaces," 25.
94. Mikhail, "The Heart's Desire," 137.
95. Andrews and Kalpaklı, *The Age of Beloveds,* 186.
96. On chess, backgammon, and other games as *liʿb* (play) and *lahw* (diversion), see Rosenthal, *Gambling in Islam,* 9–67.
97. Not all *ʿulamāʾ* shared this attitude. In his travelogue, the Shāfiʿī jurist from Medina Ibrāhīm al-Khiyārī (d. 1672) praised the Nawfura coffeehouse in Damascus. He considered such establishments open spaces where refined men could socialize and reflect on the world. Masters, *The Arabs of the Ottoman Empire,* 121.
98. As James Grehan has argued, smoking tobacco must be understood as "the extension of a new sociability that first emerged with the spread of coffee drinking." In 1611, Ahmed I (r. 1603–17) prohibited the sale of tobacco throughout the empire. As discussed below, Ahmed I's son Murad banned coffeehouses, along with tobacco, opium, and wine, in 1633. Although some Ottoman *ʿulamāʾ* discouraged the use of tobacco, others like Ghazzī supported outright prohibition. Ghazzī's campaign against tobacco was ultimately unsuccessful, however. The Ottoman Empire finally legalized tobacco in 1650, one year before his death. Grehan, "Smoking," 1362, 1365, 1375.
99. A manuscript copy of this fatwa in Ghazzī's own handwriting has been published in Ḥāfiẓ and Abāzah, *ʿUlamāʾ Dimashq wa aʿyānuhā,* 2:82–92. Regarding slovenliness, Ghazzī cites a hadith that stereotypes Jews with not cleaning under the arms (see chapter 3). Also see al-Kattānī, *Iʿlān al-Ḥujja,* 134.
100. Lefebvre, *The Production of Space,* 170.
101. Ibid., 154.
102. Boyar and Fleet, *A Social History of Ottoman Istanbul,* 190.
103. Çelebi, *The Balance of Truth,* 61.
104. Boyar and Fleet, *A Social History of Ottoman Istanbul,* 190; Mikhail, "The Heart's Desire," 139.
105. Boyar and Fleet, *A Social History of Ottoman Istanbul,* 190; Lewis, *Istanbul,* 132–33.
106. White, *Three Years in Constantinople,* 1:280.
107. ʿĀlī, *Muṣṭafā ʿĀlī's Description of Cairo,* 33.
108. al-Ghazzī, *al-Kawākib al-sāʾira,* 3:5–6; Pfeifer, "The Gulper and the Slurper," 61.
109. Çelebi, *The Balance of Truth,* 61.

110. Ibid., 156.
111. Çaksu, "Janissary Coffee Houses," 122.
112. Ibid., 124–25.
113. Kafadar, "Yeniçeri-Esnaf Relations," 113.
114. Piterberg, *An Ottoman Tragedy,* 27–28.
115. Grehan, "Smoking," 1363.
116. Çelebi, *The Balance of Truth,* 51.
117. Ibid., 61.
118. al-Ghazzī, *Ḥusn al-tanabbuh,* 5:514.
119. Moosa, *Ghazali and the Poetics of Imagination,* 34.
120. Çelebi, *The Balance of Truth,* 57–58.

8. CAN MUSLIMS WEAR EUROPEAN HATS?

1. For the original text of ʿAbduh's fatwa and commentary by Egyptian *ʿulamāʾ* of al-Azhar, see *Irshād al-umma,* 7–8, 45–47. English translation and brief commentary on the fatwa in Adams, "Muḥammad ʿAbduh and the Transvaal Fatwā." Also see Voll, "Abduh and the Transvaal Fatwa"; Kerr, *Islamic Reform,* 145.
2. Adams, "Muḥammad ʿAbduh and the Transvaal Fatwā," 15; Skovgaard-Petersen, *Defining Islam,* 128.
3. Jacob, *Working Out Egypt,* 198.
4. On these treatises, see Patel, "The Islamic Treatises against Imitation," 619–34. Also see Koningsveld, "Between Communalism and Secularism"; Harahap, "The Fatwā of Muḥammad bin Jaʿfar al-Kattānī." On Islam in modernity, see Masud, Salvatore, and van Bruinessen, *Islam and Modernity;* on "modernist" trends in Islamic thought, see Kurzman, *Modernist Islam;* on responses of the *ʿulamāʾ*, see Zaman, *The Ulama in Contemporary Islam.*
5. Ahmed, *What Is Islam?* 189–93.
6. ʿAbd-ar-Rāziq, *Islam and the Foundations of Political Power.*
7. Quadri, *Transformations of Tradition,* 165–208.
8. Tayob, *Religion in Modern Islamic Discourse,* 9.
9. Halevi, *Modern Things on Trial,* 87.
10. Adams, "Muḥammad ʿAbduh and the Transvaal Fatwā," 17; *Irshād al-umma,* 8.
11. On the relevance of intention in Ibn Taymiyya's legal conceptualization of *tashabbuh,* see chapter 5.
12. Zaman, *Modern Islamic Thought,* 108–42. On the historical development of *maṣlaḥa* in classical Islamic law, see Opwis, *Maṣlaḥa;* on its contemporary application, see Opwis, "Maṣlaḥa," 182–223.
13. Jacob, *Working Out Egypt,* 208–10. The Egyptian Medical Association wrote: "Because of its fabric, shape, colour, absence of perforation, and weight, the tarboush warms the head excessively in summer, causing profuse perspiration, irritation and headaches. From a hygienic standpoint, tarboushes are definitely harmful to eyes and head. The association believes that the best headdress for Egypt's climate in summer

is a white felt hat, perforated for ventilation. In winter, the tarboush is less harmful, but less superior still to the hat." Habib and Hesham, "The Effendi's Crown."

14. Khallāf, *ʿIlm uṣūl al-fiqh,* 210–12; Emon, *Islamic Natural Law Theories,* 123–88, 194–99; Kamali, *Shariʿah Law,* 123–40; on the contemporary application of the *maqāṣid,* see Nassery, Ahmed, and Tatari, *The Objectives of Islamic Law.*
15. I located only one copy of Ḥarāʾirī's treatise, published in 1862, at the Bibliothèque Nationale in Paris. For a brief biography of Ḥarāʾirī, see al-Ziriklī, *al-Aʿlām,* 3:131. On the fatwa, see Koningsveld, "Between Communalism and Secularism," 330–31. ʿIlīsh's response, which was composed in 1862–63, cites the text of Ḥarāʾirī's fatwa directly.
16. L'Homond and Al-Harairi, *Grammaire française de Lhomond.*
17. ʿIlīsh's response to Ḥarāʾirī's fatwa appears to have been published, but I could not find a copy in an American library: Muhammad ʿIlīsh, *Ajwibat al-ḥayārā ʿan ḥukm qalansuwa al-naṣārā* (Casablanca: Qaṭr al-Nadā, Majalla ʿIlmīya Muḥakkama, 2019). Instead, I consulted a handwritten copy of the manuscript held at the King Saud University Library: ʿIlīsh, *Risāla fī radd ʿalā man jawwaza libs al-qalansuwa.* Another copy is held at the General Library of Tetouan in Morocco: *al-Radd ʿalā Risāla Ajwibat al-ḥayārā ʿalā al-qalansuwat al-nasārā,* no. 236, 26 pp. Translations are mine unless otherwise noted. On ʿIlīsh, see al-Ziriklī, *al-Aʿlām,* 6:19–20; Koningsveld, "Between Communalism and Secularism," 335–36; *Encyclopaedia of Islam,* 2nd ed., s.v. "ʿIlaysh [*sic*]" (F. de Jong); Gesink, *Islamic Reform and Conservatism,* 89–109. al-Ziriklī notes (20, n. 1) that ʿIlīsh pronounced his name with *kasra* under the letters *ʿayn* and *yā,* so his name is sometimes incorrectly transliterated as ʿIlaysh or ʿUlaysh.
18. *Sunan Ibn Mājah, kitāb al-zuhd, bāb al-qanāʿa.*
19. ʿIlīsh's response to a petitioner's question concerning the collective obligation of Muslims living in French Algeria to emigrate is another indicator of his spatial imaginary in which colonial Europe was the enemy. ʿIlīsh responded by citing the fatwas composed at the turn of the sixteenth century by the Mālikī jurist Aḥmad al-Wansharīsī (d. 1508), who issued the opinion that Muslims living under Christian rule in Marbella, Spain, must flee to *dār al-Islām.* Verskin, *Oppressed in the Land?* 95–97.
20. al-Zayyāt, "al-Waḍʿ al-lughawī," 171; translation of this passage, with minor modifications, from Gesink, "Islamic Educational Reform," 25.
21. Gesink, *Islamic Reform and Conservatism,* 91–93.
22. On ʿIlīsh's view of *taqlīd,* see ibid., 89–109.
23. Ibid., 112.
24. Riḍā, "Mulakhkhaṣ sīrat al-ustādh al-imām," 391; translation in Gesink, *Islamic Reform and Conservatism,* 94.
25. Riḍā, "Mulakhkhaṣ sīrat al-ustādh al-imām," 391; Gesink, *Islamic Reform and Conservatism,* 95.
26. Gesink, *Islamic Reform and Conservatism,* 95.
27. Riḍā, "al-Tashabbuh wa'l-iqtiḍāʾ," 551–57. On Riḍā's response to the Transvaal fatwa, also see Halevi, *Modern Things on Trial,* 87–93.
28. On utilitarianism in modern Islamic legal thought, see Hallaq, *A History of Islamic Legal Theories,* 214–31; Hallaq, *Sharīʿa,* 443–542.

29. al-Muwayliḥi, *What ʿĪsā Ibn Hishām Told Us,* 11–13.
30. Ibid., 183–85.
31. Ibid., 183–85. Also see Von Grunebaum, *Modern Islam,* 158–59.
32. al-Muwayliḥī, *What ʿĪsā Ibn Hishām Told Us,* 11.
33. On Muwayliḥī, see ibid., 1–19.
34. Adams, "Muḥammad ʿAbduh and the Transvaal Fatwā," 16, n. 9.
35. Kāmil, "Al-Mister Muḥammad ʿAbduh," 4; discussed in Gesink, *Islamic Reform and Conservatism,* 188–95.
36. Shalabī, *al-Taʿdīl al-Islāmiyya,* 34–39.
37. Riḍā, "Libs al-qalansuwa," 710–16.
38. Ibid., 711.
39. Shabana, *Custom in Islamic Law;* Kamali, *Principles of Islamic Jurisprudence,* 369–83; Khallāf, *ʿIlm uṣūl al-fiqh,* 89–91; Gerber, *Islamic Law and Culture,* 105–15. In the Ḥanafī school, see Ibn ʿĀbidīn, "Nashr al-ʿarf"; and discussions of this treatise in Hallaq, *Authority, Continuity and Change,* 215–33; and Ahmad, *Islam, Modernity, Violence, and Everyday Life,* 83–116. And as a universal maxim in Islamic law, see Ibn Nujaym, *al-Ashbāh wa'l-naẓāʾir,* 93–104; Shabīr, *al-Qawāʿid al-kulliyya,* 229–68.
40. Riḍā, "Libs al-qalansuwa," 711.
41. Emon, "Ḥuqūq Allāh and Ḥuqūq al-ʿIbād," 325–91.
42. Riḍā, "Libs al-qalansuwa," 714.
43. Halevi, *Modern Things on Trial,* 150–54.
44. Riḍā, "Libs al-qalansuwa," 715–16.
45. Riḍā, "Fatāwā." Unless otherwise noted, selected translations of the fatwa are drawn from Haddad, "Muhammad Rashid Rida," 476–78.
46. I have translated these couplets cited by Riḍā, which were originally composed by "Illuminationist" theosopher Shihāb al-Dīn al-Suhrawardī. Also see epigraph of chapter 6. al-Ḥamawī, *Muʿjam al-udabāʾ,* 6:2808.
47. *Irshād al-umma,* 45–47.
48. Ibid., 47.
49. Lewis, *The Political Language of Islam,* 35–37; Crone, *God's Rule,* 4; Black, *The History of Islamic Political Thought,* 94–95.
50. Quadri, *Transformations of Tradition,* 165–208.
51. Ibid., 186.
52. Elshakry, *Reading Darwin in Arabic,* 186–93.
53. Âṭïf, *Frenk Mukallitliği ve Şapka.* On this treatise, see Patel, "The Islamic Treatises against Imitation," 30–31.
54. Lewis, *The Emergence of Modern Turkey,* 269.
55. Quataert, "Clothing Laws."
56. Ibid., 412.
57. Yilmaz, *Becoming Turkish,* 25.
58. Ibid., 29–39.
59. Jacob, *Working Out Egypt,* 191.
60. Badawī, *Shāhid ʿiyān ʿalā al-ḥayā al-Miṣrīya,* 113–38; Jacob, *Working Out Egypt,* 206–7.
61. Habib and Hesham, "The Effendi's Crown."

62. Ibid.
63. Reynolds, *A City Consumed,* 98.
64. "Ḥukm al-sharʿ al-sharīf fī libs al-qubbaʿa." Italian translation: *Orient moderno* 6 (1926): 300–303.
65. Halevi, *Modern Things on Trial,* 191–224.
66. Riḍā, "Fatāwā al-Manār." Selected translations of the fatwa from Haddad, "Muhammad Rashid Rida," 484–89.
67. Riḍā, "al-Tajdid wa al-tajaddud wa al-mujaddidun." Translations of Riḍā's speech from Shahin, "Muhammad Rashid Rida."
68. Salīm, "Tashabbuh al-Muslim bi'l-kāfir," 1522–26. Also see Skovgaard-Petersen, *Defining Islam,* 167–70. Italian translation of the fatwa in *Orient moderno* 12 (1932): 139–40.
69. Doubt or suspicion is an insufficient basis on which to blame the accused of having committed a criminal act; evidence beyond a reasonable doubt is needed. Ibn Nujaym, *al-Ashbāh wa'l-naẓāʾir,* 57–74; Shabīr, *al-Qawāʿid al-kulliyya,* 127–62; Zakariyah, *Legal Maxims in Islamic Criminal Law,* 80–136.
70. "Maʿa al-muftī al-akbar."
71. al-Kawtharī, *Maqālāt al-Kawtharī,* 219–28; also see the "conservative" view of Moroccan scholar Muḥammad b. Jaʿfar al-Kattānī on adopting European-style headgear grounded in an impassioned defense of the turban in al-Kattānī, *al-Diʿāma li-maʿrifat aḥkām sunnat al-ʿimāma;* Harahap, "The Fatwā of Muḥammad bin Jaʿfar al-Kattānī"; Koningsveld, "Between Communalism and Secularism," 336–39.
72. El Shamsy, *Rediscovering the Islamic Classics,* 212–17.
73. Kawtharī credits Salīm only for stating that the motive to renounce or denigrate Islam voids his legal ruling permitting Muslims to wear foreign headgear.
74. Abū Zahra, "al-Imām al-Kawtharī," 16.
75. Ahmed, *What Is Islam?* 6.
76. Shahin, "Muhammad Rashid Rida," 81.

EPILOGUE

1. *lā yushbihu al-ziyy al-ziyy ḥattā tushbiha al-qulūb al-qulūb.* The saying is attributed to Ibn Masʿūd, one of the most learned of Muhammad's Companions. See *Encyclopaedia of Islam,* 2nd ed., s.v. "Ibn Masʿūd" (J. C. Vadet). Ibn Abī Shayba, *al-Muṣannaf,* 12:210; also see the ninth-century collection of renunciant sayings attributed to Wakīʿ b. Jarrāḥ (d. 812): Ibn Jarrāḥ, *Kitāb al-Zuhd,* 1:597. ʿAbd al-Raḥmān al-Furaywāʾī, the editor of Ibn Jarrāḥ's collection, casts doubt on the attribution to Ibn Masʿūd.
2. My reflections on style draw upon sources spanning the fields of religion, literature, philosophy, and art: Hecker, "Islam: The Meaning of Style"; Sontag, "On Style"; Gombrich, "Style"; Eco, *On Literature,* 161–79; Van Eck, McAllister, and Van de Vall, *The Question of Style;* Schapiro, "Style"; Huemer, "Literary Style"; Lang, *The Concept of Style.*
3. *lā yushbihu al-ziyy al-ziyy ḥattā yushbiha al-khuluq al-khuluq wa man tashabbaha bi-qawm^{in} fa-huwa min-hum.* al-Daylamī, *al-Firdaws bi-maʾthūr al-khiṭāb,* 5:168.
4. Kister, "'Do Not Assimilate Yourselves,'" 346.

5. See, for example, a fatwa on Christmas (and other holidays) by the late Salafi jurist from Saudi Arabia ʿAbd Allāh b. Bāz (d. 1999): http://www.binbaz.org.sa/noor/11155.
6. Akhtar, *Disgraced,* 83.
7. Ibid., 84–85.
8. Ibid., 83.
9. Asad, *Muhammad Asad: Europe's Gift to Islam,* 2:888.
10. Ibid., 2:894.
11. Ibid., 2:886.
12. Ibid., 2:906.
13. Ibid., 2:900–901.
14. Ibid., 2:899.
15. Parker, "Death of a Muslim Mentor," 29.
16. A few caveats are in order, however. I do not enter into theological debates on matters such as supersessionism or salvation since my main concerns are socio-cultural. I also do not dwell on the pivotal role of the secular nation-state in defining religious difference, which the late Saba Mahmood has examined. Nor is my exploration, which is most salient to Muslims in North America, intended to impress a uniform stylistic template upon Muslims across the globe. As this book has shown, context—historical, political, cultural, and social—is unremittingly germane to religious imaginations of self and other. My intervention is not meant to end the conversation but to advance it. See Sirry, *Scriptural Polemics;* Mahmood, *Religious Difference in a Secular Age.*
17. Sirry, *Scriptural Polemics,* 181.
18. Taylor, *Modern Social Imaginaries.*
19. March, "Sources of Moral Obligation," 38.
20. Fadel, "'No Salvation outside Islam.'"
21. Ali, *Sexual Ethics and Islam,* 50–71; Ali, "Slavery and Sexual Ethics in Islam"; Brown, *Slavery & Islam;* Ayubi, *Gendered Morality.*
22. Waller, *Becoming Evil,* 171–220; Bandura, "Moral Disengagement."
23. *lā ḍarar wa lā ḍirār.* In *Sunan Ibn Mājah, kitāb al-aḥkām, bāb man banā fī haqqihi mā yaḍurru bi-jārihi.* On the hadith's function as a universal maxim in Islamic law, see Ibn Nujaym, *al-Ashbāh wa'l-naẓāʾir,* 85–92; Shabīr, *al-Qawāʿid al-kulliyya,* 163–86; Zakariyah, *Legal Maxims in Islamic Criminal Law,* 158–72.
24. Amina Wadud builds her approach to sexual difference around Q 49:13, arguing that hierarchical distinctions between men and women must be conceived not categorically but in terms of the individual. Wadud, *Qur'an and Woman,* 34–38.
25. Āl-e Aḥmad, *Gharbzadegī;* Āl-e Aḥmad, *Occidentosis;* Patel, "The Islamic Treatises against Imitation," 619–39.
26. On Salafism within and beyond Saudi Arabia, see Meijer, *Global Salafism;* Lacroix, *Awakening Islam;* Lauzière, *The Making of Salafism.*
27. Through a painstaking analysis of Islamic sources, Shahab Ahmed demonstrates how early Muslims accepted that the "Satanic Verses" (*qiṣṣat al-gharānīq,* lit., "story of the cranes") may have occurred, while contemporary Muslims cannot. The narrative is now outside the boundaries of orthodoxy. Ahmed also claims that orthodox Islam in modernity has been reduced to its prescriptive texts. Broadly consistent with Ahmed's

narrative, Thomas Bauer argues that modern Islam "suppressed its old tolerance of ambiguity and its plurality." Ahmed, *Before Orthodoxy;* Ahmed, *What Is Islam?*; Bauer, *Culture of Ambiguity,* 275.

28. Sassen, *Globalization and Its Discontents.*
29. Nguyen, *Modern Muslim Theology,* 53–72.
30. Shabana, *Custom in Islamic Law,* 37.
31. Ibn Ḥanbal, *Musnad,* 6:84.
32. Lamptey, *Never Wholly Other;* also see Sirry, *Scriptural Polemics.*
33. Huwaydī, *Muwāṭinūn lā dhimmiyyūn;* Abou El Fadl, *Reasoning with God,* 158–62. Other reformists have also argued the *dhimmī* system is historically outmoded: Abū-Sulaymān, *Towards an Islamic Theory of International Relations;* Hirschkind, "Religious Difference," 77–80; Sirry, *Scriptural Polemics,* 168–82; Nielsen, "Contemporary Discussions on Religious Minorities in Islam," 360–68.
34. Winter, "The Last Trump Card," 153.
35. Murad, *Travelling Home,* 188–214.
36. Ibid., 195.
37. Ibid., 198.
38. Ibid., 204.
39. Winter, "The Last Trump Card," 153.
40. Murad, *Travelling Home,* 189.
41. On reformist interpretations of Q 5:51 concerning friendship with non-Muslims, see Pink, "Tradition and Ideology in Contemporary Sunnite Qurʾānic Exegesis"; Sirry, *Scriptural Polemics,* 182–93.
42. Lamptey, *Never Wholly Other.*
43. Levinas, *Totality and Infinity,* 50–51, 194–98, 262.
44. "Beware the insight of the true believer, for he sees with the light of God" (*Ittaqū firāsat al-muʾmin fa-innahu yanẓur bi-nūr Allah*). *Sunan al-Tirmidhī, kitāb tafsīr al-Qurʾān, bāb wa min sūrat al-ḥijr.* Although the collector of this tradition, al-Tirmidhī, considered this hadith to be rare (*gharīb*), it was subsequently incorporated into numerous works, especially in the field of Sufism. On *firāsa* as physiognomy in Islamic thought, see Swain and Boys-Stones, *Seeing the Face, Seeing the Soul;* Hoyland, "Physiognomy in Islam."
45. On the concept of *dihlīz,* see Moosa, *Ghazālī and the Poetics of Imagination,* 275–80.
46. Murad, *Travelling Home,* 205–6.
47. Murad's singling out of the ritual practices of Quran recitation (*tajwīd*) and the call to prayer (*adhān*) is puzzling since they are performed in Arabic and by their very essence are inflected with Arab culture. While British non-Muslims may be able identify certain sartorial styles common among British Muslims as foreign, most are unable to discern whether Quran recitation or the call to prayer is performed with non-Arabic accents. Quran recitation, in particular, is not usually heard in Britain outside of mosques or the private homes of Muslims. Ibid.
48. Murad, *Travelling Home,* 189–93.
49. Jackson, *Islam and the Blackamerican,* 154.
50. Ibid., 153–54.

51. Ibid., 163.
52. The Quran repeats the phrase "Believe and do good" over seventy times, e.g., Q 103:3.
53. On the distinction between social citizenship and legal citizenship, see Anderson, *Imagined Communities,* 7.
54. Malcolm X, *The Autobiography of Malcolm X,* 180.
55. Jackson argues that at the core of Black Religion is a "sustained sentiment of protest and resistance" that conditions Blackamerican Sunni Islam. But that does not mean that the religious expressions of all Blackamerican Muslims conform to this style. He notes that Salafis are particularly suspicious of adapting Islam to American social and cultural life. Jackson, *Islam and the Blackamerican,* 32, 48–49, 52–56.
56. The presence of religious diversity in the United States is indebted to a long history of persecuted religious communities—Mormons, Catholics, Jews, and Muslims—fighting back against prejudice. Lawrence, *New Faiths, Old Fears;* Haddad, Smith, and Esposito, *Religion and Immigration;* Joselit, *Parade of Faiths;* Lee, *America for Americans.*
57. Q 5:48 (Abdel Haleem). Also see Q 11:118. On reformist interpretations of these verses, see Lamptey, *Never Wholly Other,* 51–52, 56, 176–78; Abou El Fadl, *Reasoning with God,* 153–63.
58. Compare reformist and premodern exegeses of Q 2:256 in Crone, "No Compulsion"; Sirry, *Scriptural Polemics,* 179–81; Friedmann, *Tolerance and Coercion,* 102; McAuliffe, "Fakhr al-Dīn al-Rāzī," 112.
59. On *tawḥīd* as a modern hermeneutic of social solidarity, see Rahemtulla, *Qur'an of the Oppressed,* 28–31.

Bibliography

ʿAbd al-Ghaffār, Suhayl. *al-Sunan wa'l-āthār fī al-nahy ʿan al-tashabbuh bi'l-kuffār.* Riyadh: Dār al-Salaf, 1995.

ʿAbd-ar-Rāziq, ʿAlī. *Islam and the Foundations of Political Power.* Translated by Abdou Filali-Ansary. Edinburgh: Edinburgh University Press, 2013.

Abou El Fadl, Khaled. *Reasoning with God: Reclaiming Shariʿah in the Modern Age.* Lanham, Md.: Rowman & Littlefield, 2017.

Abū Dāwūd al-Sijistānī, Sulaymān b. al-Ashʿath. *al-Marāsīl.* Edited by Shuʿayb al-Arnāʾūṭ. Beirut: Muʾassasat al-Risāla, 1998.

———. "Risāla li'l-Imām Abī Dāwūd al-Sijistānī ilā ahl Makka fī waṣf al-sunna." In *Thalāth rasāʾil fī ʿilm muṣṭalaḥ al-ḥadīth,* edited by ʿAbd al-Fattāḥ Abū Ghudda, 31–32. Beirut: Dār al-Bashāʾir al-Islāmiyya, 2005.

Abū Yūsuf, Yaʿqūb b. Ibrāhīm. *Kitāb al-Kharāj.* Beirut: Dār al-Maʿrifa, 1979.

Abū Zahra, Muḥammad. "al-Imām al-Kawtharī." In *Maqālāt al-Kawtharī,* 13–19. Cairo: Maktabat Tawfīqiyya, n.d.

AbūSulaymān, ʿAbdulḤamīd. *Towards an Islamic Theory of International Relations: New Directions for Methodology and Thought.* Herndon, Va.: International Institute of Islamic Thought, 1993.

Adams, C. C. "Muḥammad ʿAbduh and the Transvaal Fatwā." In *The Macdonald Presentation Volume,* edited by William G. Shellabear, 13–29. Freeport, N.Y.: Books for Libraries Press, 1968.

Adorno, Theodor. *Minima Moralia: Reflections on a Damaged Life.* Translated by E. F. N. Jephcott. London: Verso Books, 2005.

Ahmad, Ahmad Atif. *Islam, Modernity, Violence, and Everyday Life.* New York: Palgrave Macmillan, 2009.

Ahmed, Leila. *A Quiet Revolution: The Veil's Resurgence, from the Middle East to America.* New Haven: Yale University Press, 2011.

———. *Women and Gender in Islam: Historical Roots of a Modern Debate.* New Haven: Yale University Press, 1992.

Ahmed, Shahab. *Before Orthodoxy: The Satanic Verses in Early Islam.* Cambridge, Mass.: Harvard University Press, 2017.

———. *What Is Islam? The Importance of Being Islamic.* Princeton: Princeton University Press, 2016.

Ahmed, Shahab, and Yossef Rapoport, eds. *Ibn Taymiyya and His Times.* Oxford: Oxford University Press, 2015.

Akhtar, Ayad. *Disgraced.* New York: Back Bay Books, 2013.

Al-Azmeh, Aziz. *The Emergence of Islam in Late Antiquity: Allāh and His People.* Cambridge: Cambridge University Press, 2014.

al-Albānī, Muḥammad Nāṣir al-Dīn. *Irwāʾ al-ghalīl fī takhrīj aḥādīth manār al-sabīl.* 9 vols. Beirut: Maktab al-Islāmī, n.d.

———. *Silsilat al-aḥādīth al-ḍaʿīfa wa'l-mawḍūʿa.* 14 vols. Mecca: Maktabat al-Maʿārif li'l-Nashr wa'l-Tawzīʿ, 2001.

Āl-e Aḥmad, Jalāl. *Gharbzadegī.* Tehran: Khorram, 2011.

———. *Occidentosis: A Plague from the West.* Edited by Hamid Algar. Translated by Robert Campbell. Contemporary Islamic Thought, Persian Series. Berkeley: Mizan, 1983.

Al-Ghabbān, ʿAlī Ibrāhīm. "The Evolution of the Arabic Script in the Period of the Prophet Muḥammad and the Orthodox Caliphs in the Light of New Inscriptions Discovered in the Kingdom of Saudi Arabia." *Proceedings of the Seminar for Arabian Studies* 40 (2010): 89–101.

Ali, Kecia. *Sexual Ethics and Islam: Feminist Reflections on Qur'an, Hadith, and Jurisprudence.* London: Oneworld, 2017.

———. "Slavery and Sexual Ethics in Islam." In *Beyond Slavery: Overcoming Its Religious and Sexual Legacies,* edited by Bernadette J. Brooten, 107–22. Black Religion/Womanist Thought/Social Justice. New York: Palgrave Macmillan, 2010.

ʿĀlī, Muṣṭafā. *Muṣṭafā ʿĀlī's Description of Cairo of 1599.* Translated by Andreas Tietze. Vienna: Verlag der Österreichischen Akademie der Wissenschaften, 1975.

Alshech, Eli. "Out of Sight and Therefore out of Mind: Early Sunnī Islamic Modesty Regulations and the Creation of Spheres of Privacy." *Journal of Near Eastern Studies* 66, no. 4 (2007): 267–90.

Alter, Robert. *The Five Books of Moses: Translation and Commentary.* New York: Norton, 2004.

al-Āmilī, Muḥammad b. al-Ḥasan al-Ḥurr. *Wasāʾil al-Shiʿa.* 30 vols. Qumm: Muʾassasat Āl al-Bayt, n.d.

Amitai, Reuven. "The Mongol Occupation of Damascus in 1300: A Study of Mamluk Loyalties." In *The Mamluks in Egyptian and Syrian Politics and Society,* edited by Michael Winter and Amalia Levanoni, 21–41. Leiden: Brill, 2004.

Anchassi, Omar. "Status Distinctions and Sartorial Difference: Slavery, Sexual Ethics, and the Social Logic of Veiling in Islamic Law." *Islamic Law and Society* 28, no. 1 (2021): 1–31.

Anderson, Benedict. *Imagined Communities: Reflections on the Origin and Spread of Nationalism.* New York: Verso, 1991.

Anderson, C. A., and B. J. Bushman. "Effects of Violent Video Games on Aggressive Behavior, Aggressive Cognition, Aggressive Affect, Physiological Arousal, and Prosocial Behavior: A Meta-Analytic Review of the Scientific Literature." *Psychological Science* 12, no. 5 (2001): 353–59.

Andrews, Walter G., and Mehmet Kalpaklı. *The Age of Beloveds: Love and the Beloved in Early-Modern Ottoman and European Culture and Society.* Durham: Duke University Press, 2005.

Anthony, Sean W. *Muhammad and the Empires of Faith: The Making of the Prophet of Islam.* Oakland: University of California Press, 2020.

Appiah, Kwame Anthony. *The Lies That Bind: Rethinking Identity.* New York: Norton, 2018.

al-ʿAql, Nāṣir al-Dīn. *Man tashabbaha bi-qawm fa-huwa min-hum.* Riyadh: Dār al-Waṭan li'l-Nashr, 1991.

Aristotle. *Poetics.* New York: Hill & Wang, 1961.

Asad, Muhammad. *Islam at the Crossroads.* Gibraltar: Dar al Andalus, 1982.

———. *Muhammad Asad: Europe's Gift to Islam.* Edited by Muhammad I. Chaghatai. 2 vols. Lahore: The Truth Society, Sang-e-Meel, 2006.

Asad, Talal. "The Idea of an Anthropology of Islam." In *Occasional Papers Series.* Washington D.C.: Center for Contemporary Arab Studies, Georgetown University, 1986.

al-Aṣbahānī, Abū Nuʿaym. *Akhbār Aṣbahān (Iṣfahān).* 2 vols. Beirut: Dār al-Kutub al-ʿIlmiyya, 1990.

Aslan, Reza. *No god but God: The Origins, Evolution, and Future of Islam.* New York: Random House, 2011.

Atçıl, Abdurrahman. *Scholars and Sultans in the Early Modern Ottoman Empire.* Cambridge: Cambridge University Press, 2016.

ʿAthamina, Khalil. "The Black Banners and the Socio-Political Significance of Flags and Slogans in Medieval Islam." *Arabica* 36, no. 3 (1989): 307–26.

Âṭı̆f, Iskilipli Mehmet. *Frenk Mukallitliği ve Şapka.* Istanbul: Matbaa-i Kader, 1924.

Ayubi, Zahra. *Gendered Morality: Classical Islamic Ethics of the Self, Family, and Society.* Chapel Hill: University of North Carolina Press, 2019.

al-ʿAẓīm Ābādī, Sharaf al-Ḥaqq. *ʿAwn al-Maʿbūd Sharḥ Sunan Abī Dāwūd.* Edited by ʿAbd al-Raḥmān Muḥammad ʿUthmān. 2nd ed. 14 vols. Medina: al-Maktaba al-Salafiyya, 1969.

Badawī, Jamāl. *Shāhid ʿiyān ʿalā al-ḥayā al-Miṣriyya.* Cairo: Dār al-Hilāl, 2001.

al-Bahūtī, Manṣūr b. Yūnus. *Kashshāf al-qināʿ ʿan al-iqnāʿ.* 15 vols. Saudi Arabia: Wizārat al-ʿAdl, 2000.

Bakhit, Adnan. "The Christian Population of the Province of Damascus in the Sixteenth Century." In *Christians and Jews in the Ottoman Empire,* edited by Benjamín Braude and Bernard Lewis, 2:19–66. New York: Holmes & Meier, 1982.

Bakhtin, Mikhail. *Problems of Dostoevsky's Poetics.* Minneapolis: University of Minnesota Press, 1984.

Bandura, Albert. "Moral Disengagement in the Perpetration of Inhumanities." *Personality and Social Psychology Review* 3, no. 3 (1999): 193–209.

Bandura, Albert, Dorothea Ross, and Sheila A. Ross. "Imitation of Film-Mediated Aggressive Models." *Journal of Abnormal and Social Psychology* 66, no. 1 (1963): 3–11.

Barāzish, ʿAlī Rizā. *al-Muʿjam al-mufahras li-alfāẓ aḥādīth al-kutub al-arbaʿa.* 10 vols. Tehran: Sharikat Intishārāt Iḥyāʾ Kitāb, n.d.

Barthes, Roland. *The Fashion System.* New York: Hill & Wang, 1983.

Bashear, Suliman. "ʿĀshūrā, An Early Muslim Fast." *Zeitschrift Der Deutschen Morgenländischen Gesellschaft* 141, no. 2 (1991): 281–316.

———. "Qibla Musharriqa and Early Muslim Prayer in Churches." *The Muslim World* 81, nos. 3–4 (1991): 267–82.

———. "Qurʾān 2:114 and Jerusalem." *Bulletin of the School of Oriental and African Studies* 52, no. 2 (1989): 215–38.

Baudrillard, Jean. *Simulacra and Simulation.* Ann Arbor: University of Michigan Press, 1994.

Bauer, Karen. "Room for Interpretation: Qurʾānic Exegesis and Gender." Ph.D. diss., Princeton University, 2008.

Bauer, Thomas. *A Culture of Ambiguity: An Alternative History of Islam.* Translated by Hans Hinrich Biesterfeldt and Tricia Tunstall. New York: Columbia University Press, 2021.

al-Bayhaqī, Abū Bakr. *al-Jāmiʿ li-Shuʿab al-īmān.* 14 vols. Riyadh: Maktabat al-Rushd, 2003.

———. *al-Sunan al-kubrā.* 11 vols. Beirut: Dār al-Kutub al-ʿIlmiyya, 2003.

al-Bazzār, Abū Bakr Aḥmad b. ʿAmr. *al-Baḥr al-zakhkhār al-maʿrūf bi-Musnad al-Bazzār.* 18 vols. Medina: Maktabat al-ʿUlūm wa'l-Ḥikam, 1988.

Becker, C. H. "Zur Geschichte des islamischen Kultus." *Der Islam* 3 (1912): 374–99.

Bell, Richard. *Introduction to the Qur'ān.* Edinburgh: University of Edinburgh Press, 1953.

Benjamin, Walter. "On the Mimetic Faculty." In *Walter Benjamin: Selected Writings, Volume 2: Part 2, 1931–1934,* edited by Michael William Jennings, Howard Eiland, and Gary Smith, translated by Rodney Livingstone and others, 720–22. Cambridge, Mass.: Harvard University Press, 2005.

Ben-Naeh, Yaron. *Jews in the Realm of the Sultans: Ottoman Jewish Society in the Seventeenth Century.* Tübingen: Mohr Siebeck, 2008.

Berg, Herbert. "Competing Paradigms in the Study of Islamic Origins." In *Method and Theory in the Study of Islamic Origins,* edited by Herbert Berg, 259–92. Leiden: Brill, 2003.

Berglund, Jenny. "Princely Companion or Object of Offense? The Dog's Ambiguous Status in Islam." *Society & Animals* 22, no. 6 (2014): 545–59.

Berkey, Jonathan. *The Formation of Islam: Religion and Society in the Near East, 600–1800.* Cambridge: Cambridge University Press, 2003.

———. "Tradition, Innovation and the Social Construction of Knowledge in the Medieval Islamic Near East." *Past & Present,* no. 146 (1995): 38–65.

Berkowitz, Beth A. *Defining Jewish Difference: From Antiquity to the Present.* Cambridge: Cambridge University Press, 2012.

Bilefsky, Dan. "Muslim Boys at a Swiss School Must Shake Teachers' Hands, Even Female Ones." *New York Times,* May 26, 2016.

Black, Antony. *The History of Islamic Political Thought: From the Prophet to the Present.* Edinburgh: Edinburgh University Press, 2011.

Blake, Stephen P. *Time in Early Modern Islam: Calendar, Ceremony, and Chronology in the Safavid, Mughal and Ottoman Empires.* Cambridge: Cambridge University Press, 2017.

Blecher, Joel. *Said the Prophet of God: Hadith Commentary across a Millennium.* Oakland: University of California Press, 2017.

Bori, Caterina. "The Collection and Edition of Ibn Taymiyah's Works: Concerns of a Disciple." *Mamlūk Studies Review* 13, no. 2 (2009): 47–67.

———. "A New Source for the Biography of Ibn Taymiyya." *Bulletin of the School of Oriental and African Studies* 67, no. 3 (2004): 321–48.

Bosanquet, Antonia. *Minding Their Place: Space and Religious Hierarchy in Ibn al-Qayyim's Aḥkām Ahl al-Dhimma.* Leiden: Brill, 2020.

Bowen, John R. *Why the French Don't Like Headscarves: Islam, the State, and Public Space.* Princeton: Princeton University Press, 2007.

Boyar, Ebru, and Kate Fleet. *A Social History of Ottoman Istanbul.* Cambridge: Cambridge University Press, 2010.

Bromberger, Christian. "Hair: From the West to the Middle East through the

Mediterranean (The 2007 AFS Mediterranean Studies Section Address)." *Journal of American Folklore* 121, no. 482 (2008): 379–99.

Brown, Jonathan. *The Canonization of al-Bukhārī and Muslim: The Formation and Function of the Sunnī Ḥadīth Canon, Islamic History and Civilization.* Studies and Texts. Leiden: Brill, 2007.

———. *Hadith: Muhammad's Legacy in the Medieval and Modern World.* Oxford: Oneworld, 2009.

———. *Misquoting Muhammad: The Challenge and Choices of Interpreting the Prophet's Legacy.* London: Oneworld, 2019.

———. *Slavery & Islam.* London: Oneworld, 2020.

Brummett, Palmira. *Mapping the Ottomans: Sovereignty, Territory, and Identity in the Early Modern Mediterranean.* Cambridge: Cambridge University Press, 2015.

Buckley, R. P. "The Muḥtasib." *Arabica* 39, no. 1 (1992): 59–117.

Burbank, Jane, and Frederick Cooper. *Empires in World History: Power and the Politics of Difference.* Princeton: Princeton University Press, 2010.

Burge, Stephen R. "Reading between the Lines: The Compilation of Ḥadīṯ and the Authorial Voice." *Arabica* 58, nos. 3–4 (2011): 168–97.

Burton, John. "The Qurʾān and the Islamic Practice of Wuḍūʾ." *Bulletin of the School of Oriental and African Studies* 51, no. 1 (1988): 21–58.

al-Būṣīrī, Abū al-ʿAbbās Shihāb al-Dīn. *Itḥāf al-khiyara al-mahara bi-zawāʾid al-masānīd al-ʿashara.* 9 vols. Riyadh: Dār al-Waṭan li'l-Nashr, 1999.

Butler, Howard Crosby, and Earl Baldwin Smith. *Early Churches in Syria: Fourth to Seventh Centuries.* Amsterdam: Hakkert, 1969.

Butler, Judith. "Imitation and Gender Insubordination." In *Inside/Out: Lesbian Theories, Gay Theories,* edited by Diana Fuss, 13–31. New York: Routledge, 1991.

Çaksu, Ali. "Janissary Coffee Houses in Late Eighteenth-Century Istanbul." In *Ottoman Tulips, Ottoman Coffee: Leisure and Lifestyle in the Eighteenth Century,* edited by Dana Sajdi, 117–32. London: I. B. Tauris, 2014.

Calder, Norman. *Studies in Early Muslim Jurisprudence.* Oxford: Clarendon, 1993.

Carlebach, Elisheva. *Palaces of Time: Jewish Calendar and Culture in Early Modern Europe.* Cambridge, Mass.: Harvard University Press, 2011.

Castelli, Elizabeth A. *Imitating Paul: A Discourse of Power.* Louisville, Ky.: Westminster/John Knox, 1991.

Çelebi, Ḣājjī Khalīfa Kâtib. *The Balance of Truth.* Translated by Geoffrey Lewis. London: Allen & Unwin, 1957.

Chamberlain, Michael. *Knowledge and Social Practice in Medieval Damascus, 1190–1350.* Cambridge: Cambridge University Press, 1994.

Clery, E. J. "Women, Publicity and the Coffee-House Myth." *Women: A Cultural Review* 2, no. 2 (1991): 168–77.

Cohen, Mark R. *Under Crescent and Cross: The Jews in the Middle Ages.* Princeton: Princeton University Press, 1994.

———. "What Was the Pact of ʿUmar? A Literary-Historical Study." *Jerusalem Studies in Arabic and Islam* 23 (1999): 100–157.

Colton, C. C. *Lacon; or, Many Things in Few Words: Addressed to Those Who Think.* London: Longman, Hurst, Rees, Orme, & Brown, 1820.

Constable, Giles. "Introduction: Beards in History." In *Apologiae Duae (Gozechini Epistola Ad Walcherum, Burchardi Apologia De Barbis),* edited by R. B. C. Huygens, 46–130. Turnhout, Belgium: Brepols, 1995.

Constable, Olivia Remie. *To Live Like a Moor: Christian Perceptions of Muslim Identity in Medieval and Early Modern Spain.* Edited by Robin J. Vose. Philadelphia: University of Pennsylvania Press, 2018.

Cook, Michael. *Commanding Right and Forbidding Wrong in Islamic Thought.* Cambridge: Cambridge University Press, 2000.

Cook, Michael A., and Patricia Crone. *Hagarism: The Making of the Islamic World.* Cambridge: Cambridge University Press, 1977.

Corbin, Henry. *Suhrawardî d'Alep; fondateur de la doctrine illuminative.* Paris: G.-P. Maisonneuve, 1939.

Corradini, Richard, Max Diesenberger, and Helmut Reimitz. *The Construction of Communities in the Early Middle Ages: Texts, Resources and Artefacts.* Leiden: Brill, 2003.

Crone, Patricia. "Among the Believers." *Tablet,* August 10, 2010.

———. "The First-Century Concept of Hiǧra." *Arabica* 41, no. 3 (1994): 352–87.

———. *God's Rule: Government and Islam.* New York: Columbia University Press, 2004.

———. "No Compulsion in Religion: Q. 2:256 in Mediaeval and Modern Interpretation." *The Qurʾānic Pagans and Related Matters,* January 1, 2016, 351–409.

Culcasi, Karen, and Mahmut Gokmen. "The Face of Danger: Beards in the U.S. Media's Representations of Arabs, Muslims, and Middle Easterners." *Aether: The Journal of Media Geography* 8B (2011): 82–96.

Curtis, John, Nigel Tallis, and Béatrice André-Salvini. *Forgotten Empire: The World of Ancient Persia.* Berkeley: University of California Press, 2005.

Dakake, Maria Massi. *The Charismatic Community: Shiʿite Identity in Early Islam.* Albany: State University of New York Press, 2007.

al-Dāraquṭnī, ʿAlī b. ʿUmar. *Sunan al-Dāraquṭnī.* Edited by Shuʿayb al-Arnāʾūṭ. Beirut: Muʾassasat al-Risāla, 2004.

al-Daylamī, Abū Shujāʿ. *al-Firdaws bi-maʾthūr al-khiṭāb.* 6 vols. Beirut: Dār al-Kutub al-ʿIlmiyya, 1986.

Delaney, Carol. "Untangling the Meanings of Hair in Turkish Society." *Anthropological Quarterly* 67, no. 4 (1994): 159–72.

Deleuze, Gilles. *Difference and Repetition.* New York: Columbia University Press, 1994.

Déroche, François. *Qur'ans of the Umayyads: A First Overview.* Leiden: Brill, 2014.

De Sacy, A. I. S. *Chrestomathie Arabe.* Vol. 1. Paris: Imprimerie Impériale, 1826.

al-Dhahabī, Shams al-Dīn. "al-Naṣīḥa al-dhahabiyya li-Ibn Taymiyya." In *Bayān zagal al-ʿilm wa'l-ṭalab,* 33–37. Cairo: Maktabat al-Azhariyya, n.d.

———. *Imitating the Disbelievers.* Translated by Abū Rumaysah. Birmingham, U.K.: Daar us-Sunnah, 2002.

———. *Mīzān al-iʿitidāl.* 8 vols. Beirut: Dār al-Kutub al-ʿIlmiyya, 1995.

———. *Siyar aʿlām al-nubalāʾ.* Edited by Shuʿayb al-Arnāʾūṭ. 2nd ed. 25 vols. Beirut: Muʾassasat al-Risāla, 1982.

———. *Tashabbuh al-khasīs bi-ahl al-khamīs fī radd al-tashabbuh bi'l-mushrikīn.* Edited by ʿAlī ʿAbd al-Ḥamīd. Amman: Dār ʿAmmār, 1988.

Dhalla, Maneckji Nusservanji. *Zoroastrian Civilization: From the Earliest Times to the Downfall of the Last Zoroastrian Empire, 651 A.D.* New York: Oxford University Press, 1922.

al-Dihlawī, Shāh Walī Allāh. *The Conclusive Argument from God: Shāh Walī Allah of Delhi's Ḥujjat Allāh al-Bāligha.* Translated by Marcia K. Hermansen. Leiden: Brill, 1996.

Donner, Fred M. *The Early Islamic Conquests.* Princeton: Princeton University Press, 1982.

———. *Muhammad and the Believers: At the Origins of Islam.* Cambridge, Mass.: Harvard University Press, 2010.

———. *Narratives of Islamic Origins: The Beginnings of Islamic Historical Writing.* Princeton: Darwin, 2006.

Douglas, Elmer H. "The Beard." *The Muslim World* 68, no. 2 (1978): 100–110.

Douglas, Mary. *Natural Symbols: Explorations in Cosmology.* London: Routledge, 1996.

———. *Purity and Danger: An Analysis of the Concepts of Pollution and Taboo.* London: Routledge, 2001.

Durkheim, Émile. *The Elementary Forms of Religious Life.* Translated by Karen E. Fields. New York: Free Press, 1995.

Durkheim, Émile, and Marcel Mauss. *Primitive Classification.* Abingdon: Taylor & Francis, 2009.

Eco, Umberto. *On Literature.* Translated by Martin L. McLaughlin. Orlando: Harcourt, 2004.

El Shamsy, Ahmed. *The Canonization of Islamic Law: A Social and Intellectual History.* Cambridge: Cambridge University Press, 2013.

———. "The Curious Case of Early Muslim Hair Dyeing." *Islam at 250,* May 14, 2020, 187–206.

———. *Rediscovering the Islamic Classics: How Editors and Print Culture Transformed an Intellectual Tradition.* Princeton: Princeton University Press, 2020.

El-Hawary, Hassan Mohammed. "The Most Ancient Islamic Monument Known, Dated A.H. 31 (A.D. 652) from the Time of the Third Calif ʿUthman." *Journal of the Royal Asiatic Society of Great Britain & Ireland* 62, no. 2 (1930): 321–33.

Eliade, Mircea. "Methodological Remarks on the Study of Religious Symbolism." In *The History of Religions: Essays in Methodology,* edited by Mircea Eliade and Joseph M. Kitagawa, 86–107. Chicago: University of Chicago Press, 1959.

Elias, Jamal J. *Alef Is for Allah: Childhood, Emotion, and Visual Culture in Islamic Societies.* Oakland: University of California Press, 2018.

———. "The Sufi Robe (Khirqa) as a Vehicle of Spiritual Authority." In *Robes and Honor: The Medieval World of Investiture,* edited by S. Gordon, 275–89. New York: St. Martin's, 2000.

El-Rouayheb, Khaled. "Opening the Gate of Verification: The Forgotten Arab-Islamic Florescence of the 17th Century." *International Journal of Middle East Studies* 38, no. 2 (May 2006): 263–81.

Elshakry, Marwa. *Reading Darwin in Arabic: 1860–1950.* Chicago: University of Chicago Press, 2013.

Emon, Anver M. "Ḥuqūq Allāh and Huqūq Al-ʿIbād: A Legal Heuristic for a Natural Rights Regime." *Islamic Law and Society* 13, no. 3 (2006): 325–91.

———. *Islamic Natural Law Theories.* Oxford: Oxford University Press, 2010.

———. *Religious Pluralism and Islamic Law: Dhimmīs and Others in the Empire of Law.* Oxford: Oxford University Press, 2014.

Encyclopaedia Islamica. Edited by Farhad Daftary and Wilferd Madelung. Leiden: Brill. Online edition: http://referenceworks.brillonline.com/browse/encyclopaedia-islamica.

The Encyclopaedia of Islam. 1st ed. (1913–1936). Edited by Martijn Theodoor Houtsma et al. Leiden: Brill. Online edition: https://referenceworks.brillonline.com/browse/encyclopaedia-of-islam-1.

The Encyclopaedia of Islam. 2nd ed. Edited by Peri Bearman et al. Leiden: Brill. Online edition: https://referenceworks.brillonline.com/browse/encyclopaedia-of-islam-2.

The Encyclopaedia of Islam. 3rd ed. Edited by Kate Fleet et al. Leiden: Brill. Online edition: https://referenceworks.brillonline.com/browse/encyclopaedia-of-islam-3.

The Encyclopaedia of the Qurʾān. Edited by Jane Dammen McAuliffe. Leiden: Brill. Online edition: https://referenceworks.brillonline.com/browse/encyclopaedia-of-the-quran.

Ernst, Carl W. *Eternal Garden: Mysticism, History, and Politics at a South Asian Sufi Center.* Albany: State University of New York Press, 1992.

Ettinghausen, Richard. *From Byzantium to Sasanian Iran and the Islamic World: Three Modes of Artistic Influences.* Leiden: Brill, 1972.

Fadel, Mohammad. "Ibn Hajar's *Hady al-Sārī:* A Medieval Interpretation of the Structure of al-Bukhārī's al-Jāmiʿ al-Ṣaḥīḥ; Introduction and Translation." *Journal of Near Eastern Studies* 54, no. 3 (1995): 161–97.

———. "Is Historicism a Viable Strategy for Islamic Law Reform? The Case of 'Never Shall a Folk Prosper Who Have Appointed a Woman to Rule Them.'" *Islamic Law and Society* 18, no. 2 (2011): 131–76.

———. "'No Salvation outside Islam': Muslim Modernists, Democratic Politics, and Islamic Theological Exclusivism." In *Between Heaven and Hell: Islam, Salvation, and the Fate of Others,* edited by Mohammad Hassan Khalil, 35–61. Oxford: Oxford University Press, 2013.

al-Farāhīdī, al-Khalīl b. Aḥmad. *Kitāb al-ʿAyn.* Edited by Mahdī al-Makhzūmī and Ibrāhīm al-Sāmirāʾī. 8 vols. Beirut: Dār wa Maktabat al-Hilāl, n.d.

Faroqhi, Suraiya. "Crisis and Change, 1590–1699." In *An Economic and Social History of the Empire, 1300–1914,* edited by Halil Inalcik and Donald Quataert, 411–636. Cambridge: Cambridge University Press, 1994.

Fattal, Antoine. *Le statut légal des non-musulmans en pays d'islam.* Beirut: Imprimerie Catholique, 1958.

Ferguson, Heather L. *The Proper Order of Things: Language, Power, and Law in Ottoman Administrative Discourses.* Stanford: Stanford University Press, 2018.

Fierro, Maribel. "The Treatises against Innovations (*Kutub al-Bidaʿ*)." *Der Islam* 69 (1992): 204–46.

Fierro, Maribel, and John Tolan. *The Legal Status of Dhimmīs in the Islamic West.* Turnhout, Belgium: Brepols, 2013.

al-Fīrūzʾābādī, Muḥammad b. Yaʿqūb. *al-Qāmūs al-muḥīṭ.* 2 vols. Beirut: Dār Iḥyāʾ al-Turāth al-ʿArabī; Muʾassasat al-Taʾrīkh al-ʿArabī, 1997.

Fleisher, Cornell. "Mahdi and Millennium: Messianic Dimensions in the Development of Ottoman Imperial Ideology." In *The Great Ottoman-Turkish Civilisation,* edited by Kemal Çiçek, 3:42–54. Ankara: Yeni Türkiye, 2000.

Flood, Finbarr Barry. *Objects of Translation: Material Culture and Medieval "Hindu-Muslim" Encounter.* Princeton: Princeton University Press, 2009.

Foucault, Michel. *Discipline and Punish: The Birth of the Prison.* New York: Vintage Books, 1995.

———. "Nietzsche, Genealogy, History." In *The Foucault Reader,* edited by Paul Rabinow, 76–100. New York: Pantheon, 1984.

———. "Of Other Spaces." Translated by Jay Miskowiec. *Diacritics* 16, no. 1 (1986): 22–27.

Fowden, Garth. *Empire to Commonwealth: Consequences of Monotheism in Late Antiquity.* Princeton: Princeton University Press, 1993.

Freidenreich, David. *Foreigners and Their Food: Constructing Otherness in Jewish, Christian, and Islamic Law.* Oakland: University of California Press, 2011.

———. "The Implications of Unbelief: Tracing the Emergence of Distinctively Shiʿi Notions Regarding the Food and Impurity of Non-Muslims." *Islamic Law and Society* 18, no. 1 (2011): 53–84.

Freud, Sigmund. *Civilization and Its Discontents.* New York: Norton, 1961.

———. *Sexuality and the Psychology of Love.* Edited by Philip Rieff. New York: Simon & Schuster, 1997.

Friedmann, Yohanan. *Tolerance and Coercion in Islam: Interfaith Relations in the Muslim Tradition.* Cambridge: Cambridge University Press, 2003.

al-Gamāʿah al-Islāmīyah, and Sherman A. Jackson. *Initiative to Stop the Violence: Sadat's Assassins and the Renunciation of Political Violence.* New Haven: Yale University Press, 2015.

Geertz, Clifford. *The Interpretation of Cultures: Selected Essays.* New York: Basic Books, 1973.

Gerber, Haim. *Islamic Law and Culture, 1600–1840.* Leiden: Brill, 1999.

Gesink, Indira Falk. "Islamic Educational Reform in Nineteenth-Century Egypt: Lessons for the Present." In *Reforms in Islamic Education: International Perspectives,* edited by Charlene Tan, 17–33. London: Bloomsbury, 2014.

———. *Islamic Reform and Conservatism: Al-Azhar and the Evolution of Modern Sunni Islam.* London: I. B. Tauris, 2010.

al-Ghazālī, Abū Ḥāmid. *Al-Ghazālī on Disciplining the Soul & on Breaking the Two Desires.* Translated by T. J. Winter. Cambridge: Islamic Texts Society, 1995.

———. *Al-Ghazālī on the Manners relating to Eating: Kitāb Ādāb al-Akl, Book XI of the Revival of the Religious Sciences—Iḥyāʾ ʿUlūm al-Dīn.* Translated by Denys Johnson-Davies. Cambridge: Islamic Texts Society, 2015.

———. *Iḥyāʾ ʿulūm al-dīn.* 5 vols. Beirut: al-Maktaba al-ʿAṣriyya, 2002.

al-Ghazālī, Muḥammad. *Within the Boundaries of Islam: A Study on Bidʿah.* Translated by Aslam Farouk-Alli. Kuala Lumpur: Islamic Book Trust, 2010.

al-Ghazzī, Kamāl al-Dīn b. Muḥammad. *Intimate Invocations: al-Ghazzī's Biography of ʿAbd al-Ghanī al-Nābulusī (1641–1731).* Translated by Samer Akkach. Leiden: Brill, 2012.

al-Ghazzī, Najm al-Dīn. *Ḥusn al-tanabbuh li-mā warada fī al-tashabbuh.* Edited by Nūr al-Dīn al-Ṭālib. 12 vols. Beirut: Dār al-Nawādir, 2011. Manuscripts: Istanbul: Süleymaniye Library Tekkeler Murad, no. 69; vols. 1–2; Damascus: Asad National Library, nos. 8585–8586, copied 1024/1615 and 1026/1617, vol. 3; Dublin: Chester Beatty Library, Arabic Collection, no. 3216, copied 16 Jumādā I, 1035 (February 13, 1626).

———. *Itqān mā yaḥsun min al-akhbār al-dāʾira ʿalā al-alsun.* Beirut: Dār al-Kutub al-ʿIlmiyya, 2004.

———. *al-Kawākib al-sāʾira bi-aʿyān al-miʾa al-ʿāshira.* 3 vols. Beirut: Dār al-Kutub al-ʿIlmiyya, 1998.

———. *Luṭf al-samar qaṭf al-thaman.* Edited by Maḥmūd al-Shaykh. 2 vols. Damascus: Wizārat al-Thaqāfa wa'l-Irshād al-Qawmī, 1981.

Gibb, H. A. R. "Arab-Byzantine Relations under the Umayyad Caliphate." In *Arab-Byzantine Relations in Early Islamic Times,* edited by Michael Bonner, 65–80. London: Routledge, 2017.

Girard, René. *Things Hidden since the Foundation of the World.* Stanford: Stanford University Press, 1987.

Goldstone, Jack A. *Revolution and Rebellion in the Early Modern World.* Berkeley: University of California Press, 1991.

Goldziher, Ignaz. "Le dénombrement des sectes mohamétanes." *Revue de l'histoire des religions* 26 (1892): 129–37.

———. *Muslim Studies.* Edited by S. M. Stern. 2 vols. London: G. Allen & Unwin, 1967.

———. "Über jüdische Sitten und Gebräuche aus muhammedanischen Schriften." *Monatsschift für Geschichte und Wissenschaft des Judentums* 29 (1880): 302–15.

———. "Usages juifs d'après la littérature religieuse des Musulmans." *Revue des études juives* 28, no. 55 (1894): 75–94.

Gombrich, Ernst. "Style." In *The Art of Art History: A Critical Anthology,* edited by Donald Preziosi, 129–40. Oxford: Oxford University Press, 2009.

Görke, Andreas. "Eschatology, History, and the Common Link: A Study in Methodology." In *Method and Theory in the Study of Islamic Origins,* edited by Herbert Berg, 179–208. Leiden: Brill, 2003.

Graham, William A. *Beyond the Written Word: Oral Aspects of Scripture in the History of Religion.* Cambridge: Cambridge University Press, 1993.

Grehan, James. "Smoking and 'Early Modern' Sociability: The Great Tobacco Debate in the Ottoman Middle East (Seventeenth to Eighteenth Centuries)." *American Historical Review* 111, no. 5 (2006): 1352–77.

Griswold, William J. *The Great Anatolian Rebellion, 1000–1020/1591–1611.* Berlin: Klaus Schwarz, 1983.

Grohmann, A. "Aperçu de papyrologie arabe." *Études de papyrologie* 1 (1932): 23–95.

Habib, Nader, and Soha Hesham. "The Effendi's Crown." *Al-Ahram,* August 25, 2011.

Haddad, Mahmoud O. "Muhammad Rashid Rida." In *Islamic Legal Thought: A Compendium of Muslim Jurists,* edited by Oussama Arabi, David Powers, and Susan Spectorsky, 457–89. Leiden: Brill, 2013.

Haddad, Yvonne Yazbeck, Jane I. Smith, and John L. Esposito, eds. *Religion and*

Immigration: Christian, Jewish, and Muslim Experiences in the United States. Walnut Creek, Calif.: AltaMira, 2003.

Ḥāfiẓ, Muḥammad Muṭīʿ, and Nizār Abāẓah. *ʿUlamāʾ Dimashq wa aʿyānuhā fī al-qarn al-ḥādī ʿashar al-hijrī.* 2 vols. Beirut: Dār al-Fikr, 2000.

Haider, Najam. "The Geography of the Isnād: Possibilities for the Reconstruction of Local Ritual Practice in the 2nd/8th Century." *Der Islam* 90, no. 2 (2013): 306–46.

———. "Prayer, Mosque, and Pilgrimage: Mapping Shīʿī Sectarian Identity in 2nd/8th Century Kūfa." *Islamic Law and Society* 16, no. 2 (2009): 151–74.

Halevi, Leor. *Modern Things on Trial: Islam's Global and Material Reformation in the Age of Rida, 1865–1935.* New York: Columbia University Press, 2019

———. *Muhammad's Grave: Death Rites and the Making of Islamic Society.* New York: Columbia University Press, 2007.

Hallaq, Wael B. *Authority, Continuity, and Change in Islamic Law.* Cambridge: Cambridge University Press, 2001.

———. *A History of Islamic Legal Theories: An Introduction to Sunnī Uṣūl al-Fiqh.* Cambridge: Cambridge University Press, 1997.

———. *Sharīʿa: Theory, Practice, Transformations.* Cambridge: Cambridge University Press, 2009.

al-Ḥamawī, Yāqūt b. ʿAbd Allāh. *Muʿjam al-udabāʾ: Irshād al-arīb ilā maʿrifat al-adīb.* Edited by Iḥsān ʿAbbās. 7 vols. Beirut: Dār al-gharb al-Islāmī, 1993.

al-Ḥanbalī, Abū al-Mawāhib. *Mashyakha.* Edited by Muḥammad Muṭīʿ al-Ḥāfiẓ. Damascus: Dār al-Fikr, 1990.

Harahap, Fakhriati Jaipuri. "The Fatwā of Muḥammad Bin Jaʿfar Al-Kattānī concerning with [*sic*] the Wearing of the Turban." *Islamic Quarterly* 42, no. 3 (1998): 188–99.

al-Ḥarāʾirī, Sulaymān. *Ajwibat al-ḥayārā ʿalā al-qalansuwat al-naṣārā.* Paris: H. Carrion, 1862.

Harari, Roberto. *Lacan's Seminar on "Anxiety": An Introduction.* New York: Other Press, 2001.

al-Harawī, ʿAbd Allāh b. Muḥammad. *Dhamm al-kalām.* Beirut: Dār Fikr al-Lubnānī, 1994.

Hassan, Mona. *Longing for the Lost Caliphate: A Transregional History.* Princeton: Princeton University Press, 2018.

Hattemer, R. "Ataturk and the Reforms in Turkey as Reflected in the Egyptian Press." *Journal of Islamic Studies* 11, no. 1 (2000): 21–42.

Hattox, Ralph S. *Coffee and Coffeehouses: The Origins of a Social Beverage in the Medieval Near East.* Seattle: University of Washington Press, 1985.

al-Haythamī, Nūr al-Dīn. *Bughyat al-rāʾid fī majmaʿ al-zawāʾid wa manbaʿ al-fawāʾid.* 10 vols. Beirut: Dār al-Fikr, 1994.

Hecker, Pierre. "Islam: The Meaning of Style." *Sociology of Islam* 6, no. 1 (2018): 7–28.

Hilali, Asma. *The Sanaa Palimpsest: The Transmission of the Qur'an in the First Centuries AH.* Oxford: Oxford University Press, 2017.

Hirschkind, Charles. "Religious Difference and Democratic Pluralism: Some Recent Debates and Frameworks." *Temenos* 44 (2008): 67–82.

Hitti, Philip. *The Arabs: A Short History.* Washington, D.C.: Regnery, 1996.

Hodgson, Marshall G. S. *The Gunpowder Empires and Modern Times.* Vol. 3 of *The Venture of Islam.* Chicago: University of Chicago Press, 1974.

Holt, aka Muhammad v. Hobbs, Director, Arkansas Department of Correction, et al., 574 U.S. 352 (2015).

Hoover, Jon. *Ibn Taymiyya.* London: Oneworld, 2019.

———. "Kitāb Iqtiḍāʾ al-ṣirāṭ al-mustaqīm mukhālafat aṣḥāb al-jaḥīm; Iqtiḍāʾ al-ṣirāṭ al-mustaqīm, 'The Necessity of the Straight Path in Distinction from the People of Hell.'" In *Christian-Muslim Relations: A Bibliographical History, Volume 4 (1200–1350),* edited by David Thomas and Alex Mallet, 865–73. Leiden: Brill, 2012.

Howard, I. K. A. "The Development of the *Adhān* and *Iqāma* of the *Ṣalāt* in Early Islam." *Journal of Semitic Studies* 26, no. 2 (1981): 219–28.

Hoyland, Robert G. *In God's Path: The Arab Conquests and the Creation of an Islamic Empire.* Oxford: Oxford University Press, 2014.

———. "Physiognomy in Islam." *Jerusalem Studies in Arabic and Islam* 30 (2005): 361–402.

———. *Seeing Islam as Others Saw It: A Survey and Evaluation of Christian, Jewish, and Zoroastrian Writings on Early Islam.* Princeton: Darwin, 2007.

Huda, Qamar-ul. *Striving for Divine Union: Spiritual Exercises for Suhrawardī Sūfīs.* London: RoutledgeCurzon, 2003.

Huemer, Wolfgang. "Literary Style." In *The Routledge Companion to Philosophy of Literature,* edited by Noël Carroll and John Gibson, 195–204. New York: Routledge, 2016.

al-Hujwīrī, ʿAlī b. ʿUthmān. *The Kashf Al-Maḥjūb: The Oldest Persian Treatise on Sufism.* Edited by R. A. Nicholson. Leiden: Brill, 1911.

"Ḥukm al-sharʿ al-sharīf fī libs al-qubbaʿa." *al-Manār* 27, no. 1 (April 13, 1926): 25–32.

Hurgronje, C. Snouck. *Mekka in the Latter Part of the 19th Century.* Translated by James H. Monahan. Leiden: Brill, 1970.

Huwaydī, Fahmī. *Muwāṭinūn lā dhimmiyyūn.* Beirut: Dār al-Shurūq, 1985.

Iacoboni, Marco. "Imitation, Empathy, and Mirror Neurons." *Annual Review of Psychology* 60 (2009): 653–70.

Ibn ʿAbd al-Barr, Yūsuf b. ʿAbd Allāh. *al-Tamhīd li-mā fī al-Muwaṭṭaʾ min al-*

maʿānī waʾl-asānīd. Edited by Muḥammad ʿAbd al-Kabīr al-Bakrī, Muṣṭafā b. Aḥmad al-ʿAlawī, and Saʿīd Aḥmad al-Aʿrāb. 26 vols. Rabat: al-Shuʾūn al-Islāmiyya, 1967.

Ibn ʿAbd al-Hādī, Muḥammad b. Aḥmad. *al-ʿUqūd al-durriyya min manāqib Shaykh al-Islām Aḥmad b. Taymiyya.* Edited by Muḥammad Ḥāmid al-Fiqī. Cairo: Maṭbaʿat al-Ḥijāzī, 1958.

Ibn ʿĀbidīn, Muḥammad Amīn. "Nashr al-ʿarf fī bināʾ baʿḍ al-aḥkām ʿalā al-ʿurf." In *Majmūʿ Rasāʾil Ibn ʿĀbidīn.* N.p., 1970.

Ibn Abī Shayba, Abū Bakr. *al-Muṣannaf.* Edited by Ḥamad al-Jumʿa and Muḥammad al-Laḥīdān. 16 vols. Riyadh: Maktabat al-Rushd, 2004.

Ibn al-ʿArabī, Abū Bakr. *ʿĀriḍat al-aḥwadhī bi-sharḥ Ṣaḥīḥ al-Tirmidhī.* 13 vols. Beirut: Dār al-Kutub al-ʿIlmiyya, 1997.

Ibn Ḥajar al-ʿAsqalānī. *al-Durar al-kāmina fī aʿyān al-miʾa al-thāmina.* Edited by ʿAbd al-Wārith Muḥammad ʿAlī. 4 vols. Beirut: Dār al-Kutub al-ʿIlmiyya, 1997.

———. *Fatḥ al-Bārī sharḥ Ṣaḥīḥ al-Bukhārī.* Edited by ʿAbd al-ʿAzīz b. Bāz. 15 vols. Riyadh: Dār al-Salām, 2000.

———. *al-Iṣāba fī tamyīz al-Ṣaḥāba.* Edited by Ṭāhā Muḥammad al-Zaynī. 13 vols. Cairo: Maktabat al-Kullīyāt al-Azhariyya, 1969.

Ibn al-Ḥājj al-ʿAbdarī, Muḥammad. *al-Madkhal.* 4 vols. Cairo: Dār al-Turāth, n.d.

Ibn Ḥanbal, Aḥmad. *Musnad al-Imām Aḥmad b. Ḥanbal.* Edited by Shuʿayb al-Arnāʾūṭ. 50 vols. Beirut: Muʾassasat al-Risāla, 1993–2001.

Ibn Ḥazm, ʿAlī b. Aḥmad. *al-Muḥallā.* 11 vols. Cairo: Idārat al-Ṭibāʿa al-Munīriyya, 1929.

Ibn Hishām, Abū Muḥammad ʿAbd al-Mālik. *al-Sīra al-nabawiyya li-Ibn Hishām.* Beirut: Dār Ibn Ḥazm, 2001.

Ibn Ḥumayd, ʿAbd. *al-Muntakhab min musnad ʿAbd b. Ḥumayd.* 2 vols. Riyadh: Dār Balansiyya, 2002.

Ibn Jarrāḥ, Wakīʿ. *Kitāb al-Zuhd.* Edited by ʿAbd al-Raḥmān al-Furaywāʾī. 2 vols. Medina: Maktabat al-Dār, 1984.

Ibn Kathīr, Ismāʿīl b. ʿUmar. *al-Bidāya waʾl-nihāya.* 21 vols. Riyadh: Dār Hijr, 1997.

Ibn Khaldūn. *The Muqaddimah: An Introduction to History.* Edited by N. J. Dawood. Translated by Franz Rosenthal. Princeton: Princeton University Press, 1969.

Ibn Manṣūr, Saʿīd. *Sunan Saʿīd b. Manṣūr.* Edited by Ḥabīb al-Raḥmān al-Aʿẓamī. 2 vols. Beirut: Dār al-kutub al-ʿIlmiyya, 1985.

Ibn al-Mubārak, ʿAbd Allāh. *Kitāb al-Jihād.* Edited by Nazīh Ḥammād. Jeddah: Dār al-Maṭbūʿāt al-Ḥadītha, n.d.

Ibn Nujaym, Zayn al-ʿĀbidīn. *al-Ashbāh waʾl-naẓāʾir.* Cairo: Muʾassasat al-Ḥalabī, 1968.

Ibn al-Qayyim al-Jawziyya, Shams al-Dīn. *Aḥkām ahl al-dhimma.* Edited by Ṣubḥī al-Ṣāliḥ. 2 vols. Beirut: Dār al-ʿIlm al-Malāyīn, 1994.

———. *Iʿlām al-muwaqqiʿīn ʿan rabb al-ʿālamīn.* 4 vols. Beirut: Dār al-Kutub al-ʿIlmiyya, 1996.

Ibn Qudāma, Muwaffaq al-Dīn. *al-Mughnī.* 3rd ed. 15 vols. Riyadh: Dār ʿAlam al-Kutub, 1997.

Ibn Qutayba al-Dīnawarī, Abū Muḥammad. *ʿUyūn al-akhbār.* 4 vols. Cairo: Dār al-Kutub al-Miṣriyya, 1996.

Ibn Rushd, Abū al-Walīd Muḥammad. *The Distinguished Jurist's Primer (Bidāyat al-Mujtahid wa Nihāyat al-Muqtaṣid).* 2 vols. Reading, U.K.: Garnet, 1994.

Ibn Saʿd, Muḥammad. *Kitāb al-Ṭabaqāt al-kabīr.* Edited by ʿAlī Muḥammad ʿUmar. 11 vols. Cairo: Maktabat al-Khānjī, 2001.

Ibn Shāshū, ʿAbd al-Raḥmān b. Muḥammad. *Tarājim baʿḍ al-aʿyān dimashq.* Beirut: al-Maṭbaʿa al-Lubnāniyya, 1886.

Ibn Sulaymān, Muqātil. *Tafsīr Muqātil b. Sulaymān.* Edited by ʿAbd Allāh Maḥmūd Shiḥāta. 5 vols. Beirut: Dār Iḥyāʾ al-Turāth al-ʿArabī, 2002.

Ibn Taymiyya. *Iqtiḍāʾ al-ṣirāṭ al-mustaqīm li-mukhālafat aṣḥāb al-jaḥīm.* Edited by Nāṣir al-Dīn al-ʿAql. 2 vols. Riyadh: Maktabat al-Rushd, n.d.

———. *Majmūʿat al-fatāwā.* Edited by ʿĀmir Jazzār and Anwar Bāz. 3rd ed. 37 vols. Mansoura: Dār al-Wafāʾ, 2005.

———. *A Muslim Theologian's Response to Christianity: Ibn Taymiyya's al-Jawab al-Sahih.* Translated by Thomas F. Michel. Delmar, N.Y.: Caravan Books, 1984.

Ibn Taymiyya and Badr al-Dīn al-Baʿlī. *Mukhtaṣar al-fatāwa al-Miṣriyya li-Ibn Taymiyya.* Dammam: Dār Ibn al-Qayyim, 1986.

Ibn Wahb, ʿAbd Allāh. *al-Jāmiʿ fī al-ḥadīth.* Edited by Muṣṭafā Ḥasan Ḥusayn Muḥammad. 2 vols. Riyadh: Dār Ibn al-Jawzī, 1996.

ʿIlīsh, Muḥammad. "Risāla fī radd ʿalā man jawwaza libs al-qalansuwa." Manuscript. Riyadh: King Saud University Library, no. 2580, copied 1862–63.

Imber, Colin. *Ebuʾs-suʿud: The Islamic Legal Tradition.* Stanford: Stanford University Press, 2009.

Imbert, Frédéric. "La nécropole islamique de Qasṭal al-Balqā' en Jordanie." *Archéologie islamique* 3 (1992): 17–59.

Irshād al-umma al-lslāmiyya ilā aqwāl al-aʾimma fī al-fatwā al-Transfāliyya. Cairo: ʿAbd al-Ḥamīd Hamrūsh al-Baḥrāwī al-Azharī, 1903.

al-Iṣfahānī, Rāghib. *Mufradāt alfāẓ al-Qurʾān.* Beirut: Dār al-Qalam, 2009.

ʿIzz ad-Dīn, Mūʾil Yūsuf. *The Theory and the Practice of Market Law in Medieval Islam: A Study of Kitāb Niṣāb Al-Iḥtisāb of ʿUmar b. Muḥammad al-Sunāmī (Fl. 7th-8th/13th-14th Century).* London: E. J. W. Gibb Memorial Trust, 1997.

Jackson, Sherman. *Islam and the Blackamerican: Looking toward the Third Resurrection.* Oxford: Oxford University Press, 2005.

Jacob, Wilson Chacko. *Working Out Egypt: Effendi Masculinity and Subject Formation in Colonial Modernity, 1870–1940.* Durham: Duke University Press, 2011.

al-Jāḥiẓ, ʿAmr b. Baḥr. *Kitāb al-Ḥayawān.* Edited by ʿAbd al-Salām Muḥammad Hārūn. 2nd ed. 8 vols. Cairo: Muṣṭafā al-Bābī al-Ḥalabī, 1965.

———. *The Life and Works of Jāḥiẓ.* Edited by Charles Pellat. Berkeley: University of California Press, 1969.

James, William. *William James: Writings, 1878–1899.* Edited by Gerald E. Myers. New York: Library of America, 1992.

al-Jamil, Tariq. "Ibn Taymiyya and al-Muṭahhar al-Ḥillī: Shiʿi Polemics and the Struggle for Religious Authority in Medieval Islam." In *Ibn Taymiyya and His Times,* edited by Shahab Ahmed and Yossef Rapoport, 229–46. Oxford: Oxford University Press, 2015.

al-Jazarī, Shams al-Dīn Muḥammad b. Ibrāhīm. *Taʾrīkh ḥawādith al-zamān.* 3 vols. Beirut: al-Maktaba al-ʿAṣriyya, 1998.

Jenkins, Richard. *Social Identity.* London: Routledge, 2008.

Jones, Linda G. *The Power of Oratory in the Medieval Muslim World.* Cambridge: Cambridge University Press, 2012.

Joselit, Jenna Weissman. *Parade of Faiths: Immigration and American Religion.* Oxford: Oxford University Press, 2008.

Judd, Steven C. "Competitive Hagiography in Biographies of al-Awzāʿī and Sufyān al-Thawrī." *Journal of the American Oriental Society* 122, no. 1 (2002): 25–37.

al-Jurjānī, ʿAlī b. Muḥammad. *Kitāb al-Taʿrifāt.* Beirut: Dār al-Nafāʾis, 2007.

Juynboll, G. H. A. "Dyeing the Hair and Beard in Early Islam: A Ḥadīth-Analytical Study." *Arabica* 33, no. 1 (1986): 49–75.

———. *Encyclopedia of Canonical Ḥadīth.* Leiden: Brill, 2007.

———. "(Re)Appraisal of Some Technical Terms in *Ḥadīth* Science." *Islamic Law and Society* 8, no. 3 (2001): 303–49.

Kaegi, Walter E. *Byzantium and the Early Islamic Conquests.* Cambridge: Cambridge University Press, 1995.

Kafadar, Cemal. "Yeniçeri-Esnaf Relations: Solidarity and Conflict." M.A. thesis, McGill University, 1981.

Kamali, Mohammad Hashim. *Principles of Islamic Jurisprudence.* Cambridge: Islamic Texts Society, 2003.

———. *Shariʿah Law: An Introduction.* Oxford: Oneworld, 2008.

Kāmil, ʿAbd al-Majīd. "Al-Mister Muḥammad ʿAbduh, Muftī al-Diyār al-Miṣriyya." *Al-Babaghallo al-Miṣrī,* January 12, 1904.

al-Kandhlawī, Muḥammad Zakariyyā. *al-Abwāb waʾl-tarājim liʾl-Bukhārī.* 2 vols. Sahāranpur: al-Maktaba al-Yaḥyawiyya, Maẓāhir al-ʿUlūm, 1971.

Kant, Immanuel. *Critique of Judgment.* Translated by Werner S. Pluhar. Indianapolis: Hackett, 1987.

al-Kāsānī, Abū Bakr. *Badāʾiʿ al-ṣanāʾiʿ fī tartīb al-sharāʾiʿ*. 7 vols. Beirut: Dār al-Kutub al-ʿIlmiyya, 1986.

al-Kattānī, Muḥammad b. Jaʿfar. *al-Diʿāma li-maʿrifat aḥkām sunnat al-ʿimāma.* Damascus: Maṭbaʿat al-Fayḥāʾ, 1923.

———. *Iʿlān al-Ḥujja wa iqāmat al-burhān ʿalā man ʿmā ʿamma wa fashā min istiʿmāl ʿushbat al-dukhān.* Damascus: Tawzīʿ Maktabat al-Ghazālī, 1990.

al-Kawtharī, Muḥammad Zāhid. *Maqālāt al-Kawtharī.* Cairo: Maktabat Tawfīqiyya, n.d.

Keane, Webb. "Semiotics and the Social Analysis of Material Things." *Language & Communication* 23, nos. 3–4 (2003): 409–25.

Kendon, Adam. *Gesture: Visible Action as Utterance.* Cambridge: Cambridge University Press, 2010.

Kermani, Navid. *God Is Beautiful: The Aesthetic Experience of the Quran.* Cambridge: Polity, 2015.

Kerr, Malcolm H. *Islamic Reform: The Political and Legal Theories of Muḥammad ʿAbduh and Rashīd Riḍā.* Berkeley: University of California Press, 1966.

Khallāf, ʿAbd al-Wahhāb. *ʿIlm uṣūl al-fiqh.* Cairo: Maktabat Dār al-Turāth, n.d.

al-Khaṭṭābī, Abū Sulaymān. *Maʿālim al-sunan.* Edited by ʿAbd al-Salām ʿAbd al-Shāfī Muḥammad. Beirut: Dār al-Kutub al-ʿIlmiyya, 1996.

Kister, M. J. "'Do Not Assimilate Yourselves . . .': *Lā tashabbahū.*" *Jerusalem Studies in Arabic and Islam* 12 (1989): 321–71.

———. "'You Shall Only Set out for Three Mosques.' A Study of an Early Tradition." *Le muséon* 82 (1969): 173–96.

Kohen, Elli. *History of the Turkish Jews and Sephardim: Memories of a Past Golden Age.* Lanham, Md.: University Press of America, 2007.

Kohlberg, Etan. "Some Imāmī Shīʿī Views on Taqiyya." *Journal of the American Oriental Society* 95, no. 3 (1975): 395–402.

———. "Taqiyya in Shīʿī Theology and Religion." In *Secrecy and Concealment: Studies in the History of the Mediterranean and the Near Eastern Religions,* edited by H. G. Kippenberg and G. G. Stroumsa, 345–80. Leiden: Brill, 1995.

Koningsveld, Sjoerd van. "Between Communalism and Secularism: Modern Sunnite Discussions on Male Head-gear and Coiffure." In *Pluralism and Identity: Studies in Ritual Behaviour,* edited by Jan Platvoet, 327–45. Leiden: Brill, 1995.

Koselleck, Reinhart. "Linguistic Change and the History of Events." *Journal of Modern History* 61, no. 4 (1989): 650–66.

Krstić, Tijana. *Contested Conversions to Islam: Narratives of Religious Change in the Early Modern Ottoman Empire.* Stanford: Stanford University Press, 2014.

Kugle, Scott. *Sufis & Saints' Bodies: Mysticism, Corporeality, & Sacred Power in Islam.* Chapel Hill: University of North Carolina Press, 2007.

Kurz, Otto. *European Clocks and Watches in the Near East.* Leiden: Brill, 1975.
Kurzman, Charles. *Modernist Islam, 1840–1940: A Sourcebook.* Oxford: Oxford University Press, 2002.
Lacroix, Stéphane. *Awakening Islam: The Politics of Religious Dissent in Contemporary Saudi Arabia.* Cambridge, Mass.: Harvard University Press, 2011.
Lalani, Arzina R. *Early Shīʿī Thought: The Teachings of Imām Muḥammad al-Bāqir.* London: I. B. Tauris, 2000.
Lamptey, Jerusha Tanner [aka Tanner Rhodes]. *Never Wholly Other: A* Muslima *Theology of Religious Pluralism.* Oxford: Oxford University Press, 2014.
Lane, E. W., and Stanley Lane-Poole. *An Arabic-English Lexicon.* 2 vols. Beirut: Librairie du Liban, 1968.
Lang, Berel. *The Concept of Style.* Ithaca: Cornell University Press, 1987.
Lange, Christian. "'On That Day When Faces Will Be White or Black' (Q3:106): Towards a Semiology of the Face in the Arabo-Islamic Tradition." *Journal of the American Oriental Society* 127, no. 4 (2007): 429–45.
Laoust, Henri. *Essai sur les doctrines sociales de Taki-d-Din Ahmad b. Taimiya.* Le Caire: Impr. de l'Institut français d'archéologie orientale, 1939.
Lauzière, Henri. *The Making of Salafism: Islamic Reform in the Twentieth Century.* New York: Columbia University Press, 2015.
Lawrence, Bruce B., ed. *Messages to the World: The Statements of Osama Bin Laden.* Translated by James Howarth. London: Verso, 2005.
———. *New Faiths, Old Fears: Muslims and Other Asian Immigrants in American Religious Life.* New York: Columbia University Press, 2004.
Lecker, Michael. *The "Constitution of Medina": Muḥammad's First Legal Document.* Princeton: Darwin, 2004.
Lee, Erika. *America for Americans: A History of Xenophobia in the United States.* New York: Basic Books, 2019.
Lefebvre, Henri. *The Production of Space.* Oxford: Blackwell, 1991.
Levinas, Emmanuel. *Totality and Infinity: An Essay on Exteriority.* Translated by Alfonso Lingis. Pittsburgh: Duquesne University Press, 1969.
Levy-Rubin, Milka. *Non-Muslims in the Early Islamic Empire: From Surrender to Coexistence.* New York: Cambridge University Press, 2011.
Lewis, Bernard. *The Emergence of Modern Turkey.* London: Oxford University Press, 1961.
———. *Islam from the Prophet Muhammad to the Capture of Constantinople: Religion and Society.* Vol. 2. New York: Harper & Row, 1974.
———. *Istanbul and the Civilization of the Ottoman Empire.* Norman: University of Oklahoma Press, 1963.
———. *The Political Language of Islam.* Chicago: University of Chicago Press, 1991.

L'Homond, C. F., and Soliman Al-Harairi. *Grammaire française de Lhomond: Traduite en Arabe.* Paris: Benjamin Duprat, 1857.

Lindstedt, Ilkka. "*Muhājirūn* as a Name for the First/Seventh Century Muslims." *Journal of Near Eastern Studies* 74, no. 1 (2015): 67–73.

Little, Donald P. "Did Ibn Taymiyya Have a Screw Loose?" *Studia Islamica,* no. 41 (1975): 93–111.

Locke, John. *Two Tracts on Government.* Edited by Philip Abrams. Cambridge: Cambridge University Press, 1967.

al-Luwayḥiq, Jamīl Ḥabīb. *al-Tashabbuh al-manhī ʿanhu fī al-fiqh al-Islāmī.* Jeddah: Dār al-Andalus al-Khaḍrāʾ, 1999.

"Maʿa al-muftī al-akbar." *al-Risāla* 10, no. 449 (February 9, 1942): 11–15.

Mahmood, Saba. *Religious Difference in a Secular Age: A Minority Report.* Princeton: Princeton University Press, 2015.

Makdisi, George. "Ibn Taimiya: A Sufi of the Qadiriya Order." *America Journal of Arabic Studies* 1 (1973): 118–29.

al-Makkī, Abū Ṭālib. *Qut al-qulūb fī muʿāmalat al-Maḥbūb wa waṣf ṭarīq al-mazīd ilā maqām al-tawḥīd.* Edited by ʿĀṣim Ibrāhīm al-Kayālī. 2 vols. Beirut: Dār al-Kutub al-ʿIlmiyya, 2005.

Malcolm X. *The Autobiography of Malcolm X.* New York: Ballantine Books, 1992.

Mālik b. Anas and Muḥammad b. al-Ḥasan al-Shaybānī. *Muwaṭṭaʾ al-Imām Mālik: Riwāyat Muḥammad b. al-Ḥasan.* Edited by ʿAbd al-Wahhāb ʿAbd al-Laṭīf. 4th ed. Cairo: Wizārat al-Awqāf al-Majlis al-Aʿlā li'l-Shuʾūn al-Islāmiyya, n.d.

Mangera, Abdur-Rahman Ibn Yusuf. *Imām Abū Ḥanifa's al-Fiqh al-Akbar Explained.* California: White Thread, 2014.

Mansel, Philip. *Dressed to Rule: Royal and Court Costume from Louis XIV to Elizabeth II.* New Haven: Yale University Press, 2005.

al-Maqrīzī, Taqī al-Dīn. *Mawāʿiẓ wa'l-iʿtibār bi-dhikr al-khiṭaṭ wa'l-āthār.* 4 vols. Beirut: Dār al-Kutub al-ʿIlmiyya, 1997.

March, Andrew. "Sources of Moral Obligation to Non-Muslims in the 'Jurisprudence of Muslim Minorities' (Fiqh al-Aqalliyyāt) Discourse." *Islamic Law and Society* 16, no. 1 (2009): 34–94.

Margoliouth, D. S. *Mohammed and the Rise of Islam.* New York: G. P. Putnam's Sons, 1905.

Marlow, Louise. *Hierarchy and Egalitarianism in Islamic Thought.* Cambridge: Cambridge University Press, 2002.

al-Marwadhī, Aḥmad b. Muḥammad. *Kitāb al-Waraʿ.* Edited by Samīr b. Amīn al-Zuhayrī. Riyadh: Maktabat al-Maʿārif, 2000.

Masters, Bruce. *The Arabs of the Ottoman Empire, 1516–1918: A Social and Cultural History.* Cambridge: Cambridge University Press, 2013.

Masud, Muhammad Khalid. "Cosmopolitanism and Authenticity: The Doctrine of Tashabbuh B'il-Kuffar ('Imitating the Infidel') in Modern South Asian Fatwas." In *Cosmopolitanisms in Muslim Contexts,* edited by Derryl N. MacLean and Sikeena Karmali Ahmed, 156–75. Oxford: Oxford University Press, 2012.

———. "The Definition of *Bid'a* in the South Asian Fatāwā Literature." *Annales islamogiques* 27 (1993): 55–75.

Masud, Muhammad Khalid, Armando Salvatore, and Martin van Bruinessen, eds. *Islam and Modernity: Key Issues and Debates.* Edinburgh: Edinburgh University Press, 2012.

Matar, Nabil. "John Locke and the 'Turbanned Nations.'" *Journal of Islamic Studies* 2, no. 1 (1991): 67–77.

Mattson, Ingrid. "A Believing Slave Is Better Than an Unbeliever: Status and Community in Early Islamic Society and Law." Ph.D. diss., University of Chicago, 1999.

Mauss, Marcel. *The Gift: The Form and Reason for Exchange in Archaic Societies.* London: Routledge, 2002.

———. "Techniques of the Body." *Economy and Society* 2, no. 1 (1973): 70–88.

al-Māwardī, Abū al-Ḥasan ʿAlī b. Muḥammad. *al-Ḥāwī al-kabīr.* 19 vols. Beirut: Dār al-Kutub al-ʿIlmiyya, 1994.

al-Mawṣilī, Abū Yaʿlā. *Musnad Abī Yaʿlā.* Beirut: Dār al-Maʿrifa, 2005.

al-Mawsūʿa al-fiqhiyya. 45 vols. Kuwait: Wizārat al-Awqāf wa'l-Shuʾūn al-Islāmiyya; Dār al-Ṣafwa li'l-Ṭabāʿa wa'l-Nashr wa'l-Tawzīʿ, 1983.

Mayer, L. A. *Mamluk Costume: A Survey.* Geneva: A. Kundig, 1952.

Mazuz, Haggai. *The Religious and Spiritual Life of the Jews of Medina.* Leiden: Brill, 2014.

McAuliffe, Jane Dammen. "Fakhr Al-Dīn al-Rāzī on Āyat al-Jizyah and Āyat al-Sayf." In *Conversion and Continuity: Indigenous Christian Communities in Islamic Lands, Eighth to Eighteenth Centuries,* edited by Michael Gervers and Ramzi Bikhazi, 103–21. Toronto: Pontifical Institute of Mediaeval Studies, 1990.

McManus, I. C. *Right Hand, Left Hand: The Origins of Asymmetry in Brains, Bodies, Atoms, and Cultures.* Cambridge, Mass.: Harvard University Press, 2004.

Meier, Fritz. "The Cleanest about Predestination: A Bit of Ibn Taymiyya." In *Essays on Islamic Piety and Mysticism,* edited by Fritz Meier, 309–34. Leiden: Brill, 1999.

Meijer, Roel. *Global Salafism: Islam's New Religious Movement.* New York: Columbia University Press, 2009.

Melchert, Christopher. *Ahmad Ibn Hanbal.* Oxford: Oneworld, 2006.

———. "Aḥmad Ibn Ḥanbal's Book of Renunciation." *Der Islam* 85, no. 2 (2011): 345–59.

———. *The Formation of the Sunni Schools of Law, 9th-10th Centuries C.E.* Leiden: Brill, 1997.

———. "Ibn Al-Mubārak's *Kitāb al-Jihād* and Early Renunciant Literature." In *Violence in Islamic Thought from the Qur'ān to the Mongols,* edited by Robert Gleave and István Kristó Nagy, 1:49–69. Edinburgh: Edinburgh University Press, 2015.

———. "The Life and Works of Abū Dāwūd Al-Sijistānī." *Al-Qanṭara* 29 (2008): 9–44.

———. "The Piety of the Hadith Folk." *International Journal of Middle East Studies* 34, no. 3 (2002): 425–39.

———. "Review: Religion and Politics under the Early ʿAbbāsids: The Emergence of the Proto-Sunnī Elite by Muhammad Qasim Zaman." *Islamic Law and Society* 6, no. 2 (1999): 272–75.

Memon, Muhammad Umar. *Ibn Taimiya's Struggle against Popular Religion.* The Hague: Mouton, 1976.

Meri, Josef W. *The Cult of Saints among Muslims and Jews in Medieval Syria.* Oxford: Oxford University Press, 2002.

Merleau-Ponty, Maurice. *Phenomenology of Perception: An Introduction.* London: Routledge, 2002.

Meyer, Birgit, and Jojada Verrips. "Aesthetics." In *Keywords in Religion, Media and Culture,* edited by David Morgan, 20–30. New York; London: Routledge, 2008.

Mikhail, Alan. *The Animal in Ottoman Egypt.* Oxford: Oxford University Press, 2014.

———. "The Heart's Desire: Gender, Urban Space, and the Ottoman Coffee House." In *Ottoman Tulips, Ottoman Coffee: Leisure and Lifestyle in the Eighteenth Century,* edited by Dana Sajdi, 133–70. London: I. B. Tauris, 2007.

Miller, David. "Majorities and Minarets: Religious Freedom and Public Space." *British Journal of Political Science* 46, no. 2 (2016): 437–56.

Misch, Georg, Ralph Wieser, Joerg Burger, Marek Kralovsky, Jim Howard, Mischief Films, and Icarus Films. *A Road to Mecca: The Journey of Muhammad Asad.* Brooklyn: Icarus Films, 2009.

al-Miṣrī, Aḥmad Ibn al-Naqīb. *Reliance of the Traveller: The Classic Manual of Islamic Sacred Law.* Translated by Noah Ha Mim Keller. Rev. ed. Beltsville, Md.: Amana, 1994.

Mittwoch, Eugen. *Zur Entstehungsgeschichte des islamischen Gebets und Kultus.* Berlin: Akademie der Wissenschaften, 1913.

al-Mizzī, Yūsuf b. ʿAbd al-Raḥmān. *Tahdhīb al-kamāl.* 2nd ed. 35 vols. Beirut: Muʾassasat al-Risāla, 1983.

Modarressi Tabatabaʿi, Hossein. *Crisis and Consolidation in the Formative Period of Shiʿite Islam: Abū Jaʿfar Ibn Qiba al-Rāzī and His Contribution to Imāmite Shīʿite Thought.* Princeton: Darwin, 1993.

Moosa, Ebrahim. *Ghazālī and the Poetics of Imagination.* Chapel Hill: University of North Carolina Press, 2006.

Moosa, Ebrahim, and Sherali Tareen. "Revival and Reform." In *The Princeton Encyclopedia of Islamic Political Thought,* edited by Gerhard Böwering, Patricia Crone, and Mahan Mirza, 462–70. Princeton: Princeton University Press, 2013.

Morony, Michael G. "Religious Communities in Late Sasanian and Early Muslim Iraq." *Journal of the Economic and Social History of the Orient* 17, no. 2 (1974): 113–35.

Motzki, Harald. "Dating Muslim Traditions: A Survey." *Arabica* 52, no. 2 (2005): 204–53.

———. "The Muṣannaf of ʿAbd al-Razzāq al-Ṣanʿānī as a Source of Authentic Aḥādīth of the First Century A.H." *Journal of Near Eastern Studies* 50 (1991): 1–21.

———. *The Origins of Islamic Jurisprudence: Meccan Fiqh Before the Classical Schools.* Translated by Marion H. Katz. Leiden: Brill, 2002.

Mourad, Suleiman. "A Note on the Origin of *Faḍāʾil Bayt al-Maqdis* Compilations." *Al-Abḥāth* 44 (1996): 31–48.

Muhanna, Elias. *The World in a Book: Al-Nuwayri and the Islamic Encyclopedic Tradition.* Princeton: Princeton University Press, 2017.

al-Muḥibbī, Muḥammad. *Khulāṣat al-athar fī aʿyān al-qarn al-ḥādī ʿashar.* 4 vols. Beirut: Maktabat Khayyāṭ, 1966.

———. *Nafḥat al-rayḥāna wa rashḥat ṭilāʾ al-ḥāna.* 5 vols. Cairo: Dār Iḥyāʾ al-Kutub al-ʿArabiyya, ʿĪsā al-Bābī al-Ḥalabī, 1967.

al-Munāwī, ʿAbd al-Raʾūf b. Tāj al-ʿĀrifīn. *Fayḍ al-qadīr sharḥ al-jāmiʿ al-ṣaghīr min aḥādīth al-bashīr al-nadhīr.* 6 vols. Beirut: Dār al-Maʿrifa, 1972.

Murad, Abdal Hakim. *Travelling Home: Essays on Islam in Europe.* Cambridge: Quilliam, 2020.

al-Muwayliḥī, Muḥammad. *What ʿĪsā Ibn Hishām Told Us; or, A Period of Time.* Translated by Philip F. Kennedy and Roger Allen. Vol. 2. New York: New York University Press, 2015.

Nahshon, Edna. *Jews and Shoes.* Oxford: Berg, 2008.

Nassery, Idris, Rumee Ahmed, and Muna Tatari, eds. *The Objectives of Islamic Law: The Promises and Challenges of the Maqāṣid al-Sharīʿa.* Lanham, Md.: Lexington Books, 2018.

al-Nawawī, Muḥyī al-Dīn b. Sharaf. *al-Majmūʿ sharḥ al-muhadhdhab.* 18 vols. Cairo: Zakariyya ʿAlī Yūsuf, 1966.

Neuwirth, Angelika. "From the Sacred Mosque to the Remote Temple: Sūrat al-Isrāʾ, between Text and Commentary." In *With Reverence for the Word: Medieval Scriptural Exegesis in Judaism, Christianity, and Islam,* edited by Joseph Ward Goering, Jane Dammen McAuliffe, and Barry D. Walfish, 376–407. Oxford: Oxford University Press, 2003.

———. *The Qur'an and Late Antiquity: A Shared Heritage.* Oxford: Oxford University Press, 2019.

Neuwirth, Angelika, Nicolai Sinai, and Michael Marx. *The Qurʾān in Context: Historical and Literary Investigations into the Qurʾānic Milieu.* Leiden: Brill, 2010.

Nguyen, Martin. *Modern Muslim Theology: Engaging God and the World with Faith and Imagination.* Lanham, Md.: Rowman & Littlefield, 2019.

Nielsen, Jorgen S. "Contemporary Discussions on Religious Minorities in Islam." *Brigham Young University Law Review* 2002, no. 2 (2002): 353–70.

Noth, Albrecht. "Problems of Differentiation between Muslims and Non-Muslims: Re-reading the 'Ordinances of ʿUmar' (al-Shurūṭ al-ʿUmariyya)." In *Muslims and Others in Early Islamic Society,* edited by Robert Hoyland, 103–24. Aldershot, U.K.: Ashgate, 2004.

Ohlander, Erik S. *Sufism in an Age of Transition: ʿUmar al-Suhrawardī and the Rise of the Islamic Mystical Brotherhoods.* Boston: Brill, 2008.

Opwis, Felicitas. *Maṣlaḥa and the Purpose of the Law: Islamic Discourse on Legal Change from the 4th/10th to 8th/14th Century.* Leiden: Brill, 2010.

———. "Maṣlaḥa in Contemporary Islamic Legal Theory." *Islamic Law and Society* 12, no. 2 (2005): 182–223.

Pamuk, Orhan. *My Name Is Red.* Translated by Erdağ M. Göknar. New York: Knopf, 2001.

Parker, Geoffrey. "Crisis and Catastrophe: The Global Crisis of the Seventeenth Century Reconsidered." *American Historical Review* 113, no. 4 (2008): 1053–79.

Parker, Geoffrey, and Lesley M. Smith. *The General Crisis of the Seventeenth Century.* 2nd ed. London: Routledge, 1997.

Parker, Mushtak. "Death of a Muslim Mentor." *Middle East* 211 (May 1992): 28–29.

Partington, David H. "The 'Niṣāb al-Iḥtisāb': An Arabic Religio-Legal Text." Ph.D. diss., Princeton University, 1961.

Patel, Youshaa. "The Islamic Treatises against Imitation (*Tašabbuh*): A Bibliographical History." *Arabica* 65, nos. 5–6 (2018): 597–639.

———. "'Their Fires Shall Not Be Visible': The Sense of Muslim Difference." *Material Religion* 14, no. 1 (2018): 1–29.

———. "'Whoever Imitates a People Becomes One of Them': A Hadith and Its Interpreters." *Islamic Law and Society* 25, no. 4 (2018): 359–426.

Penn, Michael Philip. *When Christians First Met Muslims: A Sourcebook of the Earliest Syriac Writings on Islam.* Berkeley: University of California Press, 2015.

Pfeifer, Helen. "Encounter After the Conquest: Scholarly Gatherings in 16th-Century Ottoman Damascus." *International Journal of Middle East Studies* 47, no. 2 (2015): 219–39.

———. "The Gulper and the Slurper: A Lexicon of Mistakes to Avoid While

Eating with Ottoman Gentlemen." *Journal of Early Modern History* 24, no. 1 (2020): 41–62.

Pfluger-Schindlbeck, Ingrid. "On the Symbolism of Hair in Islamic Societies: An Analysis of Approaches." *Anthropology of the Middle East* 1, no. 2 (2006): 72–88.

Pink, Johanna. "Tradition and Ideology in Contemporary Sunnite Qurʾānic Exegesis: Qurʾānic Commentaries from the Arab World, Turkey and Indonesia and Their Interpretation of Q 5:51." *Die Welt Des Islams* 50, no. 1 (2010): 3–59.

Piterberg, Gabriel. *An Ottoman Tragedy: History and Historiography at Play.* Berkeley: University of California Press, 2003.

Plato. *Plato: Republic.* Translated by G. M. A. Grube. London: Hackett, 1992.

Posner, Eric. "Rick Hills on Slippery Slopes." *Slate.com,* May 30, 2008. https://slate.com/news-and-politics/2008/05/rick-hills-on-slippery-slopes.html.

Pregill, Michael E. *The Golden Calf between Bible and Qurʾan: Scripture, Polemic, and Exegesis from Late Antiquity to Islam.* Oxford: Oxford University Press, 2020.

al-Qāḍī Abū Ḥanīfa al-Nuʿmān. *The Pillars of Islam: Acts of Devotion and Religious Observances.* Edited by Ismail K. Poonawala. Translated by Asaf A. A. Fyzee. Vol. 1. New Delhi: Oxford University Press, 2002.

Qalʿarjī, Muḥammad Rawwās. *Mawsuʿat Fiqh ʿAbd Allāh b. ʿUmar.* Beirut: Dār al-Nafāʾis, 1986.

al-Qaraḍāwī, Yūsuf. *The Lawful and the Prohibited in Islam.* 2nd ed. Cairo: Al-Falah Foundation, 2001.

"al-Qawl al-mukhtār fī al-manʿ ʿan takhyīr al-kuffār." Manuscript. Riyadh: King Abdul Aziz Public Library, no. 3049.

Quadri, Junaid. *Transformations of Tradition: Islamic Law in Colonial Modernity.* Oxford: Oxford University Press, 2021.

Quataert, Donald. "Clothing Laws, State, and Society in the Ottoman Empire, 1720–1829." *International Journal of Middle East Studies* 29, no. 3 (1997): 403–25.

al-Quḍāʿī, Abū ʿAbd Allāh Muḥammad b. Salāma. *Musnad al-Shihāb.* 2 vols. Beirut: Muʾassasat al-Risāla, 1985.

al-Quḍāʿī, al-Qāḍī. *A Treasury of Virtues: Sayings, Sermons, and Teachings of ʿAlī.* Translated by Tahera Qutbuddin. New York: New York University Press, 2014.

al-Qummī, al-Ṣadūq Abū Jaʿfar Ibn Bābawayh. *Man lā yaḥḍuruhu al-faqīh.* Edited by ʿAlī Akbar al-Ghaffārī. 4 vols. Qumm: Manshūrāt Jamāʿat al-Mudarrisīn fī al-Ḥawza al-ʿIlmiyya, 1983.

al-Qurṭubī, Muḥammad b. Aḥmad. *al-Jāmiʿ li-aḥkām al-Qurʾān.* Edited by Aḥmad ʿAbd al-ʿAlīm al-Burdūnī and Ibrāhīm Aṭfīsh. 21 vols. Riyadh: Dār ʿAlam al-Kutub, 2003.

Rabbat, Nasser. "Al-Azhar Mosque: An Architectural Chronicle of Cairo's History." *Muqarnas* 13 (1996): 45–67.

Rafeq, Karim. "The Economic Organization of Cities in Ottoman Syria." In *The*

Urban Social History of the Middle East, 1750–1950, edited by Peter Sluglett, 104–40. Syracuse: Syracuse University Press, 2008.

Rahemtulla, Shadaab. *Qur'an of the Oppressed: Liberation Theology and Gender Justice in Islam.* Oxford: Oxford University Press, 2018.

Rahman, Fazlur. *Islam.* Chicago: University of Chicago Press, 1979.

———. *Major Themes of the Qur'ān.* Minneapolis: Bibliotheca Islamica, 2004.

———. *Revival and Reform in Islam: A Study of Islamic Fundamentalism.* Edited by Ebrahim Moosa. Oxford: Oneworld, 2000.

al-Rāzī, Fakhr al-Dīn. *al-Maḥṣūl.* Edited by Ṭāhā Jābir al-Alwānī. 6 vols. Beirut: Mu'assasat al-Risāla, 1997.

———. *al-Tafsīr al-kabīr.* 11 vols. Beirut: Dār Iḥyā' al-Turāth al 'Arabī, 1995.

Reinhart, A. Kevin. "'Like the Difference between Heaven and Earth': Ḥanafī and Shāfi'ī Discussions of *Farḍ* and *Wājib* in Theology and *Uṣūl.*" In *Studies in Islamic Legal Theory,* edited by Bernard G. Weiss, 205–34. Leiden: Brill, 2002.

Reynolds, Nancy Y. *A City Consumed: Urban Commerce, the Cairo Fire, and the Politics of Decolonization in Egypt.* Stanford: Stanford University Press, 2012.

———. "National Socks and the 'Nylon Woman': Materiality, Gender, and Nationalism in Textile Marketing in Semicolonial Egypt, 1930–56." *International Journal of Middle East Studies* 43, no. 1 (2011): 49–74.

Riḍā, Muḥammad Rashīd. "Fatāwā." *al-Manār* 7, no. 1 (March 18, 1904): 24–26.

———. "Fatāwā al-Manār." *al-Manār* 26, no. 6 (October 18, 1925): 421–24; 26, no. 7 (January 14, 1926): 496–98.

———. "Libs al-qalansuwa al-ma'rūf bi'l-burnayṭa aw al-tashabbuh bi'l-naṣārā." *al-Manār* 6, no. 18 (December 6, 1903): 710–16.

———. "Mulakhkhaṣ sīrat al-ustādh al-imām." *al-Manār* 8, no. 10 (July 19, 1905): 379–400.

———. "al-Tajdīd wa al-tajaddud wa al-mujaddidūn." *al-Manār* 31, no. 10 (July, 1931): 770–77; 32, no. 1 (October 1931): 49–60; 32, no. 3 (March 1932): 226–31.

———. "al-Tashabbuh wa'l-iqtiḍā'," *al-Manār* 1 (1898): 551–57.

Ridgeon, Lloyd. "Shaggy or Shaved? The Symbolism of Hair among Persian Qalandar Sufis." *Iran and the Caucasus* 14, no. 2 (2010): 233–63.

Rispler, Vardit. "Toward a New Understanding of the Term Bid'a." *Islam* 68 (1991): 320–28.

Rizzo, Mario J., and Douglas Glen Whitman. "The Camel's Nose Is in the Tent: Rules, Theories, and Slippery Slopes." *UCLA Law Review* 51, no. 2 (2003): 539–92.

Rizzolatti, Giacomo, and Laila Craighero. "The Mirror Neuron System." *Annual Review of Neuroscience* 27, no. 1 (2004): 169–92.

Robinson, Chase F. *Islamic Civilization in Thirty Lives: The First 1,000 Years.* Oakland: University of California Press, 2017.

Rosenthal, Franz. *Gambling in Islam.* Leiden: Brill, 1975.

———. *Knowledge Triumphant: The Concept of Knowledge in Medieval Islam.* Leiden: Brill, 2006.

Rothman, E. Natalie. "Visualizing a Space of Encounter: Intimacy, Alterity, and Trans-imperial Perspective in an Ottoman-Venetian Miniature Album." *Journal of Ottoman Studies,* no. 40 (2012): 39–80.

Rowson, Everett K. "The Effeminates of Early Medina." *Journal of the American Oriental Society* 111, no. 4 (1991): 671–93.

Rubin, Uri. "Between Arabia and the Holy Land: A Mecca-Jerusalem Axis of Sanctity." *Jerusalem Studies in Arabic and Islam* 34 (2008): 301–25.

———. "Ḥanafiyya and Kaʿba: An Inquiry into the Arabian Pre-Islamic Background of Dīn Ibrāhīm." *Jerusalem Studies in Arabic and Islam* 13 (1990): 85–112.

———. "The Kaʿba: Aspects of Its Ritual Functions." *Jerusalem Studies in Arabic and Islam* 8 (1986): 97–131.

Sabiq, Sayyid. *Fiqh Us-Sunnah: At-Tahara and as-Salah.* Vol. 1. Indianapolis: American Trust, 1991.

Sadeghi, Behnam. "The Traveling Tradition Test: A Method for Dating Traditions." *Islam-Zeitschrift Fur Geschichte Und Kultur Des Islamischen Orients* 85, no. 1 (2009): 203–42.

al-Ṣafadī, Khalīl b. Aybak. *Kitāb al-Wāfī bi'l-wafayāt.* Edited by Sven Dedering et al. Wiesbaden: Steiner, 1949.

Safran, Janina M. *Defining Boundaries in al-Andalus: Muslims, Christians, and Jews in Islamic Iberia.* Ithaca: Cornell University Press, 2013.

Sajdi, Dana. "Decline, its Discontents and Ottoman Cultural History: By Way of Introduction." In *Ottoman Tulips, Ottoman Coffee: Leisure and Lifestyle in the Eighteenth Century,* edited by Dana Sajdi. London: I. B. Tauris, 2014.

al-Sakhāwī, Shams al-Dīn. *al-Maqāṣid al-ḥasana fī bayān kathīr min al-aḥādīth al-mushtahara ʿalā al-alsina.* Beirut: Dār al-Kitāb al-ʿArabī, 1985.

Salamah-Qudsi, Arin. "The Idea of *Tashabbuh* in Sufi Communities and Literature of the Late 6th/12th and Early 7th/13th Century in Baghdad." *Al-Qanṭara* 32, no. 1 (2011): 175–97.

———. *Sufism and Early Islamic Piety: Personal and Communal Dynamics.* Cambridge: Cambridge University Press, 2019.

Salem, Feryal. *The Emergence of Early Sufi Piety and Sunnī Scholasticism: ʿAbdallāh b. al-Mubārak and the Formation of Sunnī Identity in the Second Islamic Century.* Leiden: Brill, 2016.

al-Ṣāliḥī, Muḥammad b. Ṭūlūn. *al-Shadhra fī al-aḥādīth al-mushtahara.* 2 vols. Beirut: Dār al-Kutub al-ʿIlmiyya, 1993.

Salīm, ʿAbd al-Majīd. "Tashabbuh al-Muslim bi'l-kāfir." In *al-Fatāwā al-Islāmiyya min dār al-iftāʾ al-miṣriyya,* 1:1522–26. Cairo: Majlis al-Aʿlā li'l-Shuʾūn al-Islāmiyya, 1997.

al-Ṣanʿānī, ʿAbd al-Razzāq. *al-Muṣannaf.* Edited by Ḥabīb al-Raḥmān al-Aʿẓamī. 2nd ed. 12 vols. Beirut: Maktab al-Islāmī, 1983.

al-Ṣanʿānī, Muḥammad b. Ismāʿīl al-Amīr. *Ḥadīth iftirāq al-umma ilā nayyif wa sabʿīn firqa.* Riyadh: Dār al-ʿĀṣima, 1994.

———. *Subul al-salām al-mūṣila ilā bulūgh al-marām.* 8 vols. Jedda: Dār Ibn al-Jawzī, n.d.

al-Sarakhsī, Muḥammad. *al-Mabsūṭ.* 30 vols. Beirut: Dār al-Maʿrifa, 1993.

al-Sarrāj, Abū Naṣr. *The Kitāb al-Lumaʿ fi'l-Taṣawwuf.* Edited by R. A. Nicholson. Leiden: Brill, 1914.

Sassen, Saskia. *Globalization and Its Discontents: Essays on the New Mobility of People and Money.* New York: New Press, 1999.

Sayeed, Asma. *Women and the Transmission of Religious Knowledge in Islam.* Cambridge: Cambridge University Press, 2013.

Schacht, Joseph. *The Origins of Muhammadan Jurisprudence.* Oxford: Clarendon, 1967.

Schaff, Philip. *History of the Christian Church.* Vol. 4. New York: Charles Scribner's Sons, 1909.

Schaff, Philip, and Henry Wace. *Select Library of Nicene and Post-Nicene Fathers of the Christian Church.* Vol. 14. New York: Charles Scribner & Sons, 1900.

Schapiro, Meyer. "Style." In *Anthropology Today: An Encyclopedic Inventory,* edited by A. L. Kroeber, 287–311. Chicago: University of Chicago Press, 1965.

Schmitt, Carl. *The Concept of the Political.* Chicago: University of Chicago Press, 2007.

Sells, Michael A. *Desert Tracings: Six Classic Arabian Odes.* Middletown: Wesleyan University Press, 1989.

Serjeant, R. B. "The 'Sunnah Jāmiʿah,' Pacts with the Ya<u>th</u>rib Jews, and the 'Taḥrīm' of Ya<u>th</u>rib: Analysis and Translation of the Documents Comprised in the So-Called 'Constitution of Medina.'" *Bulletin of the School of Oriental and African Studies* 41, no. 1 (1978): 1–42.

Shabana, Ayman. *Custom in Islamic Law and Theory: The Development of the Concepts of ʿUrf and ʿĀdah in the Islamic Legal Tradition.* New York: Palgrave Macmillan, 2010.

Shabīr, Muḥammad ʿUthmān. *al-Qawāʿid al-kulliyya wa'l-ḍawābit al-fiqhiyya fī al-sharīʿa al-islāmiyya.* Amman: Dār al-Furqān, 2000.

Shafir, Nir. "Moral Revolutions: The Politics of Piety in the Ottoman Empire Reimagined." *Comparative Studies in Society and History* 61, no. 3 (2019): 595–623.

Shahin, Emad Eldin. "Muhammad Rashid Rida." In *Modernist Islam, 1840–1940: A Sourcebook,* edited by Charles Kurzman, 77–85. Oxford: Oxford University Press, 2002.

Shalabī al-Shubrā al-Shāfiʿī, Yūsuf. *al-Taʿdīl al-Islāmiyya fī takhṭiʾat ḥizb al-fatāwā al-Transfāliyya.* Cairo: Y. Shalabī, 1904.

Shams, Muḥammad ʿUzayr, and ʿAlī b. Muḥammad al-ʿImrān, eds. *al-Jāmiʿ li-sīrat Shaykh al-Islām Ibn Taymiyya (661–728) khilāl sabʿat qurūn.* Mecca: Dār ʿĀlam al-Fawāʾid, 1999.

al-Shāṭibī, Abū Isḥāq. *al-Muwāfaqāt.* Edited by ʿAbd Allāh Darāz. 2 vols. Cairo: Dār al-Ḥadīth, 2006.

al-Shaybānī, Muḥammad b. al-Ḥasan, and Muḥammad al-Sarakhsī. *Sharḥ Kitāb al-Siyar al-kabīr.* 5 vols. Beirut: Dār al-Kutub al-ʿIlmiyya, 1997.

Shoshan, Boaz. *Popular Culture in Medieval Cairo.* Cambridge: Cambridge University Press, 1993.

Shtober, Shimon. "'*Lā Yajūz an Yakūn Fī al-ʿālam Li'Llāhi Qiblatayn*': Judeo-Islamic Polemics concerning the Qibla (625–1010)." *Medieval Encounters: Jewish, Christian and Muslim Culture in Confluence and Dialogue* 5, no. 1 (1999): 85–98.

Sijpesteijn, Petra M., ed. "Hair in the Mediaeval Muslim World." Special issue, *Al-Masāq* 30, no. 1 (2018).

———. *Shaping a Muslim State: The World of a Mid-Eighth-Century Egyptian Official.* Oxford: Oxford University Press, 2013.

———. "Shaving Hair and Beards in Early Islamic Egypt: An Arab Innovation?" *Al-Masāq* 30, no. 1 (2018): 9–25.

Simmel, Georg. *The Sociology of Georg Simmel.* Edited by K. H. Wolff. New York: Free Press, 1950.

Sirry, Mun'im A. *Scriptural Polemics: The Qur'an and Other Religions.* Oxford: Oxford University Press, 2014.

Sivan, Emmanuel. *Radical Islam: Medieval Theology and Modern Politics.* New Haven: Yale University Press, 1990.

Skovgaard-Petersen, Jakob. *Defining Islam for the Egyptian State: Muftis and Fatwas of the Dar al-Ifta.* Leiden: Brill, 1997.

Sontag, Susan. "On Style." In *Against Interpretation and Other Essays,* 15–36. New York: Farrar, Straus & Giroux, 1966.

Spencer, Herbert. *The Principles of Sociology.* Vol. 2. New York: Appleton, 1883.

Stetkevych, Suzanne P. "Archetype and Attribution in Early Arabic Poetry: Al-Shanfarā and the Lāmiyyat Al-ʿArab." *International Journal of Middle East Studies* 18, no. 3 (1986): 361–90.

Stewart, Devin. "Taqiyya as Performance: The Travel of Bahāʾ al-Dīn al-ʿĀmilī in the Ottoman Empire (991–93/1583–85)." In *Law and Society in Islam,* edited by Devin Stewart, Baber Johansen, and Amy Singer, 1–70. Princeton: Marcus Weiner, 1996.

St. Félix, Doreen. "What Will Taking the Knee Mean Now?" *New Yorker,* September 24, 2017.

Stillman, Norman A. *The Jews of Arab Lands: A History and Source Book.* Philadelphia: Jewish Publication Society of America, 1979.

Stillman, Yedida Kalfon, and Norman A. Stillman. *Arab Dress: A Short History from the Dawn of Islam to Modern Times.* Leiden: Brill, 2000.

Stilt, Kristen, and M. Safa Saraçoğlu. "Hisba and Muhtasib." In *The Oxford Handbook of Islamic Law,* edited by Anver M. Emon and Rumee Ahmed, 326–56. Oxford: Oxford University Press, 2018.

Stowasser, Barbara Freyer. *The Day Begins at Sunset: Perceptions of Time in the Islamic World.* London: Bloomsbury, 2014.

al-Subkī, Tāj al-Dīn. *Ṭabaqāt al-Shāfiʿiyya al-kubrā.* Edited by Maḥmūd Muḥammad al-Ṭanāḥī and ʿAbd al-Fattāḥ Muḥammad al-Ḥilw. 10 vols. Cairo: ʿĪsā al-Bābī al-Ḥalabī, 1964.

al-Suhrawardī, Abū al-Najīb. *Ādāb al-murīdīn.* Edited by Menahem Milson. Jerusalem: Hebrew University, 1977.

———. *A Sufi Rule for Novices: Kitāb Ādāb al-Murīdīn of Abū al-Najīb al-Suhrawardī.* Translated by Menahem Milson. Cambridge, Mass.: Harvard University Press, 1975.

al-Suhrawardī, Abū Ḥafs ʿUmar. *ʿAwārif al-maʿārif.* Cairo: Dār al-Maqṭam, 2009.

al-Sulamī, Muḥammad b. al-Ḥusayn. *Kitāb Ādāb al-ṣuḥba.* Edited by M. J. Kister. Jerusalem: Israel Oriental Society, 1954.

———. *al-Muqaddima fī al-taṣawwuf.* Edited by Yūsuf Zaydān. Beirut: Dār al-Jīl, 1999.

al-Sunāmī, ʿUmar b. Muḥammad. *Niṣāb al-iḥtisāb.* Mecca: Maktabat al-Ṭālib al-Jāmiʿī, 1986.

al-Suyūṭī, Jalāl al-Dīn. *Jamʿ al-jawāmiʿ (al-Jāmiʿ al-kabīr).* 25 vols. Cairo: al-Azhar, 2005.

Swain, Simon, and G. R. Boys-Stones. *Seeing the Face, Seeing the Soul: Polemon's Physiognomy from Classical Antiquity to Medieval Islam.* Oxford: Oxford University Press, 2007.

al-Ṭabarānī, Abū al-Qāsim Sulaymān. *al-Muʿjam al-Awsaṭ.* 10 vols. Cairo: Dār al-Ḥaramayn, 1995.

———. *al-Muʿjam al-kabīr.* 25 vols. Cairo: Maktabat Ibn Taymiyya, 1983.

———. *Musnad al-Shāmiyyīn.* 4 vols. Beirut: Muʾassasat al-Risāla, 1984.

al-Ṭabarī, Abū Jaʿfar b. Jarīr. *The History of al-Ṭabarī: Between Civil Wars; The Caliphate of Muʿāwiyah.* Translated by Michael G. Morony. Vol. 18. Albany: State University of New York Press, 1987.

———. *The History of al-Ṭabarī: Incipient Decline.* Translated by J. L. Kramer. Vol. 34. Albany: State University of New York Press, 1989.

———. *The History of al-Ṭabarī: The Victory of Islam.* Translated by Michael Fishbein. Vol. 8. Albany: State University of New York Press, 1997.

———. *Tafsīr al-Ṭabarī*. Edited by ʿAbd Allāh b. ʿAbd al-Muḥsin al-Turkī. 26 vols. Cairo: Dār Hijr, 2001.

al-Taftāzānī, Saʿd al-Dīn Masʿūd b. ʿUmar. *A Commentary on the Creed of Islam: Saʿd al-Dīn al-Taftāzānī on the Creed of Najm al-Dīn al-Nasafī*. Translated by Earl Edgar Elder. New York: Columbia University Press, 1950.

———. *Majmūʿat al-Ḥawāshī al-bahiyya ʿalā sharḥ al-ʿaqāʾid al-nadafiyya al-mushtamil ʿalā sharḥ al-ʿaqāʾid al-nasafiyya liʾl-ʿallāma al-Taftāzānī*. 2 vols. Quetta: Maktabaʾi Islāmiyya, 1977.

al-Ṭaḥāwī, Abū Jaʿfar Aḥmad. *The Creed of Imam Al-Ṭaḥāwī (Al-ʿAqīda al-Ṭaḥāwiyya)*. Translated by Hamza Yusuf. Berkeley: Zaytuna Institute, 2007.

———. *Sharḥ Mushkil al-āthār*. Edited by Shuʿayb al-Arnāʾūṭ. 16 vols. Beirut: Muʾassasat al-Risāla, 1994.

Talmon, Rafael. *Arabic Grammar in Its Formative Age: Kitāb al-ʿAyn and Its Attribution to Ḫalīl b. Aḥmad*. Leiden: Brill, 1997.

Tannous, Jack. *The Making of the Medieval Middle East: Religion, Society, and Simple Believers*. Princeton: Princeton University Press, 2018.

"Taqallub al-azyāʾ fī miʾat ʿāmm." *al-Hilāl*, December 1925.

Taussig, Michael T. *Mimesis and Alterity: A Particular History of the Senses*. New York: Routledge, 1993.

Taylor, Charles. *Modern Social Imaginaries*. Durham: Duke University Press, 2007.

Tayob, Abdulkader. *Religion in Modern Islamic Discourse*. New York: Columbia University Press, 2009.

Terzioğlu, Derin. "How to Conceptualize Ottoman Sunnitization: A Historiographical Discussion." *Turcica* 44 (2012–13): 301–38.

Tezcan, Baki. "The Ottoman Monetary Crisis of 1585 Revisited." *Journal of the Economic and Social History of the Orient* 52, no. 3 (2009): 460–504.

Tlili, Sarra. "Animal Ethics in Islam: A Review Article." *Religions* 9, no. 9 (2018): 1–18.

———. *Animals in the Qurʾan*. Cambridge: Cambridge University Press, 2012.

Tokatly, Vardit. "The *Aʿlām al-ḥadīth* of al-Khaṭṭābī: A Commentary on al-Bukhārī's *Ṣaḥīḥ* or a Polemical Treatise?" *Studia Islamica* 92 (2001): 53–91.

Toombs, Lawrence E. *Tell El-Hesi: Modern Military Trenching and Muslim Cemetery in Field I (Strata I-II)*. Waterloo: Wilfrid Laurier University Press, 1985.

Tritton, A. S. *The Caliphs and Their Non-Muslim Subjects: A Critical Study of the Covenant of ʿUmar*. London: Oxford University Press, 1930.

Trombley, Frank R. "Fiscal Documents from the Muslim Conquest of Egypt: Military Supplies and Administrative Dislocation, ca 639–644." *Revue des études byzantines* 71, no. 1 (2013): 5–38.

al-Tustarī, Muḥammad Taqī. *Qāmūs al-rijāl*. 12 vols. Qumm: Muʾassasat al-Nashr al-Islāmī, 1989.

Twain, Mark. *Tom Sawyer Abroad; Tom Sawyer, Detective.* Edited by John C. Gerber and Terry Firkins. Berkeley: University of California Press, 1982.

Tweed, Thomas A. *Crossing and Dwelling: A Theory of Religion.* Cambridge, Mass.: Harvard University Press, 2006.

Ukeles, Raquel. "Innovation or Deviation: Exploring the Boundaries of Islamic Devotional Law." Ph.D. diss., Harvard University, 2006.

———. "The Sensitive Puritan? Revisiting Ibn Taymiyya's Approach to Law and Spirituality in Light of 20th-Century Debates on the Prophet's Birthday (Mawlid Al-Nabī)." In *Ibn Taymiyya and His Times,* edited by Yossef Rapoport and Shahab Ahmed, 319–27. Oxford: Oxford University Press, 2010.

Vajda, Georges. "Juifs et musulmans selon le Ḥadīṯ." *Journal asiatique* (January–March 1937): 57–127.

Van Eck, Caroline, James McAllister, and Renée Van de Vall. *The Question of Style in Philosophy and the Arts.* Cambridge: Cambridge University Press, 2010.

Verskin, Alan. *Oppressed in the Land? Fatwas on Muslims Living under Non-Muslim Rule from the Middle Ages to the Present.* Princeton: Markus Wiener, 2013.

Voll, John O. "Abduh and the Transvaal Fatwa: The Neglected Question." In *Islam and the Question of Minorities,* edited by Tamara Sonn, 27–40. Atlanta: Scholars Press, 1996.

Volokh, Eugene. "The Mechanisms of the Slippery Slope." *Harvard Law Review* 116, no. 4 (2003): 1026–1137.

Von Grunebaum, Gustave E. *Modern Islam: The Search for Cultural Identity.* Berkeley: University of California Press, 1962.

Wadud, Amina. *Qur'an and Woman: Rereading the Sacred Text from a Woman's Perspective.* Oxford: Oxford University Press, 1999.

Waller, James. *Becoming Evil: How Ordinary People Commit Genocide and Mass Murder.* Oxford: Oxford University Press, 2007.

Ward, Seth. "Taqī al-Dīn al-Subkī on Construction, Continuance and Repair of Churches and Synagogues in Islamic Law." In *Studies in Islamic and Judaic Traditions,* edited by William M. Brinner and Stephen D. Ricks, 2:169–88. Atlanta: Scholars Press, 1989.

Watt, W. Montgomery. *Muhammad at Medina.* Oxford: Clarendon, 1956.

Webb, Peter. *Imagining the Arabs: Arab Identity and the Rise of Islam.* Edinburgh: University of Edinburgh Press, 2017.

Weiner, Isaac. *Religion Out Loud: Religious Sound, Public Space, and American Pluralism.* New York: New York University Press, 2014.

Wensinck, A. J. "Die Entstehung der muslimischen Reinheitsgesetzgebung." *Der Islam* 5, no. 1 (1914): 62–80.

———. *The Muslim Creed: Its Genesis and Historical Development.* London: Frank Cass, 1965.

———. "The Origin of the Muslim Laws of Ritual Purity." In *The Development of Islamic Ritual,* edited by Gerald Hawting, 75–93. Aldershot, U.K.: Ashgate, 2006.

White, Charles. *Three Years in Constantinople.* 3 vols. London: Henry Colburn, 1845.

White, Sam. *The Climate of Rebellion in the Early Modern Ottoman Empire.* Cambridge: Cambridge University Press, 2011.

Williams, Raymond. *Keywords: A Vocabulary of Culture and Society.* New York: Oxford University Press, 1976.

Winter, Michael. *Egyptian Society under Ottoman Rule, 1517–1798.* London: Routledge, 1992.

———. "A Polemical Treatise by ʿAbd Al-Ġanī al-Nābulusī against a Turkish Scholar on the Religious Status of the Ḏimmīs." *Arabica* 35, no. 1 (1988): 92–103.

Winter, Stefan. *The Shiites of Lebanon under Ottoman Rule, 1516–1788.* Cambridge: Cambridge University Press, 2010.

Winter, Tim. "The Last Trump Card: Islam and the Supersession of Other Faiths." *Studies in Interreligious Dialogue* 9, no. 2 (1999): 133–55.

Yarbrough, Luke. *Friends of the Emir: Non-Muslim State Officials in Premodern Islamic Thought.* Cambridge: Cambridge University Press, 2019.

———. "Origins of the Ghiyār." *Journal of the American Oriental Society* 134, no. 1 (2014): 113–21.

———. "Al-Qawl al-mukhtār fī l-manʿ ʿan takhyīr al-kuffār." In *Christian-Muslim Relations: A Bibliographic History, Vol. 4 (1200–1350),* edited by David Thomas and Alex Mallett, 924–27. Leiden: Brill, 2012.

———. "'A Rather Small Genre': Arabic Works against Non-Muslim State Officials." *Der Islam* 93, no. 1 (2016): 139–69.

Ydit, Meir. "Ḥukkat Ha-goi." In *Encyclopaedia Judaica,* 2nd ed., 22 vols., edited by F. Skolnik and M. Berenbaum, 9:580. Detroit: Macmillan, 2007.

Yilmaz, Hale. *Becoming Turkish: Nationalist Reforms and Cultural Negotiations in Early Republican Turkey, 1923–1945.* Syracuse: Syracuse University Press, 2013.

Zakariyah, Luqman. *Legal Maxims in Islamic Criminal Law: Theory and Applications.* Leiden: Brill, 2015.

Zaman, Muhammad Qasim. *Modern Islamic Thought in a Radical Age: Religious Authority and Internal Criticism.* Cambridge: Cambridge University Press, 2012.

———. *Religion and Politics under the Early ʿAbbāsids: The Emergence of the Proto-Sunnī Elite.* Leiden: Brill, 1997.

———. *The Ulama in Contemporary Islam: Custodians of Change.* Princeton: Princeton University Press, 2010.

al-Zarnūjī, Burhān al-Dīn. *Instruction of the Student: The Method of Learning.* Translated by Gustave E. von Grunebaum and Theodora Mead Abel. Chicago: Starlatch, 2003.

al-Zayyāt, Aḥmad Ḥasan. "al-Waḍʿ al-lughawī wa hal li'l-muḥdathīn ḥaqq fīhi?" In *Waḥī al-risāla,* 3:170–82. Cairo: Maṭbaʿat al-Risāla, 1950.

Ziai, Hossein. *Knowledge and Illumination: A Study of Suhrawardī's Ḥikmat al-Ishrāq.* Atlanta: Scholars Press, 1990.

al-Ziriklī, Khayr al-Dīn. *al-Aʿlām.* 8 vols. Beirut: Dār ʿIlm al-Malāyīn, 2002.

Žižek, Slavoj. *The Plague of Fantasies.* London: Verso, 1997.

Index